The Public Sphere From Outside the West

Also available from Bloomsbury

Difference and Repetition, Gilles Deleuze

*Endless Andness: The Politics of Abstraction according to
Ann Veronica Janssens*, Mieke Bal

Gandhi and Philosophy: On Theological Anti-Politics,
Shaj Mohan and Divya Dwivedi

Landscape and Travelling East and West: A Philosophical Journey,
edited by Hans-Georg Moeller and Andrew Whitehead

On Resistance: A Philosophy of Defiance, Howard Caygill

Perfecting Justice in Rawls, Habermas and Honneth, Miriam Bankovsky

The Bloomsbury Companion to Analytic Philosophy,
edited by Barry Dainton and Howard Robinson

The Bloomsbury Companion to Heidegger,
edited by Francois Raffoul and Eric S. Nelson

The Fold: Leibniz and the Baroque, Gilles Deleuze

The Theory and Reality of Democracy, Suman Gupta

The Public Sphere From Outside the West

Edited by
Divya Dwivedi and Sanil V

Bloomsbury Academic
An imprint of Bloomsbury Publishing Plc

B L O O M S B U R Y
LONDON · OXFORD · NEW YORK · NEW DELHI · SYDNEY

Bloomsbury Academic

An imprint of Bloomsbury Publishing Plc

50 Bedford Square	1385 Broadway
London	New York
WC1B 3DP	NY 10018
UK	USA

www.bloomsbury.com

BLOOMSBURY and the Diana logo are trademarks of Bloomsbury Publishing Plc

First published 2015
Paperback edition first published 2017

British Library Cataloguing-in-Publication Data
A catalogue record for this book is available from the British Library.

ISBN: HB: 978-1-4725-7193-9
PB: 978-1-3500-2834-0
ePDF: 978-1-4725-7194-6
ePub: 978-1-4725-7192-2

Library of Congress Cataloging-in-Publication Data
A catalog record for this book is available from the Library of Congress.

Typeset by Deanta Global Publishing Services, Chennai, India

Contents

List of Illustrations

Colour versions of these photographs can be found online at http://www.
bloomsbury.com/uk/the-public-sphere-from-outside-the-west-9781350028340/

List of Contributors

G. Arunima is associate professor in the Centre for Women's Studies at Jawaharlal Nehru University and a visiting fellow at Internationales Kollege Morphomata, University of Cologne, Germany. She is the author of *Colonialism and the Transformation of Matriliny in Malabar 1850–1940* (Cambridge, 1992) and *'There Comes Papa': Colonialism and the Transformation of Matriliny in Kerala, Malabar c.1850–1940* (Orient Longman, 2003). She is co-organizer for Workshops and Conferences on Love and Revolution with the University of the Western Cape and the University of Minnesota.

Howard Caygill is professor of modern European philosophy at Kingston University. He is the author of *On Resistance: A Philosophy of Defiance* (Bloomsbury Academic, 2013), *Levinas and the Political* (Routledge, 2002), *Walter Benjamin: The Colour of Experience* (Routledge, 1998), *A Kant Dictionary* (Blackwell, 1995). His recent research publications include 'Also Sprach Zapata: Philosophy and Resistance' in *Radical Philosophy* (2012) and 'Kafka and the Missing Photograph' in *Photographies* (2011).

Tina Chanter is professor of philosophy and head of the School of Humanities at Kingston University. She is the author of *Whose Antigone? The Tragic Marginalization of Slavery* (SUNY, 2011), *The Picture of Abjection: Film Fetish and the Nature of Difference* (Indiana, 2008), *Time, Death and the Feminine: Levinas with Heidegger* (Stanford, 2001) and *Art, Politics and Rancière: Seeing Things Anew* (forthcoming Polity Press). She has edited *The Returns of Antigone: Interdisciplinary Essays* (SUNY Press, 2014).

Subarno Chattarji is associate professor in the Department of English, University of Delhi. His publications include: *Tracking the Media: Interpretations of Mass Media Discourses in India and Pakistan* (Routledge, 2008), *Memories of a Lost War: American Poetic Responses to the Vietnam War* (Oxford University Press, 2001). He is co-editor of *An Anthology of Indian Prose Writings in English* (Penguin, 2004) and *Globalization in India: Contents and Discontents* (Pearson Education, 2009).

Susmita Dasgupta is a sociologist and joint chief economist of Joint Plant Committee, Ministry of Steel, Government of India. Her doctoral and postdoctoral research was on Hindi commercial cinema. She writes regularly on cinema and politics.

Christel Rashmi Devadawson is associate professor in the Department of English, University of Delhi. She is the author of *Reading India, Writing England: The Fiction of Rudyard Kipling and E. M. Forster* and co-editor with Shormishtha Panja and Shirshendu Chakrabarti of *Word, Image, Text: Nature and Time in Literature and the Visual Arts* (Orient Blackswan, 2009). Her most recent work is *Out of Line: Cartoons, Caricature and Contemporary India* (Orient Blackswan, 2014).

Divya Dwivedi is a philosopher based in India. She is assistant professor at the Department of Humanities and Social Sciences, Indian Institute of Technology Delhi and Visiting Fellow at Centre for Fictionality Studies, Aarhus University. Her forthcoming publications include *Gandhi and Philosophy: On Theological Anti-politics* with Shaj Mohan (Bloomsbury Academic), *Narratology and Ideology: Encounters between Narrative Theory and Postcolonial Criticism* co-edited with Richard Walsh and Henrik Skov Nielsen (Ohio State University Press), *Structuralism and Narratology* in Herman Rapaport (series ed.) (Orient Blackswan) and 'Anti-Mimetic Theory and Postcolonialism' in Robin Warhol, Mark Currie and Zara Dinnen (eds) *Edinburgh Companion to Narrative Theory*.

Patricia Hayes is a Zimbabwean historian based at the History Department of the University of the Western Cape. She has co-edited *Namibia under South African Rule* and *The Colonising Camera* and guest edited special journal issues on visuality and gender in African history, including *Kronos* (2000) and *Gender & History* (2006). Her recent publications include *Bush of Ghosts* (2010) with John Liebenberg and several articles on South African documentary photography.

Shannon Hoff is associate professor of philosophy at the Institute for Christian Studies in Toronto, Ontario, Canada. In 2013 she was a Visiting Fellow at the Institute for Cultural Inquiry in Berlin, Germany. She is the author of *The Laws of the Spirit: A Hegelian Theory of Justice*, as well as of numerous articles in modern and contemporary political philosophy.

Udaya Kumar is professor of English literature at Delhi University. He has been a Leverhulme Visiting Professor, Newcastle University. He is the author of *The Joycean Labyrinth: Repetition, Time and Tradition in Ulysses* (Clarendon, 1991). His recent publications include 'The Strange Homeliness of the Night: Spectral Speech and the Dalit Present in C. Ayyappan's Writings' in *Studies in Humanities and Social Sciences* (2013) and 'Self, Body and Inner Sense: Some Observations on Sree Narayana Guru and Kumaran Asan' in *The Indian Postcolonial*, Elleka Boehmer and Rosinka Chaudhuri (eds) (Routledge, 2011).

Premesh Lalu is professor and director of Centre for Humanities Research at the University of the Western Cape. He is the author of *The Deaths of Hintsa: Postapartheid South Africa and the Shape of Recurring Pasts* (HSRC, 2009), 'The Border and the Body: Post-Phenomenological Reflections on the Borders of Apartheid' in *South African Historical Journal* (2010) and 'Still Searching for "the Human"' in *Social Dynamics – A Journal of The Centre for African Studies* (2012). He is trustee of the District Six Museum.

Anish Mohammed is a multidisciplinary technologist with degrees in medicine and cryptology. He is Doctoral Research Fellow at Royal Holloway, Fellow at Singularity University and member of IEEE. His research interests and pursuits include bionics, singularity, robotics and drone algorithms, genetics, information security and techno-urbanity, on which he lectures regularly. He is currently lead security architect with Lloyds Bank UK. His recent publications include 'The New Secret' with Shaj Mohan (*Economic and Political Weekly*, 2011).

Shaj Mohan is a philosopher based in India. His philosophical monograph on *Gandhi and Philosophy: On Theological Anti-Politics* with Divya Dwivedi is forthcoming (Bloomsbury Academic).

A. Raghuramaraju is professor at the University of Hyderabad. His recent publications include *Debating Gandhi: A Reader* (OUP, 2006), *Enduring Colonialism: Classical Presences and Modern Absences in Indian Philosophy* (OUP, 2009), *Modernity in Indian Social Theory* (OUP, 2011), *Grounding Morality: Freedom, Knowledge and Plurality of Cultures*, co-edited with Jyotirmaya Sharma (Routledge, 2010), *Ramchandra Gandhi: The Man and His Philosophy* (ed.) (Routledge, 2013).

Daniel Ross is a Prometeo researcher at Yachay Tech and co-director of the award-winning documentary feature *The Ister*. He is the author of the book *Violent Democracy* (Cambridge University Press, 2004). He has translated seven books by Bernard Stiegler: the three volumes of the *Disbelief and Discredit* series; *Acting Out*; *For a New Critique of Political Economy*; *What Makes Life Worth Living: On Pharmacology*; and *States of Shock: Stupidity and Knowledge in the Twenty-First Century* (2015). The publication of the two chapters translated by him in this volume is sponsored by the Prometeo Project of the Secretariat for Higher Education, Science, Technology and Innovation of the Republic of Ecuador.

John Russon is professor of philosophy at the University of Guelph in Canada. Among his books on Hegel are *Reading Hegel's Phenomenology* (Indiana, 2004) and *Infinite Phenomenology: The Lessons of Hegel's Science of Experience* (Northwestern, forthcoming). His original philosophical contributions include *Bearing Witness to Epiphany: Persons, Things and the Nature of Erotic Life* (SUNY, 2009) and *Sites of Exposure: A Philosophical Essay on Art, Politics and the Nature of Experience* (Indiana, 2016).

Bernard Stiegler is a French philosopher who is also a founder of the philosophical, political and cultural group Ars Industrialis, head of the Institut de recherche et d'innovation (IRI) that he created at the Centre Georges-Pompidou and founder of the philosophy school at Épineuil-le-Fleuriel. He is the author of the *Technics and Time* series (3 volumes), the *Disbelief and Discredit* series (3 volumes), *What Makes Life Worth Living: On Pharmacology*, and *States of Shock: Stupidity and Knowledge in the Twenty-First Century* (2015).

Tridip Suhrud is the author of *Writing Life: Three Gujarati Thinkers*, *Hind Swaraj Vishe*, *Reading Gandhi in Two Tongues and other essays* and *Kavi Ni Choki*. He has edited and translated (with Suresh Sharma) a bilingual edition of Gandhi's *Hind Swaraj*. His translation of Narayan Desai's four-part biography of Gandhi was published as *My Life Is My Message*. He is currently the director of Sabarmati Ashram.

Sanil V is professor at the Department of Humanities and Social Sciences, Indian Institute of Technology Delhi. He was the Watumall Distinguished Professor at Department of Philosophy University of Hawaii, USA, 2010, and Directeur d'études associés at Maison des sciences de l'homme, Paris. His recent publications include 'On Hating One's Own Children' in Jyotirmaya Sharma and A. Raghuramaraju (eds) *Grounding Morality: Freedom, Knowledge and the Plurality of Cultures* (Routledge, 2010), 'The Diagram of Vastu Purusha: From Meaning to Measurement' in Amiya Dev (ed.) *Science, Literature, Aesthetics: A Project of History of Indian Science Philosophy and Culture* (PHISPC, 2009) and 'The Impersonal Image' in *Journal of the Indian Council of Philosophical Research*.

Milind Wakankar is associate professor at the Department of Humanities and Social Sciences, Indian Institute of Technology Delhi. He is the author of *Subalternity and Religion: The Prehistory of Dalit Empowerment in South Asia* (Routledge, 2010). His recent publications include 'The Function of Rajwade's Fantastic in Realist Novels: Re-imagining Realism in Marathi Utopianism' in *South Asia Review* (2010) and 'The Question of a Prehistory' in Gyanendra Pandey (ed.) 'Subaltern Citizens', Special Issue of *Interventions* (2008). He also translates from Marathi and Hindi.

Acknowledgements

Thanks are owed to the Indian Council of Philosophical Research and the Indian Institute of Technology Delhi for supporting an earlier conference on The Idea of the Public Sphere, from which some of the chapters in this book resulted. We are grateful to Rachit Anand and Tanya Desai for the immense editorial help in preparing the manuscript. Above all we would like to thank the Philosophy editor at Bloomsbury, Colleen Coalter, who complemented our vision and guided the volume expertly and inexorably to its completion.

Introduction:
From Outside the West: Whence? Whither?

Divya Dwivedi and Sanil V

Used by Jürgen Habermas for simultaneously a historical formation and a normative ideal held up to later times, the term 'public sphere' has undergone, by turns, extension, criticism, suspension, qualification, update and contestation. It persists in contemporary philosophy and social theory because it refers to certain institutions that make the *public use of critical reason* possible. It harks to the Kantian characterization of enlightenment in terms of the public use of reason and to the earlier parallel in Greece distinguishing between the *polis* and the *oikos* (roughly city and home). In the Greek context, especially in the early forms of democracy, the ability and right to speak in public gatherings was fundamental to the concept of a citizen. Indeed the democratization of civic space accompanied the reorganization of public institutions from Solon to Demosthenes. But such freedom was a short-lived phenomenon, as the equality of man was tempered by the notion of reason. The political man, for Aristotle, was a rational agent. With the European Enlightenment, this idea moved to centre stage where it became universal. Later, liberal philosophy developed the idea of public sphere as an arena where a reasoning and debating public constitutes itself as the bearer of public opinion. Though the eighteenth-century public sphere was meant to be inclusive, the right of admission depended on education and the ownership of property. The civil society formed the private realm and included the economy and other social institutions like family. In classical liberal political thought, the public sphere was characterized by egalitarian practices of sociability, free discussion and decision by majority. The private sphere consisted of family, cultural and religious bonds and the economy and was governed by private law. The property-owning, autonomous private individuals who were nourished by the intimate relationships within the family and the sense of solidarity received from tradition and culture constituted the public. At the same time, this compelled the property-owning private person to transcend his personal interests and transform himself into a citizen.

It became important in the debate on the public sphere to consider how far this idea could be abstracted from its eighteenth-century European bourgeois origins and which trajectories, outside this context, its historical developments traced. Post-Kantian transformations of the idea of critique, the crisis in the self-understanding of social sciences, radically new conceptions of democracy proposed by feminists and new social movements, decline of the social democratic nation state, irruption of religion into insurrectionary politics and structural demands of economic and administrative systems have all challenged the viability and significance of the very idea of the public sphere. More recent contributions examined the colonial determinations of the concepts of reason, culture and politics that informed the idea of the public sphere. Categories besides class, globalizing capital and media technologies have been brought to bear on this debate, and they include gender, religion, race and ethnicity as well as now biopolitics and geopolitics and mediatization of politics. It has been implied that the public sphere, in its historical specificity and normative ideality, is merely concomitant with a certain image whose title is 'the West': the name for a selective, retroactive construct of a way of life which supremacistically arrogates to itself universality, critique and, thereby, world government.

This volume takes this as a point of departure: not that the public sphere is embedded in Western hegemony so much as that this term is ravelled in several layers of discourse – historical, theoretical and metaphysical. To consider this name 'the West': it is, among other things, a short form that is expanded differently by, say, nineteenth- and twentieth-century discourses on history, science, education, international relations and economics that arose in Europe and the United States, as compared to the early twentieth-century anti-colonial discourses that arose in Africa and Asia, which were followed by yet other, namely postcolonialist and poststructuralist, discourses that arose in the post-globalization academia (Dirlik 1994). With the latter it was already difficult to assign a location to them on a map which could orient discourses in geography. The West and its 'outside' are not merely geopolitical or cultural domains that house possibly different kinds of publics. The idea of the West is inseparable from the call for the public use of reason that founds the modern public sphere. The West is an idea that was handed down not from myth and tradition but from a public act of naming itself as 'The West'; though the development of this idea makes abundant use of both myth, for example, of Europa, and of tradition such as the relative geographic isolation that was perforated by the Silk Route. In this sense, the Western public sphere is not a specific domain of the global public sphere with its own geopolitical location and specific history. Nevertheless, it is in the name West that the culture and its symbolic resources were for the first time connected to the public as a fact of reason. When we speak of a public sphere outside the West here, it implies not only the contributions that arise out of geopolitical regions that are not included in the West, but also, most importantly, theoretical directions that are not easy to clarify within the perfect geometric form of the sphere. For Hegel, the origin of West was tied to the sphere of truth discovered by Parmenides, who lived in a region now in Italy. Since both chronography and geography are political, it is important to acknowledge the historical alignment of ideas of 'west', 'public', 'critical' and 'public sphere' and to register their fraught and for the large part occluded relationship with the outside of the 'west', where the 'outside' was also determined by 'the west'. The endeavour of this volume is to pursue a third and equally important obligation: to admit the opening of the 'west' as well as of its 'outside' to other 'outsides' by new developments that are underway, that are not unmistakable and that presage unfamiliar spatialities and futures.

Habermas's early writings identified the public sphere as a mediating institution between two other institutions firmly distinguished from each other: the individual embedded in the private, sustaining realm of kinship and home on the one hand, and on the other the state which was in charge of law and policy but whose governance reached into private matters of social propriety and mental and physical health. Habermas identified corresponding facets of the public sphere, addressing both sides in the literary and political public spheres. The former included literary journals, periodicals and the institutions, such as coffee houses and salons, which were spaces for members of the public to critically discuss art and literature, drawing on the emotional resources they developed within the private sphere of the family. The acts of writing and reading could be said to come to circulate in the society and at the same time constituted the channel of ideas by the activation of the new institutional networks. The political public sphere, which was born out of the literary sphere, was a place where people critically analysed the actions of the government and kept a check on the state. However, attributing rationality or truth-value to opinion has been a matter of controversy in philosophy. How can mere opinion, even if held by the majority of the public, claim rationality? Philosophers like Hobbes and Locke tried to grant opinion the potential for rationality by identifying it with conscience. But both placed opinion in the private sphere. Rousseau transformed this private and critical opinion into a general will which was more than the result of competing private interests but still less than a debating public. Kant invested publicity with the rational potential to unite politics and morality, which according to Foucault was the conception of 'a way out'. For Kant, publicity was the principle of a legal order and a method of enlightenment. By placing this idea in a philosophy of history, he read the emergence of a public sphere as a sign of progress and derived the sociological preconditions for a political public sphere. The Kantian identification of public opinion with reason was critiqued by Hegel, who brought out the antagonistic character of the public sphere. The conflicting nature of civil society could be reconciled only by the force of the state. Public opinion, for Hegel, was too fragile for this task. For Marx, both the bourgeois constitutional state and public opinion were ideological. Hegel made the public sphere redundant by making the state absorb the civil society. Marx destroyed it by proposing the collapse of the state into society.

The institutions that came up in eighteenth-century Europe and later spread to other societies were the result of an institutional restructuring of Europe, which was uneven across the continent. This transformation was also credited to kings (Frederick the Great with making reason available to the public) and queens (Maria Theresa of Austria with her abolishment of superstitions) by contemporaries. The way the public sphere was transplanted in other continents was further distinct. The American public sphere functioned under its own unique conditions and goals, such as Washington's hope that 'our arrival would result in the extinction of both the savages and the predators which are distinguished only in their anatomy'. Not only later historical developments, as has been frequently pointed out in the critical responses to Habermas, but also other, simultaneous movements, protests and voices in eighteenth-century Europe defied and were muffled by the hegemonic bourgeois public sphere. It has been suggested that the response to them actively shaped the bourgeois public sphere. Hence its limited description from which the ideal of communicative action amenable to rational legitimation of implicit discourse ethics was abstracted for political liberalism requires reconsideration (Klancher 1987; Eley 1992; Negt and Kluge 1993; Calhoun 1993, 2010).

Several critics of the eighteenth-century European model of the public sphere point out that various sections of the society like women, ethnic minorities, the mentally disabled and criminals are excluded from this sphere. They argue that these exclusions are constitutive of the public sphere where who-can-speak-what is determined (Negt and Kluge 1993; Fraser 1985). The political philosophy of new social movements did not accept the state as the privileged locus of the analysis of power. They have given up the holistic notion of a societal totality. For them, the public sphere is part of the civil society, which is characterized not by rational deliberation but by struggles for discursive hegemony. Social theory has recognized the complexity of the functional differentiation of partially autonomous spheres like the economy and administrative systems, which do not allow their internal transformation through direct democratic means. Politics can no longer be conceived as a channelling of the solidarity potential available at the level of concrete traditions or lived experience into democratic procedures. Politics involves complex issues of identity and self-fashioning, which take place in collectives that need to be conceptualized differently from the available notions of the public (Laclau and Mouffe 1985). Social historians have claimed that in Europe there was never a single public sphere but many, thus shifting from the exclusion model to one of parallel and oppositional 'counterpublics' defined by, rather than irrespective of, interests and characterized by non-uniform strategies (Fraser 2007). The normative presupposition of a rational debate does not find any clear application in understanding the logic of multiple publics. The vast numbers today defined as 'sans-papiers' are seen as forming a 'clandestine public' that does not share the classic forms of publicity (Kroser 2005; Pojmann 2008; Castles, Haas and Miller 2013; Bloch, Sigona and Zetter 2014). It is deprived of political status but is nevertheless incorporated by indirectly legitimating the interests of the production process at a transnational level. A reconsideration of the moral and emotional resources of the private sphere and the forms of solidarity they can engender suggests those dimensions of the category of 'subaltern counterpublics' which are not always oppositional or counter-hegemonic.

To observe formations of public sphere outside the West, so to speak, requires a critical parsing through resemblances and differences. For example, the formation of a debating public through English education, circulation of newspapers, birth of the genres of novel and autobiography and social reform movements against caste difference have been seen as its signs in the context of Indian societies (Bhargav 2005). The nevertheless increasing presence of religion and caste in the modern political arena is often seen as the residue of a secularization process that began with the social reform movement but remained incomplete or was thwarted midway. However, when 'interest' as articulated by civil society in India is found to be confined to secular items such as corruption, as in the professedly apolitical anti-corruption campaign organized around Anna Hazare in 2011 and 2012 in India (see Devadawson in this volume), problematization of religion, caste and economic inequalities recede in priority. They are not assumed to be of public interest, since such consideration would 'hurt the public sentiment'/opinion. The 2007 UN Resolution on Combating the Defamation of Religion is a sign of this as a wider phenomenon in our times. This indicates the need for a re-examination of the distinction between the private and the public, leading to a different, and more critical, self-understanding of modernity in India.

Globalization is redefining the place and significance of the nation state and the idea of citizenship. It is increasingly felt that democratic decision-making reduces the efficacy of a market-driven economy. Policy decisions are better left to technological or management expertise. Political parties are taking the form of corporations that lobby for vested interests. Media, while extending its reach, has become a manipulator of public opinion instead of being a facilitator of critical debates. Some cultural critics argue that the public has become a mere consumer of information and that the public has transformed itself into the masses. The masses who enjoy their public image in the rise and fall of public opinion ratings are dangerously reflective and are capable of being the localized and contingent subjects of unpredictable political events. It's a juncture at which it would be worth asking if there is a 'way out' of the public sphere. The debates in the British courts regarding the private lives of celebrities, and the collapse of Rupert Murdoch's British tabloid the *News of the World* in 2011 over illegal phone hacking, raise another question – Is public interest something which entertains the public? Something which keeps the public interested? Or is it what ought to be of interest to the public? The 'ought' here shows up as moral – certainly, the morality of being a public. But the fate of this word 'interest' is conjoined with the concept of the public sphere. Interest as of today is held between the positivism of opinions and the normativity of the ought, both conditioned and produced by public opinion management.

In response to some of the criticisms of the idea of public sphere, John Rawls formulated a political theory of justice attempting to provide the principles that govern universalization of interests in a just society, principles expected to elicit the rational agreement of everyone and attached to public institutions (1987, 1997). Habermas incorporated several criticisms, particularly relating to counterpublics and to religion in the public sphere (see parts III and V in this volume) and proposed a discourse ethics which anchors the validity of norms in the possibility of a rationally founded agreement on the part of all those who might be affected, insofar as they take on the role of participants in a rational debate (1996, 2006). The idea of an institutionalized public sphere grounded in the communicative structure of the lifeworld provides the normative background for criticizing the manipulation of public opinion by the media (Dahlgren 1991, 1995). Observations on the contemporary trends of mediatization of politics have mostly extended and sometimes qualified the Habermasian narrative (Lipmann 1997; Esser and Strömbäck 2014). This is a narrative of decline from the eighteenth-century bourgeois public sphere owing to the progressive nationalization and professionalization of politics into party systems, isolating it increasingly, in the form of electoral politics, from the home; and the emergence of national public spheres owing to new communicational and media technologies and paradigms, instrumentalizing them increasingly for globalizing market forces (Roberts and Crossley 2004).

Recent public protests in places outside the West – mainly in Asia and Africa – go beyond the critical resources of the counter public sphere. In what terms can the massive public participation in the political events of the Jasmine Revolution and the Arab Spring, the unabating protests in Greece and Spain and Iran's so-called Twitter Revolution be understood? They announced themselves as collectively occupying a unique space like the city square or a street – acts of defiance which were not those of conquest or trespass but of occupying a public space. The protesters in many cases did not have an organization, leadership or coherent set of clearly articulated demands or programmes. The act of occupying an empty space that is not a private property exposed the fact that the public spaces were preoccupied by the state and police. This public of occupation is not exactly a debating public. As W. J. T. Mitchel says, the strategy of occupation is to anticipate the adversary by snatching the initiative and pre-empting his arguments. Instead of making a charter of demands these movements opened up a space for the articulation of any such demands (2012).

The chapters in this volume include contributions from philosophy, aesthetics, sociology, history, critical media and technology studies, and film and literary studies. They have been gathered here to suggest that the public sphere can be said to be a *migratory concept* in the manner in which family resemblances between socially and institutionally different formations resonate with the idea of 'public use of critical reason' and with the critical task of speaking to the spectre of the contemporary. In the overlaps and intervals between these nineteen chapters, the readers will hopefully discern questions of how other outsides to the 'West' open and what relations beyond continuity/discontinuity they establish with past formations. The five parts of the volume address different aspects of this opening of the past and future, of the occident and its other, onto each other.

Civil society, state and economy, the three components of the model in which the public sphere is articulated, have transformed in ways that cannot be comprehended in the late Habermasian terms of 'system' and 'lifeworld' (1984). What is the status of the public/private division in today's world of WikiLeaks, Snowden revelations and secret laws, celebrity Instagrams and cloud-leaks, and Snapchat and *citizen porn*? The first part, 'Secret Munitions: Genealogies of Crypto-Politics', considers the relation of the public/private distinction with the 'West', analysing those dimensions in its genealogy that have only now begun to reveal themselves, and paradoxically so, in the form of secret. The four chapters by Bernard Stiegler, Howard Caygill, John Russon and Shaj Mohan address the manner in which secret enters and structurally redefines the system–lifeworld model. Cohen and Arato conceived each of these two parts as comprising a public and a private subsystem (1992). Revisiting the Greek legacy, the dimension of *polis* can be seen as not just an exemplum of communicative action but also a source of a blind universalism that shows that the liberalism in the idea of public sphere is an Occidentalism. The relegated *oikos*, the hearth where cultural difference or ethos germinates, is the surviving of something 'between Europe and Asia' but neither East nor West, the thought of which might break the spell of globalized capitalist economy and expansionist technology, premised as they are on the insistence on rational discourse between individuals (see Russon). New technologies contribute, in ways that demand thinking beyond media logic, to new political configurations and hence to new possibilities and impossibilities of political action. Stiegler contrasts the Greek epoch of democracy opened by the technology of writing with the reigning telecracy which resists what digitization makes possible. Rather than a simplistic hope or despair scenario, the digital must be recognized first of all in its signature upon things, which is where secret turns up as the secret of the digital epoch of politics according to Caygill. The *public–private* division is displaced by that between the *secret* and the *accessible*. The asymmetry of the relation between the state and society is now complicated by a new engagement between violence and secrecy, both monopolized by the state via digital technology. The idea of the lifeworld colonized by a decoupled politico-economic system in the new regime appears increasingly irrelevant as the so-called lifeworld voluntarily institutes itself in corporate social media, uploading and transmitting its erstwhile privacy (see Mohan). If there are other munitions to be forged for this lopsided crypto-politics, they are less secret than obscure and require a relook at the past as well.

The second and third parts look at yet other contexts in the nineteenth-century world increasingly bound together by colonial capitalism, imperialism and their attendant governmentality. A function of it is what can be called geo-power, which through discourses of geo-graphing, science and race induces actions towards the ordering and management of space (Ó Tuathail 2005). Against this background, the chapters by Udaya Kumar, Tridip Suhrud, Subarno Chattarji and A. Raghuramaraju in the second part, 'Births of "Public": Translating Media, Travelling Contexts', inquire into the emergences of publics outside the West. In attempting to sustain discourse ethics as an ethics, the necessity, for Habermas, of including religion in the public sphere entailed an asymmetrical burden: that of translation on the part of the religious citizens and that of imagination on the part of the secular citizens (2006). This part points to a more elaborate role of translation in considering the idea and reality of public sphere. The printing press technology in these contexts acted with respect to and unfolded different social structures, ideas and energies. Instead of simply marking the difference between East and West, between vernacular and global public spheres, this part presents a multilevel scene of translation, destabilizing the valency of these calibrations of the public. In the examples of both Ramakrishna Pillai (see Kumar) and Gandhi (see Suhrud) inaugural moments entail translational exactions at the semantic, idiomatic and cultural levels, devising political ideas to institute communications in non-bourgeois, non-parliamentary settings, with very different models of state, princely in the case of nineteenth- and twentieth-century southern India, and colonial in the case of late nineteenth-century South Africa. Chattarji considers the postcolonial dimensions of English Studies in the highly corporatized and mediatized context of late twentieth- and early twenty-first-century India – a multilingual country with unceasing language politics since colonial times – and of the managerial rationality of the university unfolding globally today.

The following part, Seeing/Doing: Mediatization, Passive Publics and Dissents in Images, introduces crucial nuances, from the perspective of visual arts and media, into the historical and sociological studies on the advent of modernity outside the West which, consciously or not, grant normative privilege to the idea of public sphere, marked specifically by colonial modernity (Joshi 2001; Orsini 2002; Kalpagam 2002). The restriction to the visual, in fact, permits a critical vantage on those constructions of non-Western societies and their public sphere formations which were informed by notions of passivity, non-individuality, susceptibility to the spectacular and an absence of certain traits of reason (Muthukumaraswamy and Kaushal 2004; Debord 1995; Roberge 2010). The order of the visual pertains not only to aesthetics and represented content but also to issues of technology; of access – who can access what; of visibility – of whom by whom, under what conditions, inducing which effects;

and of regime – composition, framing, relation to discourse and feedback (McLuhan 1964; Lundby 2009; Hjarvard 2013). The chapters by Patricia Hayes, G. Arunima, Christal Devadawson and Susmita Dasgupta explore the various levels of the materiality of the visual in relation to the private, the public and the political. Photographic technology, explored by Hayes in the South African context, enables documentation and surveillance but also gets ravelled in channels that link the photographer, the viewer and the viewed in the politics and history of colour. Colour itself belies therein its history. Similarly, the visual is coded with social meaning such that the interventions of art in domains of previously constituted artefacts – for example, auratic religious objects – generate new circuits of desire. Arunima demonstrates the work of art at work in relation to caste, gender, modernity and *publicity* in the case of India's possibly first *public artist*. In more recent times, new social movements (Arab Spring, Occupy), social media, the global crisis of capitalism and older paradigms of television news are plugging into each other to produce certain – visual – determinations of public protest even as the contours of their politics appear foggy (Hallin and Mancini 2004). The shape of crowds, relayed in live crane-mounted TV cameras as well as in the rhizomatic collages *spontaneously* born of netizens, images forth the 'public' in 'resistance'. Devadawson registers the differential between such images and those in an older visual genre – of political cartoon – in their attempts to resist the relay. Interesting conclusions may be drawn from a comparison of this discussion with Dasgupta's account of the public sphere in terms of framing in popular Indian cinema through its history: from its sole reign before the television and cable eras to the current milieu of paparazzi culture and star-studded reality TV.

The fourth part, 'Inside Out: Individuation, Digitization and New Global Publics', dwells on the implications of digitization both on the idea of public and on contemporary and future politics. Is the internet a new chance for a revitalized public sphere, for a new universalism? The chapters by Stiegler, Premesh Lalu, and Mohammed and Mohan refrain from the narrow definition of politics, which restricts it to policy, formal political institutions, politicians and other state actors (Esser 2013), in order to consider another transnational public that has been identified in the electronic networks of social media, such as Facebook, Twitter and blogging sites (Keen 2007). *YouTwitFace* has been a witticism for the manner in which different services have been linked together in spheres of seamless continuity between news, business, advertisements, entertainment, personal relationships, group conflicts, political mobilization and alternative realities – a continuity that facilitates the conversion of persons into data and appears to increase freedom to the same extent that it increases surveillance (Goldberg 2010). The availability of virtual publics on the internet has led some to claim that technology is no longer a mere means but is constitutive of our social being. Stiegler's second and longer contribution extends his earlier meditation on psychic, collective and technological individuation (1998) to digital technology and, using the metaphor of pharmacon, points to the various possibilities of private sphere and psychic individuation that it can both open and destroy through encoding. The critical appraisal by Premesh Lalu of the project to digitize archives in post-apartheid South Africa disentangles the technological and the historical and political threads in this example of digitization at work, cautioning about the distorted futures attendant upon an archive selectively lapidified and subordinated to a digitally assisted and obsolete narrative, in this case that of the Cold War. Another aftermath of digitization, the big data paradigm, can be seen as a governmentality based on control more than surveillance, one that is bringing about a 'totally administered society' by eliminating all contingency (see Mohammed and Mohan).

The last part, (Whose?) Inclusion (Where?), provokes us to consider whether the ideas of multiple publics, counterpublics and subaltern publics remain theoretical adjustments to the normative ideal of public sphere and whether they are politically escapist or transformist (Calhoun 2010). The outside or exteriority, as the chapters by Shannon Hoff, Divya Dwivedi, Tina Chanter and Milind Wakankar show, is not a geographical notion. The presence and the participation of migrants in the mediatized polity, the technological fissuring of the conceptual model of the modern public sphere which relied on the private/ public distinction and the delocalized form of financial capital discussed in several of the chapters in this volume, point towards the complexity that must be borne in mind when we speak today of both the public sphere and the West. Hoff rearticulates 'public' and 'private' in terms of the familiar and the strange and, stressing the continuities between the two, she introduces the intimate as a hidden movement of affects with various histories and each forming different strata in the public. Chanter upends Ranciére's definition of politics as the negotiation of the public–private divide with her proposal that the aesthetic unconscious ushers in new possibilities of interrupting the old fences. One such is the old myth of Vampire, ascribed to a certain East – of the West – and now transforming into new tropes of migration, refugeehood and biopower in contemporary films and fiction, bringing intimations of other schematics in politics but something outside them as well (see Dwivedi). In this figure the theme of exclusion from the public can be read as an invitation to permit politics. Another old fence is the Indian caste system, and neither its origin nor its history can be conceived from the perspective of freedom, according to Wakankar, unless the division built into conceptuality itself is investigated for its incipience in an originary negativity, which is prior to the publicness that constitutes all philosophical concepts. Only by going to the origin of sociality as such can the opposition to caste be inaugurated, as some dalits' writings show.

There have been various enquiries in recent times into the birth of the new political structure and the institutions it facilitated, for example, in the works of Althusser and Foucault. On the other hand there have been claims that the public sphere insists even if the structure with which it coincided has come to a pass. Should we still retain some version of the liberal notion of the public sphere – enlarged and revised – and propose it as a normative basis for a critical analysis of our society? Or, should we give up this very idea? Or, is it time to propose radically new concepts of deliberating collectives that fundamentally differ from the prevalent view of the public sphere? Is it the case today that we are developing a new political structure and the public sphere as proper name refers to certain other things in it; perhaps it names certain confusions. Yet, will the concept of the public sphere as the will to the problematic have another epoch? In that case, as it is customary, should we prepare for another act of naming, a baptism? This would imply the fate of this concept today determining the being of the public.

Part One

Secret Munitions: Genealogies of Crypto-Politics

The chapters in this part seek the philosophical genealogies for this epoch of leaks, exposés, secret laws and paparazzi in order to recognize the politics unfolding in the context of new technologies. The assessment of the present state of the public sphere varies from one essay to the next as do the genealogies, although certain philosophers emerge as anchor points in the grounding of the division – Locke, Kant, Derrida, Carl Schmitt, Heidegger, Nagel and Malebranche. The concept of 'secret' is explored by Howard Caygill in its relation to the state, by John Russon in the relation between democracy and individual differences, and by Shaj Mohan in its opposition to another concept, the obscure. These explorations, however, find an illuminating *praeambulum* in the short piece by Bernard Stiegler, 'Democracy, Consumerism and Industrial Populism', which exhorts us to prepare to seize the opportunity given by the new epoch of the digital – being understood as training, or what he calls education.

It is to be noted that technology is analogue when a signal is produced, processed and received continuously without dividing it into units. Nevertheless, at the level of analogue technology several selections happen, of which noise reduction is an important example. On the other hand, digital implies, literally, digits or that which is separated by units, whereby something, when recorded, is already received into discrete quanta. Stiegler uses 'analogue' as a metaphor for an era dominated by the press, the radio and the television. This era was eventually dominated by television as *telecracy*. Digital for him is the new era of the internet and social media, the era that allows everyone to publish in so many ways, and he indicates a real battle between the two eras. Telecracy suppressed democratic actions and created the public as the sphere of populism; indeed, the most threatening for democracy is to misunderstand itself and turn into populism. Against this, what is required according to Stiegler, is education. He traces a history of technologies at war, starting with the Greek epoch of thought determined by writing – without writing no mathematics is possible beyond elementary counting. As thought itself assumed a new form at this transition, Socrates and Protagoras were both punished by the old guard. A similar epochal change of guard occurred with the printing press, but the technology that changed for worse, in the sense of blocking any further the change of guard, is telecracy.

Arguably, today, WikiLeaks and Snowden would show a change of guard with the arrival of the digital. This change too will be resisted by the new old guard: in the United States, the Boomers, who work with telecracy and its populism. Stiegler exhorts us to explore *how can one make this opportunity of the digital into an epoch for democracy?* Indeed, this change of guard already instructs in the contemporary relationship between state and the civil society, as explored in Caygill's chapter. Snooping into the lives of the citizen while keeping its own conduct a secret, the state elicits civil society's demand for a revelation of all state secrets to the public, as well as the need to keep its own life a secret from state surveillance machines. The revelations might indicate an accidental but rectifiable deviation from an open and equal relation between the state and the society. Instead, Caygill argues that this is an asymmetrical relationship that is not one of war or duel fought on the shared terrain of the political. The modern state is the monopolist of not only violence but also secrets. Politics can no longer afford the enlightenment luxury of being open. Enlightenment is characterized by both the appeal for the public use of reason and the formation of secret societies like the Freemasons whose political strategy was to transform politics into morality. This morality is the crypto-politics of the civil society that tries to camouflage itself from the secret surveillance of the state and at the same time resorts to stealthy means to indirectly occupy it. Caygill disagrees with Agmaben's view that the non-political domain of the surveillance state, able in its sovereignty to declare states of exception, is the no man's land between the private and the public for which we lack a conceptuality. Rather, we have always been living in this no man's land. Through the works of Hobbes, Kafka, Benjamin and Chamanyou he shows the incipience of a conceptuality for this domain which is neither that of democratic debate nor of military conflict, but of man hunt, whose anti-political nature we must recognize. The modes of resistance by camouflage and secrecy are played out within the same logic of hunting. The hope evinced by Assange is that strong cryptography could be a means of resistance against state surveillance. Caygill raises a note of caution that attempts to use strong cryptography to constitute a new public sphere should not underestimate the link between violence *and* secrecy and criticizes Agamben and Assange both for not holding on to the *and*.

The relation of secrecy to democracy is discussed quite differently in Russon's chapter, taking as its point of departure Derrida's insistence that 'democracy must recognize the right to secrets', by which Derrida means the private space per se. Russon finds the ground for thinking private space in Greek idea of *Oikos*. The European idea of democracy is built on the Universality of Man – either you are that or we have got to make you that – which is intolerant to the difference one makes at home through one's culture. Russon identifies the *Oikos* as the place kept out of the *Polis*, in whose privacy one could create one's individual differences, be individualized. Moreover, he lays a different stress on Greek than is typically assigned to the history of Europe: 'the people who lived between Asia and Europe'. He alludes, hence, to a politics that is neither oriental nor occidental. Occidental would be the universalizing system that cannot brook cultural difference or ethos. Based on an idea of 'anyone', the Universal Man, it forgets the 'everyone', all the little actual differences. Russon questions the idea of a liberal public sphere as a domain of rational discourse between discrete, disembodied and self-defined rational individuals, a view that has sponsored a globalized capitalist economy and an expansionist technology. For Russon, the private, that is the secret or the non-public, is where we *dwell* in the Heideggerian sense. The Euro democratic project, which has resulted in pure capitalistic-surveillance-command-control excess, has technologically cut off the dwelling. Instead, he suggests that we must seek a new economics of dwelling or *oiko-nomos*.

Mohan takes yet another view of secrecy where the surveillance model is redundant, as we live with full knowledge that we have no private life: the public/private distinction vanishes with the voluntary, total transmission of individuals who broadcast anyway – both what they wish to and what they do not, such as phone calls, location sharing in apps and metadata. Both the state and corporations harvest this transmission, one in the name of security and the other of profit. Mohan emphasizes three epochs in a mutual tension. The first is represented by Thomas Nagel's idea of privacy as still something to be fought for to prevent the overload of stimuli in the social system which carefully balances the public/private divide in order to reproduce itself. Privacy activism, privacy rights and demands for strong privacy laws continue an older moralism. The second epoch, of the secret, assumes that power is hierarchically denominated by the availability of encryption, where the activists and the government are in a war for decryption. The state avails of legal means such as 'key disclosure laws' to win. This epoch is found in Derrida's *I Have a Taste for Secret*, which shows the extreme tragedy in taking recourse to a secret that cannot in principle be decrypted, although its decryption is *to come*. Derrida implies that the domination of the secret is the total transmission or the exposure of all things. The third epoch, for Mohan, coincides with the metaphysics of the obscure. The chapter finds different axial points for articulating the obscure: in the epistemology of Malebranche and Leibniz, in the Kantian training programme of Reason and in the concept of *precursor* in Canguilhem and Deleuze. Mohan argues that, while a politics of secrets is necessary and its being underway is unquestionable as it demands us to strengthen our cryptography, we need to pay heed to the new politics unfolding before us – the obscure which is not codable within the other epochs, yet always available. Resonating with Stiegler, he suggests that we train with the new obscure figures who might mis-appear as degenerates, since being degenerate is one of the ways something or someone becomes a precursor, the way the Marquis de Sade was.

Democracy, Consumerism and Industrial Populism

Bernard Stiegler
Translated by Daniel Ross

Populism is a constitutive inclination of democracy. Only by subjecting itself to constant critique can democracy contain this inclination. A democracy that loses the capacity for self-critique is headed for serious trouble: it will begin to decompose, to become distorted, and it is in this fact that its essential fragility lies. It is for this reason that opponents of democracy claim that populism, far from distorting democracy, in fact reveals its true nature. Hence Socrates and Plato.

To struggle against populism and against the opponents of democracy we must again become capable of critique, to critique the tendency democracy has, more than any other regime, to generate populism. Democracy means the implementation of the public thing (the common weal or the *res publica*) in such a way that everyone can take part in it, and hence its critique must be carried out at every level of society. This is why democracy begins with the institution of a form of education that allows everyone to recognize the value of the knowledge that grounds the critical processes through which it constantly reinvents itself.

Without a vigorous education system, real democracy becomes merely formal, discredited and ruined from within. Furthermore, the educational system is intrinsically tied to the technics of publishing that make possible the *res publica*, of which democracy would be one possible regime among others – and, specifically, its critical regime.

Do we live today in a regime of this kind? Certainly not: the system of publication through which the public thing can be constituted has been mutating for several decades, but we have barely begun to think this transformation. Through this transformation, the public thing has become the thing publicized by publicists, 'parliaments are becoming depopulated' by the mass media (Benjamin 2003, p. 277, n. 27), marketing has become the new 'instrument of social control' (Deleuze 1992, p. 6) – and the market is thereby phagocytically engulfing the movement of that universal which democracy claims for itself.

In this new state of public things, formed and transformed by publicists at the service of the 'creative destruction' (Schumpeter 1976) constitutive of 'market society', the citizen has been dissolved into the consumer to the extent that television has been imposed as 'telecracy', replacing real democracy with formal democracy and leading either to non-participation or to populisms. This elimination of democracy by telecracy does not begin politically: it is first an economic programme founded on the organization of structural obsolescence, ever more directly soliciting the drives of consumers via 'trash TV' and everything that goes with it, culminating in recent decades in a form of capitalism based on the drives.

Drive-based capitalism engenders an addictive consumption that combines with the short-termist inclinations of speculators who are themselves controlled by the drives. This state of affairs, established via a globalization driven by exclusively speculative financialization, has resulted in an industrial populism within which political populisms proliferate.

Industrial populism draws upon the analogue technologies designed to capture attention that were implemented by the United States at the beginning of the twentieth century, as described by Al Gore in *The Assault on Reason*: the mass media, he argues, has ruined democratic life as it was conceived by the 'founding fathers' of American democracy (Gore 2007). Analogue publishing technologies have transformed citizens into consumers by diverting their desire towards commodities, so much so that the 'creative destruction' theorized by Schumpeter has led to generalized disposability – and, along with it, to disgust with oneself and hatred of others.

Families, churches, schools, representative bodies, political parties and democratic institutions of political representation together form the apparatus through which individual and collective desire is produced by diverting the drives from their goal. Through the mass media, marketing has systematically short-circuited these social structures, without which it is impossible to transform short-termist drives into the socio-economic investments of all kinds that form what we call the future.

The analogue media have annihilated the idealization processes without which there can be no ideas, nor any knowledge, nor that shared critical consciousness in the absence of which there can be no real democracy. At the same time, the global economic crisis, by revealing the carelessness and negligence of this planetary organization of obsolescence and the submission of the public thing to the short-term dictates of marketing, has led to systemic disinvestment and generalized distrust.

The critical ideas that have been derived from rational idealization processes – including those of mathematical idealities – required the appearance of that form of writing which, in the seventh century BCE, opened up public space as the implementation of a system of publication *à la lettre*: there is no public thing without publishing technology. The latter has not ceased to evolve: if 'literal' technology was the condition of appearance of the Greek *politeia*, we who reclaim this heritage are no longer people *only* of the book. During the twentieth century, we became the addressees of the analogue media that brought us telecratic industrial populism, while in the last twenty years digital technologies have totally reshaped the public and private spheres.

The WikiLeaks affair constitutes a significant moment in this regard, a moment in which we are witnessing the entrance of 'digital natives' into the national and international public things. And while they may be met by formalist democratic protests, such protests, far from taking the measure of what digitization is bringing, show that there is still a failure to grasp the immense changes that analogue technology has wrought upon the modern democratic model deriving from the printed letter, wherein formed Humanism, the Reformation and the Republic of Letters.

Socrates was a native of the letter. In *The Greeks and the Irrational*, Dodds stressed that it was in the context of the conflict of the generations, when the gerontocracy felt threatened by the 'Enlightenment' that formed as a result of the *pharmakon* that is the letter, that Protagoras and Socrates were condemned, one to exile and the other to drink the hemlock (Dodds 1951, p. 189).

As for the analogue natives, those 'baby boomers' who in the twenty-first century are ageing, who for quite some time have ceased to be natives of the letter or of printing and who have become acritical in the face of the transformation of public things by publicists, they can and must reckon with the *new generation* who, rejecting consumerism by appropriating for themselves the system of digital publication, still need them on their pathway towards a new critique of democracy and political economy. Only a democratic renaissance of this kind will be capable of combatting populism.

References

Benjamin, W. (2003), 'The work of art in the age of its technological reproducibility',
    in Howard Eiland and Michael W. Jennings (eds), *Selected Writings, Volume 4:*
    1938–1940, 251–83, Cambridge, MA and London, England: Harvard University Press.
Deleuze, G. (1992), 'Postscript on the societies of control', *October*, 59, 3–7.
Dodds, E. R. (1951), *The Greeks and the Irrational*, Berkeley and London: University of
    California Press.
Gore, A. (2007), *The Assault on Reason*, New York: Penguin.
Schumpeter, J. A. (1976), *Capitalism, Socialism and Democracy*, London: Allen &
    Unwin.

2

Arcanum: The Secret Life of State and Civil Society

Howard Caygill

The state would leech into the veins and arteries of our new societies,
gobbling up every relationship expressed or communicated, every web page
read, every message sent and every thought googled, and then store
this knowledge, billions of interceptions a day, undreamed of power, in vast
top secret warehouses, forever. It would go on to mine and mine again this
treasure, the collective private intellectual output of humanity, with ever more
sophisticated search and pattern finding algorithms, enriching the treasure
and maximizing the power imbalance between interceptors and the world of
interceptees. And then the state would reflect what it had learned back into the
physical world, to start wars, to target drones, to manipulate UN Committees
and trade deals and do favours for its vast concealed network of industries,
insiders and cronies.

Julian Assange, October 2012

For his 'Thought for the Day' broadcast on P. J. Harvey's *BBC Today* programme (2 January 2014) Julien Assange chose to meditate on the political theology of secrecy: 'Documents disclosed by NSA whistleblower Edward Snowden show that governments dare to aspire, through their intelligence agencies, to a God-like knowledge of each and every one of us but they hide their actions behind official secrecy. As our governments and corporations know more and more about us we know less and less about them.'[1] Assange counters this blasphemy of state with a warning from the Gospel of St Matthew: 'There is nothing concealed that will not be disclosed, or hidden that will not be made known, what you have said in the dark will be heard in the daylight, what you have whispered in the ear in the inner rooms will be proclaimed at last from rooftop to rooftop.'

If this is Matthew X: 28 then neither Greek nor Latin refers to the *arcana* or 'inner rooms', but it is entirely appropriate that they should now begin to emerge from the text of the gospel. For Assange state secrecy is but the other side of the imposed ignorance of civil society and against it he wages a literally apocalyptic struggle, one of unveiling that reveals not just the secrets but the very *arcana* or secret places of the state to the *Öffentlichkeit* or open space of civil society. Yet this should not be understood as a Clausewitzian 'war as politics by other means' but rather as a struggle in which secrecy becomes the means of waging *both* war and politics.[2] In this struggle, not only must the secret life of the state be revealed to civil society, but civil society too must learn to conceal itself from surveillance; it can no longer afford the Enlightenment luxury of being open or *öffentlich*. The escalating struggle waged on the terrain of cryptography aims to compromise the secret life of the state while enhancing that of civil society and provides a pressing occasion for rethinking the terms according to which we have understood the relationship between state and civil society.

Secrecy, war and the manhunt

The recent revelations of *secret* laws, of *secret* courts with *secret* verdicts, of *secret* deals with internet providers, of massive but *secret* surveillance programmes, of the *secret* systematic exchange of information between intelligence agencies of sovereign states in order to circumvent domestic law have been quite properly decried by press and public opinion – the classic institutions of traditional civil society. But the terms of critique are largely moral, only occasionally political and rarely strategic. The actions of the US National Security Agency and other *arcana* are deplored as if they were a deviation from the normal and upright behaviour that some seem still to expect from the state. It is also assumed that such deviations can be corrected by reforms implemented through political actors and institutions, if they are petitioned fervently enough to do so.[3] There is also the forlorn hope that this surveillance was unintentional, an accidental outcome of the technology that allowed the *arcana* inadvertently to harvest information illegally.[4] These actions are defended by the neo-Machiavellian argument that states must conceal their own secrets and expose those of civil society in order to provide the latter with security. Yet the sheer scale of state secrecy and surveillance should alert us that something more essential is working itself through; it should provoke the suspicion that this is not an accidental deviation from a 'normal' open and equal relation between state and civil society but reveals a constitutive asymmetry that was always present in this relation and has ever since been jealously guarded by one of its parties.

The revelations should make us to think again, not only about state secrecy but also about the concept of the political and the very character of the relationship between state and civil society. The recent actions of the *arcana* of state might be viewed as a declaration of war by the state against civil society, except that this would be too optimistic a scenario. To view state/civil society relations in terms of war places us in the Clausewitzian scenario of a duel, one in which state and civil society figure as opposed parties who tacitly agree on the terrain and the limits according to which they will play or fight out their differences. Politics, especially representative politics, is one such terrain, but it is important not to assume too quickly that the essence of the state is necessarily political in this way. Perhaps politics is rarer than we think, and, coming back to the *arcana*, if there is a shared terrain between the state and civil society it is to be found not so much in politics as in the possibility that both state and civil society are anti-political. In this view, the anti-political secret of civil society would be morality and that of the state, war and the manhunt. Following Gregoire Chamayou's challenging analyses in *The Man Hunts* and *Theory of the Drone* the suspicion arises that the secret life of the state is not at all political, that, contrary to Aristotle, citizens are rarely 'political' but more usually 'hunted animals'. In this view the life of the state is dedicated at best to war and at worst to the hunt – whether actual or virtual – and the reason of state is at best strategic in its pursuit of the logic of war or at worst cynegetic or guided by the logic of the hunt.

The Snowden revelations permitted a rare glimpse of the *arcanum* of the state, those places where it lives its secret life behind the moral, political and even military camouflage in which it routinely conceals itself. Like the ever-expanding hidden room or *arcanum* of Mark Danielewski's *House of Leaves*, or the arcana of Kafka's *The Trial and Castle*, each secret place leads to another and each state has back doors into the arcana of its neighbours. In a sense this is well known, and the WikiLeaks and Snowden revelations only confirm long-held suspicions.[5] Indeed one of the most widely read novels of the twentieth century already told millions of readers all they needed to know about the *arcanum*. The protagonist of Kafka's *The Trial*, in his chase through the *arcanum* of the Court (Gericht) comes closest to its constitutive secret when he meets the court painter and whistle-blower Titorelli who advises him on his case at the same time as discreetly warning him to retreat and not inquire too closely into the *arcanum* that he seeks. As an artist he has his own literal *arcanum*, a locked chest containing the hereditary secrets of the court painter for the representation of power:

> There are so many complicated and various and above all secret rules laid down for the painting of the different grades of functionaries that a knowledge of them must be confined to certain families. Over there in that chest, for instance, I keep all my father's drawings, which I never show to anyone. (Kafka, p. 131)

The chest of secrets – literally the '*arcanum*' – allows him indirectly to represent the more deadly arcana of the court to its victims. Titorelli is indeed working on a portrait when Josef K. stumbles into his studio – a portrait of a judge sitting on a chair in front of an allegorical figure – and continues painting while Josef K. watches:

> 'It still needed a few more touches,' the painter replied, and fetched a crayon from a table, armed with which he worked a little at the outline of the figure but without making it any more recognizable to K. 'It is justice,' said the painter at last. 'Now I can recognize it,' said K. 'There's the bandage over the eyes, and here are the scales. But aren't there wings on the figure's heels, and isn't it flying?' 'Yes,' said the painter, 'my instructions were to paint it like that; actually it is justice and the goddess of victory in one.' 'Not a very good combination, surely,' said K., smiling. (Kafka, p. 126)

Josef K., not for the first or last time in the course of *The Trial*, has fatally misunderstood the first warning – that justice and victory – Nike, that is, military victory – are the same: victory is the meaning of the pantomime of justice that he is pursuing, but it can never be *his* victory. Josef K., in other words, is being warned that he should not behave as if he were in a court of justice, but must realize that he is and has always been engaged in battle. But the painter goes further, as far as he can (Tintorelli is a whistle-blower who succeeds in concealing his indiscretion from the court by using the 'safe platform' of painting but at the cost of being too subtle to effectively warn Josef K.), first by giving the represented judge a dark halo – a warning of the demonic – and then by altering the allegorical figure of justice:

> But the figure of Justice was left bright except for an almost imperceptible touch of shadow: that brightness brought the figure sweeping right into the foreground and it no longer suggested the goddess of Justice, or even the Goddess of Victory, but looked exactly like a Goddess of the Hunt in full cry. (Kafka, p. 127)

Yet, even after this revelation, Josef K. still cannot see that nested within the *arcanum* of justice as war and victory is the further *arcanum* of the hunt. If he can't heed the first warning that what appears to be a court of justice is really a battlefield – the Clausewitzian insight, which is bad enough – how can he be expected to move to the second *arcana* which is that the battlefield in its turn is really a manhunt for which he is the prey. The artist advises that the best he can do is delay the pursuit by evasion and by adopting the posture of prey, but in any case his fate is sealed. Kafka thus anticipates Gregoire Chamayou's insight that the *arcanum* of the state is not political, is no longer war but is becoming, perhaps secretly always was, the manhunt.

Kafka began work on *The Trial* just days after the outbreak of the First World War – which as an anarchist fellow-traveller he naturally opposed and even despised – and initially wrote the arrest and execution scenes that begin and end the novel consecutively, as one nasty short story. The rest of the novel comprises pantomimic delaying tactics, a catalogue of Josef K.'s strategic and cynegetic errors. In the first draft of *The Trial* Josef K., it seems, was not even arrested: the famous opening line 'Someone must have slandered Joseph K., for one morning, without having done anything wrong he was arrested' first read 'Someone must have slandered Joseph K., for without having done anything wrong he was caught'. The word *Gefangen* – 'caught' or 'captured' – of the first draft was later crossed out and replaced by *Verhaftet*, 'arrested'.[6] In the original version Josef K. was prey caught in a trap awaiting the return of the hunter and execution – the scenario was emphatically not juridical but one of a manhunt in pursuit of a randomly chosen victim, the one who this time fell into its trap.

In writing *The Trial* Kafka attempted to extend indefinitely the delaying narrative between the capture and the decreed execution, a compositional strategy that proceeded in the reverse direction to Titorelli's revelations, first by obscuring the manhunt by regarding it as a declaration of war between Josef K. and the Court and then by obscuring this in turn under the moral claim to be pursuing justice. After filling the time between his character's capture and execution with stories of war and moral quests for justice, Kafka returned and juridified the opening scene of captured prey and the hunt by turning it into the beginning of a trial. This was not intended to soften or divert the cynegetic narrative but rather to emphasize that *imagining* he had been arrested was Josef K.'s cardinal error, for far from being a heroic duellist or defendant, he was just captured prey awaiting extermination. This predicament however was extended to the problem of the *arcanum* of the Court; what was this institution that provoked Josef K. to nurse so many illusions? It seemed to profess the pursuit of justice, but when more closely examined, it revealed itself to be first a machine of war that offered security in exchange for obedience and then, under further scrutiny, an eliminatory manhunt. Kafka would not be alone in having such thoughts about the meaning of the war during the summer and autumn of 1914 nor during the four years of state-sponsored mass killing that would follow.[7]

Arcanum and the concept of the political

Another response, one of the most sustained yet fragmented efforts to look again at the state and its relationship to the political following the massacres of the First World War, was undertaken by Carl Schmitt, whose *Concept of the Political* offers a view of this relation through the optic of sovereignty. I'd like to look at another of Schmitt's post-war attempts to reframe the relation of state and civil society, namely the concept of the political *arcanum*, proposed towards the end of his 1923 *Roman Catholicism and Political Form*, a text whose impact has been most pronounced in recent Italian thought.[8] It is important to remember that Schmitt's works from the early 1920s were hypotheses, internally inconsistent experiments in understanding the contemporary transformations of the political. One hypothesis was that the sovereignty of the modern state was contrived as a solution to the religious *stasis* or civil wars of the early modern period (*The Concept of the Political*); another was that political concepts are secularized theological ones (*Political Theology*) and a third, less well known than the other two, was that the modern state is arcane, that is, possessed of *arcana* or secret chambers. This was the argument of *Roman Catholicism and Political Form*.

In *Roman Catholicism and Political Form* Schmitt reflects on the political from the standpoint of the church, an institution exceptional for being a party to the very civil war that sovereign politics was invented to overcome, an exception moreover that survived into the contemporary world. For Schmitt the church embodies a political reason distinct from economic and technical rationalities: 'Catholicism is eminently political in distinction from such an absolute economic objectivity. Political indeed does not mean the manipulation and domination of certain factors of social and international power as maintained by the Machiavellian concept which by isolating a single factor outside political life reduces it to simple technique' (Schmitt, p. 33). Politics, in other words, entails more than good government and should not be associated exclusively with the actions and aspirations of the state. Schmitt continues by claiming that 'No political system can endure even for a generation by the technique of the conservation of power alone. The "political" has within it the idea – granted that there is no politics without authority – that there is no authority without an *ethos* of conviction' (Schmitt, p. 35). The church has such an ethos, which for Schmitt means that it is an eminently political institution, even serving in his view as a place of refuge for the political, for the 'Church has not only the *ethos* of justice, but also that of its own power, that is in its turn raised to the *ethos* of glory, of splendour and honour' (Schmitt, p. 63). Yet this claim to justice and glory that constitutes the political character of the church serves also, Schmitt suggests, to dissemble its political power.

The case of the church shows how the secret itself becomes the *arcanum* of political form in modernity. In the church the *arcanum* is 'its own power' camouflaged within the ethos of justice and of glory – but what then is the *arcanum* of the secular state? Schmitt towards the end of the book looks for what can take the place of glory as the *arcanum* of the modern political and discovers that, in the secularized state, the *arcanum* assumes the form of the secret itself. The state, while appearing to be related to the political, obeys, above all, the *arcanum* of secrecy – it's very *arcanum is* secrecy. The secular state will enhance its power not through an ethos of justice and glory, nor through the claims to offer security or care for its citizens, but through the ethos of the secret. Schmitt evokes Mozart's *Magic Flute* as the hymn to a crypto-enlightened politics, one that for him began the dissolution of the political: 'The eighteenth century remained sure of itself and had the courage to support the aristocratic concept of the "secret." In a society that no longer possesses this assurance, there will be no more *arcana*, or hierarchy, or secret diplomacy; above all there will no longer be politics, for every great political implies the *Arcanum*' (Schmitt, p. 68). This description of the passage from enlightenment to democratic liberalism with, for Schmitt, the democratic dissolution of the political is a preface to his diagnosis of the present, which is no longer liberal but involves the emergence of a new, post-political *arcanum* that combines corporate power and government: 'It would seem as if this kind of secret would be particularly understandable for technical-economic thought and from here might represent the beginning of a new uncontrollable power' (Schmitt, p. 68). The state viewed from this perspective may be defined, in a *detournement* of Weber, as much in terms of its claim to possess a monopoly in the legitimate use of the instruments of secrecy as in its more familiar claim to a monopoly in the legitimate use of the instruments of violence. The thinking of the relationship between the two monopolies is an important aspect of any meditation upon the character of the current and emergent relation between state and civil society.

Perhaps one of the most sophisticated examinations of the political *arcanum* to emerge from the matrix of Schmitt's reflections is Reinhart Koselleck's book from the early 1950s *Critique and Crisis: A Study of the Pathogenesis of the Bourgeois World*.[9] Koselleck's text is largely an elaboration of Schmitt's core theses, but one that emphasizes the role of the *arcanum*: this debt is warmly acknowledged in the preface to the first edition.[10] Koselleck is indebted to Schmitt for the view that the doctrine of sovereignty is developed as a response to religious civil war, that reason of state is katechontic, that the state, to be coherent, must be absolute and that the emergence of the state/ civil society relation is best understood through the concept of the *arcanum*. Koselleck's historical narrative moves from Hobbes and the absolute state to the intersection of an at-once public *and* secret opposition to this state-form in the 'republic of letters' and the masonic secret societies. This is the very meshing of *Öffentlichkeit* and the *arcanum* of civil society that would give us, among other things, Kant's encrypted answer to the question 'What is Enlightenment', published in his preferred journal in the Republic of Letters, the *Berlinische Monatsschrift*, which was also the mouthpiece of a secret society.

Koselleck argues that neither the claims of the state nor those of civil society are essentially political. The *arcanum* of the state consists in its political camouflage concealing a strategic technology dedicated to containing civil war by its monopolies of violence and secrecy. This meta-political conception of the state is opposed to, but also complicit with, a meta-political or moralized civil society whose own political *arcanum* is its conduct of civil war under the guise of morality. Modernity, for Koselleck, is essentially meta-political: within it, the arcana of strategy confront those of morality both to the exclusion of politics. For example, 'the moralizing of politics was far more an unleashing of the civil war, one that in the collapse, in the Revolution was not perceived as civil war but as the mere fulfilment of moral postulates' (Koselleck, p. 156). This, for Koselleck (as perhaps for Arendt in her contrast of the American and French revolutions in the almost contemporary *On Revolution*), is the meta-political condition of modernity, or as he himself put it, 'the civil war under whose laws we still live' (Koselleck, p. 156).

But there is a striking asymmetry in Koselleck's account of the *arcanum*; he focuses solely on the moral *arcanum* of civil society, barely mentioning the corresponding *arcana* of the state. He takes for granted that the state has the right to its secrets and that the reason of state is arcane and its secrecy to be respected. This concession is evident at a crucial point in his discussion of Hobbes's *Leviathan*. Koselleck follows Schmitt in situating *Leviathan* almost exclusively in the context of the religious civil wars unleashed by the Reformation,[11] seeing the claims of sovereignty as founded on the relegation of religious faith from the realm of politics and war to that of private conscience and morality: in his reading of Hobbes, 'The necessity of founding the state transforms the moral alternative of good and evil into the political one of peace and war' (Koselleck, p. 20). But there is also a further inconspicuous transformation at work here, for the distinction of peace and war described here as 'political' conceals something else. Koselleck though avoids confronting this question – that of the *arcanum* of state – and focuses almost exclusively on uncovering the *arcanum* of civil society.

In introducing his discussion of secrecy that plays a central part in his analysis of the *arcanum* of modernity as the *arcanum* of civil society (not the state) Koselleck cites *Leviathan*, Part II, chapter XXI 'On the Kingdom of God by Nature' and Part III, chapter 40 'On the Rights of the Kingdom of God, in Abraham, Moses, the High Priests and the Kings of Judah'.[12] These are key sections of *Leviathan*, the first departing from the condition of 'anarchy' or 'absolute liberty' in which there 'neither are Soveraigns, nor subjects', which Hobbes immediately defines as 'the condition of war'. From the ultimate sovereignty of God, Hobbes moves to a distinction between the honour and worship of God – honour involves the 'inward thought, and opinion of the power, and goodness of another' while worship involves 'external signs appearing in the words and actions of men' – what Hobbes also calls 'culture' and that he sees encompassing labour and education on the one hand and 'the art by which men's wills are to be wrought to our purpose' (Hobbes, p. 399) on the other. There follows some further crucial distinctions within the concept of worship. The first elucidates a problem raised by the infamous frontispiece to *Leviathan* – namely why, in the image of the sovereign or mortal God and commonwealth, some of the men who form the body cover their heads with their hats and others do not. In Hobbes's time covering or uncovering the head was not a matter of individual taste; it was a sign of treasonous insolence and defiance to keep your hat on in front of majesty. In his frontispiece which shows covered and uncovered subjects, Hobbes seems to be illustrating the phenomenon of *commanded* worship. *Free* worship issues from the worshipper, *commanded* worship from the worshipped – in the former, worship concerns the 'opinion of the beholders' while in the latter 'not the words, or gesture, but the obedience is the worship' (Hobbes, p. 400). If the state was founded in free worship then the opinions or religious beliefs of the subjects would matter, while under commanded worship it doesn't matter what they think or what they wear or what they say as long as they obey.

A late echo of this position resonates in Kant's citation of Frederick the Great in 'Answering the Question: What is Enlightenment' – remember, an encrypted text – argue as much as you like as long as you obey. It doesn't matter whether you wear your hat before the sovereign, as long as you are an obedient subject. Kant's distinction between the public and private use of reason is anticipated in Hobbes's modulation of the distinction between commanded and free worship into one between public and private worship (note how the place of Hobbes's 'worship' was assumed by 'reason' in the following century): private worship 'is in secret Free: but in the sight of the multitude, it is never without some restraint, either from the Laws, or from the opinion of men; which is contrary to the nature of liberty' (Hobbes, p. 401). This is the passage cited in a fragmented way by Koselleck; he ignores the context of the discussion of honour and worship and cites only the words 'in secret free' as a description of free conscience. His motive in linking this truncated citation with the reference to Part III chapter 40 of *Leviathan*, while never fully spelt out, is nevertheless apparent: chapter 40 is concerned with the problem of conditional obedience – the ancient Hebrews according to Hobbes 'always kept in store a pretext, either of Justice, or of Religion, to discharge themselves of their obedience, whenever they had hope to prevail' (Hobbes, p. 510). This is a clear description of the *arcanum* as a secret reserve, a secret capital or store of defiance on the part of the ruled. As we saw in Schmitt's discussion in *Roman Catholicism and Political Form* the ethos of glory, expressed in the monopoly of worship, were essential to the political *arcanum* of the church. The 'secular' discussions of worship in Hobbes point us towards the *arcanum* of secular power that is secrecy itself. Power is closely tied to the capacity to keep or reveal a secret. Koselleck, however, looks away too quickly from this connection between sovereign power and secrecy and the claim to a monopoly of secrecy, focusing on the contestation of that claim by civil society and its own *arcanum* or secret reserve of defiance.

By compressing Hobbes's discussions of honour and worship into a description of conscience, Koselleck prepares for his almost exclusive attention to the *arcanum* of civil society. After citing 'in secret free' he interprets it as permitting an individual and politically irresponsible 'migration into conscience' to take place, one in which the not entirely subjected subject of civil society conceals its true relation to the state ('state' is Koselleck's not Hobbes's term). From this, he draws the following programmatic conclusion:

> The splitting of subjects into private and public (*das Etatische*) is constitutive for the genesis of secrecy. The Enlightenment will subsequently extend the inner realm of the conscience but every claim to the political (*das Staatliche*) remains perforce covered by the veil of secrecy. The dialectic of secrecy and enlightenment, of uncovering and mystifying, is already laid down in the roots of the absolute state. (Koselleck, 29)

What is here called the 'dialectic' of secrecy and enlightenment rooted in the absolute state is quickly revealed as an aspect of the *arcanum* of civil society – the transformation of politics into morality effected by both open enlightened critique and by the secret societies. Koselleck points to the 'astounding parallels' between the histories of the Republic of Letters (the exclusive focus of Jonathan Israel's later influential account of the Radical Enlightenment) and the freemasonic lodges; for him they are the 'two social formations that decisively shaped the era of the Enlightenment on the continent' (Koselleck, p. 49): enlightenment and secrecy are thus and seemingly against all expectation 'historically twinned'.

But the simultaneous publicity and secrecy of enlightenment and freemasonry was but an aspect and not the whole of the *arcanum* of civil society. Another predominant feature was the political strategy of transforming politics into morality:

> With the renunciation of politics the freemasons also established themselves as the better conscience of politics. The separation of morality and politics implied a moral verdict on the dominant politics. For as long as the politics of the absolute monarchs dominated, the freemasons hid their secret under the cloak of moral innocence and political absence. One thought, one enlightened, one embodied the spirit and was a bearer of the light. On the basis of the masonic lodges a new system of values was consciously installed beside the existing political order. But that political actuality began to be regarded as the negation of the moral positions already incorporated in the lodges ... demonstrated that political absence in the name of morality was an indirect political presence. (Koselleck, p. 67)

What happened was in fact a crypto-politics – this was the secret or arcanum of civil society recognized as such by the Freemasons and, following them, by Koselleck: 'In addition to the function of the arcanum as protecting and enabling the moral work of the free masons emerged the further function of concealing the indirectly political character of this work, that as such belonged to the true content of the arcanum itself' (Koselleck, p. 72). The conservative, Schmittian but maybe also Arendtian critique of the moralizing of politics informing this narrative becomes quickly apparent: the insincere, dissembled moral politics of civil society replaced political realism – whose open political objectives were maintaining peace and security – with the political realization of a moral (for Arendt 'social') utopia, a mutation of the political that would tend in the extreme towards terror and intolerance.

In this account of the pathogenesis of civil society – now we can see what Koselleck meant by both the 'pathogenesis' and the '*burgerliche Welt*' of his subtitle – there is an astonishing absence. When confronted with the moral dissemblances of civil society it appears as if the state had no secrets, no *arcanum* and, what is more, was the open, honest even naive protector of the 'political'. This of course *is* precisely its *arcanum*; the state does not have secrets but *is* secrecy. This aspect of the political arcanum is expressed negatively in Koselleck's account. Why did the secret societies need the first degree of the *arcanum* – the *protection* of the 'moral inner space' by means of secrecy – if they were not at risk of surveillance, and who would be observing them if not the state (and perhaps the church)? Only at one point in his detailed analysis does Koselleck openly concede that the *arcanum* of civil society was a coherent strategic response to the *arcanum* of the state: 'The secrecy of the illuminati opposed the mysteries of the superstitious and the arcanum of politics' (Koselleck, p. 6). But nothing more is said of this mysterious *arcanum* of politics; it remains in Koselleck precisely that, an *arcanum*. The civil war in short continues – 'The difference between state and society intensified into a conscious and clear offensive posture (*Kampfstellung*)' (Koselleck, p. 76). Except that now 'The political action programme consists in the indirect and stealthy occupation of the state' (Koselleck, p. 77) by the secretive forces of civil society. The *arcanum* of civil society – the protection of its moral secret – is revealed by Koselleck as the effective or 'pure political function' of 'camouflaging the attack, the indirect occupation of the state' (Koselleck, p. 77). The recourse to the language of the hunt at this point is striking, the *arcanum* of civil society is 'camouflage', for while hiding itself from the scrutiny of the state it makes an indirect and stealthy approach to capturing it.

Before leaving Koselleck's still fascinating book it might be worth observing that methodologically its revelation of the *arcanum* of civil society is inseparable from preserving that of the state. The state is cast in the implausible role of the last redoubt of the open and direct expression of the political, assailed in its naivety by civil society's dissembling, insidiously concealed politics of morality that led to the historically disastrous results of moral or utopian 'politics'. But is the state really that innocent, a basically sincere institution that in its bluff political way is incapable of arcane machinations? Obviously not, but the fact that its *arcanum* remains all but invisible in Koselleck's account is not just the contingent shortcoming of a classic of post-war political theory and historiography, but points to a constitutive feature of modernity that has been prominent again in the responses to the contemporary uncovering of the *arcana* of the state by WikiLeaks and Snowden. While the messengers and whistle-blowers are cast as immoral conspirators for revealing the state's arcana and allegedly endangering the security of its citizens, it is also claimed that what they have revealed is not the essence of the state – its combination of secrecy and violence – but a moral deviation by some of its agencies or individual servants or an unanticipated outcome of the surveillance technology that inadvertently gathers more information than is legally or morally acceptable. Just as with Koselleck's historiography, there is an enormous desire to protect the *arcana* of state from closer scrutiny; it must be protected from intrusion against the secretive institutions of civil society that are dedicated to revealing them.

If we return to Koselleck's point of departure in his reading of Hobbes's *Leviathan* I think we can understand this desire to protect state secrecy better. First of all it is necessary methodologically to suspend the Schmittian axiom (that he didn't even believe himself in the end) that the essence of the state is political. Perhaps the state is there to ensure that politics doesn't happen: this is certainly the case for Hobbes whose Leviathan aspires to the once-and-for-all suspension of political difference with the katechontic aim of ending the existing and preventing all future civil wars. We have already seen the way Koselleck interprets this by emphasizing upon the secrecy of conscience. We saw there, as Koselleck did not see, or did not want us to see, that the discussion of honour and worship informing the secret concerned above all the question of obedience. I suspect that here, with obedience, we have an entry to the *Arcanum*, or the secret life, of the state. What then is obedience and where is it located with respect to the monopolies of violence and secrecy?

Security and obedience

The disproportionate and violent response to the work of Assange, Manning and Snowden suggests that their defiance, that is to say their openly disobedient exposure of the secret life of the state, touched a fundamental nerve. Yet it is important not to assume – with Agamben – that this response is driven primarily by concerns with endangered *security*. While the response to the revelations is indeed obsessively posed in terms of the alleged threats to security that they pose, Agamben's claim in *Comment l'obsession sécuritaire fait muter la démocratie* (*Le Monde diplomatique*, January 2014) that security 'seems to have supplanted all other political concepts' implicitly confines itself to the choice of terrain chosen by the apologists for state secrecy. His intuition seems correct, however, when he notes that 'The growing multiplication of security techniques [*dispositifs securitaire*] bears witness to a change in political conceptuality, to the point that one might legitimately ask not only whether the societies in which we currently live can still be described as democratic, but also and above all whether they can still be considered to be political societies' (Agamben, p. 56). He sees a process of 'depoliticization' in course, but even while citing Hobbes in connection with the 'zone of indifference between the public and the private' – the space of surveillance – he considers this process more a deviation or corruption than the manifestation of the essence of the state. He links the surveillance activities of the contemporary state with its view of the citizen as a potential terrorist and asks again, 'What is a state, what is a society guided by this axiom. Can it still be called democratic, or even political?' (Agamben, p. 56). Agamben concludes that 'by placing itself under the sign of security, the modern state exits from the domain of the political and enters into a no man's land in which it is difficult to grasp the geography and its limits and for which we do not possess the conceptuality' (Agamben, p. 59). But this only holds if it is conceded that there has been an epochal change, that the modern state is no longer political. Yet the analysis of Hobbes's *Leviathan* suggested that it never was political, that it had to be forced to concede the political, sometimes by using its own means, namely violence and secrecy.

The assumption that the state is *essentially* a political institution that has been diverted by an obsession with security informs Agamben's prescription for political action – his 'need to rethink traditional strategies of political conflict' (Agamben, p. 59). His rethinking departs from the principle of avoiding escalation, recognizing that any violent opposition to the security state will provoke a disproportionately violent response to the perceived threat to its monopoly of violence. It also breaks with the 'political tradition of modernity that thinks radical political change in the form of a political revolution that acts as the constituent power of a new constitutional order' (Agamben, p. 59). Against the violent claims to constituent power, and in the light of the categorical imperative to avoid escalation, Agamben proposes a *destituent* power, one 'purely destituent, that will not be captured by the security apparatus and driven into a vicious spiral of violence. If one wishes to halt the anti-democratic drift of the security state, the problems of the forms and means of such a destituent power will be the essential political question that we must think in the years to come' (Agamben, p. 59). The call for destituent power, however, reveals a number of problems with Agamben's premises. It is a power that remains fundamentally oriented to *evading capture* by the state, that is to say it is one that considers itself to be vulnerable prey for the hunter state. The turn to a 'politics' of prey, one that seeks to hide and to avoid escalating confrontation, is precisely the politics of obedience pursued on its part by Leviathan. It entails a 'politics' of secrecy that falls behind even that of the enlightened secret societies patiently described by Koselleck. In their terms, Agamben's destituent politics is held at the level of the first *arcanum*, of hiding from the eye of the state rather than proceeding the further *arcana* of a secret politics that sets out to reveal and hunt the hunter.

Agamben is, in short, inviting us to devote the coming years to rethinking the political in a direction already pursued by the Radical Enlightenment. This is a consequence of his claim that we have left the 'domain of the political' in order to enter into a 'no man's land' (in English in the original) of whose geometry we are ignorant and for whose limits we lack conceptuality. Except that we have always been there, that it is not a 'no man's land' and we do indeed possess the conceptuality necessary to understand it. By suggesting otherwise, Agamben is implicitly preserving the *arcanum* of the state. First of all, according to the reading developed above, the domain of the political is and has always been intermittent and fugitive, secured against the state. We are not, in other words, in the course of an epochal exit from political societies but at another stage in the struggle to maintain their existence. Furthermore, we have not entered into a 'no man's land' – a space of war and military struggle – but are in another kind of space, one that is nevertheless well charted and for which we possess conceptuality. This is the space of the game reserve, of the hunt that corresponds to the conceptuality of the cynergetic state most recently analysed by Chamayou in *Theory of the Drone*. Chamayou provides us with the beginnings of a conceptuality and a detailed mapping of the space between state and civil society that is no longer the open forum of democratic debate and will-formation nor the no man's land of military conflict.

Chamayou's *Theory of the Drone* extends the anti-Clausewitzian theses of his book on the manhunts to shifts in contemporary military doctrine. He traces the development from a political/strategic model of warfare incorporated in a counter-insurgency model of control to an anti-terrorist cynergetic model of hunting and eliminating dangerous prey. The strength but perhaps also the weakness of his analysis is its focus on elimination. He is interested in the use of the drone for this purpose and the reconfiguration of global space from one of politicon and military confrontation to the space of elimination – the 'kill box'. His ethical outrage at this development is expressed in the attention he lends to moral issues surrounding the use of drones (he correctly considers the phrase 'drone warfare' to be a contradiction in terms, an expression of nostalgia for the epoch of war) and this, along with timing of the publication of his book shortly before the Snowden revelations, distracts him from an important strategic insight. This is the link between secrecy and the hunt. While aware that drones are used for much of the time to observe and build up patterns of association between observed targets in order to justify elimination, he does not relate this to the sheer scale of surveillance that has been revealed. He shows, against Agamben's claims about the indiscernibility of no man's land and the absence of conceptuality, that the state comports itself as a hunter in a landscape occupied by potentially dangerous prey. However, even his account falls short of imagining just how precisely this landscape has been charted and mapped. The collection of metadata permits precise knowledge of potential prey and their habitats, identified by their degree of potential deviation from a norm of obedience. This linked with the increasingly precise technology of elimination and tightly focused operational definitions of permitted elimination marks an advanced stage in the realization of the hunter state and its complementary pursuit of security and its allergy to politics.

As in his *Manhunts* book, Chamayou's *Theory of the Drone* proposes an ethical critique that gains its force by the careful, almost loving description of the enormities of domination. He is less adept in describing and assessing emergent strategies for defying such domination. In *Manhunts* he was very careful to avoid Agamben's option now revealed as 'destituent power'; *homo sacer* after all is the hunted man or woman. To evade the hunter by hiding and raising camouflage – the Enlightenment secret society's first *arcanum* – is a limited form of resistance suited to survival but not to the pursuit of the good life through politics. This secret life of civil society renounces the aspiration to be a *zoon politicon* in favour of survival as a hunted animal. Nevertheless his analyses of potentials for resistance in *Theory of the Drone* are more extensive and focus on weak links in the control of drones, largely due to their dependence on GPS and on encrypted internet communications; nevertheless they remain episodic and do add up to a wider strategic doctrine of resistance. By focusing on the state and its combination of a monopoly of violence and secrecy/surveillance, he does not look to the emergent politics of secrecy associated with the internet. Both Agamben and Chamayou, in spite of their differences, conclude from the imprudence of challenging the state's monopoly of violence that are leaving the epoch of politics and entering that of security. They do not, however, reflect systematically on the increasing intermeshing of the claims to the monopoly of the means of violence and the means of secrecy that seem constitutive of the contemporary state, nor do they appreciate the significance of the emergent strategies for contesting the state's claim to the monopoly of secrecy as a form of politics rooted in the Enlightenment dialectic of secrecy and revelation.

In his 'Thought for the Day', Assange framed his biblical reflections in terms of Aristotle's definition of the human as a 'knowing' and thus a 'political' animal and the contribution of Protestantism to the Enlightenment. He thus pointed to an important historical nexus that informs the two aspects of his work – the first *arcanum* of protecting civil society from state surveillance and the second *arcanum* of contesting the state's claim to an effective monopoly of secrecy. In the dialogues published as *Freedom and the Future of the Internet*, Assange and his colleagues reflect explicitly on the 'architecture' of surveillance and strategies for resisting it. They depart from the premise that civil society is now largely digital and must consequently express its emancipatory desires through the internet while recognizing the corollary that the state is aware of this and is responding pre-emptively in order to defend its monopolies of violence and secrecy. Although published in 2012 their conversation is fully aware of the extent and degree of state surveillance of digital communications – that is to say of contemporary civil society as the site for the exchange of goods, ideas and affections – now confirmed by Snowden's revelations. Their reflections on the possibilities for resistance depart from the premise that the state is founded on an asymmetry of information with respect to civil society, that it is constitutionally arcane and will defend its claim to secrecy by all means. In response they propose a two-step politics of secrecy reminiscent of the Radical Enlightenment: the first step is to reveal the *arcana* of the state – its secret architecture – and to make visible the implementation and defence of its claim to the monopoly of secrecy. The revelation that the state is an *arcanum*, that it is constituted in and by secrecy and is in this sense essentially anti-political, is the first step towards resistance. Linked to this is the realization that the secrecy of the state with respect to civil society depends on the surveillance of civil society and its relation to the state pursued towards the limit of omniscience. Yet since this is accomplished by a precisely articulated and concealed machinery of surveillance, hunt and elimination, the political response to it cannot be restricted to the evasive manoeuvres of Agamben's destituent power – the tactic of the first *arcanum* of radical enlightenment – but must extend to the second *arcanum* of securing protected spaces against the attention of the state and the protected exchange of ideas and the empowerment that this brings, an *Öffentlichkeit* protected from and not by the state.

Any radical politics founded in the emergent global civil society empowered by but also dependent on digital technology has to confront the problem of the *arcana* of state and civil society and the question of the legitimacy of the state's claim to a monopoly of the means of violence and secrecy. Assange and his colleagues remain ambivalent on this issue. On the one hand they clearly suspect a link between the pursuit of a monopoly of secrecy through mass surveillance and the development of elimination strategies by means of drones and other means of violence, but they also place great faith in the power of secrecy or 'code'. In Assange's view the challenge to the monopoly of secrecy also compromises the Hobbesian claim to secure obedience through the fear of real or potential coercion rooted in the monopoly of the means of violence: 'Strong cryptography can resist an unlimited application of violence' and for this reason 'is the ultimate form of non-violent direct action' (Assange et al., p. 5). Cryptography, the *arcanum*, is war *and* politics by other means. Yet in turning to strong cryptography to open a new *Öffentlichkeit* or arcane civil society it is important not to forget the connection between violence and the *arcanum* – Assange's 'soldier under the bed'. It is this connection that needs to be better understood when contemplating the revelations of state secrecy and surveillance and the increasing adoption by some states of the means of violence suited to the practice of the manhunt.

My thanks to Michael Dillon, Maja Zehfus and members of the Northern Theory Group for their critical comments on an earlier version of this chapter.

Notes

1 http://www.bbc.co.uk/news/uk-politics-25573643, last accessed 1 May 2014.
2 Some tactical aspects of this struggle are discussed in Assange et al.'s *Cypherpunk*, an unjustly overlooked text; they are also raised to the Kleistian condition of being the very secret of world history in Neill Stephenson's novel *Cryptonomicon*, much read in the hacker community.

3	See Ryan Liza's illuminating investigation of the overseeing role of the US Senate Committee on Intelligence in *The New Yorker*, 16 December 2013.

4	This was the line of defence adopted by the National Security Agency (NSA) – it was adopted in public by the US director of public intelligence James R. Clapper who, before the Senate Committee on Intelligence on 2 March 2013, admitted that data collection might take place 'inadvertently' but not 'wittingly' as well by council for the NSA when under scrutiny before a secret Foreign Intelligence Surveillance Act (FISA) court. See Liza, op. cit.

5	It should be remembered that Manning and Snowden are but the most recent in a long line of whistle-blowers who had substantially revealed the extent of NSA surveillance as early as 2004. See footnote 44 of Assange et al., for a chronicle of revelations concerning NSA activity prior to Snowden.

6	Most of the examples for the usage of *Gefangen* in the Duden *Deutsches Universal Wörterbuch A–Z* involve captured soldiers and prisoners of war.

7	For a self-consciously revisionist account of the problem of the 'mass-killing' that is hidden behind the term 'First World War' see Stéphane Audoin-Rouzeau and Annette Becker, *14–18, retrouver la Guerre*, Éditions Gallimard. Paris, 2000.

8	Roberto Esposito refers directly to Schmitt's arguments from *Roman Catholicism and Political Form* in a wide-ranging dialogue with Massimo Cacciari, 'Dialogo sulla teologie politica' *Micromega* 3/25, Spring 2014, p. 6.

9	Koselleck's book was presented as a thesis in 1954 at the University of Heidelberg, then published in 1959 by Verlag Karl Alber and republished with Suhrkamp in 1973.

10	The bibliography refers to Schmitt's *Political Theology, The Law of the Earth, The Leviathan in Hobbes's Doctrine of the State* and *The Dictator*.

11	'Paradigmatisch fur die Genese der modernen Staatstheorie aus der situation der religiosen Burgerkriege ist Hobbes, auf den sich Spinoza berufen hat' (Koselleck, p. 17).

12	He also cites Hobbes's discussion of conscience from the *Elements of Law II, 6, 3*.

References

Agamben, Giorgio (2014), 'Comment l'obsession securitaire fait muter la democratie', *Le Monde diplomatique, Maniere de voir 133, Fevrier-Mars 2014: Sourriez vous etes surveilles*, Paris.

Assange, Julien, Jacob Appelbaum and Andy Muller-Maguhn (2012), *Cypherpunks: Freedom and the Future of the Internet*, New York and London: OR Books.

Chamayou, Gregoire (2010), *Les chasses à l'homme: Histoire et philosophie du pouvoir cynérgétique*, Paris: La fabrique editions.

Chamayou, Gregoire (2013), *Theorie du drone*, Paris: la fabrique editions.

Hobbes, Thomas (1982), *Leviathan or the Matter forme and Power of a Commonwealth*, ed. T. Macpherson, Harmondsworth: Penguin Books.

Kafka, Franz (2008), *The Complete Novels*, trans. Willa and Edwin Muir, London: Vintage Books.

Koselleck, Reinhard (1973), *Kritik und Krise: Eine Studie zur Pathogenese der bürgerliche Welt*, Frankfurt-am-Main: Suhrkamp Verlag.

Lizza, Ryan (2013), 'State of Deception: Can the Intelligence Community be Reformed?' *New Yorker*, 16 December.

Schmitt, Carl (2010), *Cattolicesimo Romano e Forma Politica*, trans. Carlo Galli, Bologna: Il Mulino.

3

On Secrets and Sharing: Hegel, Heidegger and Derrida on the Economics of the Public Sphere

John Russon

The public sphere is the shared space in which people meet. How we understand this 'meeting', however, has substantial political consequences. The tradition of European liberalism has typically interpreted the public sphere as the domain of rational discourse between human individuals. This liberal conception is premised on the notion of a discrete and self-defined rational individual and, whereas this conception has been highly politically liberatory, specifically through recognizing the rights of individuals to define themselves beyond the oppressive terms of predetermined political and cultural situations, this disembodied sense of human persons has also sponsored an economic and technological expansionism that is absolved in advance from recognizing the moral authority of the boundaries that define natural and cultural specificity. For this reason, the supposedly 'universal' notion of the liberal public sphere has in fact been in service of the expanding political and economic domination of the non-Western world by powers historically rooted in the European West.

Hegel, Heidegger and Derrida offer us powerful resources for criticizing the early modern conception of persons and, with this, they offer us the terms for a redefined conception of the public sphere. Hegel demonstrates that rational individuality is always subtended by social systems of interpretation, with the result that the meeting of persons is not an encounter of homogenous individuals but is first and foremost an encounter of cultural systems that precisely fail to meet: the public sphere is thus better understood as the domain of intercultural opacity than as transparent rationality. I will pair the discussion of these Hegelian ideas with Derrida's discussion of the inherent ambiguity in the notion of democracy, such that it must simultaneously be committed to the maintaining of sharing and of what cannot be shared. I will finally pair this critique of traditional liberal conceptions of democracy with Heidegger's critique of technology, to understand why it is that the problematic conceptions that underlie the liberal vision ultimately sponsor an exploitative globalization.

Politics and recognition

It is the ancient Greeks, who lived in the areas surrounding the Aegean Sea, straddling the continents we now call Europe and Asia, from whom we have inherited both the word and the notion of the *'polis'*. We now take both the word and the notion 'politics' for granted, forgetting that 'political life' is not a naturally occurring human condition but is a developed way we have of dealing with each other, a way that has been refined and transformed throughout history.[1] Our contemporary interpretation of 'politics' is most prominently informed by the ideas of the English philosopher John Locke and other thinkers of the European Enlightenment who have defined the tradition of 'liberalism'. To Locke, we owe the notion of the universal equality of persons and the idea that a just political power rests upon the consent of the self-conscious individuals subject to it.[2] It is on the basis of these liberal principles that we have come to approach our understanding of politics through the distinction between 'private' and 'public', where private life is the arena in which individuals exercise their self-conscious freedom of choice to determine their mode of personal life and the disposition of their personal property according to their own values and public life is the arena in which individuals interact with others, crucially governed by the requirement that one's individual action not transgress against the equal rights of other individuals. Political power is understood as the use of force to protect against such transgression on behalf of individuals, a use of force that is to be 'transparent' – that is, defensible in public in terms that are in principle meaningful to any rational individual. This understanding of politics in terms of 'public' and 'private' in fact differs significantly from the understanding of it among the ancient Greeks, for whom the fundamental concern is not 'individual in relation to individual and in contrast to the state' but is instead '*oikos* in relation to *oikos* and in contrast to the *polis*'. This distinction between the ancient and the modern interpretations is politically significant, and is indeed highly relevant to the contemporary interpretation of 'the public sphere'.

For the Greeks, the fundamental 'unit' of human life is not the individual but the *oikos*, which is commonly translated as 'family' or 'household' but which more exactly means the human environment that is one's 'own'. Playing upon the word 'family', we might translate *oikos* more expansively as 'the familiar', a notion of something that is inherently social and situated. The *polis*, on the contrary, is understood as the human reality that is constituted when members of different *oikoi* come together to develop a shared environment and a shared practice, acting in advance as agents of this new, collaborative reality rather than as agents of their respective *oikoi*. This notion of 'the political' differs from our typical, modern conception in two important ways. (1) It understands the relevant participants in political – 'public' – discourse to be, not indifferent individuals, but participants already defined by specific communities. (2) It understands political discourse to be the practice of forming a new, shared reality, rather than as the generation of policies to regulate a formal space of alienated engagement. Hegel's analysis of the nature of self-conscious individuals reinvigorates this ancient conception as a means of criticizing the liberal interpretation of political life.

The most powerful and important insight of Hegel's phenomenological investigation of human experience is the observation that each of us develops her sense of herself through negotiation with the ways in which other people give us feedback about ourselves. More precisely, we have a 'desire for recognition [*Anerkennung*]' – that is, we need our sense of self-worth to be confirmed by others, and our developed sense of self-identity is fundamentally formed from the terms of this interpersonal dialogue (Hegel 1977, paras 174–85):

> Each is for the other the middle term, through which each mediates itself with itself and unites with itself; and each is for itself, and for the other, an immediate being on its own account, which at the same time is such only through this mediation. They *recognize* themselves as *mutually recognizing* each other. (Hegel 1977, para. 184)

We enact such a dialogue individually with individual others, but such individual exchanges are themselves contextualized and informed by the broader, historical accumulation of terms through which people in general have come to acknowledge the nature of people in general. Our formative interpersonal exchanges are thus themselves conduits through which our culturally established terms for recognizing each other are perpetuated, transmitted and transformed. Through the 'surface text' of individual engagement, the larger and deeper scripts of cultural belonging are being performed.

What this means is that individuals are never simply individual. The very fabric of individual existence is social discourse, so our individuality is always really a way of taking up the established terms of intersubjective life: each person is a way of expressing a communal self-perception, or 'Spirit' [*Geist*], which Hegel defines as,

> this absolute substance which is the unity of the different independent self-consciousnesses which, in their opposition, enjoy perfect freedom and independence: 'I' that is 'We' and 'We' that is 'I'. (Hegel 1977, para. 177)

Self-perception is thus inherently relational – it is essentially a sense of how we fit with each other and with the surrounding world – and it is thus as much a perception of the world as it is a self-perception.

> [Spirit] is the *self* of actual consciousness ... which opposes to itself ... an objective, actual *world*, but a world which has completely lost the meaning for the self of something alien to it, just as the self has completely lost the meaning of a being-for-self separated from the world. (Hegel 1977, para. 439)

Our sense of self is essentially our sense of belonging: it is how we define the terms of the inter-human world in which we recognize ourselves as belonging. We bring such a cultural worldview in our train whenever we act and in whatever we say.

The Greeks distinguished the *oikos* from the *polis* and imagined the political sphere to be the domain of interaction in which we rise above the merely familiar – the *oikos* – and engage with each other in (comparatively) neutral terms. What Hegel's analysis of 'recognition' draws our attention to, however, is that the domain of familiarity extends well beyond the household that the Greeks called '*oikos*'; more broadly, we participate in a *Volk* – a 'people' or a 'nation' – that is our cultural domain of familiarity, of feeling 'at home', and thus the terms that define the *oikos* in fact infect in principle our participation in political life. Hegel's name for this domain of cultural familiarity is '*Sittlichkeit*' or 'ethicality'.

> The *realm of ethical life* ... is nothing else than the absolute spiritual *unity* of the essence of individuals in their independent *actual existence*; it is an intrinsically universal self-consciousness that takes itself to be actual in another self-consciousness. ... The single individual consciousness ... is only this existent unit in so far as it is aware of the universal consciousness in its individuality as its *own* being, since what it does and is, is the universal custom. It is in fact in the life of a people or nation that the *concept* ... of beholding, in the independence of the 'other,' complete *unity* with it ... has its complete reality. (Hegel 1977, paras 349–50)

Within our intra-communal 'political' life, we share our implicit 'ethical' commitments, and, since they are the very terms in which we as individuals recognize each other, these commitments are largely invisible to us. While a 'political' community might explicitly and self-consciously posit specific laws for the regulation of behaviour, there nonetheless remains behind this explicit positing an implicit system of shared commitments, an 'unwritten law' or '*nomos*' that governs behaviour not as an external regulation but as the very formative logic of the social fabric. In this sense, intra-communal politics thus precisely fails to be the true site of the *polis* inasmuch as properly political behaviour was to be the engagement of those from different *oikoi* beyond the terrain of familiarity. Indeed, when familiarity is construed in this way, we can see that it is precisely in cross-cultural exchanges, in the encounter between *different* 'political' communities, that the site for true political interaction is engaged.[3]

It is in extra-communal political life that the real challenge of establishing a rapport between members of different *oikoi* – different 'ethicalities' – is engaged. But let us reflect phenomenologically on the form such engagements take. In extra-communal political life our ethical commitments, which are invisible and comfortable in intra-communal political life, become thematic and problematic. In the political encounters between people of different 'ethical' societies, we precisely meet those with whom we do not have established terms of mutual recognition. In this situation, our own implicit commitments stand out to the other as strange and inappropriate dimensions of behaviour, even as they are invisible to us; simultaneously, the modes of ethical behaviour that are obvious and inconspicuous to our others stand out to us as odd and inappropriate. We always imagine others, so to speak, 'to speak with an accent', whereas we imagine our own 'speech' to be neutral; in fact, however, culturally speaking, there is no such 'unaccented speech'[4]: it is only in and through our culturally 'coloured' ways of establishing terms of interpersonal recognition that we become able to participate in the shared human world at all, and our participation in political life, whether within or beyond our community, will always bear within it the traces of our historical and cultural particularity.[5]

This common but problematic interpretation of cross-cultural political engagement as something that takes place between a 'neutral' party and an 'accented' party has significant and real political problems attached to it, not, of course, with matters of language specifically, but with matters of (cultural) value. The concern for the 'rights of women' is a prominent and clear example of a situation fraught with these interpretative difficulties of 'neutrality' and 'accent'. It is common for liberal theorists in the West to be critical of the 'abuses' of women's 'rights' in non-Western (prominently Muslim) cultures.[6] The moral motivations for such critiques are principled and significant, but they are nonetheless interpretively problematic: in particular, in such criticism, 'woman' is a notion that is (typically) taken to be neutral. Though from the perspective of a culture that views persons as individuals, it seems obvious and unproblematic to look at a human situation and see an interaction between 'a woman' and 'a man' or something similar, from the perspective of another culture – which could be ancient Greek or could be various contemporary Muslim or Hindu cultures – what might be obvious is that one sees 'a family'. Whereas in the individual-centred perception, the persons are independent units and the family a derivative construction based upon them, in a family-centred perspective, the family is the unit and the individuals are derivative units abstracted from that context. In other words, the very meaning of 'woman' (or, *mutatis mutandis*, 'man') is fundamentally different in these contexts, in one case being an ontologically autonomous unit, in the other an ontologically derivative aspect of the real unit (the family). For that second perspective, the norm of the proper functioning of the family may well be what appears neutral and the forceful isolation of the woman from this context what appears accented, rather as one might consider the hand outside the context of the functioning of the body an artificial reality produced by forceful isolation. While the concern with women's rights is without a doubt a highly important theme, so too is the concern with the health of the family; and, most importantly, neither is neutral. In neither case, then, is it a matter of the simple perception of an obvious fact; rather, on each side, we have an *interpretation* of human nature and, while there might be very good – even compelling – reasons to deem one or the other interpretation superior, this does not remove the fact of its being an interpretation.[7] Analogous problems shape cross-cultural communication wherever the interpretative dimension of the terms in which we address the world is denied and those terms are presumed to be unproblematically neutral. This recognition of the inescapable interpretative dimension of our social experience is of primary importance for understanding the nature of the public sphere.

The ancient Greek model of the *polis* points to the public domain as the arena in which we meet with each other and communicate together about our shared interests; what we should notice, though, is that, in political interaction between cultures, the meetings of individuals precisely enact a kind of non-communication because the basic terms for the interpretation of the world – the basic parameters of *nomos* – are not shared. For this reason, the fundamental error in cross-cultural politics is the assumption that there is a neutral body of political terms, a universal rationality that defines the grounding values of human interaction. What is required instead is the recognition that the political world is essentially and necessarily an arena defined by the conflict of interpretations, and that the political imperative is precisely the cooperative establishment of shared terms of interpretation. In place of presuming that we are in a zone where it is already possible to communicate and where we are thus meeting with others, we must precisely begin by acknowledging the fact of a non-meeting.[8]

The public domain is thus precisely the arena in which we do not know in advance who we are encountering: what is presented to us is the absence, the hiddenness of the other. Compared to the obviousness of the world of our *Volk*, the world articulated through our *nomos*, the other is strange, her ways secret. And, indeed, for that other herself – and similarly for the *nomos* that is present in ourselves – those strange ways are themselves precisely not transparent, for they are taken to be obvious perceptions of fact rather than historically sedimented and socially enacted practices of interpretation. Hegel's analysis of 'ethicality' thus reveals the secret that precedes individuals, the founding 'past' that provides the very terms through which we are able to be present to others. Let us now turn to Derrida for the secret of our future.

Publicity and secrecy

In the wake of Locke and the Enlightenment tradition, 'democracy' has been broadly advocated as the only just political regime. As Derrida writes in *Rogues*,

> Today in what is called the European tradition (at the same time Greco-Christian and globalatinizing) that dominates the worldwide concept of the political ... the democratic becomes coextensive with the political. (Derrida 2005, p. 28)

Precisely what it means to be 'democratic', however, is not transparent, and reflecting further on this notion can help us again to recognize the one-sidedness of the Western, liberal tradition.

Like the word and the notion 'politics', the word and the notion 'democracy' comes from the ancient Greeks. Its core notion, etymologically speaking, is the idea that people should govern themselves – basically the same meaning as 'politics'.[9] This idea of self-governance, however, though easy to state, has no unambiguous realization; indeed, Derrida in *Rogues* refers to 'the semantic

vacancy or indetermination at the very center of the concept of democracy'
(Derrida 2005, p. 24). 'Democracy' names an unconditional value – that
people should govern themselves – but that value can only be enacted through
determinate measures based on decisions about how to interpret 'people' and
'governance', and every form of its realization will thus be only a one-sided
enactment of that notion of self-governance. For this reason, democracy, like
politics itself, has historically taken various forms, forms that each have their
own ground for being deemed legitimate realizations of the notion of 'self-
governance'; hence Derrida refers to 'a *future of the very concept* and thus of
the language of democracy, an *essential historicity of democracy*' (Derrida
2005, p. 25). In its finite realization, though, every so-called democracy – every
'conditional' democracy: that is, democracy 'on the condition that' we interpret
this or that as what is essential to its realization – is as much open to legitimate
criticism in terms of the unconditioned notion of 'self-governance' as much as it
is legitimated by that notion. There is thus no pure or 'neutral' democracy: there
are only democra*cies*, each an ambivalent realization of the notion, as much
a betrayal as an endorsement of its concept.[10] To see the political force of this
ambivalence, we can, following Derrida, note two essential but opposed notions
that are constitutive of our core sense of what makes democracy worthy of our
moral endorsement.

First, as Locke-inspired liberalism has insisted, democracy insists that
legitimating appeal must be made to the comprehension and consent of self-
conscious individuals: politics must be 'transparent' and political power must rest
on *reasons* that in principle any individual could grasp and to which any individual
could agree: justice must be public.[11] The institutional acknowledgement of
the right of the public is as old as the original Greek democracy and Roman
republic. In both Greece and Rome, institutions were established for publishing
the laws. In Rome, the plebeians regularly held assemblies to discuss their
collective situation in the context of patrician oppression, a voice institutionally
recognized in the establishing of the office of the 'tribunate', which was to
serve as a popular check against the unjust actions of legislators. A similar
acknowledgement of the living 'reason' of popular self-reflection emerged in the
seventeenth- and eighteenth-century development (through such vehicles as *The
Spectator* of Addison and Steele) of the newspaper as a tool for informed public
discourse. Simultaneously, however, in both the ancient and the modern world,
this notion of legitimation by the public has empowered tyrannical populist
demagogues who rely upon popular ignorance to gain political power, and in
the modern world it has precisely encouraged the growth of the oligarchical

power of advertisers and the so-called news media to shape public opinion and hence political decision-making. This first notion, the emphasis on legitimation through publicity, though intended as a voice against tyranny and oligarchy, can equally encourage the growth of non-democratic power in the context of cultivating a norm of populist homogeneity.[12] This principle, ambivalent in itself, is also set off against a second principle of democracy.

The second principle, with which the notion of the inherent publicity of whatever is legitimate is coupled, is the equally important idea that democracy should allow us to live life on our own terms and should protect our ability, precisely, to be private. This second value, however, sits uncomfortably with the first. As Derrida writes,

> A democracy must be public and phenomenal through and through, something of the Enlightenment. But since it must also recognize, in the name of democracy, the right to the secret, things again get complicated. (Derrida 2005, p. 65)

Against the homogenizing tendency of the norm of 'publicity', democracy can precisely be understood as the endorsement of heterogeneity, the protection of people to shape their worlds in unique and determinate ways and thus to enact boundaries that determine who will and who will not be invited in: to have 'secrets' that we do not share and that make us intentionally different from others whom we exclude from our circle. To understand how this is, as Derrida says, a 'complication', we must again reflect on two different ways of interpreting persons.

Democracy intends to endorse and realize the freedom of all. This 'all', however, is an interpretively ambivalent term. The tension, essentially, is that between interpreting 'persons' generically – as each the same, each 'anyone' – and interpreting 'person' singularly – as each different, each 'unique'. Derrida describes this intrinsic tension in *On the Name*, drawing again on the language of 'the secret':

> It's a matter of maintaining a double injunction …: the desire to be inclusive of all, thus understood by all … and the desire to keep or entrust the secret within the very strict limits of those who hear/understand it *right*, as secret, and are then capable or worthy of keeping it. (Derrida 1995, pp. 83–4)

In insisting that it speaks to 'everyone', democratic politics must address 'anyone' – that is, it must address a generic subject not defined by any specialized characteristics. Such an 'inclusive' orientation, however, is inherently homogenizing, precisely excluding from political recognition those aspects of our lives that are premised on exclusivity. And yet, it is equally the mandate of democracy precisely to protect our heterogeneity: to allow us to live our lives on our own terms, terms precisely which differentiate us from and exclude others. In our unique lives, we determine for ourselves those with whom we will associate, the interpersonal bonds that will define us, the projects we will undertake with others and the terms in which we will take up those projects. Within these worlds shared with others, we do not exist as generic, atomic individuals; on the contrary, through our desires, choices and associations, through our love relations, our educational apprenticeships, our material conditions and our social bonds, we take on irreducibly multiple and intertwined identities that are incomparable to the identities of others and that do not answer to the 'logic' of individuality, either in their form of agency or in the norms to which they answer. Through our capacity to choose, we precisely become non-individual participants in exclusive networks into which others are not immediately welcome to enter. Democracy, in other words, is inherently the endorsement of our 'right' to renounce liberal individuality.[13] Democracy is to be the freedom for all, but there is no single form of freedom that fits all of us, and, in insisting that there is a generic (individual) form of freedom, the supposedly inclusive 'democracy' precisely becomes a regime that fails to recognize – excludes – every actual person.[14] In contrast to the Enlightenment vision that has resulted in a public domain that is construed as the homogeneous arena where liberal individuals meet, we should instead recognize the public domain as the site of heterogeneity where new, exclusive forms of (non-)identity are constantly emerging.

Economic and technological globalization

Rights are understood to accrue to human individuals intrinsically, and they are thus no more limited by the historically contingent boundaries of nation states than they are by the naturally given conditions of gender, race or age. Indeed, it was precisely for the sake of overcoming the limitations of political boundaries that Malcolm X in the 1960s appealed to a notion of human rights, rather than a notion of civil rights, in championing the cause of black Americans against entrenched cultural oppression in the United States.[15] On the one hand, this notion of 'human' rights promises a liberation from which no one can legitimately be excluded and thus invokes a promise of a universal justice.

On the other hand, it is a notion that in principle can be invoked to justify the refusal to acknowledge the rights of national sovereignty. In other words, the agent of 'human rights' does not need to ask for permission to enter the domain of another, for she has defined herself as already speaking and acting on the other's behalf. In our discussion of 'neutrality' and 'accent', we already saw the problem in principle with this as a theoretical approach; it is also a political problem in practice because it defines a form of human action that absolves itself of answerability to precisely the institutions that are a community's resources for self-governance. Though in principle a programme for universal liberation, the norms of liberalism have in fact underwritten a quite different reality, for their justification in principle of a disregard of the essentiality of national sovereignty has facilitated the expansion of (European) economic power as a para-political institution that is not answerable to legitimate government.

While it is not intrinsic to liberal politics explicitly to endorse in principle any particular model of knowledge or economics, in fact the cultural championing of a politics of individual rights developed hand-in-hand with the scientific revolution and the rise of capitalism in and as the emergence of (early) modern Europe and its global expansion. The new science and the emerging capitalism effectively relied upon the 'rights' of the individual in the domains of knowledge and economics respectively, and the politics of 'human rights' licensed this culture and enshrined its premises in law. The technological and economic successes of this culture made Europeans highly attractive advisors to non-European regimes seeking to 'modernize', and these European views came to shape the functioning of non-European cultures while simultaneously installing Europeans in very powerful positions within those cultures.[16] Both because of the historical intertwining of these cultural enterprises and because of the shared premise of the irreducible authority of the individual, liberal politics and the global expansion of (European) capitalism are intimately linked. There is a further link, though, rooted in the metaphysical implications of this shared interpretation of the nature of persons.

Since the choosing individual is construed as being able to determine the value or significance of any and all particularities, the particular world about which the individual makes such choices comes to be construed as merely instrumental, as a reality that is simply 'for' choice: in short, property. It is precisely this instrumental view of the world, under the name of 'enframing' [*Ge-stell*], that Heidegger argues is distinctive of the problematic 'technological' worldview that is characteristic of the modern world (Heidegger 1993, pp. 324–8).

Though humans have always used machines to mediate and enhance their relationship to the world, the distinctly 'technological' worldview, as Heidegger deploys that term, construes the world as an objective 'standing-reserve' (*Bestand*) for deployment: forests are 'lumber', rivers are 'hydro-electric power', geological formations are 'oil-fields' and so on (Heidegger 1993, pp. 320–3). Heidegger writes,

> The revealing that rules in modern technology is a challenging [*Herausfordern*], which puts to nature the unreasonable demand that it supply energy which can be extracted and stored as such. ... Everywhere, everything is ordered to stand by, to be immediately on hand, indeed to stand there just so that it may be on call for a further ordering. (Heidegger 1993, pp. 320, 322)

For technology, nature holds no secrets: this is an approach to the natural world in which all the given forms, all natural boundaries, are erased, and the very materiality of existence is construed as plasticity, a resource available for re-formation and, as such, fundamentally a 'valuable' unit for our projects. Indeed, this interpretation of nature simultaneously shapes our humanity; Heidegger writes:

> The forester who measures the felled timber in the woods ... is today ordered by the industry that produces commercial woods, whether he knows it or not. He is made subordinate to the orderability of cellulose, which for its part is challenged forth by the need for paper, which is then delivered to newspapers. ... The latter, in their turn, set public opinion to swallowing what is printed, so that a set configuration of opinion becomes available on demand. (Heidegger 1993, p. 323)

This technological view is not the self-conscious intention of any particular individual (though it might be that as well) but is precisely the '*ethos*', the 'obvious' interpretative orientation that animates our behaviour at the level of our social institutions and cultural practices, that sponsors the exploitation of the planet for the sake of economic gain (with the result that we are in fact destroying the very environment upon which we depend).

This technological interpretation of nature as, essentially, an economic resource, when coupled with the sense of the universal rights of all individuals to choose their own values unconstrained by the demands of specific national or other inter-human realities, produces a sense of government, ultimately, as nothing more than a referee for managing economic behaviour and ensuring that the contracts of exploitative, property-bearing individuals are honoured.

Liberalism thus in principle and not just as a matter of historical coincidence has an inherently 'economic' interpretation of the public sphere on its horizon and is thus complicit in the spread of global capitalism.[17]

The liberal notion of individual rights manifestly aims to be culturally neutral and to empower a self-governing public sphere. In fact, however, the reality of this political programme has been the replacement of the authority of self-governing publics to establish the boundaries of their own cultural identities with the authority of global economic powers to define the terms of natural and social existence. Paradoxically, the principle that affirms a respect for the rights of the other is precisely the principle that takes itself to be empowered in advance to disregard the other's boundaries – to disregard the 'otherness' of both the cultural and the natural other.

Recuperating dwelling

For the Greeks, the *oikos* is the familiar world in which we make a home: our dwelling. As Heidegger writes, such dwelling, or being at home in the world, is essential to our human existence:

> The way in which you are and I am, the manner in which we humans *are* on the earth, is *buan*, dwelling. ... The old word *bauen*, which says that man *is* insofar as he *dwells*, this word *bauen* however *also* means at the same time to cherish and protect, to preserve and care for. (Heidegger 2013, p. 147)

The world of capitalist economics, however, is one in which such a 'home', with the boundaries it entails, is denied any weight such that the world is always 'anyone's' world but not the world of anyone in particular. Indeed, as Hannah Arendt writes, the modern, technological world rather than 'cherishing' and 'caring for' the earth is premised on the denial of its essentiality, when in fact 'the earth is the very quintessence of the human condition' (Arendt 1988, p. 2). Whereas the technological worldview that has co-opted the public sphere is a way of dwelling in the world that precisely denies the necessity of dwelling, it is incumbent upon us to reinterpret our way of living with each other, precisely to shelter the heterogeneous forms of shared human life: we must precisely develop a new *oiko-nomos*, a new 'economics' of dwelling.[18]

The liberal individual is construed as detached in principle from all natural and social bonds, but no such individual can actually exist. No doubt it is to some extent true that the determinate features of our experienced world are objects about which we can choose, but this description is neither exhaustive of nor adequate to our relationship to those features. More fundamentally, the determinate conditions of our world – material and social – are the very medium and fabric of our existence: just as the power to see is precisely the power *of* the eye and the power to grab the power *of* the hand (or, more exactly, of the person as an 'en-eyed' and 'en-handed' body), so are our powers of choice the powers *of* our situated existence. Our determinacy is not, primarily, the *object* of our choosing but our very embodiment – that from which our power emerges. Our very ability to exist as free individuals rests on our ontological embeddedness in a natural and social world that is not itself a product of our freedom.[19] It is only by thus living from or 'dwelling' in a non-thematic and non-effaceable materiality that we can be free individuals, and the protection of our freedom thus presupposes the protection of our formative and sustaining environments, both natural and social. It is incumbent upon us to develop a new way of inhabiting the public world that acknowledges and supports our need, first and foremost, to dwell.

Notes

1 See Aristotle, *Politics*, Book I, Chapters 1–2, in Jonathan Barnes (ed.), *The Complete Works of Aristotle*, vol. 2, pp. 1986–8, for the idea that the *polis*, though the environment necessary for the fulfilment of human nature, is not something naturally occurring.

2 John Locke, *Second Treatise of Government*, Chapter 2, section 6 and Chapter 4, section 22.

3 In fact, communities are not monolithic, and, as Uma Narayan argues in *Dislocating Cultures: Identities, Traditions and Third-World Feminism*, the boundaries of any person's 'ethical' commitments do not necessarily align with externally defined cultural boundaries.

4 For an extended discussion on the theme of 'accented' speech and its political relevance, see Eduardo Mendieta, 'The Sound of Race: The Prosody of Affect'.

5 For a study of our political responsibilities in cross-cultural settings, see John Russon, 'Heidegger, Hegel and Ethnicity: The Ritual Basis of Self-Identity', pp. 509–32. See also Réal Fillion, *Multicultural Dynamics and the Ends of History: Exploring Kant, Hegel and Marx*.

6 On this topic of women's rights in the context of cross-cultural criticism, see in particular Ayelet Shachar, 'Group Identity and Women's Rights in Family Law: The Perils of Multicultural Accommodation', pp. 285–305, and Shannon Hoff,

'Hegel and the Possibility of Inter-Cultural Criticism', in *Unity of Opposites? Hegel and Canadian Political Thought*, ed. Susan Dodd and Neil Robertson.

7   For these conflicting interpretations of human nature, see Locke, who argues in *Second Treatise of Government*, Section 2 that such individual freedom is our natural condition; and Aristotle, who argues in *Politics*, Book I, Chapters 1–2 that our natural environment is one characterized in general by relations of dependence and in particular is fully realized only in a political community.

8   This is the central thrust of Derrida's contributions to his famous (non-)encounter with Gadamer in Paris in 1981. For the texts and discussion, see *Dialogue and Deconstruction: The Gadamer-Derrida Encounter*, ed. Diane P. Michelfelder and Richard E. Palmer.

9   See Derrida's extensive and insightful discussion of this etymology throughout Part I, Chapter 2, 'License and Freedom: the *Roué*'; on the history of this Greek notion, see Charles W. Fornara and Loren J. Samons II, *Athens from Cleisthenes to Pericles*.

10 For related reasons, Derrida remarks (*Rogues*, p. 26) that ' "democracy" is neither the name of a regime nor the name of a constitution. It is not a constitutional form among others.'

11 Compare John Rawls, 'The Idea of Public Reason Revisited', pp. 765–807.

12 The historical emergence, and the ambivalent dynamism, of the public sphere is studied in detail in Jürgen Habermas, *The Structural Transformation of the Public Sphere*. On the complex meaning of 'public opinion', see also Jacques Derrida, 'Call It a Day for Democracy', in *The Other Heading: Reflections on Today's Europe*, trans. Pascale-Anne Brault and Michael Naas, pp. 84–98.

13 On this theme of the resistance of human identity to the model of liberal individuality, see especially *Rogues*, Chapter 6, 'The Rogue that I Am.' See also pp. 14–15 on the tension between the '*autos*' of self-governance and the affirmation of heterogeneity.

14 This is the point of Hegel's analysis of the French Revolution; see *Phenomenology of Spirit*, M582–95. For discussion of this material, see Shannon Hoff, 'The Ideal Nation and the Real Nation', Chapter 6 of *The Laws of the Spirit: A Hegelian Theory of Justice*, pp. 109–29.

15 See, for example, 'The Ballot or the Bullet', in *Malcolm X Speaks: Selected Speeches and Statements* (New York: Grove Weidenfeld, 1994).

16 An excellent and accessible overview of this history is found in Tamim Ansary, *Destiny Disrupted: A History of the World through Muslim Eyes* (New York: PublicAffairs, 2009). I discuss related themes in John Russon, *Sites of Exposure: A Philosophical Essay on Art, Politics and the Nature of Experience*.

17 On the critique of liberal democracy as in principle committed to exploitative capitalism, see Bruce Gilbert, *The Vitality of Contradiction: Hegel, Politics, and the Dialectic of Liberal-Capitalism.*

18 On these themes of dwelling and technology, see John Russon and Kirsten Jacobson, 'Space: The Open in Which We Sojourn', in *The Bloomsbury Companion to Heidegger*, ed. François Raffoul and Eric S. Nelson, pp. 349–51. See also Kirsten Jacobson, 'The Experience of Home and the Space of Citizenship', pp. 219–45.

19 See Arendt, *The Human Condition*, p. 2: 'The human artifice of the world separates human existence from all mere animal environment, but life itself is outside the artificial world.' Compare Heidegger, 'The Question Concerning Technology', p. 323: 'Man can indeed conceive, fashion, and carry through this or that in one way or another. But man does not have control over unconcealment itself, in which at any given time the actual shows itself or withdraws.'

References

Ansary, Tamim (2009), *Destiny Disrupted: A History of the World through Muslim Eyes*, New York: PublicAffairs.

Arendt, Hannah (1988), *The Human Condition*, 2nd edn, Chicago: University of Chicago Press.

Aristotle (1984), 'Politics', in Jonathan Barnes (ed.), *The Complete Works of Aristotle*, Volume II, Princeton: Princeton University Press.

Derrida, Jacques (1992), 'Call It a Day for Democracy', in Pascale-Anne Brault and Michael Naas (trans.), *The Other Heading: Reflections on Today's Europe*, Bloomington: Indiana University Press.

Derrida, Jacques (1995), *On the Name*, trans. John P. Leavey Jr., Stanford: Stanford University Press.

Derrida, Jacques (2005), *Rogues: Two Essays on Reason*, trans. Pascale-Anne Brault and Michael Naas, Stanford: Stanford University Press.

Fillion, Réal (2008), *Multicultural Dynamics and the Ends of History: Exploring Kant, Hegel and Marx*, Ottawa: University of Ottawa Press.

Fornara, Charles W. and Loren J. Samons II (1991), *Athens from Cleisthenes to Pericles*, Berkeley: University of California Press.

Gilbert, Bruce (2013), *The Vitality of Contradiction: Hegel, Politics, and the Dialectic of Liberal-Capitalism*, Montreal and Kingston: McGill-Queens University Press.

Habermas, Jürgen (1991), *The Structural Transformation of the Public Sphere*, trans. Thomas Burger, Cambridge, MA: MIT Press.

Hegel, G. W. F. (1977), *Phenomenology of Spirit*, trans. A. V. Miller, Oxford: Oxford University Press.

Heidegger, Martin (1993), 'The Question Concerning Technology', in David Farrell Krell (ed.), *Basic Writings*, New York: HarperCollins, pp. 324–8.

Heidegger, Martin (2013), 'Building, Dwelling, Thinking', in Albert Hofstadter (trans.), *Poetry, Language, Thought*, New York: Harper Perennial, pp. 143–59.

Hoff, Shannon (2014), 'The Ideal Nation and the Real Nation', Chapter 6 of *The Laws of the Spirit: A Hegelian Theory of Justice*, Albany: State University of New York Press, pp. 109–29.

Hoff, Shannon (2015), 'Hegel and the Possibility of Inter-Cultural Criticism', in Susan Dodd and Neil Robertson (eds), *Unity of Opposites? Hegel and Canadian Political Thought*, Toronto: University of Toronto Press, forthcoming.

Jacobson, Kirsten (2010), 'The Experience of Home and the Space of Citizenship', *Southern Journal of Philosophy*, 48: 219–45.

Locke, John (1993), 'Second Treatise of Government', in David Wooten (ed.), *Political Writings*, Indianapolis: Hackett.

Menieta, Eduardo (2015), 'The Sound of Race: The Prosody of Affect', in *Radical Philosophy Review*, forthcoming.

Michelfelder, Diane P. and Richard E. Palmer (eds) (1989), *Dialogue and Deconstruction: The Gadamer-Derrida Encounter*, Albany: State University of New York Press.

Narayan, Uma (1997), *Dislocating Cultures: Identities, Traditions and Third-World Feminism*, New York: Routledge.

Rawls, John (1997), 'The Idea of Public Reason Revisited', *The University of Chicago Law Review*, 64: 765–807.

Russon, John (1995), 'Heidegger, Hegel and Ethnicity: The Ritual Basis of Self-Identity', *Southern Journal of Philosophy*, 33: 509–32.

Russon, John (2015), *Sites of Exposure: A Philosophical Essay on Art, Politics and the Nature of Experience*, Bloomington: Indiana University Press, forthcoming.

Russon, John and Kirsten Jacobson (2013), 'Space: The Open in Which we Sojourn', in François Raffoul and Eric S. Nelson (eds), *The Bloomsbury Companion to Heidegger*, London, New Delhi and New York: Bloomsbury, pp. 349–51.

Shachar, Ayelet (1998), 'Group Identity and Women's Rights in Family Law: The Perils of Multicultural Accommodation', *The Journal of Political Philosophy*, 6: 285–305.

X, Malcolm (1994), 'The Ballot or the Bullet', in *Malcolm X Speaks: Selected Speeches and Statements*, New York: Grove Weidenfeld.

4

On the Relation Between the Obscure, the Cryptic and the Public

Shaj Mohan

It is so difficult to find the beginning. Or, better: it is difficult to begin at the beginning. And try not to go further back.

–Ludwig Wittgenstein

Remarking in *I Have a Taste for Secret* on the relation between the public and the secret, Derrida opposed them to one another but also found that an absolute concept of the secret insists from outside this relation. It is illuminative that Derrida did not asseverate a distinction between the secret and the private. Like an assayer, instead, he found a mark on the secret that propelled him to hold it up to the obscure liminality that occurred in the text between truth, a category understood as both epistemological and confessional, and the public, another category understood until then to be the ground of politics. Perhaps, he feared that the end of politics lays in the *absolutisement* of the public. Held against it, but not opposed to it, was the absolute secret which could do no more than lend a dark illumination[1] to the relation between the total opening, as the public, and death (absolute secret is not death, but akin to it).[2] We can extract a proportional articulation from this text: in inverse proportion to the expansion of the public, which has no resource of its own but what it takes from the secret, there recedes death – death understood as the thinkable of the secret. Derrida demands of us to think the secret in a way that would not determine it as the obverse of something to be revealed, something that would appear to us either in the spin of chance or in the decryption of its sign. This is possible only if the thinking gives up distinctions and clarity in order to assay this secret which finds the mark in itself – the secret thought of the secret that secretes itself and exposes itself only as the autopoiesis[3] of secret, and with no component other than itself.

Derrida here articulates not the isolation of the secret thought into its own domain, for we would then have had to call it the regularity of mysticism or the ineffable. Instead, he brings the secret thought of death into the exposed thought of life in a rigorous construction – 'that which has a relation to death, that which is carried off by death – that which is thus life itself' (2001, p. 58). We can call this construction of thought *the obscure* by securing for it, against the grain of deconstruction, an objective reality, namely, the construction of exteriority. In sofar as this thought reveals something essential about our time, it also battles another ground for politics, as will be discussed ahead.

Around the same time,[4] the American philosopher Thomas Nagel was engaged in a similar inquiry into the exposure of all things to all things. For Nagel, too, at stake was death, of conversations, speech, the common life, due to 'the importance of concealment as a condition of civilisation' (Nagel 2002, p. 4). He too anticipated the arrival of a new form of dictatorship with the dictator not determined as yet, or a dictatorship, perhaps, without a dictator. However, Nagel thought along another set of distinctions and determinations: the public, the private and the obscure. Both Nagel and Derrida speak of the ratio between two categories or institutions – the secret and the public for Derrida and concealment and exposure for Nagel – in considering which, Kant's observations on the essence of ratio in politics are illuminative.

The obscure animal

In 'What Is Enlightenment', which Foucault identifies as obscure,[5] Kant gives reason to politics. For Foucault obscurity is not the impenetrability of the stylistic aspect of a text but the constitution of a distinct object of thought that is exogenous to the domain of the given, imposing a new rigour for the conceptual while constituting the outside – exogenesis. This is not to assume that reason abstracts from political practice concepts understood as the propositional relations between terms, but to bring into exposure the zones of negotiation or to give relief to the war zones through concepts understood as the determinants of relations.

It is well known that Kant was not explicitly proposing the critique of enlightenment, but responding to the question posed by a journal in such a way that it appeared to be the essential question of the time or a crisis. Crisis and critique are related in concept and etymology. Crisis is the arrival of anything existent to the limit beyond which it can either return to a lower or higher threshold. A man in the care of an intensivist is in a life-threatening condition which has broken the regular relations of his internal milieu. He can exit the intensive care system, or the crisis, either as lifeless or as a life less or more than what he was. Another critical state is the chrysalis, even though it occupies a long while in the life of the organism, since what appears thereafter is an existence of new potentialities. Crisis implies the offer of an exchange of a determinate group of potentials for another, and its overcoming consists precisely in the negotiation of the exchange. Critique is performed as an estimation of the potentials of a system, the limits of the potentials, their broken internal milieu, understood as the system which distinguishes exteriority, and also their preparedness to develop new potential differences. Ultimately, critique is prescriptive as it gives a new regimen for the system, whereas criticism refers to the criteria of the regimen and its maintenance, as when the doctor says 'you smoke too much' or 'you are not eating enough carbohydrates'. Clearly, 'What Is Enlightenment' is not a criticism but a text, which, in its movement of generating a crisis, draws new lines of demarcation. It is also a critique understood as examining the conditions for an organic state of reason.[6]

The liberal interpretation of this text is that mankind will remain in a state of immaturity as long as it does not show the courage to reason, decide and act in all the domains of life – religion, army, school. For that, the king must give room for men to reason without restraint in public as long as they obey in their work space. This will bring about the maturity of mankind and *clarify* the essence of mankind as reason itself. Kant here appears to be setting a contract with the emperor in the form of the conditions for the possibility of man's transition from his state of minority to that of majority. The conditions are the distinction between the two offices, and the period in which this happens is an 'age of enlightenment'. However, the tone of the text is menacing and suggests an obscure imminence. Its arguments constitute an organism that is in preparation to negotiate the unknown gradients: it lays down the training ground to clarify man, like a metal, to the freedom that he essentially is.

Minority – 'the inability to make use of one's own understanding without direction from another' (Kant 1999, p. 17) – involves, for Kant, being directed. Majority is the power to be non-directable, which implies to be obscure[7] (not cryptic) with respect to directions. A public in a minority has two possible courses. It can be in a state that is equal to or less than that of a machine: if the former, it will need directions at all moments of action, and when the authorities are unable to provide them it will stand around as an army frozen in the cold of the withdrawal of command or an organism in shock. If the public is less than a machine, it will not obey new orders; that is, if it is ordered through the instilment of prejudices and if the new orders appear to conflict with those prejudices, it will disobey:

> The public, which was previously put under this yoke by the guardians, may subsequently itself compel them to remain under it, if the public is suitably stirred up by some of its guardians who are themselves incapable of any enlightenment; so harmful is it to implant prejudices, because they finally take their revenge on the very people who, or whose predecessors, were their authors. (Kant 1999, p. 18)

Or, the same minor public can, under the dominance of other prejudices, take a revolutionary course, overthrowing the emperor even if this will not allow them the transition into majority:

> A revolution may well bring about a falling off of personal despotism and of avaricious or tyrannical oppression, but never a true reform in one's way of thinking; instead new prejudices will serve just as well as old ones to harness the great unthinking masses. (Kant 1999, p. 18)

The emperor is a function of the state of the public – majority or minority – which also determines that of the authorities. This is the imminence of which Kant reminds the emperor: that a revolution might not change things much for the people, it might even give them a much worse new ruler, but it can certainly turn out nasty for the present ruler.

To produce a majority in mankind requires a gradual and modulated distribution of reason across two political categories – the public office where one reasons freely and the private office where one obeys conditionally – given by reason itself, through which it will circulate to overcome every determination to obedience to bring about a preparedness for any kind of gradient. Since we are free to reason in public and criticize the very grounds of the private offices where we obey as much as we can, our obedience has a theatrical form. It is absolute if it is given unthinkingly. Conditional obedience involves the questioning of the plan of command. For example, the plan to move an army to the East to capture the amber mines for building a bigger army to be moved westward later can be publically questioned although the orders pertaining to it are obeyed. The obedience of a machine is determined causally while its degrees of freedom are grounded in the body plan. A pulley system has no freedom to execute the action of grinding directly unless it participates in the body plan of a grinding mechanism. However, the animal has more degrees of freedom since the perceptions according to which it is directed to act are registered by it in gradients; in other words, the animal has its condition or internal milieu, which is its exteriority. Until mankind arrives at full maturity, one pretends to obey. The pretended obedience in the private office is not strict as it is only according to one's conscience and the training of the conscience. It is in the public office, where one reasons about the very plans of the structures of obedience, that the training in reason takes place.

Reason is given only in proportion to one's own training in it, as Kant clarifies in another obscure text, 'On Education'. It concerns training in character, which for him was preparation without plan: 'With regard to th[is] training – which we may indeed call also, in a certain sense, physical culture – we much chiefly bear in mind that discipline should not be slavish' (Kant 2003, p. 47).[8] The distribution of reason in accordance with the categories instituted by it *plans* a system of the ontogeny of reason whereby it can come to majority – that is, to the greatest degree of freedom – without need of the very categories that modulated its coming to perfection. Thus, man trains to be the animal that has the maximum exteriority. It is clear from this text that freedom is used as the right to pretend to obey – 'indeed the least harmful of anything that could even be called freedom: namely, freedom to make *public use* of one's reason in all matters' (1999, p. 18). Instead of the pretended freedom (corresponding to the categories that train reason) and the pretend obedience, the reality of freedom is an experience of the majority of man to which corresponds the question 'How to orient oneself in thinking?' In the eponymously titled text, man, understood as Freedom, appears before himself as a dark night in the desert with no star to guide it. Freedom, we can say, is the obscure that we are to become, such that disorientation is our disposition towards the maximum exteriority opened by it. Kant's example for training in obscurity is to imagine that you are in your study in pitch darkness and your mischievous friend has disarranged the furniture. How would you find your way around? Reason's objective reality is such obscure exigency which does not come with a plan.[9] Freedom constitutes man as an animal that does not respond causally to the world. This is consistent with Kant's practical metaphysics. Reason is the power to be free; politics is the training through the categories of *the public* and *the private* to be the obscure animal. The sense we might get in Kant's *clarification* of man into the obscure animal is of a being subject to *no* plan, but, in fact, it is characterized by a preparedness for *any* plan, which is the very definition of *the degenerate*. Yet, is this being of reason man? Or is it the 'monstrous exception, absolutely outside the pale of humanity'? (Blanchot, p. 71) Reason emerges as an obscure constitution of mankind that grounds it well for any imminence and demands reading the rest of Kant quite differently. Foucault writes, 'I believe that it is necessary to stress the connection that exists between this brief article and the three *Critiques*' (1984, p. 37). Preparedness, or being-before, is what defines the obscure in Kant.

The obscure as the degenerate

Kant's use of the words public and private is quite foreign today. For us, public designates the places where we act under constraints, including tolerance, which Kant considered arrogance. Private is the domain where we speak and do things freely and out of which we let ourselves into the controlled exposure of the public. While the terms public and private still remain in use as political categories their use as the negotiation of two distinct places has come to an end today. Nagel shows the difficulties in our desire to somehow retain a little bit of the two places, to which we must return. He too speaks of a pretend zone of action, although he sets the stage of action differently: 'Everyone knows that there is much more going on than what enters the public domain, but the smooth functioning of that domain depends on a general non-acknowledgement of what everyone knows' (2002, p. 7). We do not pretend to obey but we pretend to not know without appearing to be mendacious. For Nagel, the distinction between the private and the public regulates the movement of stimuli (that which causes an action), which reason can also be. Once a certain content enters from the private into the public, the distinct transducers of both domains come into operation, and the resulting overload of stimuli may be dangerous for this organism:

> What is allowed to become public and what is kept private in any given transaction will depend on what needs to be taken into collective consideration for the purposes of transaction and what would, on the contrary, disrupt if introduced into the public space. (Nagel 2002, p. 12)

The danger of overload also attends a movement of stimuli from the public towards the private. Examples of it are the regulation of age-appropriate censorship and of social gatherings. The plans for the regulation of the movement of stimuli itself are made in public and, hence, the Kantian public exists vestigially in Nagel's schema – 'The attempt to control public space is importantly an attempt to control the cultural and ideological environment in which young people are formed' (Nagel 2002, p. 21).

Nagel attests, as well, to the Kantian training programme instituted by the *public–private* distinction, but where the Kantian programme sought to develop reason to constitute us as the obscure animal, Nagel assumes that the human animal has a critical limit for receiving stimuli (overload) and forming adequate responses (either too much or too little), such that 'it is essential to permit creatures as complex as ourselves to interact without social breakdown' (Nagel 2002, p. 28). The overload is also capable of breaking down individual lives and Nagel mentions in his essays those who could withstand such overloads and also those who crumbled. A special case for him is provided by the biographies of Bertrand Russell and Ludwig Wittgenstein, both authored by Ray Monk. Nagel asks, 'Why does a great philosopher, or a great artist, or a great scientist, forfeit his privacy forever …?' (p. 63) He compares the quality of the works and lives of both philosophers: Russell's philosophical work and private life were guided by the search for clarity which would often make him deliver his private life into an argument in the public – 'Granted, in Russell's case there is more excuse than usual for comprehensive attention since he himself went public about so much' (p. 63). There is a moral appreciation of Russell: he lived an open life and cared little to hide what could be considered damaging for his career, and hence he was a remarkably brave man. Wittgenstein's life is characterized by a different moral quality, that of obscuring the beleaguered life: he was 'consumed by shame and by the desire to hide' and to Nagel 'he comes across as an insufferably selfish and heartless human being' (p. 64). The quality of life parallels the work, Wittgenstein's characterized 'as deep or obscure' and Russell's by 'his distrust of obscurity' (p. 71).

The greatness of Nagel's texts on concealment lies in this reticulation of what is man: instead of clarification he asks, in the domain of publicity, for ridges and patterned surfaces which are minimal and decorative, introduced and maintained through the deft hands of great socializers, where the circulation of stimulus between the public and private is to be determined maturely in order to secure the autopoiesis of the social system – to be the simple hum of a feedback loop, the one that can be left alone forever, were best. Politics is the maintenance of the social system and Nagel admits to the conservatism inherent in this project. He finds in this inquiry, in gradations, a very troubling quality of being: the obscure – to be tactful is better than reticence, to be reticent is better than being conceited, conceited rather than secretive, secretive rather than obscure and deep, obscure being the most degenerate. The gradations are governed by the publicly given rules to clarify each quality of expression, 'because the conventions that govern them are generally known' (p. 6). The obscure is without convention. The gradations are also determined according to a theory of self-relation: we practice tactfulness in society according to the relation we have with ourselves such that we know what we want and we know well the conventions through which we can pursue our wants. The interior sentiment through which we know ourselves must be proportionate to the exterior sentiment in which we find ourselves invested in others. We train in order to divide ourselves into a harmonious unity under the category of clarity; 'Ideally the social costume shouldn't be too thick' for then we will move towards the obscure gradient of self-relation. Is the obscure a self-relation or any relation at all? It can be considered a relation if it designates the negative direction of the form of transparency such as 'water is more transparent than wax'. However, this would be a relation of opacity, not obscurity. Is it a positive moral quality such as courage, wisdom, generosity, truthfulness and moderation? Nagel suggests that the obscure could designate the opposite of good morals. The Nazi interpretation of art would be an instance of such opposition: since it was limited to the representations of *Blut und Boden*, modern art appeared to them as the obscure, and its works were called 'Degenerate Art' in their exhibitions. What then of Derrida's insistence on the secret, which in its absolute form is a non-relation? Why did he oppose the totalitarianism of exposure, not with the private, but with the secret?

Resistance of the obscure

What really is a secret? Where does it stand in relation to the gradients of knowledge and truth, moral values and persuasion? A secret in its informal sense is something whispered in the ear with the restriction '*you can't tell this to anyone else*', as children are taught. Secret, here, is a function of the technology of promise. When children are taught to make a promise they are also taught of the consequences of breaking it, be they supernatural or real. Locked by the promise, the secret, then, performs a training; it introduces a discipline into the faculty of speech that divides secrets into those which can appear anywhere, those which can appear within the community of the promise and those which may never appear. The secret initiates the child into the order that is more than that of the promise. It reveals society as reticulated by the speakable and the unspeakable; it reveals in language the power to expose and conceal; and it reveals a hierarchy of secrets according to the gradients of power: *the adults have more secrets than us and the state has more than the adults.*[10] Michel Foucault's re-introduction of the Greek notion of *parrhesia* concerns the conditional unlocking of the secret, guaranteeing the condition in which the coming open of the secret may not involve consequences to the speaker. Parrhesia implies someone who can grant it – 'speak freely and you shall not be harmed however harmful what you have to say may be' – but can also withdraw it. Hence, it is also a game of power, of life and death and, today, of whistle-blowing. Secret implies consequences, and a statement such as 'the sky is blue today' can rarely be worthy of being a secret though 'the sky does not rotate around the earth' is worth it. For the same reason, what is held to be a secret is also something particular which has immediate relation to the events around it beyond the adage *'secretiveness is corrosive'.* Hamlet hid his knowledge of the secret of his father's murder so that it would not immediately enter the events around him to change their tempo; the drama is a game proportioning tempo to the gradation of knowledge from the appearance of the obscure-spectre-being towards the clarity of poison.

The secret is essentially something distinct, and a thing is transformed to the level of secrets precisely due to its power to make the indistinct dissolve in truth. This formal relation of invertible transformation defines cryptology – the secret is in principle something transformed from the domain of exposure through technology, be it promise or polynomials, such that it can be reverted into exposure again. Otherwise, there never was any secret. A statement S transformed into the secret Sk with the key k never existed if k is lost. It is first the plain text and then the cypher text as a function of the key, and then back again, whether through a symmetric key (freed from promise) or an asymmetric one (interrogation), into the same plain text.[11] The secret is indifferent to the political categories of the public and the private, the way a pen, a gun or a computer would be – a species of the functional indifference of the technological which, once perfected, is concerned only with the dependent and the independent. The moral ambiguity of the secret is derivative of its indifference. In our time it is the most controlled technology or munition.[12] The control ranges from restricting the power of computation that individuals can have so that they may be able to decrypt secrets by force, or the key disclosure laws whereby individuals are forced to disclose their keys if the state asks.[13] The state is determined as the entity that possesses a monopoly over the technology of secrets; the crypto-hierarchy of our world is traced by the power one has to encrypt:

> Our assessment of power hierarchy is indexed by the infrastructure of the secret.
> The state has the maximum secrecy and it legislatively restricts the acquisition
> of the secret infrastructure by anyone else. Not only does the state possess the

maximum secret infrastructure and restrict its use by others, it also, hence, possesses everyone else's secrets. Businesses are next in line and the civilians must speak the truth, always. (Mohan and Mohammed 2011, p. 13)

We have arrived from the problematic of truthfulness and tactfulness to that of secrets and leaks, from 'one must always speak the truth' to 'anyone with a clean conscience should have nothing to hide' (Osang 2013). Privacy is not opposed to publicity today; the continuity between the expressions exchanged between the two domains has made their respective transducers redundant. In this sense surveillance is no longer the issue; when almost everything is visible anyway, the term now refers to the nearly continuous recording of what is being exposed. Richard Allen Posner, the jurist and serving judge of America, found the emergence of this transition a call for new grounds for jurisprudence. At the level of privacy,

> People have become blasé about having their personal belongings x-rayed, and their persons searched and at the same time they are also not yet ready to make use of encryption programs to conceal their electronic communications than invite strangers to read their correspondence. (2008)

Judge Posner, Edward Snowden, Julian Assange and Derrida are on the same jurisprudential plan when they insist on encryption as the new language. We are in a new training programme with an indeterminate plan: either we school ourselves towards the modulation of the different technologies of exposure to the liminal zone where the inter-species of the private animal is found, with its genus discovered retrospectively, or we cross-train with the cypherpunks, Wittgenstein, the Anonymous, Pussy Riot, Femen, Richard Posner, the cyber delinquents, Julian Assange, the crypto-degenerates, and with Leibniz, towards gradients of dis-exposure. The discipline of dis-exposure, insofar as it merely opposes the totalitarianism of total exposure with cryptography, will not be enough to realize a new political problematic. Perhaps this is what prompted Derrida to think, against total exposure, of an absolute secret wholly asymmetrical to the functional relation between the key, the plain text and the cypher text. But 'Why elect the word "secret" to say this?' (Derrida 2001, p. 58) instead of the obscure? The asymmetrical secret or the absolute secret is a logical object and a messianic subject. As the former, it is a text enciphered by an infinite key and as the latter it is a Hermes who is to come but will never arrive in time. Derrida releases into politics neither the concept of the monstrous – which he discovered and left behind in his early writings for its relation to the inter-species in the texts of Leibniz and Canguilhem – nor the obscure, which is too empiricist for deconstruction. *I Have a Taste for Secret* is also about the secrets of deconstruction into which we cannot go here, though this is required to think the present exigency of politics.[14] What we reckon with here is that the resistance to the obscure in Derrida resists the entirety of politics with the same symmetry as Kant resisted revolution in politics: as something which may never bring about a majority – 'I have an impulse of fear or terror in the face of a political space' (2001, p. 59). Yet, the obscure unwittingly shows in the Derridean logic: the resistance of the obscure (or the plan of its resistance in Derrida) is the obscure resistance (as it reveals itself to the plan).

The obscure prince

The obscure can easily be given negative determinations. It obscures itself in propositions – 'A proposition also becomes obscure when it contains such a concept' (Leibniz 1956, p. 449). Yet, to conceive the obscure in terms of the obscure is the difficult task of philosophy. It is not something we obtain at the end of reasoning, though it describes the quality of concepts, following from the epistemology of Malebranche, inherited and modified by Leibniz and Hegel. Leaving out the problem of deciding whether concepts are received or given, and the different entities constituted by the two relations which entirely determine the orientation of the systems they describe, something can be understood of the obscure from the old epistemology. Concepts, understood as the representations under which there is recognition, are classified into four – obscure, confused, clear and distinct.[15] For Malebranche we move in a gradient of the light from the modalities of the mind to the *lumen illuminans*. The distinct is the concept in which the recognition of an object is complete through its differences; you distinctly learn that a secret is being told from the promise extracted from you, '*you shall not speak of it*'. A distinct concept where all its differences are known and are denominated, and also given the clear intuition of its reality, is found in the Hegelian Idea, or Truth as a quality. The obscure stands against the Idea but is not a negative determination of the Idea. It can be known adequately – that is, *as the obscure* – through its differences, though it cannot be denominated and it is given in intuition just as intuition is given in it for Malebranche. As in proposition, where a confused predicate of a clear subject leaves the entire proposition confused ('*There is something about Mary*'), so it is with the obscure, which therefore does not lend itself to syllogistic articulations of any kind.

Yet, Malebranche and Leibniz insisted that we begin everything with the obscure concept. We have sufficient ground to state from within the domain of concepts that with the obscure we arrive in the terrain of metaphysics, although it is not an object reserved for metaphysics. Artists, perhaps, are the most intimate with it. If philosophy is marked by the desire of principles then art is characterized by the eroticism of the obscure.[16] In politics it appears as something which cannot be held in the grounds of the present law: we need only think of Gandhi in his *Yeravada Mandir* (prison/temple). Rarely does the obscure grasp someone from the supine clarity of thinking, from a movement of address between propositions, into the disposition of disorientation such that he infects all regions with the obscure, constituting him as an obscure prince. Marquis de Sade was a prince who would not rule anywhere but would rather infect the juridical concepts with obscurity, which *clarifies* the rules such that they are no longer useful for ruling. Maurice Blanchot, the progeny of Sade or (same thing) the degenerate, writes: 'In a dozen different ways, Sade formulated the idea that man's wildest excesses call for secrecy, for the obscurity of the farthest depths, the inviolable solitude of a cell' (1965, p. 38).

How then do we recognize the obscure? In his metaphysics, Gilles Deleuze used an obscure expression derived from Canguilhem, 'the obscure precursor' (2004, p. 154); adjectivally, the obscure shows itself as the being-before. De Sade was neither a programme that was implemented nor a possibility that is being currently realized. Rather, he stands before us as the being-before of the unrealizable just as he had when the Bastille was being stormed, amidst the reign of terror, and when Napoleon ordered him back into prison. The figure of De Sade also serves as a warning – the obscure prince must reign alone in prison. A precursor is not the same as the cause of something; causality entails distinct relations between causes and effects and the order of causes. A precursor is not an agent for which a passive body can be set the way Cartesianism distinguishes between the active *res cogitans* and the passive *res extensa*. Instead, it is something or someone who cannot be cast into an epoch, bygone or present. As being-before, it constitutes its own epoch – the Difference Engine of Babbage, the metaphysics of Arthur Schopenhauer, the physics of Alfred North Whitehead. It is more even than what Nietzsche referred to as 'born posthumously'. Yet, the obscure is not exhausted by the precursor just as no adjectives are, in that they have their own formal reality while being adjoined to something else.

The indifference of the obscure to the public and the private is not that of a technology such as the secret. Instead, the obscure as concept grasps and releases the region of such distinctions. Labour and home are examples of such a neat division, and what objectively determines them – the capitalist mode of production – is not something we do, nor is it the place we return to after a day's work. The obscure in art is something that shocks us when we realize that there is nothing we have at our disposal to recognize this work. Even after the senses have tired of the novel object of art, the obscure in it insists on grasping us. For example, the problem of the presentation of two dimensions in painting with analytic cubism – where mathematics, through Maurice Princet and Poincaré, determined the course of colours – results in a series of paintings testifying to the discharge between two philosophical objects, *Idea* and the *obscure*. In the domain of politics, Anonymous is obscure. But who are they? And what do they stand for? Gabriella Coleman, the ethnographer of Anonymous, writes:

> Mutability and dynamism continue to be a staple of Anonymous' activism and historical development. As a result, it is difficult to forecast when or why Anonymous will strike, when a new node will appear, whether a campaign will be successful and how Anonymous might change direction or tactics during the course of an operation. (2013, p. 7)

A lazy erasure of the obscure in Anonymous would be to call them anarchists, which is another rigorously obscure concept: no two things are similar in being obscure, just as being distinct does not entail similarity – for example, a group and a set are two distinct mathematical objects. Politics today demands movements in two equally important directions – on the one hand the seizure of encryption for all and on the other the construction of obscure bodies and movements. The Anonymous movement, if it can be so called, co-ordinates these two directions of encryption and obscurity.[17] In the public sphere, we are in the presence of an obscure complex (i.e. a relation between finite terms that are each obscure) composed of Pussy Riot, Femen,[18] Anonymous[19] and Occupy movements: it is a new principality with obscure sovereigns. This appearance of obscure-politics is something the media, the sociologists and the philosophers have not been keen to speak about, except in the familiar terms – activist groups, anarchism and communism-that-is-late, respectively. Philosophical participation in the public sphere today can involve finding designations for the new *polis* right before us. Encryption has displaced privacy and publicity; surveillance has been made redundant by the amorous denudation of the sheath between the two; the distinction between stimulus and response is confused since the delay between the two in the realms of eroticism and the stock market is shorter than we can think. Here, the philosophical exigency would be to invent a necessity for the obscure-politics such that there will be sovereigns, precursors and more 'until finally everything *is* expressed, is revealed, but also everything is plunged back again into the obscurity of unformulated and inexpressible thoughts' (Blanchot, p. 39).

This chapter is dedicated to G. Shankar and Habitat.

Notes

1   The dark illumination as God is a concept that grounds the hierarchies in the corpus of Pseudo-Dionysius, and deconstruction's relation to it can be seen in the hyper-polemics between Derrida and Jean-Luc Nancy. Our concerns are no longer the ineffable or the hyper-effable in theology, but the obscure as reality, formal as well as material.

2   Derrida refuses here to outline the absolute secret. It is certainly neither a concept nor is it Idea, unless we call it negative idea. Instead, he gives us a taste of it – 'Clearly, the most tempting figure for this absolute/secret is death' (2001).

3   Francisco Varela's concept of *autopoiesis* is not circular in the sense of a loop, and it is certainly cybernetic in origin. Yet there is the obscure, proper to philosophy, and Derrida poetically circulates it between death and exposure (2001). In Derrida too we find a species of cybernetics, even a feedback which constitutes an enclosed entity.

4   This was in the mid-1990s and these two philosophers were responding differently to something wholly new taking place: the public revelations of the then American president Bill Clinton's private life and its trial led by Kenneth Starr.

5   He says, 'beneath its appearance of simplicity, it is rather complex' (Foucault 1984, p. 33).

6   State has to be understood as a regimen capable of any kind of crisis.

7   What is obscure is not the state obtained by coming to majority. But, having come to that and hence gaining the courage to exercise reason freely, which means to act freely, renders one into an object that is thrown into the dark desert with no stars. Majority is defined by that circulation of reason constitutive of the desert, the dark night, the plan of the body and the sense of being unanchored – lost at sea for Foucault.

8   Kant instructs us not to order our servants around in the presence of children. Such indirect instruction in obedience too will be detrimental to the development of their reason (2003, p. 47).

9   See Kant (1996).

10   The determination of *who can possess how many secrets* and the power to make the secret, either by one's legal right to refuse to speak it or the right to possess the technology to encrypt without limits, under the law came into effect in the mid-twentieth century. In America it was also a matter of serious discussion and dissent, though limited to cryptographers and hackers.

11   The secret has another relation to truth: that something is held in reversible transformation implies that it must be distinct and true, and further that this truth can have consequences, very likely negative for the one who holds the key. See Mohan and Mohammed (2011).

12   The USA is not alone in considering cryptography to be a munition at the level of tanks and fighter jets. The legal and intellectual battle between computer programmers and the American government for securing the right to secrecy for all is known as the 'Crypto Wars'. It is amusing that there is no Wikipedia entry yet for Crypto Wars. See Doctorow for the most recent developments.

13   Key disclosure laws vary across states. In India any encryption key is state property (Govt. of India 2009). The USA on the other hand gives complete property rights to encryption keys according to a Supreme Court ruling of 2012 (Electronic Frontier Foundation 2012). Also see Lee (2012).

14   However, its roots are evident in 'Introduction to Origins of Geometry'.

15   We need not consider the differences between Leibniz and Malebranche here. The uses of the terms, concept and idea, would undergo radical modifications in philosophy between Malebranche and Hegel. What remains consistent in these philosophers is the power of being invested in the obscure, the maximum.

16   There are too many moments to choose from art. But none can state it as well as 'Red Square: The Painterly Realism of a Peasant Woman in Two Dimensions by Kazimir Severinovich Malevich. The parallelogram of red against white might sum up the painting. Though it resists the very two-dimensionality of form by setting sail into the title and recreating the problematic of painting – is it to represent or is it to present or is it to deny both that one paints, by creating the obscure which is outside the brawl for recognition?

17   We do not, of course, refer here to 'security through obscurity' where its practitioner assumes that the ignorance of the other regarding the security procedures would be enough security. For example, you assume that nobody in their right mind would think that the password to your email account is 'password'.

18   See http://femen.org/.

19   See http://anonnews.org/f and http://www.aljazeera.com/category/organisation/ anonymous.

References

Blanchot, M. (1965), 'Sade', in *Justine, Philosophy in the Bedroom, and Other Writings*. Compiled and Translated by Richard Seaver and Austryn Wainhouse, 37–72, New York: Grove Press.

Coleman, G. (2013), *Anonymous In Context: The Politics and the Power Behind the Mask*, Ontario: The Centre for International Governance Innovation.

Deleuze, G. (2004), *Difference and Repetition*, London: Continuum.

Derrida, J. (2001), *I Have A Taste For The Secret*, Cambridge, MA: Polity Press.

Electronic Frontier Foundation (2012), *Electronic* Frontier Foundation. [Online] Available at https://www.eff.org/press/releases/appeals-court-upholds-constitutional-right-against-forced-decryption [Accessed 08 May 2014].

Foucault, M. (1984), 'What Is Enlightenment?', in P. Rabinow (ed.), *The Foucault Reader*, 32–50, New York: Pantheon Books.

Govt. of India (2009), DeitY or Department of Electronics and Information Technology. [Online] Available at http://deity.gov.in/sites/upload_files/dit/files/downloads/itact2000/it_amendment_act2008.pdf [Accessed 08 May 2014].

Hegel, G. W. F. (1969), *Hegel's Science of Logic*, New York: Humanity Books.

Kant, I. (1996), 'What Does It Mean To Orient Oneself In Thinking?', in A. W. Wood (ed.), *Religion and Rational* Theology, 1–18. Cambridge: Cambridge University Press.

Kant, I. (1999), *Practical Philosophy*, Cambridge: Cambridge University Press.

Kant, I. (2003), *On Education*, New York: Dover Publications, Inc.

Lee, T. B. (2012), Ars Technica. [Online] Available at http://arstechnica.com/tech-policy/2012/02/appeals-court-fifth-amendment-protections-can-apply-to-encrypted-hard-drives/ [Accessed 08 May 2014].

Leibniz, G. W. v. (1956a), 'Philosophical Papers and Letters, Volume 1', Chicago: The University of Chicago Press.

Leibniz, G. W. v. (1956b), 'Philosophical Papers and Letters, Volume 2', Chicago: The University of Chicago Press.

Mohan, S. and Mohammed, A. (2011), 'The New Secret', *Economic and Political Weekly*, 26 March, XLVI (13): 13–15.

Nagel, T. (2002), *Concealment And Exposure & Other Essays*, New York: Oxford University Press.

Osang, A. (2013), Spiegel Online. [Online] Available at http://www.spiegel.de/international/world/edward-snowden-neighbor-joyce-kinsey-brands-him-a-traitor-a-937369-druck.html [Accessed 08 May 2014].

Posner, R. A. (2008), 'Privacy, Surveillance and Law', *The University of Chicago Law Review*, 75 (1): 245–60.

Part Two

Births of 'Public': Translating Media, Travelling Contexts

Discussions on the public sphere often treat it as either a normative ideal or an existing formation that is itself constantly under negotiation for inclusion. The 'public', far from being given, are born through specific efforts that stand in relation to certain institutions and to the way institutions are conceived in various instances. This part explores the material processes and strategies, not always internally consistent, through which the idea of 'public' is formed, its conditions and its crises. This enquiry is not guided by the question, which perhaps is less relevant now, whether Habermasian assumptions measure up to the social and political realities, whether the public sphere is an ideal type. Frequently in contributions which desire to recuperate the public, the production of the public is obfuscated. Two unstated questions put before us by each of the chapters in this section might be as follows: *what are the guiding rules under which the 'media' speaks as the voice of the public sphere? And what are the conditions under which these rules are created?* The contexts through which this exploration is undertaken here are spatially and temporally as diverse as an eighteenth-century southern Indian princely state, a late nineteenth- and early twentieth-century political thinker and leader against British colonialism in South Africa and India and the university–media relation in post-globalization India. Read alongside each other, these chapters contribute more than an insight into a specific socio-historical juncture.

The questions about the rules and conditions of media received very significant responses in the last century, by Raymond Williams, Marshall McLuhan, Noam Chomsky and Edward S. Hermann respectively, which point to a kind of framing. The chapters by Udaya Kumar and Tridip Suhrud place translation at the heart of the framing whereby a public is created, and both focus on the way journals and newspapers strove to forge the voice of the public, indeed the public itself. In the public sphere of the state of Travancore, which no longer exists, in the early part of the last century, the domain of Malayalam speakers and readers has a kind of public defined by the unique structure of sovereignty that the editor Ramakrishna Pillai, studied by Udaya Kumar, confronts and exploits: the king is himself a servant of the temple deity, who is in effect the treasurer; the people are servants and the served – they understand their relation to the king as that of children to their mother. The minister or *dewan* is the real ruler, who, for all the services he performs for the king, is not the only one guilty of misrule but is also responsible for protecting the king from the blames for misrule and corruption. To address the two kinds of servants while isolating the governance of the *dewan*, Pillai isolates a frame of two dynamics within which the people in general may become a collectivity. First, Udaya Kumar analyses Pillai's translation strategies for terms from the discourse of the Western public sphere, to which the concerned society of Travancore, as well as the contemporary Malayalam language, does not correspond perfectly. Second, Pillai attempts to cast the role of the newspaper as simultaneously neutral and an active political agent, so that the public can both hear itself in the press and receive the real (discriminatory) effects of the speech thus generated. Udaya Kumar identifies 'the performative dimension' of the newspaper, for instance in Pillai's resort to shame and scandal as ways of instituting a public presumed to be universal but made visible in terms of caste and sexuality.

Suhrud's painstaking philological analysis of the beginnings of Gandhi's journal *Indian Opinion* shows a similar method operating in the better-known founder of a postcolonial 'public', one that also concerns the discontinuity between the Western discourse and the Indians. To create a connection between the two, Pillai, like Gandhi, was trying to 'introduce an agentive notion' by resorting to the ancients (*Pracinasamitikal*, p. 8) where councils elected their sovereigns. Suhrud, too, locates translation issues where this Western invention, through transplantations, emerged as variants of an original theme everywhere else. Like Pillai, Gandhi's beginnings in creating a public, too, involved loyal subjects to the king and editing newspapers. However, the crucial difference is that Gandhi was not interested in translating accurately or efficiently. Rather, he saw the two languages, Gujarati and English, speaking to two different publics. The Gujarati audience had their own concerns and milieu, and their own power, while the English readership, the colonialist addressee for Gandhi, saw things in terms of the Western language of equality, fraternal bonding, freedom and colonial oppression. Gandhi tried to produce the basis for a critical stand in them that was reflective. The editor tried to create a sufficiently reflective public out of the rich and poor Indians by creating a discourse that spoke to both levels, appealing to the sense of guardianship in the former and to that of ancient continuities in the latter while bringing them on some level with the Western idea of public sphere, rights and laws and striving for the right balance at every step.

Both essays might be read as explorations of a paradigm, raising the important question whether they are different sorts of paradigms, and if so, do they intersect or oppose? While the readers of this volume would draw their own conclusions, a possible suggestion is that in cultivating (through a choice of exemplars) in *himself* a voice of the public or conscience of a nation to come soon, the person of Gandhi ceases to be a paradigm and becomes a unique event instead. The process whereby Gandhi the editor sets about making the public aware of itself as a collection of people with shared concerns and direction creates out of Gandhi a kind of public being who embodies all these things: a mixture of legal English language and the very crude local language. Suhrud shows how the Gandhian manifesto *Hind Swaraj* was the end point of this process where Gandhi perfectly became the Indian Public Sphere.

Chattarji's chapter, concerned with the contemporary rifts that define 'public' today, focuses on the university, media and technology in a globalized context. Chattarji registers the idea of the university as the place which can and should be able to produce critical reflection of the public, to intervene in public discussions and make the assumptions of these discussions explicit, while the reality of the university (not in India alone but also in US contexts compared by Chattarji) is a kind of invisibility in this role. The university itself, Chatttarji shows through the mutations of the university in technology and business schools, no longer wishes to be a critical institution or is not permitted to be one by its management. It is made visible to the public only occasionally as an object of some media reports, particularly in the admission season. The media prefers to function by warding off the university as the site and agent of critical reflections – by abusing such reflections as are forthcoming as 'lefty', for instance. The media's own interests in public causes, including the anti-corruption movement (See Devadawson's chapter in the third part) and the Delhi Gang-Rape case, appears mysteriously inconsistent, which in itself should be a matter of public interest, and, beyond the Chomsky/Herman Model, we are lacking the means, theoretical and infrastructural, to ask them. An implicit theme of this chapter in common with the previous ones is the level of the people in the constitution of the 'public', and Chattarji's suggestion is worth serious consideration everywhere today in the scenarios of education fund cuts, dissolution of humanities departments and restructuring of disciplines (of which the FYUP, or Four-Year Undergraduate Programme, of the University of Delhi is instructive). He takes the example of English Studies in India, which serves simultaneously as a training ground for job seekers and as a potential public good as the place that develops the reflective apparatus for the future. Highlighting the disturbing role of the judicial institutions in curtailing protests by educators and streamlining the university to corporate interests, this chapter cautions that if the university and the media remain uncritical, without intellectual advancement and structural autonomy the resultant 'dumb' democracy would be indistinguishable from a dictatorship.

Raghuramaraju juxtaposes three models of the public sphere as found in a Western philosopher (Descartes), a cosmopolitan poet (Rabindranath Tagore) and a social scientist (A. M. Shah) in order to locate the birth of the modern Indian public sphere at a specific intersection of the West and the East, modern and the pre-modern and also of the city and the village, as though caught between each of the two sides. For Descartes, according to Raghuramaraju, the modern Ideal city is constructed out of a rational order unlike the ancient cities that gradually evolved out of villages. Similarly modernity is born out of disinheriting the past and the public sphere by excluding the private. In India, as Tagore observed, the past remains a contemporary of the present and the village coexists with the city. Both the village and the city are public spaces, and the former is under threat from the latter. Shah too acknowledges the coexistence of the village and the city but finds that the threat runs in the reverse direction – from the village to the city. The village intrudes into the city as wandering cows, narrow lanes and unruly and slow traffic. Raghuramaraju calls the village the structural unconscious of the city. He argues that Indian social sciences that follow the Cartesian model have failed to see the work of this unconsciousness that happens in front of their eyes. The Indian philosophical traditions could help these sciences to see what the Western Cartesian model obstructs them from seeing.

5

Ambivalences of Publicity: Transparency and Exposure in K. Ramakrishna Pillai's Thought

Udaya Kumar

This chapter tracks a moment of emergence of concepts of the public and publicness as tools of self-conscious reflection in early twentieth-century Travancore. Now part of the Kerala State in South India, Travancore was a princely state governed by a maharaja under indirect rule by the British. Our focus is on the interventions of K. Ramakrishna Pillai (1878–1916), a political journalist and literary critic, who played a seminal role in initiating a discourse around the idea of the public in Malayalam. Pillai's writings and interventions in the literary and political domains bring to light vital tensions that ran through invocations of the 'public' in Kerala at the beginning of the last century, a moment of important shifts in vocabulary for describing social and political domains.

The setting: The state, the people and the population

Travancore was a Hindu state, and this was reflected in the language of politics and administration: the kingdom was, according to a self-description introduced by King Marthandavarma in the eighteenth century, governed by the maharaja as the ritual servant of Sree Padmanabhaswamy, the principal deity of the State Temple in Trivandrum. The primary political relationship was between the sovereign and his subjects: customary descriptions of kings praised them for their 'prajavatsalyam', their compassionate affection for their subjects. Travancore came increasingly under indirect British rule from the early 1800s and, by the end of the century, idioms of governmentalization were predominant in the language of administration. The arrangement of administrative functions worked through a division of powers: sovereign power was vested in the king and his Palace Darbar; distinct from this, the dewan headed the administration, held executive powers and advised the king on all important matters. No official body of popular representation existed in Travancore in the nineteenth century. A legislative council was established in 1888; it was chaired by the dewan and consisted of government officials and nominated non-officials. The decisions of the council did not have mandatory power, and the maharaja could disallow any bill passed by it.[1] Sri Mulam Prajasabha or Popular Assembly, established in 1904, was the first body to have elected members; but its aim was to enable the maharaja to 'ascertain at first hand the wants and wishes of His people through their representatives, and also to elicit their opinion' on various measures of governance.[2] The dewan chaired this assembly and his rulings set limits on what could be brought before the assembly and what was worthy of presentation to the sovereign for consideration. The dewan disallowed moves to introduce a notion of the 'voice of the assembly' as a whole, distinct from the views of individual members who primarily expressed the grievances of their representative constituencies.[3] It was only in the 1920s that franchise was expanded and statutory powers vested with the Legislative Council.

The configuration of political power in Travancore – and the absence of recognized rights of popular representation – had a major role in shaping conceptions of the people and the public. This is evident in the new mass petitions demanding adequate representation for non-Brahmin castes in government employment: the Malayali Memorial of 1891 spearheaded by leaders from the Nayar, Christian and Ezhava communities and signed by more than ten thousand petitioners was followed five years later by the Ezhava Memorial, with more than 13,000 signatories. Both petitions made ample use of the newly available census data and grounded their claims in demography and statistics on income and employment.[4] The 'population', central to techniques of governmentality, was invoked as the proper object of the state's policies and interventions.

The governmental category of the 'population' may however need to be distinguished from the political category of the 'people'. Based on the same empirical referent, these mobilize what appears to be two distinctive virtual entities: while the population points to a plane of consistencies amenable to classification and identification of patterns and tendencies, the category of the people refers to a level of political agency and conceptions of rights and liberty. The language of ritual sovereignty in late nineteenth-century Travancore spoke of subjects (*praja*) defined by their devotion to the sovereign, reciprocated in turn by the king's compassionate affection. The mass petitions in late nineteenth-century

Travancore displayed an overlap between these different invocations of the people – as an object of sovereign power and of governmental arrangements, and as a locus of political will. The petitions referred to the rightful entitlements of various sections of the population and the indifference of the administration towards disadvantaged communities; at the same time, they also made gestures of ritual supplication before sovereign authority. While the discourse of claims was directed at the state administration headed by the dewan, the language of entreaties was deferentially addressed to the maharaja. The Ezhava Memorial of 1896, authored by Dr P. Palpu, concluded by describing the petitioners as 'humble subjects weeping before their affectionate King as children do before their mother', while marshalling proof of unfair governance and indirectly threatening conversion to other religions or migration to territories under direct British rule.[5]

Changes in the language of political articulation were not confined solely to the juridical instrument of the petition. A variety of forms of writing emerged in the late nineteenth century which had the state as its implicit, if not avowed, addressee. The newspaper was the most prominent space for such writing. While ostensibly addressed to an anonymous group of interested readers, the newspaper's implicit interlocutor – while talking about political matters – was the state, especially the government. The emergence of newspapers in Kerala goes back to the history of periodical publications initiated by Christian missionaries in mid-nineteenth century.[6] By 1910, political and community affairs decisively overtook religious matters as the principal focus in periodical publication: of the twenty-eight periodicals published then in Travancore, ten were concerned with religion, while two were focused on education and the rest were preoccupied with political and community affairs.[7] Criticism of unfair policies of the government and corruption among officials formed the core of political affairs discussed in newspapers.

Ramakrishna Pillai was strongly attracted to political journalism very early on and, at the age of twenty-one, was offered the editorship of a new newspaper, *Keraladarpanam*. His inaugural editorial reflected on the duties of newspapers, an awareness of which he found lacking among journalists in Kerala. Pillai used phrases with strong moral connotation – *dharmadharmangal* and *krtyakrtyangal* – to indicate these responsibilities. The editorial identified two major objectives for newspapers: to advise administrators on their duties (*dharmopadesam*) and to educate the population by offering them 'indelible knowledge' (*orikkalum maychu kalayuvan padillatha vidhathilulla arivu*).[8]

Naming the public

The word used in the editorial to refer to the population of readers of the newspaper was *janasangham*: literally, people as a collectivity. Ramakrishna Pillai repeatedly sought to find adequate phrases to mark this community. Interestingly, he did not use words that meant 'readers' (*vayanakkar*) or 'subscribers' (*varikkar*); nor did he use the word *janam* or people in an unqualified way. Pillai's formulations implied that the newspaper's proper addressee was not the people as such in their unqualified, non-mobilized existence; nor was it an empirically circumscribed group of actual readers of subscribers. The word *janasangham* indicated a degree of collective convergence. Pillai's subsequent writings began to employ two words, synonymously, to refer to this constituency: *pothujanam* and *janasamanyam*. Both these formulations added to the word *janam* (people) an element suggesting commonality or generality (*pothu-* and -*samanyam*).

It is likely that Pillai's search for demarcating this conceptual space came from his encounter with the concept of the 'public' in Western political discourses. *Pothujanam* has acquired in Malayalam the status of a translational equivalent for the English word 'public'. Malayalis were familiar with the English word, primarily through its use in the context of administration. For instance, a Public Works Department was set up in Travancore in 1860, which absorbed the earlier Maramath Department (which then became the 'Pothumaramath' Department). An official discourse around public facilities such as roads and travellers' bungalows began taking shape at this time. Access to 'public roads' (*pothunirathu*) near Hindu temples for lower castes became a point of contention in the 1920s. Such adjectival uses of the English word 'public' were translated into Malayalam by the use of the prefix '*pothu-*' which meant 'common' or 'general'. This, however, did not serve as an equivalent of the 'public' used as a substantive. '*Pothujanam*' and '*janasamanyam*' were Pillai's responses to this lack. But what does it mean to add the prefix '*pothu-*' to the Malayalam word for people, '*janam*'? What is involved in adding a dimension of commonality or generality to the concept of the 'people'?

Innovations in uses of language may not always follow careful conceptual thinking, and it may be risky to extract theoretical formulations from an analysis of neologisms. However, the gesture implied in such formulations demands consideration as a resource for speculative understanding. The word '*pothujanam*' does not work in the same way as '*pothunirathu*' (public road) or '*pothumaramathu*' (public works), as *janam* already designates an entity that is inclusive and general. The prefix seems to add an extra dimension of commonality: as if the concept of the people were being intensified, or raised to a higher power, re-emphasizing its characteristic as the space of the common. The people, a dispersed entity, is conceived here not as a coherent collective as in Pillai's earlier formulation '*janasangham*' but as gathered together in its exposedness to itself and in a shared recognition of its commonality. We need to probe further: what do the sense of self-visibility and the sense of commonality shared by the public involve?

An early response to this can be seen in Ramakrishna Pillai's editorial for the first issue of *Keralapanchika* in 1901, where he identified two principal functions for newspapers: 'Newspapers have two principal functions: firstly, they should formulate (*svarupappetuthuka*) the opinion of the public (*janasamanyathinte abhiprayathe*); secondly, they should act in accordance (*anuvarthikkuka*) with public opinion.'[9] There is an interesting tension between these two duties, which goes to the heart of Pillai's conception of the public. On one hand, the newspapers express or follow public opinion; on the other, public opinion – or even the public – did not always exist: it was for the papers to constitute a public as the bearer or proper subject of public opinion. In another editorial, Pillai clarified this further:

> The public (*janasamanyam*) is but a collective (*sangham*) that has not achieved any concrete form (*murthibhavichittillatha*). As we know, this unformed collectivity expresses its thoughts and wishes (*manogatangal*) through newspapers and public speakers. However ... in this province, we rarely have opportunities to listen to the thoughts and wishes of the public in forums where speeches are made. People here are neither ready nor desirous to address the public through speeches. Instead, it has been the newspapers that have performed this function.[10]

The newspaper is seen as the voice of an unformed collectivity that does not possess a distinctive means of expression of its own. This distinguishes the public from other collectivities – like political parties or religious organizations – which possessed greater concreteness of form. It appears to be in the nature of the public that it lacks a voice of its own and needs representation by an exterior agent. However, the public – by virtue of its lack of concreteness of form – does not authorize its representatives. The public speakers and newspaper editors authorize themselves by claiming to express the thoughts and wishes of this unformed collectivity; by addressing the people and persuading them to the legitimacy of these opinions, they constitute a public. The mode of address of the newspaper has a performative element: it brings into existence the 'public' whose opinion it claims to express. The concept of the public seems to possess a virtual dimension: all invocations of the public presuppose its existence, but the public cannot manifest itself without the modes of address through which it is invoked.

The public and the political

What is the matrix within which Pillai conceived the production of a public and public opinion? The agentive dimension of *pothujanam* is evident in the editorial we cited earlier, where Ramakrishna Pillai wrote about the relation between newspapers and public opinion. The editorial began by framing the public in terms of a relationship between masters and servants:

> It is well known that a proper awareness of the relationship between masters (*yajamananmar*) and servants (*dasanmar*) has not yet arisen in this country. On account of this defect, servants are sometimes prone to assume the postures of masters and masters those of servants.[11]

At first sight, this may appear as a synoptic description of sovereign power. The relationship of the subjects (*praja*) to the Maharaja of Travancore was articulated in a ritualized language of supplication. However, as we saw earlier, the governance of Travancore was carried out by the dewan and a bureaucracy. Political criticism of the government often maintained a distinction between the maharaja and the governmental apparatus led by the dewan. Ramakrishna Pillai's editorial places the latter – the dewan and the government officers – as servants. But their master is not the maharaja; it is the *janasamanyam* or the general public that is described as the master. 'A "public servant" is the servant of the general public (*janasamanyam*) of that country.'[12] The subjects (*praja*) of the maharaja's sovereign power are turned into masters; they are the sovereign agents who command officers of the government.

Ramakrishna Pillai's political criticism came under increasing strain while addressing relations between the maharaja and his prominent officers. The later editorials of *Swadeshabhimani*, which led to the expulsion of Ramakrishna Pillai from Travancore and the confiscation of the press, suggested an increasing collusion between the dewan, the officials of the palace and the maharaja himself. The power that controversial officers like Sankaran Thampi or Antharama Iyer wielded, Pillai argued, was disproportionate to their official standing. Their proximity to the maharaja protected their illegitimate actions from public scrutiny.

Ramakrishna Pillai returned to the theme of sovereign power several times and tried to produce an account that would reconcile kingship with the political agentiveness of the people. In 1907, he published two essays in *Keralan* on *rajyabharanam* (governance), where he considered the authority of kings as grounded in popular will. 'It is essential for the king-subject pair that the subjects agree to abide by the rules set by the king. The doctrine of sovereign rule is grounded in this consent.'[13] In the ultimate instance, Pillai privileged the subjects over their sovereign. 'We must understand that if we weigh the King against his subjects, the subjects will emerge as heavier. However, neither the king nor his subjects should let an occasion arise for such comparison.'[14] In Travancore, sovereign power is 'shared and protected' by the British. Pillai saw this in a positive light, since the British had overcome the opposition between the king and the subjects. In their country, the people had emerged victorious in a long history of conflict with their kings, and the sovereign's will had come to merge now with the desires of the subjects.[15] After his expulsion from Travancore in 1910, Ramakrishna Pillai revisited this theme and tried to ground his arguments about popular consent in history. He wrote two essays in 1912, under the titles 'Rajadhikaram' (The Authority of the King) and 'Pracinasamitikal' (Ancient Councils), where he argued that in ancient India kings were chosen by the people and that sovereignty was vested in equal measure in the village council, the council of elders and in the king elected by them.[16] These seem to be Pillai's efforts to introduce an agentive notion of the people into the frame of ritualized sovereignty.

Scandalous exposure and public decorum

One of the ways Ramakrishna Pillai addressed the relations between the people and the rulers was by invoking notions of decorum. Just as ritual obeisance was part of appropriate decorum before the maharaja, the public domain also possessed its own sense of decorum. A sense of decorum places obligations on people to behave within a range of acceptable norms. An instance of strong violation of public decorum is found in the phenomenon of scandal.[17] In scandalous situations the decorum that holds together the public domain is disrupted. In such moments, Ramakrishna Pillai saw a possibility for political criticism: they offered a context for forging certain modes of address that constituted the public as a political subject.

The disruption of decorum in scandal seems to reveal an important aspect of publicness. It shows that the public is configured not only in terms of access and transparency but also of exposure. Concealment and truthfulness, accountability and evasion, appear as key terms in considering publicness along the axes of transparency and access. When we consider publicness as a mode of visibility where human subjects and their actions stand exposed, it is shame and dignity that come to the foreground. Scholarship on shame has at times usefully attempted to distinguish it from moral condemnation. Bernard Williams identified improper or undesired exposure as the key constituent of the experience of shame[18] (1993, p. 78). An early text of Emmanuel Levinas linked shame to a problematic of visibility and inhabitation[19] (2003). Giorgio Agamben has developed Levinas's arguments further, and analysed shame as experienced in acts of spectation[20] (1997, pp. 87–135). In cases of shameful public exposure, it is not solely those actors who appear in a disreputable light that are affected; shame also applies to the spectators; the public as the involuntary subject before whom actors stand exposed also suffers a loss of decorum. Righteous indignation is not the only public response to the eruption of scandals; in addition to the idiom of moral condemnation, we also see expressions of a sense of offence resulting from the outrage of the public's dignity. Scandal journalism works on its audience by drawing on both these responses: through its mode of address, it constitutes a public that is morally indignant as well as outraged in its sense of dignity.

The trope of improper exposure recurred frequently in Ramakrishna Pillai's journalistic writings. An early example of this is an editorial published in 1901, which criticized a custom prevalent at the Sri Padmanabhaswamy Temple in Trivandrum which required Nayar women from certain families to participate bare-breasted in some festivals. Pillai concluded his chapter by making a distinction between two spaces of exposure:

> Since the procession with the idol within the walls of the temple engenders only the feeling of religious devotion, the people who assemble there, given their familiarity with this custom, may not consider it special. However, people of various castes (*nanajatikkar*) gather at the festivals of *vetta* and *arattu* not for the *darshan* of the deity but for spectacle; therefore, such naked forms will only induce in them disapproval and scorn towards Nayar women.[21]

Cherayi Ramadas, in a sustained critique of Ramakrishna Pillai's approach to the question of caste, points out that citations of this editorial usually leave out a crucial passage, which links the problem of improper exposure explicitly to caste and religious identities. The passage runs as follows:

> We can agree to women leaving their breasts uncovered when walking with lit lamps within the Seevelippura of the Temple. This is because only a few castes which obey Hindu religion enter the temple. However, on the occasion of *vetta* and *arattu*, they walk half-naked like savage women for a long distance beginning from the western gate of the temple in front of several thousands of people crowding on both sides of the street, especially those considered as low castes such as Channars, Ezhavas, Muslims, Pulayas and Parayas. We do not think that the Europeans, who have a stricter sense of the proprieties of public behaviour (*sabhayogyamaya maryada*), or the Malayalis who follow their culture (*parishkaram*) through association with them, will like this or feel anything other than aversion and sadness.[22]

Scandal as a mode of political criticism

These passages bring together two important dimensions of the framing of improper exposure in Ramakrishna Pillai's writings: sexuality and caste. The image of bare-breasted Nayar women invoked in the editorial stands at the threshold of a modern idea of publicness. Deeply embedded in temple rituals associated with the royalty of Travancore and attended only by upper-caste Hindu devotees, these half-naked female figures become icons of cultural depravity in front of a less exclusive gathering on the road side. It is interesting that the exposure is offensive to a third party rather than to the women or the crowd that witnesses them: it is the Europeans and the Malayalis who have imbibed European norms of public behaviour that occupy the space of the normative gaze and are affected. Conflicting notions of exposure and publicness seem to undergird this editorial: Pillai identifies with the sentiments of proponents of Western ideas of public propriety; nonetheless, traditional norms which mandate women to appear half-naked in the upper-caste religious space inside the temple are accepted. The reference to the '*hinajati*' or low castes and Muslims sexualize the spectacle: they, Pillai suggests, have come not to take *darshan* but to enjoy the sight of the procession, and the Nayar women here become objects of a sexualized gaze that transgresses caste boundaries.

Ramakrishna Pillai's political criticism was primarily directed at the corruption and the illegitimate privileges enjoyed by some of the royal officials, such as Sankaran Thampi and Anantharama Iyer, and the dewan's complicity in permitting this. Reports on these irregularities were at times inflected by a dimension of sexual impropriety which accentuated the sense of shamefulness and outrage. A marital alliance the maharaja entered into in 1899 typified the combination of the political and the sexual: the lady in question was formerly involved in a similar relationship with Sankaran Thampi, who – it was widely believed – facilitated the king's new marriage. Although this was not contrary to the customary practice of *sambandham* which permitted such remarriages for Nayar women, Ramakrishna Pillai's later references to it, written at a time when the marital and inheritance practices among the Nayars were undergoing major changes, resonated with the new patrilineal sexual morality and its opprobrium towards the 'primitiveness' and 'immorality' of Nayar *sambandham* arrangements. Given Thampi's rapid rise in the royal circles and the extra-judicial powers he exercised, the marriage epitomized, for Pillai, an illegitimate exchange of political and sexual favours.

Scandal journalism directed at the government predictably came into conflict with the proprieties set by the person of the maharaja and the division between the private and the public lives of government officials. Ramakrishna Pillai, until very late in his career in Travancore, did not make the king a direct object of his criticism. The king's morality and intentions were presented as beyond reproach, and the powerful royal servants were accused of abusing his trust and polluting the sanctity of the palace with their corrupt practices. An editorial from 1908 on the misuse of the king's palace by royal servants and the extended kin of royal consorts concluded:

> In the capacity of royal servants or through association with the king's wife, these
> people and their families have intruded into the inner quarters of the maharaja.
> We cannot forget that as a result, the glory of the royal palace, established in
> the proximity of Sree Padmanabha and sanctified everyday by vedic rituals, has
> been vitiated by immensely terrifying, cruel and distressing incidents.[23]

The restraint exercised in relation to the king was matched by the virulence of the criticism directed at the royal servants and the dewan. The criticism of the dewan made ample use of tropes of improper exhibition of shameful behaviour. An example of this is found in the essays Pillai wrote in 1903 on the visit of a Tamil actress, Balamani, and the enthusiastic reception she received in Trivandrum.[24]

Ramakrishna Pillai ascribed a destructive, seductive spell to Balamani by combining several tropes: the perilous allure of theatrical exposure, the actress's manipulative charms and sexual promiscuity, the deleterious effects of popular theatre on the public and the possibility that the actress may capture in her net the very authorities who are meant to protect the public from falling into her snare. At the conclusion of her visit, a gold necklace was gifted to the actress by her admiring public, and the Dewan of Travancore presented it to her on their behalf. He invited widespread criticism by placing the gold chain around her neck rather than in her hands. Pillai's editorial loudly lamented:

> O, Travancore state! The predicament you have reached! You who were governed by noble ministers with high ideals who evoked fear and wonder among the inhabitants of neighbouring states, we cannot understand what sin you have done to be trapped now under the misgovernment of a wicked minister taken in by female charms.[25]

The theme of exposure with sexual innuendoes continued in his criticism of Dewan Rajagopalachary and arguably precipitated Pillai's expulsion from Travancore in 1910. The dewan's behaviour during a royal procession during the jubilee celebrations was the context: Pillai criticized Rajagopalachary for viewing the procession from the upper storey of a girls' school which was occupied by several respected women and which directly faced another building where women from the royal household were standing. The editorial saw in this a scandalous violation of female dignity. It placed the incident in question in a litany of sexually improper acts on the part of the dewan, ranging from wearing improper clothes which exposed his body in the presence of women and colleagues to stories about people attempting to gain the dewan's favour by procuring women for him. It concluded by invoking earlier examples of royal propriety, especially during Visakham Tirunal's reign, and suggested that had he been the king, the present-day dewan would have been horse-whipped for his behaviour.[26]

How does a writer refer to disgraceful incidents in the royal court without dragging the king and the royal family into the lurid limelight of public scandal and inviting royal wrath and public opprobrium? Pillai's method comprised strategic public interventions that deployed a range of genres and modalities of voice. The genres he used occupied a space between the discourse of reporting which advanced verifiable truth claims and the idiom of fiction which purportedly presented an imaginary narrative but left the door open to allegorical readings and inferences. A fictional representation, which does not directly claim any allegorical meaning, is put into circulation at a moment when the incidents and circumstances presented prompt their popular reception as a code for recent events. This allows the work to evade charges of defamation and address the reader in a dual tongue: at an apparent level, the work appears as a simple fictional narrative that evokes outrage, anger and compassion; at another level, the work silently appeals to the reader's knowledge of recent events, prompts an allegorical reading and turns the emotions produced in the reader into political responses. This dual address assumes that the reader of the plays is also a reader of newspapers and a receptor of hearsay and political information. The ambivalence of address produces a public that moves across the boundaries between literary and political domains.

Ramakrishna Pillai's only novel, *Narakathil Ninnu*, and the two large political novels he published – *Udayabhanu* and *Parappuram* by K. Narayana Kurukkal – use this technique.[27] While Kurukkal's novels adopt fictional settings such as the Mahabharata war or the life of a family, Pillai's own novel is about villainous officers in the palace and their posthumous destinies. The allegorical reference of the characters in *Narakathil Ninnu* would be obvious to any reader familiar with Pillai's newspaper writing and Travancore politics of the times. Pillai wrote this novel four years after his departure from Travancore, and this may explain the narrowing distance between the fictional text and its implied reference.

In an earlier essay, I discussed the relations between Ramakrishna Pillai's fictional and journalistic procedures.[28] Scandal journalism, in order to avoid charges of libel, usually refrained from naming the persons attacked and spelling out the allegations in verifiable detail but supplied enough suggestive information to help readers identify them. They went beyond the idiom of reportage and worked by interpellating the reader into a community of complicity based on a presumption of shared knowledge. Political fiction, from the other side of the divide between fiction and fact, worked by feigning a tone of aesthetic naiveté and invited the reader to directly relate the events in the novel to what lay outside the world of art. The address of the fictional work too involved a gesture of interpellation into complicity: this gesture saw through claims of aesthetic autonomy and regarded it as a screen for transacting risky political business. The literary and political public spheres in Ramakrishna Pillai's writing were tied to each other in mutual invagination through gestures of interpellation and complicity.

We saw that Ramakrishna Pillai's conception of publicness was marked by two prominent attributes, which appear to point in two directions. On one hand, the public is the domain of access and transparency; the purpose of newspapers was to bring to light what was concealed from public vision and to make the public take note of things it overlooked. On the other hand, the public also is the domain of exposure which produced the experience of dignity and shame. Shameful exposure was a threat to the loss of public decorum and to the very possibility of a public. Ramakrishna Pillai's political criticism frequently drew on the experience of witnessing shameful exposure. In doing this, scandal journalism and sensational fiction risked rehearsing the very loss of decorum which they were trying to counter and master. The language or moral righteousness and the experience of scandalous outrage often appeared in an intimate embrace in these modes of writing.

Publicness: Sites of ambivalence

The complexity of these modes also reveals the fault lines in the constitution of the new sense of publicness produced by political and literary opinion-making in Ramakrishna Pillai's times. The discourse on *'pothujanam'*, we saw, invoked the public as a virtual entity which included everyone as a potential participant in collective processes of deliberation and opinion-making. The experience of scandal, however, brought to light the threatening presence of subjectivities, relations and practices which posed a challenge to the norms that governed the virtual domain of publicness. The sexual dimension of improper exposure that cropped up time and again in Ramakrishna Pillai's writing on political scandals pointed to the shameful persistence of disavowed sexual practices such as *sambandham* in the modern public domain. This prompted constant exorcism through the expression of moral indignation at the loss of decorum that the public as a collective spectator suffered.

An equally difficult challenge to the virtual, inclusive idea of the public in Ramakrishna Pillai's writings is posed by caste identities. Ascribed caste distinctions and structures of exclusion intrude on Ramakrishna Pillai's writing. The passage discussed earlier about Nayar women appearing without breast cloth before spectators who belong to *hinajati* (low castes) is an example of this. Pillai seems to imply that such appearance inside the temple is immune from sexualization. However, the distinction is not solely a spatial one, nor is the issue purely that of improper bodily exposure. As Cherayi Ramadas points out, it is conceived in terms of caste: the spectators inside the temple comprise upper caste Hindus; those on the street side have among them people who belong to *hinajati*, including not only Hindu lower castes, but also Muslims. This allowed Pillai to define the upper caste Hindu spectators as forming a devotional public and the street-side spectators as a crowd drawn there not by the 'desire for the *darshan* of the deity' but by an ordinary, vulgar curiosity for spectacle. Before the gaze of the latter public, Nayar women, in their semi-nakedness, suffer a loss of dignity. Ramadas highlights the contradictions in this argument: is Pillai suggesting that the semi-naked appearance of Nayar women enhances the devotional sentiment among the *savarna* castes? Pillai's concern for Nayar women during temple festivals sat uncomfortably with his silence on the restrictions on covering the body that women from untouchable castes were forcibly subjected to in Travancore at that time.[29] His articulation of disgraceful bodily exposure draws rather on a sense of shame associated with the sexual transgression of caste hierarchies. A similar trope, we may recall, was used in the criticism of Dewan Rajagopalachary's appearance on the balcony of the Fort Girls' School. Could Pillai's virulent criticism of the Tamil Brahmin Dewan for offending the dignity of the upper caste Malayali women implicitly be drawing on idioms of outrage at caste-sexual contamination?

Ramakrishna Pillai's public interventions revealed interesting tensions on caste and community questions. He viewed with respect Sree Naryana Guru's initiatives for the uplifting of the Ezhavas, praised the community's aptitude for industry and recommended their admission to schools alongside upper caste children.[30] At the same time, he opposed campaigns for admitting children from the untouchable Pulaya caste in schools along with children from the Hindu upper castes. He made a distinction between matters of custom (*acharam*) and matters of comprehension in education. Upper castes who had centuries of access to education and the former agrestic slave caste of Pulayas, Pillai argued, cannot be considered to be at the same level of intellectual abilities. It would be unwise to admit them into the same classroom.

> In the cultivation of intelligence (*buddhikrishi*), to place alongside each other castes who have been cultivating their intelligence for so many generations and castes who have been cultivating the fields for so many more generations is like tethering to the same plough a horse and a buffalo.[31]

Ramakrishna Pillai repeatedly asserted that this was solely a matter of intellectual abilities and that the low castes had a right to access in all 'public matters':

> We believe that one cannot deny the claim that low castes like Pulayas and Parayas have the right and the reason to approach other castes and that they must be permitted to enter public spaces and public affairs along with other castes. Pualayas and Parayas, like Brahmins and Nayars, are among God's creations. These castes are, like them, the subjects of the Government. Therefore they must indeed be granted equal rights to enter public affairs.[32]

In spite of Ramakrishna Pillai's claim that this was solely a matter of education, the editorial on 'horses and buffaloes' resonated with the rhetoric of caste insults. The use of the word *krshi*, the Malayalam word for agriculture, in the extended sense of cultivation enabled a contrast between *buddhikrshi* (cultivation of the intelligence) and *nilamkrshi* (cultivation in the field). This was as an insulting reminder of the uncultured status of the Pulayas, whose predecessors worked as slaves in agricultural fields. Such an invocation of undignified pasts worked as a humiliating act of exposure within the decorum of public discourse. The Pulaya subject, seeking entry into the arena of a shared public discourse, was debarred through the double entendre of a caste-coloured discourse on intellectual abilities. As in his political criticism, Ramakrishna Pillai adopted a double-voiced language in the case of caste identities and their differential relationship to the experience of dignity.

Such instances of ambivalence are scattered throughout Pillai's writings: he argued against the mention of 'Ezhavas' in association with toddy tapping in a school textbook, displaying a sensitivity to the offence such caste references can create in a classroom.[33] However, allusions to caste inferiority became an important issue in the debate that followed Ramakrishna Pillai's harsh review of Pandit K. P. Karuppan's play *Balakalesam* in 1915. Pillai's review, the rejoinders by Karuppan and T. K. Krishna Menon and the further response from Pillai – all betray an intensity of engagement far in excess of the questions of literary value and the procedures of publication which formed the ostensible objects of their focus. Double-tongued phrases involving images of boats, waves and oars come up in the essays, in oblique reference to Karuppan's caste community and its traditional occupation of fishing. Caste stigma and its invocation, injurious to the very assumption of an inclusive public, energizes and threatens the fragile economy of Pillai's discourses on the public.

Ramakrishna Pillai was among the pioneering thinkers who advanced an account of the public for making political and literary claims. At the same time, he was also a proponent and interventionist in the contestatory field of public discourses. In this chapter, I tried to show how Pillai's writings invoke two sets of notions around publicness. The first set highlights inclusiveness and the right to access; it sets transparency and truthfulness as normative ideals. Accompanying this, and often mobilized in the service of this, we find a second set of concerns: they regard the public as a field of visibility and exposure; questions of dignity and shame shape this field. The exposure of disgraceful acts – even when in the name of truth – produces an experience of shame in the public realm, harming the sense of decorum essential to this domain. Sexuality and caste appear as particularly significant sites of such exposure. My attempt has been to examine the transactions between transparency and exposure in Ramakrishna Pillai's writings and track their consequences for considering publicness as value and experience.

Notes

1 T. K. Velu Pillai, *The Travancore State Manual, Vol. II: History*, p. 683.

2 Diwan V. P. Madhava Rao's address at the first session of the Sri Mulam Assembly, quoted in T. K. Velu Pillai, *Travancore State Manual, Vol. II: History*, p. 683.

3 See *Proceedings of the Fifth Session of the Sree Mulam Popular Assembly of Travancore*, pp. 82–3.

4 The first systematic census of Travancore was taken in 1875.

5 For the full text of the petition, see Velayudhan Panikkassery, *Do. Palpu* (Dr Palpu), pp. 42–4.

6 For an account of early newspapers and periodicals in Malayalam, see G. Priyadarshan, *Malayala Patrapravartanam: Prarambhaswarupam* [Newspapers in Malayalam: Early Formations].

7 'Thiruvitamkurile Pathrapravarthanam,' *Malabari*, 3 February 1911. Papers of Swadeshabhimani Ramakrishna Pillai, Nehru Memorial Museum and Library, New Delhi, Box 2, File dates: 1910–12.

8 K. Ramakrishna Pillai, 'Pathrangalude Chumathala,' (The Duty of Newspapers), editorial in *Keraladarpanam* on 14 September 1899, reprinted in *Bhayakautilya Lobhangalkkethire!: Swadeshabhimaniyude Sampurna Mukha Prasangangal* (Against Fear, Slyness and Greed!: The Complete Editorials of Swadeshabhimani), volume 1 of *Swadeshabhimaniyude Sampurna Kritikal* (The Complete Works of Swadeshabhimani), pp. 35–7.

9 Editorial in *Keralapanchika*, M. E. 1076 Medam 10 (22 April 1901), quoted in K. Bhaskara Pillai, *Swadeshabhimani*, p. 47.

10 'Pothujanadasanmarum Varthamanapathrangalum' (Public Servants and Newspapers), Editorial in *Keralapanchika*, M. E. 1077 Kumbham 13 (24 February 1902), reprinted in *Bhayakautilya Lobhangalkkethire!*, p. 48.

11 K. Ramakrishna Pillai, 'Pothujanadasanmarum Varthamanapathrangalum', p. 48.

12 Ibid., pp. 48–9.

13 K. Ramakrishna Pillai, 'Rajyabharanam – I' (Governance – I), *Keralan*, April–May 1907, reprinted in *Swadeshabhimaniyude Bhashasiddhantavum Sahitya Chintakalum*, p. 516.

14 K. Ramakrishna Pillai, 'Rajyabharanam – I', p. 518.

15	Ibid., p. 519.

16	K. Ramakrishna Pillai, 'Rajadhikaram' (The Authority of the King), *Sudarshanam*, January–February 1912, reprinted in *Swadeshabhimaniyude Bhashasiddhantavum Sahitya Chintakalum*, pp. 533–4. See also his 'Pracinasamitikal' (Ancient Councils), *Atmaposhini*, April–May 1912, reprinted in *Swadeshabhimaniyude Bhashasiddhantavum Sahitya Chintakalum*, pp. 539–50.

17	For a discussion of political scandal, gossip and rumour, see John B. Thompson, *Political Scandal: Power and Visibility in the Media Age*, pp. 11–28.

18	Bernard Williams, *Shame and Necessity*, p. 78.

19	Emmanuel Levinas, *On Escape, De l'evasion*.

20	Giorgio Agamben, *Remnants of Auschwitz: The Witness and the Archive*, esp. pp. 87–135.

21	K. Ramakrishna Pillai, 'Thiruvitamkur Maharajavu Thirumanassukondu Kalpichu Erppetuthenda Oru Samudayika Parishkaram' (A Social Reform that Needs to Introduced by the Command of His Highness the Maharaja of Travancore), *Keralapanchika*, 27 September 1901, cited in K. Bhaskara Pillai, *Swadeshabhimani*, p. 40.

22	Cherayi Ramadas, 'Stutipathakarude Swadeshabhimani' (Praise-singers of Swadeshabhimani), *Ayyankalikku Adarathode* (To Ayyankali, with Respect), p. 201. Ramadas cites this from *Swadeshabhimani Masika*, July 1925.

23	K. Ramakrishna Pillai, 'Valiya Kottaram II' (The Great Palace II), *Swadeshabhimani*, 22 July 1908, reprinted in *Bhayakautilya Lobhangalkkethire!*, p. 288.

24	The essay, signed 'Keralan', was published in *Malayali* on 4 April 1902. Cited in K. Bhaskara Pillai, *Swadeshabhimani*, pp. 70–1.

25	'Balamaniyum Sammanadanavum' (Balamani and the Presentation Ceremony), *Malayali*, 13 June 1903, cited in K. Bhaskara Pillai, *Swadeshabhimani*, p. 72.

26	K. Ramakrishna Pillai, 'Garhyamaya Natatha' (Disreputable Conduct), *Swadeshab-himani*, 24 August 1910, reprinted in *Bhayakautilya Lobhangalkkethire!*, p. 466.

27	See K. Narayana Kurukkal, *Parappuram* (Rockface), 3 vols (1908); *Udayabhanu* (The Morning Sun), 4 vols (1905). K. Ramakrishna Pillai, *Narakathil Ninnu* (1914), reprinted in *Swadeshabhimaniyude Novelum Jivacaritrakrtikalum* (Swadeshabhimani's Novel and Biographical Works), *Swadeshabhimaniyude Sampurna Krtikal* (The Complete Works of Swadeshabhimani), vol. 4, (Thiruva-nanthapuram: Kerala Granthasala Sahakarana Sangham, 2010), pp. 327–452.

28	Udaya Kumar, 'The Public, the State and New Domains of Writing: On Ramakrishna Pillai's Conception of Literary and Political Expression', pp. 413–41.

29	Cherayi Ramadas, 'Stutipathakarude Swadeshabhimani', p. 201.

30	See K. Ramakrishna Pillai, 'Vyavasayasilaraya Ezhavar' (Industrious Ezhavas), *Keralan*, April–May 1905, reprinted in *Bhayakautilyalobhangalkkethire!*, pp. 76–8; 'Ezhavarude Klesangal' (The Grievances of the Ezhavas), *Keralan*, May–June 1905, reprinted in *Bhayakautilyalobhangalkkethire!*, pp. 93–5.

31 K. Ramakrishna Pillai, 'Vidyabhyasakkuzhappam' (Trouble in Education),
    Swadeshabhimani, 2 March 1910, reprinted in *Bhayakautilyalobhangalkkethire!*,
    pp. 415–16. This idea is developed further two days later: 'Vidyabhyasapramadam'
    (Error in Education), *Swadeshabhimani*, 4 March 1910, reprinted in
    Bhayakautilyalobhangalkkethire!, pp. 417–19.
32 K. Ramakrishna Pillai, 'Vidyabhyasapramadam', p. 417.
33 K. Ramakrishna Pillai's review of the school textbook of Malayalam for the
    first standard in *Malayali*, 14 November 1903, cited in K. Bhaskara Pillai,
    Swadeshabhimani, pp. 89–9.

References

Agamben, Giorgio (1997), *Remnants of Auschwitz: The Witness and the Archive*, trans.
    Daniel Heller-Roazen. New York: Zone Books.
Kumar, Udaya (2007), 'The Public, the State and New Domains of Writing:
    On Ramakrishna Pillai's Conception of Literary and Political Expression', *Tapasam:
    A Quarterly Journal of Kerala Studies*, 2 (3–4): 413–41.
Levinas, Emmanuel (2003), *On Escape, De l'Evasion*, trans. Bettina Bergo. Stanford:
    Stanford University Press.
Narayana Kurukkal, K. (1949), *Parappuram* (Rockface), 3 vols (1908), Trivandrum:
    B. V. Book Depot.
Narayana Kurukkal, K. (1949), *Udayabhanu* (The Morning Sun), 4 vols (1905),
    Trivandrum: Kamalalayam Book Depot.
Panikkassery, Velayudhan (2002), *Do. Palpu* (Dr Palpu). Trissur: Current Books.
Priyadarshan, G. (1982), *Malayala Patrapravartanam: Prarambhaswarupam*
    [Newspapers in Malayalam: Early Formations], Trissur: Kerala Sahitya Akademi.
Proceedings of the Fifth Session of the Sree Mulam Popular Assembly of Travancore
    (1908), Trivandrum: The Government Press.
Ramadas, Cherayi (2009), *Ayyankalikku Adarathode* (To Ayyankali, with Respect),
    Ernakulam: Uparodham Books.
Swadeshabhimaniyude Sampurna Kritikal (The Complete Works of Swadeshabhimani)
    (2009), Thiruvananthapuram: Kerala Grandhashala Sahakarana Sangham.
Thompson, John B. (2000), *Political Scandal: Power and Visibility in the Media Age*,
    Cambridge, MA: Polity Press.
Velu Pillai, T. K. (1996), *The Travancore State Manual, Vol. II: History* (first pub. 1940;
    rpt.), Thiruvananthapuram: Kerala Gazetteers.
Williams, Bernard (1993), *Shame and Necessity*, Berkeley: University of California Press.

6

The Crisis of English Studies and the Public Sphere in India

Subarno Chattarji

Introduction

Humanistic studies in general and English Studies in particular have occupied a somewhat tenuous position in the Indian academy as well as civic spheres beyond. The question 'What do you do?' is less one of mystified indulgence (how can one's profession be to merely think and analyse?) and more of a managerial impatience that perceives humanistic research as irrelevant self-indulgence. Within contemporary contexts of global capital and the perception of education as a commodity necessary for India's development, English Studies is both under threat and a desirable good. The latter seems to drive policy imperatives and administrative structural changes that instrumentalize the disciplinary field to fulfil particular ends within new conceptualizations of knowledge economies. This political-bureaucratic-ideological juggernaut both wishes and has begun to reshape the discipline in ways which have consequences not only for the idea of English Studies in disciplinary terms – what should be taught, in what ways, to whom, for what ends – but also in altering the landscape of the academy, its practitioners and so-called stakeholders. Arguably, the practice of criticism in English Studies has been in a perpetual state of crisis, but this chapter will argue that the evisceration of analytical, ethical, intellectual spaces and values has further aggravated that critical sense of siege. Simultaneously this reorientation serves to diminish public spheres in its marginalization of the university as a locus for thought and dissent. What is noteworthy and troubling is the level of popular indifference – as manifested in media debates and policy–academy interface – towards this repositioning as if such reorientations were an inherent good or inevitable and therefore protest was or is a sign of redundancy, a refusal or inability to cope with 'global', 'professional' standards and standardization. This chapter will attempt to outline some of the constitutive elements of crisis within the Indian university and its implications for English Studies, placing both within an idea of the 'aesthetic public sphere', one which is deeply implicated in the everyday practices of the polity. Such debates occur not only within the university but crucially in media spheres, which have come to typify a commonsensical notion of publics and their definitional boundaries.

Intellectuals, the media and activism

Writing in 2006 Domna Stanton pace Bourdieu outlined the manner in which 'media intellectuals' were diminishing the possibilities of critique in public spaces: 'For all too often today, mediatization substitutes for activism and effective intervention: intellectuals have become chatterers instead of challengers of repressive regimes through writings and actions of contestation' (Stanton, p. 8). Stanton's contempt is well-placed but could be further nuanced within contexts of power and the crisis of legitimacy in the public sphere. One aspect of the power–legitimacy crisis are the obvious divergences between the two: as the state, its institutions and non-state actors such as corporations have appropriated larger domains of power and capital, their legitimacy has increasingly come under scrutiny and threat. Thus, on the one hand securitization and militarization of public spaces is more ubiquitous than ever[1] and on the other hand, citizenry in varied contexts – Tahrir Square, Wall Street, the steps of St Paul's Cathedral or India Gate – express anger, discontent, disenchantment and the object of their collective ire seem to be instruments of state and corporate power. At the crux of what may be termed a collective, commonsensical apprehension of inequities and injustices are precisely the modes of mediatization that Stanton alludes to. Such modes have altered and accelerated since 2006 and their proliferation is often perceived as a primary driver of protest movements and revolutionary change. There is, however, some scepticism regarding new media as a cutting-edge instrument of freedom. Evgeny Morozov's *The Net Delusion* is perhaps the most persuasive analysis of the manner in which the lure of what he terms 'Slacktivism' creates illusory, impermanent publics of easy protest, the promise of 'cyber-utopia':

> The idea that the Internet favors the oppressed rather than the oppressor is marred by what I call cyber-utopianism: a naive belief in the emancipatory nature of online communication that rests on a stubborn refusal to acknowledge its downside. It stems from the starry-eyed digital fervor of the 1990s, when former hippies, by this time ensconced in some of the most prestigious universities in the world, went on an argumentative spree to prove that the Internet could deliver what the 1960s couldn't: boost democratic participation, trigger a renaissance of moribund communities, strengthen associational life, and serve as a bridge from bowling alone to blogging together. And if it works in Seattle, it must also work in Shanghai. (Morozov 2011, p. xiii)

Morozov goes on to analyse the ways in which 'cyber-utopianism' gives rise to 'internet-centrism', an approach that perceives alternatives to authoritarianism in terms of technological determinism, of the kind outlined by Raymond Williams: '"If the medium –whether print or television – is the cause," wrote Williams in his best-selling *Television: Technology and Cultural Form*, "all other causes, all that men ordinarily see as history, are at once reduced to effects." For Williams, it was not the end of *history* that technology was ushering in; it was the end of *historical thinking*. And with the end of historical thinking, the questions of justice lose much of their significance as well' (Morozov 2011, p. 292).

Morozov's analysis is valuable not just in problematizing internet freedoms but also in contexts where the means of protest are perceived to intrinsically validate the political and ideological ends of protest, creating what Williams presciently called the 'end of *historical thinking*'. Thus, for instance, the Anna Hazare phenomenon was lauded in media domains because it seemed to offer a 'solution' to the 'problem' of corruption, without quite delving into 'questions of justice' or the easy articulation of democratic free will and anger that the protestors represented. In a different context – that of anti-globalization and anti-Iraq War protests in the United States and United Kingdom – Suman Gupta offers an argument that encapsulates the somewhat contradictory radical impulse underlying such protests, contradictions that manifest themselves in discursive radicalism within the university–public sphere relationship. Gupta writes:

> To seek a position outside the universalist, totalist, solidarist, materialist, class-and-labour-analysis-based discourse of Marxism's many political agendas, while taking possession of the anti-establishment, egalitarian, radical, empowering

edge of Marxist discourse, is the primary common ground that most social movements, research and analysis share (in common with cosmopolitan, radical, deliberative democrats). (Gupta 2006, p. 108)

The university and structures of power

The inability of the university as an institution and of academics to speak 'truth to power' is not merely a result of academic administrators being implicated in networks of power and privilege (although this co-option plays a definite role). The co-option is one of personnel as well as of language in the ways in which terms such as 'choice', 'flexibility', 'elitism', 'exit points', 'efficiency' and 'empowerment' are deliberately mobilized to attain precisely their meaningful opposites to secure certain institutional ends.[2] In opposition, a turn towards discursive radicalism, which does not substantively alter debates or structures of academic governance, falls short of creating alternative public spheres. Rather such dissent seems to ossify into varying types of absolutist stances and desires located often in moral (and moralistic) grandstanding. Perhaps, the dual drive – to belong, to exercise power on the one hand and to refuse participation as a mode of protest on the other – is indicative of the kind of intellectual angst Ariel Dorfman writes of when confronted by interrogators at a US airport post-9/11: 'Do we want to be dangerous and persecuted, or do we want to be aloof and left alone? Are we members of a community, or do we thrive on independence of opinion?' (Dorfman 2006, p. 43). Dorfman goes on to argue for the need to be 'relentlessly complex', to 'think oneself, ourselves, out of a catastrophe' (p. 47), but it is this relentless complexity which seems to be absent from much of the mediatized (and non-mediatized) public space occupied and created by intellectuals in India, particularly within the university. The occupation of moral islands splinters rather than consolidates solidarities, allowing for occasions of fertile debate but more often than not silencing those very contraries that would allow for complex interventions within circuits of power. Rather than debate there exists within varied oppositional groups and stances a kind of 'fraternity terror', constitutive of intellectual failure (a point I return to anon).

Having seemingly placed responsibility for the transformation of the university into an unseemly battleground squarely on the academic, it is necessary to highlight institutional shortcomings. There is a lack of democratic, transparent structures and mechanisms of dispute resolution and union–administration interface, primarily because the university is structured to replicate the bureaucratic power frames beloved of our political class.[3] Within these attitudinal norms negotiation, debate, discussion and deliberative reasoning are impediments to the achievement of managerial ends, which are by definition for the 'greater good' of the institution, the students and the society at large. Arguably, administrative fiats to curb dissent are long-established practices. What is relatively new to the university are juridical modes of making criticism and protest impossible and legally illegitimate and this trend fits in with larger patterns of surveillance and securitization post-9/11. The surveilling of university employees takes formal and informal forms including old-fashioned gossip culled from colleagues and students, Facebook updates, biometric attendance and the rewards for 'loyalty'. The institutional gaze perceives all critical voices as violating democratic functioning or 'fringe elements' motivated by 'unacceptable' ideological agendas. The latter is important because, while protest is ideological (usually characterized as 'leftist' and therefore intrinsically tainted), the strategies of the university ostensibly exist in non-ideological spaces of pure motivation and action.[4] The intolerance of dissent is reflective of wider societal norms and fears where, for instance, to 'like' a post critical of the arrangements for Bal Thackeray's funeral leads to the arrest of the originator as well as her friend. A climate of consensus created by coercive means as well as through incorporating and rewarding those who offer no critical insights is especially inimical to the university. A type of authoritarianism is put in place – the paradoxical trumpeting of democratic 'free speech' in domains that are policed fairly substantially – and this is a fundamental violation of the role of the university where loyal subservience is preferred over critical engagement, replicating a system of patronage available in wider public domains. As Arvind Rajagopal argues in a different context, key elements of the colonial administrative frame and attitude continued to exist in India post-1947:

> Crucially, the legal and political structure of the colonial state was largely retained, while English language dominance actually expanded in importance. As a result, the public continued to be positioned as a deficient entity to be contained, improved, or transcended, rather than one to be meaningfully engaged with by the state. (Rajagopal 2009, p. 8)

The university increasingly perceives its own publics as entities that must be 'contained, improved, or transcended' and it is interesting that judicial interventions (in matters that are exclusively the domain of the university) use the language of improvement, indeed moral chastisement. For instance, in

'Nandini Dutta & Ors. Versus University of Delhi And Anr.' the Hon'ble Judges of the High Court of Delhi noted:

> We are at a loss to understand when the matter is sub-judice and we are addressing the lis, why should there be any need and cause for 'peaceful protest'. There can be difference of opinion, but that has to be expressed with dignity and virtuosity, which is expected from a teacher. In view of the aforesaid, we hope and trust that the teachers of the university do not disrupt teaching schedules or harbour the notion of 'peaceful protest' by teaching outside the classroom or in tents, but follow the semester system as per our previous directions. Interest of the students and the institution is paramount. ... As advised, at present, we are not inclined to proceed for contempt, but we command that all teachers of the University of Delhi and all colleges affiliated to the said University shall cooperate in all aspects and teach in the semester mode and not proceed on the path of deviation which would, in the slightest manner, bring them in the net of the violators of the orders of the Court, for the order of Court has to be treated with respect regard being had to its sanctity in a country governed by Rule of Law.[5]

Apart from the obvious lexical registers, what is valuable in the legalese are the ways in which 'peaceful protest' is delegitimized not merely as deviant or immoral but as inimical to the best interests of the students and the university, thereby placing the protesting teaching self outside the bounds of the institution in which s/he is invested and out of which investment the best possibilities of protest and debate may arise. That the university increasingly depends on the law to contain and threaten its constituents is indicative of the symbiotic relationship between the university and the judiciary, which further diminishes public spaces for intellectual and reasoned disagreement.

English Studies and the public sphere

Where, to return to the ostensible focus of this chapter, within this moral-legal-surveillance matrix does English Studies (ES) figure? There seems to be a dual and contradictory attitude towards ES and its placing: it is perceived as valuable in its ability to train and equip citizens for particular kinds of labour but 'irrelevant' as critical capital, except when that capital is tied to or enhances labour. Ien Ang, in a discussion on cultural complexity and the ways in which managerial worlds manage complex knowledge, makes the distinction between 'deterministic knowledge' and 'creativity' (Ang 2011, p. 789). Ang cites IBM's

2010 *Capitalizing on Complexity* report and quotes IBM President Samuel Palmisano:

> What we heard through the course of these in-depth discussions ... is that events, threats and opportunities aren't just coming at us faster or with less predictability; they are converging and influencing each other to create entirely unique situations. These firsts-of their-kind developments require unprecedented degrees of creativity – which has become a more important leadership quality than attributes like management discipline, rigor or operational acumen. (IBM Corporation 2010, p. 4)

What is fundamental to Palmisano's embrace of 'creativity' is that it is deterministic and serves larger corporate goals in a global world where one must be aware of 'threats and opportunities', indeed transform threats into opportunities through a particular definition of 'creativity'. To translate the IBM model to the university, excess capital insofar as it is invested in the humanities is not to foster critical or creative arenas of thought and knowledge, but a deterministic means-ends paradigm where 'use value' is paramount, although the networks that create and constitute 'value' are not analysed or conceptualized with any clarity. Thus, for instance, the call centre is represented as a locus of technological and economic prowess, a part of a knowledge economy, a sign of global modernity: all this without considering everyday practices of labour, disjunctions in economic relationality that sustain these centres, the problems of women in the workforce and in city spaces that are distinctly unfriendly if not dangerous to women, and so on. The university is an active partner in a field of knowledge exchange wherein ES is a marker of class and capital, belonging and desire. When ES 'strays' from its remit and offers critical and/or oppositional insights it is contained through some of the structures and means I outlined earlier.

The university and the public sphere

The close relationship between the university and market mechanisms is one that was envisioned by John Sperling, founder and CEO of Apollo Group, parent company of the for-profit University of Phoenix, who defined his chain in the following words: 'This is a corporation. ... We are not trying to develop [students'] value systems or go in for that "expand their minds" bullshit' (cited in Donoghue 2006, p. 156). Sperling did not care to hide behind platitudes and saw his endeavour purely in commercial terms. The intersection of the university and capital is problematic in Sperling's formulation but it becomes even more so when public universities manage their domains as if they were private enterprises. While private universities have existed in India for a while, and there is a recent surge of such institutions, major Indian universities are funded by public money and those monies are now being bent towards private ends insofar as educational models suit the needs and visions of particular knowledge economies. Arguably, all universities navigate these circuits of knowledge, capital, labour and productivity, as graduates wish in the final analysis to be employed. The relationship between the university and the state in the United States, for example, has always been a troubled one whether it was Michigan State University's training programme for South Vietnamese personnel during the Vietnam War or the College of the Americas which provided counter-insurgency know-how deployed in the guerrilla wars and subsequent human rights violations in Central America. What seems unique about the moment in India are the ways in which the university is being transformed into what Robert Maynard Hutchins, then president of the University of Chicago, called 'the strangest of modern phenomenon, an anti-intellectual university' (cited in Donoghue 2006, p. 156). Or, perhaps not entirely unique, as Hutchins made the observation in 1936 and his fears are being fulfilled today.

The valorization of the for-profit university model in a rapidly globalizing and urbanizing India is perhaps unsurprising given that it posits a direct (and simplistic) relationship between college degrees and social mobility, that is, the means of entry into the knowledge economy validated by policy makers inside and outside academia.[6] At the same time questions of access and equity ought to occupy primary positions, especially in universities funded by public money, highlighting issues such as: in what manner is the university a public good? How is this good to be sustained and strengthened? How will the university enable access to historically disenfranchised constituencies? In what ways does the drive to a knowledge–market relation disempower the very groups most in need of the social and cultural capital invested in a university degree? In the intersection of the drive to 'reform' university curricula and structures and the needs of the market, such questions are ignored and 'reform' furthers elite assumptions (a point made eloquently by Babu and Rowena).

The implications of corporatization are, as Linda Hutcheon argues, not merely those 'external' to the university but inherent to the functioning of colleagues and faculties. While writing of 'saving collegiality' Hutcheon shows how the internalizing of market models creates a looking-out-for-oneself ethos that is fundamentally detrimental to collegiality and the pursuit of ideas:

> comparatists, of all people, should be the first to see the intellectual and professional benefits of the congenial and the collaborative. Our failure to do so may mean that, despite our ideological protests against the commercialization and corporatization of the academy (and the attendant rhetoric), we have somehow absorbed the business model of competition along with the individualist model of looking out only for ourselves. What this development in turn suggests is that we are unknowingly perpetuating that model by passing it on to our students as part of their professionalizing process: the opposition must be removed or destroyed; our intellectual profits must be maximized by minimizing the intellectual profits of others. (Hutcheon 2006, pp. 62–3)

Collegiality is not just a matter of 'professional intelligence' or a sentimental community of scholars, but a mode of resisting the binary oppositions that permit university administrations to discipline and punish and reward to suit particular ideological ends. Arguably Hutcheon's position is mediated by a desire to be 'outside' the corporate or the market but she nevertheless highlights the manner in which academics play to the us-versus-them model at the same time that they protest against it. The moral (moralistic) grandstanding I mentioned earlier is located within this competitive matrix and replicates the oppositional stances created and mediated by the university and its juridical allies, so that 'deviance' is as much a crime among the academic fraternity as it is in the opinions of learned judges.

Anti-intellectualism

One of the consequences of this unenviable mirroring is the rise of anti-intellectualism and/or the banishing of analytical thought to exclusive enclaves (which enclaves are often desired by their progenitors so as to remain 'untainted' by the world) or the reduction to sound bites on television programmes. Ratna Kapur articulates these consequences in stark terms:

> The narrow foundational binaries on which the liberal intellectual project is based have led to three inevitable consequences: the rise of a right-wing intellectual ideology, a fading of progressive intellectualism, and a resort to action in the trenches without political intellectual thought or vision. (Kapur 2006, p. 26)

Kapur's prognosis overstates and homogenizes the shortcomings of 'the liberal intellectual project', and yet she gestures towards the increasing disengagement of humanistic academic knowledge from the public sphere which diminishes both. Ien Ang citing the historian Russell Jacoby points to the endless urge to 'complexify' within 'a hermeneutics of suspicion' that serves to destabilize 'facts', for instance (Ang 2011, p. 785). Ang goes on, *pace* Bruno Latour, to show how climate-change sceptics use precisely the same academic tools to eviscerate scientific facts and writes:

> The argument here is not that we should return to the linear reductionism of positivism, but that it is not enough for scholars to revel in the complexity of things. There's no denying that the world is complex, and arguably increasingly so, but the recognition of this complexity – in both the political and the academic realms – cannot be left hanging. (Ang 2011, p. 785)

Climate change is one example of the problematic relationship between academia and the world and while the former is visible in that debate there are other realms where academic presence is absent or minimal. The imagining and critique of power – what Gorton Ash calls 'the incestuous relationship between private and public power' – is necessary yet absent in influential public spheres such as the mainstream media. The Radia tapes scandal wherein close ties between prominent media persons and corporate houses as well as the government were revealed was a non-event not merely because of media silence and complicity but also because of the lack of public intellectual interventions arguing for structural changes in the ways in which media and power are negotiated in India.[7] Ang's caution regarding complexity for the sake of complicating rather than explicating might seem, as he is aware, a return to positivistic thinking, but it could equally be seen as an urging towards explication and interruptions within circuits of power and knowledge that are seemingly impervious to or deliberately invisibilize academic insights, reasoning and critiques. Such interruptions do occur (as in the robust debate played out in the print media vis-à-vis the University of Delhi's FYUP) but they seem to me to be driven by crises and are reflexive in the immediacy of the responses. Such immediate fire-fighting is arguably necessary in the face of institutional intransigence and refusal to enter into administratively discomfiting but necessary debates and negotiations. However, in entering the public sphere almost solely in contexts of crises the interventions often fail to stake out an agenda, a set of arguments or publics that are not driven solely by opposition. If this is true – and it seems to be to some extent, at least – such oppositional frameworks suit the media landscape perfectly as nothing is more newsworthy than conflict and the us-versus-them narrative set by the media often obscures more complex issues such as the role of the university in twenty-first century India, the position of teachers therein, the modes of disseminating knowledge and the place and value of the humanities within that structure.

'The aesthetic public sphere'

Jonathan Roberge in his essay 'The Aesthetic Public Sphere and the Transformation of Criticism' considers the place of the activity defined as 'criticism' within a political–cultural dimension. 'Criticism,' Roberge writes, 'is not just one activity among many; it is rather a complete mediation whose role and influence are central or pivotal to the reproduction of the social whole' (Roberge 2011, p. 436). This apposite and obvious observation underpins the circulation of ideas, power and the spaces created by and within the university that I have outlined earlier. The non-deliberative and often authoritarian enactments of the futures of the university in India are enmeshed in this constantly shifting realm of criticism and culture. Although, Roberge's concern is neither the university nor India his argument that 'the distinctive way that politics and culture interact is deeply affected by the current forms of criticism as these forms make sense of the eternal ambiguity of society's self-interpretation' is relevant to my sense of the university as a space at the edges of and simultaneously central to the 'ambiguity' of India's 'self-interpretation'. (Roberge 2011, p. 436)

While disempowering its own publics and the function of criticism within, the university seeks to reinvent itself as 'relevant' to certain streams of the national conversation. The problem, however, is not merely the university and its self-representations but also, as Roberge argues, with the role of critics within the dynamics of the marginal–central interplay between the critic and the world. 'In all circumstances, critics are necessarily engaged in a series of justifications about their legitimacy to discuss the justifications of others. ... Its [criticisms'] autonomy is never assured, and its role never quite guarantees as to whether it is necessary' (Roberge 2011, p. 440). This might help us understand the attempts by power to delegitimize or disinter the voices of critics at the same time as those attempts attest to the power of critical interventions in public debate. These interventions are possibly constitutive of what Fraser in his critique of Habermas terms 'subaltern counterpublics', the manner in which political exclusion fashions alternate modes of critical engagement and thereby expand domains of publics, for in a fundamental sense the drive of the 'anti-intellectual university' is to shrink such deliberative spaces. That the humanities to a greater and social sciences to a somewhat lesser extent are perceived as 'disruptive' or 'deviant' is both a back-handed compliment and an index of their interstitial position and relation with power and reason, authority and justice.

Implications of the production of dissent in mediatized worlds

Two brief observations on mediatization and its concomitant production of 'chatterers'. One is the construction of a 'conflict' between a reasonable/visionary/authoritarian university and a reasonable/deviant/obstructive 'minority' (depending on where one stands in the ideological spectrum). Both sides claim 'eminence' and academic credibility, both claim the best interests of the university as drivers of their position, yet within media and juridical domains there is a not-so-subtle destitution of the teacher, the academic and her realm of ideas. The narrative is bipolar: teachers are respected in Indian culture, they are repositories of learning and knowledge on the one hand, and teachers are overpaid and underworked, they are fundamentally lazy and obstructive and so on, on the other. It is a classic manoeuvre of idolizing and demonizing from which arises the need to discipline and to legislate the demonic, the unruly and the deviant.

My second observation relates to the silence and passivity by-and-large of the largest constituency within the university: students. Ideologically driven campuses such as Jawaharlal Nehru University seem to be the exception and within dominant media narrative constitute the demonic 'left'. It is interesting that in the FYUP debate at the University of Delhi the only student group publicly mobilized was from the North Eastern states who posited the imposition of Hindi in human rights discourse. Student bodies within the university seem rather quiescent or indifferent although they are valuable 'stakeholders' and the seeming reason for the visionary changes.[8] The media has, particularly since the Anna phenomenon, projected an idea of 'youth' in India as drivers of change, hope and the future. This narrative was repeated with the irruption of protest and the seeming creation of public spaces of protest in the reactions to the Delhi gang rape in late 2012–early 2013. The protests were necessary expressions of rage, frustration, impotence and possibility. In mainstream media discourse, however, some questions remained unanswered or were never raised, questions such as, to what extent were the protests political in their commitment to the endowment of gender equality, of private and public safety for women and of gender sensitization? How were the protests constituted as an event and how are the debates arising thereof to be conceptualized in terms of 'subaltern counterpublics'? How do we understand the excess – of emotion, anger, outrage – generated and articulated by the media (the demand for capital punishment, for instance, as opposed to more nuanced insights into the ways in which networks of family, law, caste, economics, public and private corruption contribute to the oppression of girls and women)? The point is not that 'youth' protests were media-driven but that once mainstream media – television in particular – lost interest, the interruptions at India Gate and Jantar Mantar were as if they had never been. A larger point seems to me to be the discontinuity between the anti-corruption and anti-rape protests and the relative silences within the university which, if true, further the gap between the everyday and the world of 'learning', that which is idealized and must be left within a domain called the university, just as it is the duty of teachers to be virtuous and not indulge in 'peaceful protest' lest the sanctity of the university be defiled.

In a sensitive article on the Delhi rape Jason Burke characterized the '"inbetween" world' of the rapists:

> By then [2030 as per a McKinsey report] the dominant feature of modern India may well not be the rural village or the picturesque forts and saris of the tourist brochures but the nondescript, semi-finished, ragged-edged, semi-urban, semi-rural world that is simultaneously neither and both of them. (Burke 2013)

The six suspected rapists certainly inhabited this 'inbetween' world.

Burke draws out connections and continuities that the aftermath of the protests seems not to take into account (or which they do, but the media is not as focused as it was post 16 December). This is not to imply that media blindness disempowers or diminishes protest movements, but mediatization plays a definitive role in creating discursive domains for the protests and their afterlife. Michel de Certeau's distinction between 'strategy' and 'tactics' is perhaps useful in my attempt to perceive the in-between and betwixt not as disenfranchising (as Burke does) but as empowering, whereby tactics as Certeau puts it are not so much acts of resistance as modes of accommodating oneself, of creating space for oneself within larger structures (Certeau 1984, p. 27).[9] Within the university tactical distanciation, the need to be 'relentlessly complex' while being conscious of the pitfalls of complexifying and the concomitant drive towards reason and justice might enable less confrontational, more thoughtful public spaces. Or it may not, as tactical spaces and options shrink and the university defines itself increasingly within authoritarian discursive lexicons.

Notes

1   For an analysis of cities as sites of hyper-security and militarization see Stephen Graham, *Cities under Siege*. The April 2013 lockdown of Boston was another instance of heavy-duty policing which blurs lines between police and army–war functions.

2   The Four-Year Undergraduate Programme (FYUP) at Delhi University is a contemporary instance of such co-option. See Chandrachur Singh, 'Why Delhi University's four-year degree is a good idea', *The Hindu*, 4 May 2013, http:// www.thehindu.com/opinion/op-ed/why-delhi-universitys-fouryear-degree-is-a-good-idea/article4681046.ece# (Accessed 5 May 2012). For an analysis of the dismemberment of affirmative action in the FYUP see Hany Babu and Jenny Rowena, 'FYUP: A Critique from a Social Justice Perspective', Roundtable India, 2 May 2013, http://roundtableindia.co.in/index.php?option=com_content&view=article&id=6514%3Afyup-a-critique-from-a-social-justice-perspective&catid=119&Itemid=132 (Accessed 3 May 2013).

3   For a critique of managerial interventions in the University see Apoorvanand and Satish Deshpande, 'Wanted: Intellectual leaders, not CEOs', *The Hindu*, 1 December 2012, http://www.thehindu.com/opinion/lead/wanted-intellectual-leaders-not-ceos/article4151232.ece (Accessed 20 April 2013). Apoorvanand and Deshpande write of the necessity of the 'fortitude and humility' of 'intellectual leadership', qualities often absent in the new university.

4   Dissent(ers) is/are placed within a realm of unreason or irrationality, motivated (when such irrational motivations can be divined) purely by ideology, automatic resistance to change, obstructiveness combined with dilatory tactics and a herd mentality. For an argument along these lines, albeit implicitly, see Harish Trivedi, 'Is Delhi University Dying?' *Times of India*, 29 May 2013: 22. The only valid response to such unreason is administrative diktat and the valorization of managerial celerity wherein discussions which meandered for nine years can be telescoped to non-discussions over months or weeks. The messiness of deliberative, rational discursive democracy is cleansed and new, non-obstructive public spheres are created. As Trivedi writes, 'There's hardly been a more exciting time to be a college teacher in DU – or a college student.'

5   'W.P. (C) No. 2764/2011 Nandini Dutta & Ors. Versus University of Delhi and Anr.' In the High Court of Delhi at New Delhi, 16 May 2011: 5, 8–9. I am grateful

to the then Registrar of the University of Delhi who circulated this judgement to all staff in the university and thereby brought it to my attention. Interestingly the legal use of 'virtuosity' seems to exclude possibilities of intelligence, skill and ability which may be deployed by teachers in and outside the class.

6 For an analysis of the policy and academic implications of shifts in conceptualizations of the knowledge economy see Chaudhuri, *Thesis Eleven*, ed. Rajan, pp. 7–22.

7 I have looked at aspects of the Radia tapes issue in ' "Culture(s) of corruption": Media representations and anxieties', in *Covering and Explaining Conflict in Civil Society*, pp. 91–103.

8 Exceptions to this quiescence include the 'referendum' on FYUP conducted by the All India Students' Association (AISA) on 22 August 2013 and a spurt of protests by the Akhil Bharatiya Vidyarthi Parishad (ABVP).

9 I am grateful to Aruni Mahapatra for pointing me towards Certeau albeit in another context. See his 'Piracy as Tactics: Reimagining Creativity as Forms of Access', in *The Virtual Transformation of the Public Sphere*, ed. Desai, pp. 108–20.

References

Ang, Ien (2011), 'Navigating complexity: From cultural critique to cultural intelligence', *Continuum: Journal of Media & Cultural Studies*, 25 (6): 779–94.

Apoorvanand and S. Deshpande (1 December 2012), 'Wanted: Intellectual leaders, not CEOs', *The Hindu*, http://www.thehindu.com/opinion/lead/wanted-intellectual-leaders-not-ceos/article4151232.ece (Accessed 20 April 2013).

Ash, T. G. (2 May 2012), 'From Chongqing to Chipping Norton, money and politics have got too cosy', *The Guardian*, http://www.guardian.co.uk/commentisfree/2012/may/02/chongqing-chipping-norton-money-politics?CMP=EMCNEWEML1355 (Accessed 3 May 2012).

Babu, H. and J. Rowena (2 May 2013), 'FYUP: A Critique from a Social Justice Perspective', Roundtable India, http://roundtableindia.co.in/index.php?option=com_content&view=article&id=6514%3Afyup-a-critique-from-a-social-justice-perspective&catid=119&Itemid=132 (Accessed 3 May 2013).

Burke, J. (3 January 2013), 'In the wake of the Delhi bus rape, what is the future for India?' *The Guardian*, http://www.guardian.co.uk/world/2013/jan/02/delhi-bus-rape-future-india?CMP=EMCNEWEML1355 (Accessed 10 May 2013).

Chaudhuri, S. (May 2011), 'What is to be done? Economies of Knowledge', *Thesis Eleven*, 105 (1): 7–22.

de Certeau, M. (1984), *The Practice of Everyday Life*, trans. Steven Rendall, Berkeley: University of California Press.

Donoghue, F. (2006), 'Prestige', *Profession 2006*, 155–62, New York: The Modern Language Association of America.

Dorfman, A. (2006), 'The Lost Speech', *Profession 2006*, 40–7, New York: The Modern Language Association of America.

Gupta, S. (2006), *The Theory and Reality of Democracy: A Case Study in Iraq*, London, New York: Continuum.

Hutcheon, L. (2006), 'Saving Collegiality', *Profession* 2006, 60–4, New York: The Modern Language Association of America.

Kapur, R. (2006), 'Dark Times for Liberal Intellectual Thought', *Profession 2006*, 22–32, New York: The Modern Language Association of America.

Mahapatra, A. (2013), 'Piracy as Tactics: Reimagining Creativity as Forms of Access', in Gaurav Desai (ed.), *The Virtual Transformation of the Public Sphere: Knowledge, Politics, Identity*, 108–20, New Delhi: Routledge India.

Morozov, E. (2011), *The Net Delusion: The Dark Side of Internet Freedom*, New York: Public Affairs.

Rajagopal, A., ed. (2009), *The Indian Public Sphere: Readings in Media History*, New Delhi: OUP.

Roberge, J. (2011), 'The aesthetic public sphere and the transformation of criticism', *Social Semiotics*, 21 (3): 435–53.

Singh, C. (4 May 2013), 'Why Delhi University's four-year degree is a good idea', *The Hindu*, http://www.thehindu.com/opinion/op-ed/why-delhi-universitys-fouryear-degree-is-a-good-idea/article4681046.ece# (Accessed 5 May 2012).

Stanton, Domna C. (2006), 'Introduction', *Profession* 2006, 7–12, New York: The Modern Language Association of America.

Trivedi, H. (2013), 'Is Delhi University Dying?' *Times of India*, 29 May: 22.

7

Indian Opinion and the Making of a Satyagrahi

Tridip Suhrud

I

The *Hind Swaraj* opens with a dialogue that characterizes the mode of argumentation in the book. A direct question is posed by the Reader and the response from the Editor seeks to allude to a ground much deeper than the question entailed. Reader asks: 'Just at present there is a Home Rule wave passing over India. All our countrymen appear to be pining for National Independence. A similar spirit pervades them even in South Africa. Indians seem to be eager after acquiring rights. Will you explain your views in this matter?' The Editor responds:

> You have well put the question, but the answer is not easy. One of the objects of a newspaper is to understand the popular feeling and to give expression to it; another is to arouse among the people certain desirable sentiments; and the third is fearlessly to expose popular defects. The exercise of all these functions is involved in answering your question. To a certain extent, the people's will has to be expressed; certain sentiments will need to be fostered, and defects will have to be brought to light. (2010)[1]

Why does Gandhi refer to the role of the newspaper in answer to the question related to pining for National Independence? The answer to this question requires an understanding of the role of *Indian Opinion* in making of the Satyagrahi consciousness in colonial South Africa.

II

In his unsigned editorial of the first issue of the *Indian Opinion* on 4 June 1903 Gandhi made the purpose of the multilingual (Gujarati, English, Hindi and Tamil) mouthpiece of the Indian community in South Africa clear.

> We need offer no apology for making an appearance. The Indian community in South Africa is a recognized factor in the body politic, and a newspaper, voicing its feelings, and specially devoted to its cause, would hardly be considered out of place; indeed, we think it would supply a long felt want.[2]

He emphasized that Indians resident in British South Africa were loyal subjects of king-emperor and laboured under legal disabilities which were the result of prejudiced minds of the colonists. He hoped that these 'misunderstandings' would be removed by placing facts in their true light. The *Indian Opinion*, Gandhi hoped, would also become a moral guiding force for the Indian community, bereft as it was of institutions that guide conduct. He wrote:

> We are far from assuming that the Indian here are free from all the faults that are ascribed to them. Whenever we find them to be at fault, we will unhesitatingly point it out and suggest means for its removal. Our countrymen in South Africa are without the guiding influence of the institutions that exist in India and that impart the necessary moral tone when it is wanting ... It will be our duty, so far as it may be in our power, to supply these wants by inviting contributions from competent writers in England, in India and this sub-continent. (Ibid., p. 377)

The *Indian Opinion* was published by International Printing Press, started by Madanjit Vyavaharik with encouragement, including financial, from Gandhi (Hofmeyer 2013).[3] The fact of an Indian-owned printing press was enough to arouse murderous passions among white South Africans. In 1897 Gandhi, returning from India to Durban, was received by a lynch mob that nearly killed him. Many of those who had gathered at the dockside were in fact printers. Their passions were aroused by Gandhi's 'Green Pamphlet' and rumours that he had brought along with him from India compositors and a printing press. By October 1904 Gandhi had taken over all responsibilities of the newspaper himself. Writing to Gopalkrishna Gokhale on 13 January 1905 Gandhi reported:

> When I saw that Mr Madanjit could not carry on the paper without pecuniary assistance and as I knew that he was guided by thoroughly patriotic motives,

I placed at his service the bulk of my savings. That, however was not enough, three months ago I took over the whole responsibility and management ... My own office is at present being worked in the interests of *Indian Opinion* and I have already become responsible to the extent of nearly £3,500. (*CWMG*, vol. 4, p. 332)

The paper had an impact far more fundamental than draining of pecuniary resources. It shaped Gandhi's language. In the very second week of its publication Gandhi is told by one of his compositors, a man named Virji, via Mansukhlal Nazar, for some time the editor and printer of *Indian Opinion*, to use fewer words that require the Gujarati letter 'a', as there were fewer of those in the letterpress (Bhana and Hunt, p. 112). Gandhi was later to remark that the term 'economy' assumed a new meaning for him. His sparse, unadorned, direct Gujarati prose had much to do with his early training in writing for the *Indian Opinion*, with its scant resources.

Ever a careful observer of his audiences Gandhi knew that *Indian Opinion* was both printed word and oral. It was read and read out to those who were unable to read. In his 'Foreword' to the *Hind Swaraj*, he foregrounded this fact. 'The Gujarati subscribers of *Indian Opinion* number about 800. I am aware that, for every subscriber, there are at least ten persons who read the paper with zest. Those who cannot read Gujarati have the paper read to them' (*Hind Swaraj*, p. 9). This necessitated different styles and forms in Gujarati and English. His Gujarati writings drew upon images and a lexicon which relied heavily on the oral and the folk, while he could employ the more formal, almost legal prose in English. This meant that Gandhi often wrote two different articles on the same issue and did not rely upon translation from English to Gujarati or vice-versa. In the second issue of the paper Gandhi explained the inherently unequal, devouring relationship between the white South Africans and Indians. He used the story from Aesop's *Fables* of the lion and the lamb to conclude that 'In our days the European lion wishes to repeat the feat on the Indian lamb' (*CWMG*, vol. 3, p. 403).

The year 1903 would also see a plague in parts of South Africa – much of the public debate around the causes of the plague were centred around the insanitary conditions prevalent in 'Collie Locations'. Gandhi played an important part in the relief effort and nursed patients at the risk of contracting the disease. He also was part of the efforts which set fire to some 'Collie Locations', where the disease had become uncontrollable. However, he vociferously challenged the public discourse of the 'dirty' Indian. While so doing, it was his responsibility to point out to Indians the fact of some locations being dirty. He carried on two different kinds of interventions through the *Indian Opinion*. In his English writings he challenged the exaggerated and imaginary reports of unsanitary conditions, while in his Gujarati writing he chided his compatriots and urged them to clean up their environs. In the English section he wrote under the title 'An Insanitary Report'. He contended:

> It is evident that the Sanitary Inspector, when he paid his night visit, had the saying in his mind, namely, that 'if you want to hang a dog, call it a bad name'. Really, it is monstrous how responsible officers can let their imagination cloud their reason entirely and allow themselves to make what are libellous statements. (Ibid., p. 423)

While in the Gujarati section he wrote using a metaphor from horse riding, 'Teji ne Takoro' (A signal to the alert), wherein he advised:

> It is apparent that the officer exaggerated in his report, but we cannot be satisfied with criticising him. We cannot even use the justification that the Sanitary Department does not care for Indian locations. Our duty is clear, and that is that we must live with all possible cleanliness. We must consider as to who we are, how for thousands of years our forefathers have lived in clean environs that we are proud of it even today in India; what are the injunctions of our religions etc., etc. We have come to this country to earn a livelihood, we earn some money through hard work, why then can we not maintain the cleanliness that we keep in our country here as well? Especially, because we are disliked here, does it not behove us to live such that no one can put a blemish on us? Just because we live here are we to forget our customs? There are poor in the villages of India, but are we to forget as to how carefully they keep their huts clean? Is it becoming of us to live in squalor? There are no elders to observe and check us here. Are we to give up our humanity? (*Gandhiji No Aksherdeha*, vol. 3, p. 394)

He often used coarse, crude language to further his argument, an observation that was made regarding the language of *Hind Swaraj* also.[4] But life and vigour dwelt in his language. He described India as 'a sister-in-law of the *Raj*' (*Gandhiji No Aksherdeha*, vol. 3, p. 427), alluding to the Gujarati saying 'a poor man's wife is everyone's sister-in-law'.

He often took issues which had immense symbolic and emotive significance for the Indian community. One such issue was regarding conduct in the courtroom. We know that during his very first week in South Africa during a visit to the court, Barrister Gandhi had steadfastly refused to remove his headgear, even under the instructions of the court. A little over a decade later he took up the issue of rules of conduct in the courtroom insofar as they pertained to witnesses of Indian origin. The issue arose from a query by Sir Henry Bale, the Chief Justice of Natal, who inquired as to why an Indian witness, Manorath by name, appeared before him without his head-dress. Sir Henry expressed his desire to have the issue settled by seeking the opinion of the Chief Justice of the Calcutta High Court regarding practice in India. Gandhi took up the matter and asked a pointed question in Gujarati: 'Are we to remove our headgear or footwear?' (Ibid., vol. 4, p. 340). He reminded the Indians that removal of footwear would be the proper form of respect in India but in South Africa the established convention was a *Salaam*, both while entering and exiting the witness box. He also reminded the community: 'Our condition here depends greatly on our conduct' (Ibid.). In his intervention in English he was forthright with the Chief Justice and stated that Sir Henry had made 'much ado about nothing'. He went on to remind the Chief Justice that the matter had been settled through a judicial pronouncement.

> We may remind His Lordship that, when he was in the practice and ornamented the Natal Bar, he was Senior Counsel in the case of Cassim Abdulla & Bennett, wherein Mr Cassim Abdulla sued Mr Bennett, the Magistrate, for damages on the account of the Magistrate having ordered forcible removal of the head-dress of a witness in a case before him. He was then able to secure a dictum from the judge that the British Indians were not to be forced either to remove their head-dress or their boots, but they were to *Salaam* on entering the court. This practice has been followed ever since, and it would be a pity to re-open the question. (*CWMG*, vol. 4, p. 26)

In 1904 Gandhi began a bold new experiment. The International Printing Press and the *Indian Opinion* moved to the Phoenix Settlement. It was an experimental space from its inception and the community was conceived around print culture. Gandhi explained the move to Phoenix to his readers. 'The situation could only be saved by heroic measures. Patchwork was useless. Palliatives were dangerous. There remained then an appeal to the devoted workers and friends in favour of adopting a novel and revolutionary project' (Ibid., pp. 319–20). He could see that the Phoenix experiment could become a forerunner of many such experiments, including his own. 'It is a bold experiment and fraught with momentous consequences. We know of no non-religious organisation that is or has been managed on principles above laid down. If it succeeds, we cannot but think that it would be worthy of imitation' (Ibid., p. 320).

III

Since the beginning of 1904, as if anticipating the move to Phoenix and the struggles of the Indian community that lay ahead, the *Indian Opinion* had begun to assume a moral tone. This was signalled by a shift of emphasis from rights to duty. For Gandhi, rights were not only incumbent on performance of duties but emanated from such observance. Gandhi wrote two essays on 'Sacrifice' (Ibid., pp. 115–17 and pp. 121–2) wherein he sought in the langue of the *Gita* to remind his readers that 'Life is sustained by sacrifice' (Ibid., p. 115).

With the move to Phoenix the *Indian Opinion* began to echo Gandhi's idea that a people become one nation when they become a moral community. This argument was to later become pivotal to the arguments of *Hind Swaraj*. A moral community needed exemplars. Gandhi began a series of biographical sketches with a clear view that the readers and listeners would not only read about these lives but also follow them in their own practice:

> we believe that we are bound to benefit from a knowledge and constant contemplation of the lives of such devout men and women, and we therefore propose to give the stories of their lives from time to time. We hope that the readers of this journal will read their lives and follow them in practice and encourage us. We have suggested earlier that each one of our subscribers should maintain a file of the *Indian Opinion*. We remind them of it on this occasion. (*CWMG*, vol. 5, p. 45)

He wrote biographical sketches of varying length on figures as diverse as Maxim Gorky, Joseph Mazzini, Elizabeth Fry, Abraham Lincoln, Florence Nightingale, Ishwar Chandra Vidyasagar, George Washington, Raja Sir T. Madhav Rao, Sir Thomas Munro, Badruddin Tyabji and Mount Stuart Elphinstone among others. The biographical note on Mazzini gives an indication as to the tone of the writing and the lessons that Gandhi wanted the Indian community to take from these exemplars.

> He was a pious and religious man, ever free from selfishness and pride. Poverty was for him an ornament. The sufferings of others he regarded as his own. There are very few instances in the world where a single man has brought about uplift of his country by the strength of his mind and extreme devotion during his own lifetime. Such was the unique Mazzini. (Ibid., p. 28)

Not all his readers were pleased with the moral tone or the choice of the subjects. Gandhi began to publish a biographical sketch of Prophet Mohammed called

'Prophet Mohomed and His Caliphs' based on the biography of the prophet by Washington Irwin. He could publish only six parts of it due to hurt sentiments and protests by the Muslim community. They appeared to be displeased with descriptions of pre-Islam pagan Arabia and the narrations concerning the prophet's marriage. Gandhi discontinued the series. The memory of this stayed with him. He recalled this experience in 1932 to Mahadev Desai.[5] Gandhi probably discontinued the series as he felt that he did not have sufficient *adhikar*, right and capability, to narrate the life of the prophet if it offended the sentiments of the faithful. But in other matters he remained steadfast to his convictions. Many members of the Indian community were offended by the sharp rebukes on the plague question that he repeatedly administered. Gandhi argued that he was doing his duty.

> It is, we believe, the supreme duty of this who are in position to offer guidance in such matters to enlighten people and lead them along the right path. We say this without the least fear; for whatever we have written so far will have been in vain if we try to flatter our readers out of fear. (*CWMG*, vol. 5, pp. 114–15)

IV

The day was 11 September 1906. The Jewish-owned Empire theatre in Johannesburg was packed from floor to ceiling with men of Asiatic origin. Men, because there was not a single woman in that audience. They had come together to declare their opposition to the Asiatic Registration Act or the Black Act, which required every man, woman and child of eight years or upwards of Asiatic origin to submit to registration by providing prints of all ten fingers; failure to register was an offence under the law and the defaulter could be punished with deportation. Always a keen observer of his audience Gandhi thought he read 'in every face the expectation of something strange to be done or to happen'.

Before we go on to the meeting itself, it is necessary to ponder the relationship between humiliation and language. Gandhi describes the mode through which he not just comprehended but also internalized the hatred and humiliation embodied in the Black Act. He describes the act of reading:

> I took the Transvaal Government Gazette extraordinary of August 22, 1906, in which the Ordinance was published, home from the office. I went up a hill near the house in the company of a friend and began to translate the … Ordinance

into Gujarati for Indian Opinion, as I read the sections of the Ordinance one after another, I saw in it nothing except hatred for Indians. (*Satyagraha in South Africa*, pp. 91–2)

Mark the two dislocations or relocations that happen. Between 'office' and 'home' and from 'English' into 'Gujarati'. The true meaning and the hatred that confirmed the ordinance comes home, as it were, to Gandhi in these spatial and semantic relocations. The meeting of 11 September had been called to frame the communities' possible response to the ordinance. Abdul Gani, Chairman of the Transvaal British Indian Association, presided.

The meeting was expected to pass several resolutions, the most significant of which was the Fourth Resolution by which 'The Indians solemnly determined not to submit to the Ordinance in the event of its becoming law in the teeth of their opposition and to further all the penalties to such non-submission' (Ibid., p. 95).

Gandhi was to confess later that he had not understood all the implications of the resolution he had helped to frame. The resolution was duly proposed, seconded and supported by various speakers. Among the speakers was Sheth Haji Habib, an old and experienced resident of South Africa. Deeply moved, he invoked Khuda. He used two terms, 'Khuda Kasam' (an oath taken in the name of God) and 'Khuda' as '*hazar nazar*' (within the presence of God and with God as witness.) When Sheth Haji Habib came to the solemn declaration, Gandhi was 'at once startled and put on my guard. Only then did I fully realize my responsibility and the responsibility of the community' (Ibid., p. 96).

Gandhi was aware that it was part of public life all over the world to pass resolutions which were either amended or were not observed by all concerned. Gandhi seized the moment, as he was to do time and again, intervened in the meeting and clarified the true nature of the proposed manner of passing the resolution. 'To pledge ourselves to take an oath in the name of that god with him as witness is not something to be trifled with. If having taken such an oath we violate our pledge we are guilty before God and man' (Ibid.). He ended the long intervention on a personal note. He spoke of his personal responsibility:

I am fully conscious of my responsibility in the matter. It is possible that a majority of those present here may take the pledge in a fit of enthusiasm or indignation but may weaken under the ordeal, and only a handful maybe left to force the final test. Even then there is only one course open to someone like me, to die but not to submit to the law. It is quite unlikely but even if everyone else flinched leaving me alone to face the music, I am confident that I would never violate my pledge. (Ibid.)

This long reminder of the defining moment is to remember that Satyagraha in its moment of conception is a covenant, a covenant of the self with God as Truth. This element of pledge would become a central feature of Gandhi's thought and practice of Satyagraha.

With the advent of Satyagraha the *Indian Opinion* had to assume the role of clarifying the philosophical principles of Satyagraha, or passive resistance as it was called then, and also to provide news of protests, arrests, trials, jail experiences and negotiations within the community and with the colonial government. It was the first real test of the strength of the community and its capacity for sacrifice. Gandhi did not fail to remind the people:

> Till now the strength of the Indian community has not been tested. It has remained a secret hidden in closed fist, as it were, and no one has taken its measure. The prevailing idea is that Indians are cowardly and lacking in spirit. But, by good fortune, the community's strength is now being tested in Transvaal ... In this trial of strength the community has proved its superiority, up to the time of writing this at any rate. (*CWMG*, vol. 7, p. 97)

Gandhi had to explain his conviction that Truth force or soul force was the real force in the world. The finest exemplar of this conviction was, for Gandhi, Socrates. He wrote a six-part series, 'Story of a Soldier of Truth', on the life and death of Socrates.[6] With the advent of Satyagraha Gandhi saw himself addressing the Indians not only in South Africa but also in India. In the preface to the 'Story of a Soldier of Truth' Gandhi wrote: 'We have much to struggle for, not only in South Africa but in India as well. Only when we succeed in these [tasks] can India be rid of its many afflictions. We must learn to live and die like Socrates. He was, moreover, a great Satyagrahi. He adopted Satyagraha against his own people' (Ibid., p. 173). Prefiguring what he was to say in *Hind Swaraj*, Gandhi asked Indians to diagnose the disease and remedy it.

> When the disease is diagnosed and its true nature revealed in public, and when, through suitable remedies, the body [politic] of India is cured and cleansed both within and without, it will become immune to the germ of disease, that is the oppression by the British and the others. (Ibid., pp. 173–4)

Gandhi sought to clarify the duty of civil disobedience by invoking Thoreau.

> Passive resistance is one of the most approved methods of securing redress in given circumstances, and that is the only course law-abiding and peaceful men can adopt without doing violence to their conscience. Indeed, it would appear that it is a method they must adopt if they have a conscience, and it revolts against particular legislation. (Ibid., p. 211)

He provided a nine-part paraphrase in Gujarati of Ruskin's *Unto This Last*. In one of the most creative acts of translation he chose to render *Unto This Last* not as *Antyodaya* (welfare of the last person) but as *Sarvodaya* (welfare of all). An act of translation, in its deep faithfulness and fidelity, is a creative act; it introduces transpositions in the semantic universe.

Gandhi was not content with providing the stories of exemplars. He desired that the Indian community in South Africa and their white sympathizers share the ideals of Satyagraha. He devised modes of participation by readers in this quest. One such mode was to announce competitions for readers' contribution. In June 1906 he announced a prize of £1 for a poem composed in Gujarati or Hindi/Urdu in support of the jail resolution adopted by the Indian community in its struggle. He laid down the conditions: 'The Poem should cite modern and ancient examples of bravery, Muslim as well As Hindu. Others too may be included. The poem should contain reasons that have been advanced from time to time for adhering to gaol resolution' (*CWMG*, vol. 7, p. 5). Twenty entries were received and a poem by Ambaram Maganji Thaker was awarded the first prize.[7] The other competition was far more fundamental. It sought Gujarati equivalents of four terms: passive resistance, passive resister, cartoon and civil disobedience. His nephew and one of his closest co-workers suggested the term *sadagraha* (insistence upon good) for passive resistance, which Gandhi changed to Satyagraha. The third competition was for an essay on Satyagraha and carried a prize money of £10, which was won by Mr Maurice, an Indian Christian.

The *Indian Opinion*, with the advent of Satyagraha, sought to become inclusive in other ways also. It had as a matter of policy hitherto avoided questions that did not directly concern Indians in that country.

> Ever since the birth of this journal, it has studiously restricted itself to the questions affecting Indians in South Africa ... we must recognise our own limitations and not enter into questions of high policy, or questions that do not directly affect Indians in this country. (*CWMG*, vol. 7, p. 1)

Mtonga, a black South African, was tried by an all-white jury and found guilty but, convinced of his innocence, the governor granted him reprieve. Gandhi challenged the very idea of a trial by jury in an unequal society. 'The inherent condition of success of trial by jury is that the accused is tried by his equals. It is an insult to man's intelligence to content that there is any such trial in South Africa, when the question is as between whites and blacks' (Ibid.). This was not merely the result of the exigencies of the Satyagraha; it alludes to a deeper process in Gandhi's own evolution. He had begun to be aware of the structures of oppression that affect the human condition and not just the injustice done unto Indians.

The *Indian Opinion* also grew with the struggle. In 1903 it started with a four-page Gujarati section, which later grew to eight, twelve and later sixteen pages, with 1,100 paid subscribers. With this, the responsibilities of the Phoenix community also grew; it could no longer remain content with service to others. 'But we can no longer be content with merely bringing out a paper. Those who have chosen to settle in Phoenix wish to educate themselves and to extend the benefits of that education to the entire Indian people' (Ibid., vol. 9, p. 85). One such fundamental principle was the idea of self-restraint of the Satyagrahi. As part of the Satyagraha campaign in Johannesburg volunteers were placed to picket the office of the Registrar of Asiatics to dissuade Indians from offering themselves for registration as mandated by law. What the pickets had to exert was moral force and not resort to other coercive means, which for Gandhi was the violation of the idea of Satyagraha.

> A watchman's duty is to watch, not to assault. We have not the slightest hesitation in saying that if anyone in Johannesburg seeking registration is assaulted, our success will turn into failure just at the last moment; like a ship sinking when about to reach the harbour. Our whole struggle is based on our submitting ourselves to hardships, not inflicting them on anyone else, be he an Indian or European. (Ibid., vol. 7, p. 258)

The struggle took a new form with Gandhi offering a compromise where the Indian community agreed to submit to voluntary registration as against the one mandated by law. So fine was the distinction between voluntary submission and one mandated by law that many Indians were dismayed. Gandhi was assaulted and he suffered grievous hurt. To explain the nature of this compromise and the principle of voluntary submission, Gandhi took recourse to the form of dialogue, a form that has come to be associated in modern times with his *Hind Swaraj*, which he was to write some twenty-one months later. This dialogue, 'A Dialogue on Compromise', is, like the *Hind Swaraj*, a dialogue between Reader and Editor (Ibid., vol. 8, pp. 76–86). Gandhi said that there are two kinds of readers: those who read not to be enlightened but to pick holes and those who fail to see the point and are truly asleep. This dialogue, he said, addressed itself to the second kind and not to those who feign sleep. The dialogue opens with the question of qualification, of the right to ask questions. He states:

> You should have the following qualifications for asking questions; you should ask them in the presence of god, with sincere and patriotic intention ... this condition applies to us no less. In fact, ours is a greater responsibility and we are obliged to observe those conditions the more scrupulously. (Ibid., p. 77)

V

Gandhi spoke of *Hind Swaraj* as his seed text. As the seed comes to life, it is extinguished. Life within the seed may lie still and silent for long. But its beginning marks the end of the form from which it began. *Hind Swaraj* was written between 13 and 22 November 1909 on way to South Africa from England, aboard the steamer *Kildonan Castle*. Ten days of almost continuous writing on the ship's stationery were marked by a restless intensity that Gandhi had never known before. He wrote when he could no longer 'restrain' himself. This text was printed with meticulous exactness in the *Indian Opinion* (in two instalments, on 11 and 18 December 1909). Gandhi's own sense of his relationship with the text is complex and elusive. Three days after drawing the final line on the text, Gandhi wrote to his spiritual companion Hermann Kallenbach about his experiences aboard the *Kildonan Castle*. Almost as an afterthought, in the postscript he wrote: 'I have written an original book in Gujarati' (*CWMG*, vol. 96, pp. 36–8). It is a strangely ironical claim, utterly unlike him. This is perhaps the only instance of Gandhi making a claim of that kind.

In the foreword to the text Gandhi wrote:

> These views are mine, and yet not mine. They are mine because I hope to act according to them. They are part of my being. But, yet, they are not mine, because I lay no claim to originality. They have been formed after reading several books. That which I dimly felt received support from these books. The views I venture to place before the readers are, needless to say, held by many Indians not touched by what is known as civilisation, but I ask the reader to believe me when I tell him that they are also held by thousands of Europeans. (*Hind Swaraj*, pp. 9–10)

What does this 'mine' and yet 'not mine' indicate? Gandhi suggests that the claim of the text being his rests not so much upon the authorship but on conduct.

He said that the views were his because 'I hope to act according to them'. He reiterated this claim in the last line of *Hind Swaraj*. 'I have endeavoured to explain it [Swaraj], and my conscience testifies that my life henceforth is dedicated to its attainment' (Ibid., p. 98). He once again made this claim in 1930 when he published a Gujarati translation of the *Bhagvad Gita* as *Anasakti Yoga*. He was by his own admission not a scholar of Sanskrit, he was a son of a Vanik and yet he claimed that his translation of the text was superior to any other translation in Gujarati. He made a unique claim: he and his associates at the Satyagraha Ashram had made an attempt to lead their lives in accordance with the teachings of the *Gita*, which he described as their 'spiritual guide book'. Gandhi invoked his *adhikar* in the following terms: 'But I am not aware of the claim made by the translators of enforcing the meaning of the *Gita* in their own lives. At the back of my reading there is the claim of an endeavour to enforce the meaning in my own conduct for an unbroken period of forty years. For this reason I do harbour the wish that all Gujarati men and women wishing to shape their conduct according to their own faith, should digest and derive strength from the translation here presented' (Desai, p. 127).

VI

In February and March of 1918 the textile-mill workers of Ahmedabad went on a strike, which was met with a lockout by the mill owners. Anasuya Sarabhai, Shankerlal Banker and Gandhi came to lead the mill workers' strike. Gandhi, like in South Africa, administered the pledge of Satyagraha to the workers of Ahmedabad. He was required to explain the principles of Satyagraha to them as also the nature of the means to be adopted and eschewed during the struggle. He wrote a series of leaflets which were read out during the meetings of the striking mill workers. The principles of Satyagraha required illustration. But unlike in South Africa Gandhi did not invoke Tolstoy, Ruskin, Thoreau, Socrates or even figures such as Pralhad. He chose to speak to them about his co-workers in South Africa. In leaflet number 8 issued on 5 March 1918 Gandhi invoked three of his colleagues:

> In this leaflet, we are not going to talk about satyagrahis who have won fame in the world. It would be more profitable for us and inspire us with strength to know what suffering common men like ourselves have found it possible to go through. (*CWMG*, vol. 14, p. 237)

Gandhi spoke of Hurbatsingh, a seventy-five-year-old indentured labourer who went to prison and died in jail. The other exemplar was Transvaal businessman Ahmed Mohomed Cachalia, who adopted voluntary poverty, courted imprisonment several times and later become a servant of the community. The third was Valliamah, a girl of seventeen who despite fever courted imprisonment and died soon after her release from prison. Gandhi told his audience: 'The Satyagraha of all the three was pure. All of them suffered hardships, went to jail but kept their pledge' (Ibid., p. 238).

For Gandhi and his co-workers in South Africa this would have been a moment of immense satisfaction. They had become the exemplars. The experiment in forging a people, a community aware of its rights, ready to perform duties those rights enjoined upon them and willing to undergo self-suffering to secure justice, had become the beacon for the people of India and the oppressed elsewhere. *Indian Opinion* was integral to this.

Notes

1 Henceforth, *Hind Swaraj.*
2 Henceforth *CWMG.*
3 See Hofmeyr (2013), the only history of the press and the *Indian Opinion.*
4 Vinoba Bhave, one of the closest associates of Gandhi and a man with an acute sense of language and the literary traditions of India, described the language of *Hind Swaraj* as 'crude'. See *Vinoba Sahitya* (Wardha: Paramdham Prakashan), vol. 20, p. 365.
5 See, *Mahadevbhai Ni Diary*, vol. 1, p. 259.
6 *CWMG*, vol. 8, pp. 172–4, 185–7, 196–9, 212–14, 217–21, 227–9. Almost simultaneously he wrote a four-part biographical sketch of Mustafa Kamal Pasha.
7 For the poems on Satyagraha published in the *Indian Opinion*, see, *A Fire That Blazed In the Ocean: Gandhi and the Poems of Satyagraha in South Africa, 1909-1911*, introduced and Translated by Surendra Bhana and Neelima Shukla-Bhatt (New Delhi: Promilla & Bibliophile South Asia, 2011).

References

Bhana, S. and Hunt, J. D. (1989), *Gandhi's Editor: Letters of M. H. Nazar 1902-1903.* New Delhi: Promilla & Co.

Desai, M. (1946), *The Gospel of Selfless Action or The Gita According to Gandhi.* Ahmedabad: Navajivan.

Desai, M. *Mahadevbhai Ni Diary*. Ahmedabad: Navajivan, 1948.

Gandhi, M. K. (2010), *M K Gandhi's Hind Swaraj: a Critical Edition*, ed. and trans. S. Sharma and T. Suhrud. New Delhi: Orient BlackSwan, pp. 11–12.

Gandhiji No Aksherdeha (Ahmedabad: Navajivan), vol. 3, translated from original Gujarati by Tridip Suhrud.

Govt. of India. *The Collected Works of Mahatma Gandhi*. New Delhi: Publications Division.

Hofmeyer, I. (2013), *Gandhi's Printing Press: Experiments in Slow Reading*. Cambridge, MA: Harvard University Press.

Vinoba Sahitya. Wardha: Paramdham Prakashan, 1993.

8

In Search of a Suburb: Exploring the Relation Between City and Village in India

A. Raghuramaraju

While equating *Advaita* with Indian philosophy is politically problematic, there are certain remnants of this sophisticated philosophical school that underlie Indian thinking. This school of Indian philosophy profoundly teaches us to see what is not there in front of us and not see what is there. Whether this trait from India is captured philosophically by this branch of philosophy, thus providing a clearly formulated principle to the already existing, albeit in a scattered manner, phenomena, or it provides an axiom from which this phenomena is created and derived, is an open question that will not be pursued here. What will however be pointed in this context is that at least on some intellectual levels there is a tendency to prefer extremities that do not either consequently or programmatically enable one to see what is in front of them but see or at least vaguely see what is not in front of them. Most of the discussion in social sciences and philosophy in India has embraced this path. Western theories and society have become a new *Brahman*, and Indian society remained a mere *maya* to them. Indian debates or mere discussion on secularism in India is a good example of this (see Raghuramaraju 2011, particularly the chapter on secularism). However, literature, films, mass media, consumers and a large part of civil society, though allowed the influence from the outside, did not however lose sight of what is in front of them. In contrast, social theory in India, with this preoccupation with the new absolute or *Brahman* called the West, surreptitiously fulfilled their primordial urge during colonial or even postcolonial times.

With this background, this chapter discusses three models of the public sphere as available in Descartes the philosopher, Rabindranath Tagore and A. M. Shah the social scientist. I will conclude how to view the public sphere in India that accounts for and has been accounted for in the interaction between the West and India. This chapter will explore elucidation of this instance. Let me begin with the question regarding the presence of the public sphere in the West as clearly elucidated by Descartes in his attempt to disinherit the pre-modern as a precondition to enter modernity. He says:

> There is not usually so much perfection in works composed of several parts and produced by various different craftsmen as in the works of one man. Thus we see that buildings undertaken and completed by a single architect are usually more attractive and better planned than those which several have tried to patch up by adapting old walls built for different purposes. Again, ancient cities which have gradually grown from mere villages into large towns are usually ill-proportioned, compared with those orderly towns which planners lay out as they fancy on level ground. Looking at the buildings of the former individually, you will often find as much art in them, if not more, than in those of the latter; but in view of their arrangement – a tall one here, a small one there – and the way they make the streets crooked and irregular, you would say it is chance, rather than the will of men using reason, that placed them so. And when you consider that there have always been certain officials whose job is to see that private buildings embellish public places, you will understand how difficult it is to make something perfect by working only on what others have produced. Again, I thought, peoples who have grown gradually from a half-savage to a civilised state, and have made their laws only in so far as they were forced to by the inconvenience of crimes and quarrels, could not be so well governed as those who from the beginning of their society have observed the basic laws laid down by some wise law-giver. (Descartes 1985, pp. 116–17)

This account by Descartes, the father of modernity, is a wonderful and fascinating description of not only what the public sphere should consist of but also what a public sphere in the modern West is, and what it is and is not in modern Indian society. The reason I do this is because it very aptly describes modern Indian society as following what Descartes warned against by listing the problems associated with the gradual growth of society as opposed to a clearly planned one.

To begin with, Descartes is against gradual growth of cities or societies and prefers planned ones, that too by a single individual; the former does not enable perfection and the latter kind of societies have come up at most with ad hoc and post-facto rules to take care of inconveniences. Underlying this account is the need to disinherit the past, dismantle it and start absolutely afresh: this is clearly laid down in Lockean *tabula rasa* and man-in-the-state-of-nature – other philosophical synonyms of this term. That is, the exit of the pre-modern is the precondition to the entry of the modern. So, the beginning of the modern is the disinfected and sharply demarcated public space with clearly laid down rational rules. This public space does allow the private its interests and preferences but only those that strictly conform to the instrumental rationality and nothing outside it. So, there is a homogeneous relation between public and private within modernity. Anything that is private is not allowed, particularly those that belong to the pre-modern.

This arrangement is brilliantly choreographed within the liberalisms of both Benthamite and J. S. Mill traditions. Mill comes up with the distinction between the public and the private or other-regarding and self-regarding. What is important to remember is that the allowing of the private precedes their reducing actions to utilities, utilities to generation of pleasures that are to invariably meet the requirement of measuring through felicific calculus. So it is not that the liberal utilitarians are interested in the private sphere and then offer utilitarian doctrine: it is exactly the other way around. The reduction of actions as either private or public into utilities ensures both types of actions, particularly the former, into meeting the requirement of modern reason. While Mill, contra Bentham, is willing to allow quality to utility, he, however, would not at all concede any from the pre-modern. This strict adherence to keeping the pre-modern outside the boundaries of the modern qualifies them to be the champions of modernity. They made sure that the pre-modern remains outside. This is what made someone like David Hume a different type of utilitarian, who had to remain outside mainstream utilitarianism as he made a case for customary morality.

While modernity demands these draconian decisions to be implemented within the boundaries of modernity and has largely succeeded within the West, this package with this success in its roundtrip carried by colonialist advances towards the non-West seeks to accomplish the same task. It has succeeded, though partly, in this venture. There are many in societies like India who exaggerated this with generalizations and concluded the grading, while the examining process is still going on. Interestingly, the dissenters to modernity too joined with modernists in this procedural lapse. However, unlike in the West, in societies like India large social and political spaces remained outside the purview of modernity. Similar to that of equating the answer sheet with the question paper, or even worse the syllabus or even the subject, the success of modernity is equated with Indian society. The latter is larger than what is covered by modernity. The physical space of the pre-modern that eluded the attention of modernity is not only larger, but also deceptively eluded the attention of modernity. Seen under the floodlights of modernity, the academic activity in India did not account for those that remained outside these bright lights.

I shall come to the philosophical aspect of it later in the chapter. Let me elaborate the reasons why I began with Descartes. In contrast to this clear description by Descartes, which pictures the predicament of modern Indian society, let us look at how Indian society has responded to the canon set by modernity. Let me discuss two versions, one by Tagore and the other by sociologist A. M. Shah, to get an idea of the Indian scene. Tagore in his short essay, way back in 1924, titled, 'City and Village', while presenting a critique of city right in the beginning, says:

> The standard of living in modern civilization has been raised far higher than the average level of our necessity. The strain, which such rise of standard makes us exert, increases in the beginning our physical and mental alertness. The claim upon our energy, again accelerates its growth; and this, in its turn, produces activity that expresses itself by the rising of life's standard still higher.
>
> When this standard attains a degree of great deal above the normal, it encourages the passion of greed. The temptation of inordinately high living, normally confined to a negligibly small section of the community, becomes widespread. This ever growing burden is sure to prove fatal to any civilization that puts no restraint on the emulation of the self-indulgent. (Tagore 1924, p. 215)

In contrast to this modern civilization made available in the cities, villages, says Tagore, are closer to nature. Comparing them to women, he argues:

> Villages are like women. In their keeping is the cradle of the race. They are nearer to nature than towns; and are therefore in closer touch with the fountain of life. They have the atmosphere which possess a natural power of healing. It is the function of the village, like that of women, to provide people with their elemental needs, with food and joy, with the simple poetry of life, and with those ceremonies of beauty which the village spontaneously produces and in which she finds delight. But when constant strain is put upon her through the extortionate claim of ambition; when her resources are exploited through the excessive stimulus of temptation, then she becomes poor in life, her mind becomes dull and uncreative; and from her time-honoured position of the wedded partners of the city, she is degraded to that of maidservant. While, in its turn, the city, in its intense egoism and pride, remains unconscious of the devastation it constantly works upon the very source of its life and health and joy. (Tagore 1924, pp. 219–20)

It must however be noted that village is also a public space, but it does not meet the standards of the modern definition of the public space. Here let us remember that vill*age* has a long age in the pre-modern societies and modernity seeks to relegate it to the past, thus terminating its existence so that it can now make its entry. This sequential relation between age-old village and city prevents their coexistence and almost makes them mutually exclusive, both spatially and temporally. Going against this canon, in Tagore we have an account of moralizing the virtues of the village in the context of highlighting the vices of the city. Keeping aside this moral dimension, what is interesting to me is the assumed underlying relation between the village and city. The preoccupation with the moral might make us not recognize the social dimensions, which are significant. To begin with, in his account, unlike the mutual exclusion between the village and city, the former is envisaged as coexisting with the latter. This repudiates the canon set by modernity. Further, there is his moral dimension, which can be problematic for the kind of identification he makes and comparisons he offers. I want to focus on the social dimension. Having pointed out this contesting variation in Tagore, now let me bring into discussion his account where he goes one step further and recommends an interesting relation between the village and the city. He says:

> People, as a whole, do and must live in the village, for it is their natural habitation. But the professions depend upon their special appliances and environment, and therefore barricade themselves with particular purposes, shutting out the greater part of universal nature, which is the cradle of life. The city, in all civilizations, represents this professionalism, – some concentrated purpose of the people. That is to say, people have their home in the villages and their offices in the city.
>
> We all know that the office is for serving and enriching the home, and not for banishing it into insignificance. (Tagore 1924, p. 222)

Thus, this makes a case for the coexistence of two public spaces simultaneously. Even going against the grain of the moral intentions of the author that consist in criticizing the city and eulogizing the virtues of the village, the use of patriarchal comparisons notwithstanding, this account gives us a different combination. Here let us note two things. One, Tagore recognizes the massive entry of the modern consumerist culture that threatens to wipe out the village culture. This is evident when he says that 'Kuvera ... represents the multiplication of many whose motive force is greed. ... But the goddess, Lakshmi, who is the Deity of prosperity, is beautiful. ... By some ill-luck, Lakshmi has been deprived of her lotus throne in the present age, and Kuvera is worshiped in her place'

(Tagore 1924, p. 220). Two, he is making a moral case in favour of the village or a compromise between both. As already indicated, it is these moral aspects that drew the attention of some. Going against the grain, I want to focus on the structural aspect of this combination, namely, the envisaged coexistence of both village and city, possibly returning to the moral aspects subsequently.

While Tagore seems to be worried about the threat to the village by the city, an eminent sociologist A. M. Shah, while delivering a special address at IDRC-TTI workshop on Rural-Urban Linkage, at Institute of Rural Management, Anand, 21 August 2012, a revised version later published under the title 'The Village in the City, the City in the Village' (2012), too reports the coexistence of village and city in India when he says that an 'important commitment of urbanisation in India is that villages located outside the boundaries of a city get included in it over time' (Shah 2012, p. 17). He then goes on to claim that 'contrary to the general view that urbanisation involves migration of people from the village to the city, it also involves migration of people from city to the village' (Shah 2012, p. 19). Shah concludes by saying, 'There are false images of the relation between the rural and the urban society and, in turn, of Indian society and culture in general. This needs to be corrected' (Shah 2012, p. 19).[1] This simultaneous coexistence of village and city or town is distinctly different, even opposed, to what Descartes desired. While Shah, the social scientist, takes nearly more than a quarter of a century to realize this aspect of Indian society, Tagore, the artist, articulated it much before. Further, while Shah seems to concur with Tagore about the coexistence of two incompatible social spaces, there is a subtle but significant difference between them. Shah in this lecture reveals some interesting facets where the village seems to threaten the city. This is not there in Tagore, who is preoccupied with the reverse threat. Let us look at these. In the context of making a plea for the need to study the 'impact of these village enclaves on city life' intensely, he says:

> I may mention only one well-known impact. The village cows, buffaloes, donkeys, pigs and other animals roam around the city streets and even arterial roads. They cause traffic jams, and damage cars and other vehicles. Their droppings and urine foul the streets. They attack pedestrians, sometimes resulting in serious injuries and even death. (Shah 2012, p. 18)

Introducing two other factors – namely, religion and democracy – into the discussion he goes on to say:

> The problem seems to defy solutions. Cows are sacred and get fed by devout Hindus; they are overfed during festivals. They also eat all kinds of garbage, even

waste paper and plastic sheets. The owners of these animals live in the village enclave. They have become a vote bank, and often behave arrogantly, sometimes even violently. They and their animals cannot be removed. (Shah 2012, p. 18)

To reinforce his point, he goes on to narrate another incident of this intrusion.

I may narrate in this context the experience of the Delhi School of Economics (DSE) about the land on which it is located. After this land, belonging to the nearby Chandrawal village, was acquired in 1950 or so, its titled was disputed. When I was the director of the DSE in 1973–75, I used to receive summons about it from the court. The peasants of Chandrawal also claimed the grazing rights on this land. They used to bring their cattle for grazing even during the teaching hours. Their women came to cut grass on the open space. After the women had bundled the cut grass, she would ask one of our gardeners to lift the bundle and put it on her head. The woman and the gardener, face to face, exchange giggles. The Chandrawal peasants never allowed us to lock our gates, and threatened to kill our watchmen. The distinguishing teachers and students were experiencing the village in the city. (Shah 2012, p. 18)

So, this graphic account givens us a counter account of the relation between the village and the city. From the social scientist, we hear the impact of the village on the city. This aspect, largely muted in discussion on the nature of the city or modernity in India, gives us a different account of the coexistence. This account, along with the other from Tagore, gives us a different and even a spectacular picture of Indian society. This picture, however, eluded the attention of social scientists in India who are preoccupied or intoxicated by the theories that theorize the mutual exclusion combination in the West. Shah himself admits this when he says:

The architectural, economic, social, cultural and political changes that take place in these village enclaves in cities should be a subject of research. It is easy to dismiss them as slums, but that would be shirking the responsibility of understanding the nature of this increasingly important segment of urban society. More generally, even after a village is included in the city, the problem of rural-urban linkage remains and makes the categories 'rural' and 'urban' even more fuzzy than we have known them to be for long. (Shah 2012, p. 18)

This statement, which is an assessment of the state of affairs in social sciences, moves further to explore the reason for the apathy in analysing Indian society. One of the reasons is that they are preoccupied with the mutually exclusive model and the theories based on this model. It is clear from Shah's account that it has not taken them any further.[2] Having made this point, let me discuss another account, which gives us some more ideas about the relation between city and man.

Let me also discuss how Sumit Sarkar configures the relation between Dakshineswar temple and Belur Math.

> Dakshineswar temple, where Ramakrishna had lived for thirty years, and Belur Math, founded by his most illustrious disciple, face each other today on opposite banks of the Bhagirathi presenting in many ways a vivid study in contrasts, even oppositions. The temple, like any major Hindu sacred site, is thronged with crowds which cut across class divides, noisy, colourful, not over-sensitive to dirt. The holiness of the place permits women to shed inhibitions and bath in the river ghat along side men folk. The approaches are cluttered with shops selling a variety of mementoes, trinkets, eatables, and the atmosphere resembles that of a bazaar or mela. Solemnity reigns to some extent only inside the central shrine of Bhavatarini Kali, and, more evidently, in the corner room where Ramakrishna used to stay: here devotees sit, ponder, or pray. Belur Math is much more of an upper-middle-class devotional-cum-tourist spot: almost aggressively hygienic, it is full of guards and notices warning visitors off from bathing in the river or spoiling the lawns. An image of Ramakrishna, fully clothed in spotless white, constitutes the central shrine. A glass curtain preserves it from physical proximity or the touch of devotees or visitors. Asked where Vivekananda and his associates had themselves stayed, a swamiji points vaguely in the distance. He is much more interested in telling us that the main building had been constructed by Martin Burn in the 1930's and that Kamala Nehru and Indira Gandhi had been regular visitors.
>
> And yet Dakshineshwar and Belur remain tied together by indissoluble links, each shedding its lustre on the other: leaving us with the problems of extremely varied worlds which still for some reason require a stable centre in the figure of Ramakrishna. Diverse appropriations of a founding father are of course common and not at all exceptional. While still worth exploration in terms of implications and contexts, the theme most relevant for our present study is the persistence of a need for affiliations with Ramakrishna across decades of sweeping change. (Sarkar 1997, p. 343)

Along with the reality status of the pre-modern religious space, Sarkar brings out its contrast with the modern *math*. In both Shah and Sarkar, the living reality status of the pre-modern village is recognized, and not merely to eliminate it, as it is in Descartes, or for fear that it will be eliminated, as echoed in Tagore. An important aspect of Sarkar's account is that he goes one step further towards Shah in highlighting the positive and the human aspects associated with a pre-modern religious space like Dakshineshwar temple and the identification of limitations surrounding Belur Math. The dirt, which is the site of vice for Shah, becomes some sort of an identity or a virtue for Sarkar. With this let me claim that, unlike in the West, where the cities adhere to the modern canon, there is no city, except, perhaps, Chandigarh, which is not an extension of a village or a group of villages.

I am not only referring to the village cluster that Shah refers to, where a village is included after the growth of a city. I am not even referring to those villages that get included in the city subsequent to the growth of the city. I am saying that all the cities in India are situated just outside the village. To recall Foucault here, like the excluded institution of the clinic, mental asylum and prison, these institutions from the pre-modern in societies like India exist right in the centre of the city, sometimes performing destructive functions like not enabling the growth of cities or dirtying the roads with their droppings; they also provide an important alternative in an interactive manner. For instance, while learning speed and growth from the city, the narrow roads of the village also teach the city, in turn, how to walk slowly. This counter provides a radical alternative and offers psychological comfort. It is this underlying structural unconscious contribution that seems to be at the root of cities craving to be nearer to the villages. There seems to be a tendency, provided by their coexistence, where cities, despite inconveniences and threats, seem to, at least unconsciously, feel the craving to be near the villages in India. More importantly, the cities seem to feel insecure without a village being near them, hence their proximity. This is despite the fact that villages do not enable the progress of the city. While cities teach villages how to pick up speed, the village teaches the city to go slow. This is best exemplified when one watches SUV vehicles that have to move at a snail's pace on a narrow road, not in a village that is outside the city, but in a village that is right inside the city. While cities make villages run, the latter in turn makes the former to walk. There is a need to explore this psychological tendency more elaborately.

These villages are not the slums of the cities, but they belong to the pre-modern that coexists with the modern. Having highlighted this variance, I want to stress that this is done only to elucidate the sociological aspect. I do not want at this level to bring moral and political aspects into the discussion. I do not for instance claim that this difference is preferable. In fact, as it stands, I might prefer the clarity associated with the Western model of mutual exclusion of the village and the city or pre-modern and the modern. This is despite the fact that there is lot of violence associated with this transformation. Further, there is reductionism in this combination. However, the reason for my highlighting this variance is not to advance my preference for it. I find in this variance not virtue but a de facto virtue. There is a possibility to convert this difference and through closer negotiations arrive at developments where the difference is converted into a virtue.

My purpose here is only to highlight the existence of the variance and point out that social scientists in India failed to see what is in front of them. This observation is corroborated by those like Shah who belong to these disciplines. One of the reasons why they failed to see what is in front of them is their preoccupation with and training in the theoretical models that brilliantly capture the realities within the West.

This is what underlies the public sphere in India. Let me recall, there is a public sphere in the West that excludes the pre-modern. The exit of the pre-modern there is a prerequisite to the entry of the modern. In contrast, India provides an instance where this modern canon is not adhered to. Rather, it provides a different combination, where the public sphere, such as cities, have to coexist with the pre-modern social institutions like villages. This is shown in Tagore, in Shah and in Sarkar. This is not to ignore the violence that the city exercises on the village, as pointed out by Tagore. A brutal instance of this is evident in the case of frequent road widening that, along with brutaliz\ing the streets and roads, defaces the front aesthetic elevations of the houses, the face of these dwellings. Extending this, I have argued how this Indian combination reveals some interesting instances that await theorization. While this complex picture defies the modern canon, the social scientists, as confessed by Shah, have failed to see what is before them. The underlying reason for this inability to see the city in conjunction with village and instead to see the village and then the city is not the individual incompetence of those who engage in social theory. This is not even due only to their fascination for Western theories or due to the impact of colonialism. Rather, there seems be a larger cultural trait lurking behind this.

Let me explain this. As mentioned right in the beginning, there are two important aspects in Advaita Vedanta. One is to see what is not there, namely *Brahman*. The other one is not to see what is there, as that is *maya* or illusion. I have no problem with the first one, whereas the second one is problematic. It is problematic as it disturbs in viewing the present. While we seem to have rejected the *Advaita*, the underlying aspects, though in a modified sense, seem to have survived. One instance of this survival is not seeing what is in front of us. So, this disguised form of the *Advaita* trait seems to be in operation within social theory in India. Rather than seeing this as arising out of *Advaita*, I would want to claim that *Advaita* has captured philosophically this cultural trait of Indians. That is, rather than problematizing how *Advaita* is equated as Indian philosophy and explicating the underlying politics, I would like to explore the success of *Advaita* as rooted in its capturing this cultural and, as one of my students puts it, enduring, albeit in a modified and almost disguised[3] form, 'national trait'. While social scientists in India maintained a safe distance from philosophy, particularly from Indian philosophy, except in the case of some, if my argument has some validity then there is a need to revisit these brands of philosophies from the subcontinent to refurbish and revitalize social sciences in India. There is an additional need to read Western philosophy more closely than it is done now, particularly Descartes, to understand better what is before us. Lastly, but desperately, I want to highlight how social theory in India has delayed realization, when some of their findings were anticipated much earlier in literature. So they may have to relook at the need to relate themselves to the literary domains: thereby a lot of time can be saved. This will enable social theory in India to avoid equating the question paper with the subject.

As an appendix let me recall Shah's reference to the sociology of urination on the streets and its detrimental effect on the lives of people. Sudipta Kaviraj too refers to the politics of urinating. He reports:

> An English daily once printed an amusing photograph of a common street scene in Calcutta. It showed a municipal sign proscribing urination with the order 'Commit no nuisance', and a row of unconcerned citizens right underneath engaged in this odious form of civil disobedience. ... There can be some interesting speculation about whether the defiant citizens knew English. (Kaviraj 2011, p. 239)

What is problematic here is not only the language but the implementation of political packages. Elucidating the requirements for implementing democracy and liberalism J. S. Mill, in his *On Liberty*, claims literacy as an essential requirement. In India, democracy is sustained by those who are non-literates. Given the circumstances, it must be admitted, they have done better or at least did not mess it up.

Their situation can be best captured by the following folk story. Once upon a time, there was a king who had seven sons. They went hunting and caught seven fishes; they put all of them for drying. However, one of them did not dry – upon being asked why, it answered the grass heap obstructed the sun from falling on it; the heap answered a similar enquiry by saying that the cow did not eat it; the cow answered that the cow-boy did not take it for grazing; the cow-boy reported that the child was crying; the child answered that he was bitten by an ant; and the ant claimed that the boy put his finger inside its ant-hill. Similarly, the one who urinated can be defended by saying that they were not consulted in choosing democracy for India. I will stop before this becomes an issue in political philosophy, where it is further probed that the advent of democracy, even in the West, is not through a democratic process, as they were forced to be free, à la Rousseau.

Notes

1   The village that I am referring to is different from the idea of the slum highlighted by Ashis Nandy. Referring to slums, Nandy says:

> The urban slum consists of people who are uprooted and partially decultured, people who have moved out of traditions and have been forced to loosen their caste and community ties. That does not mean that slum has no access to cultural traditions. Often the resilience of cultures is seen in the most dramatic fashion in the urban slum. Two processes are central to an understanding of this resilience.
>
> First, the slum recreates the remembered village in a new guise and resurrects the old community ties in new forms. Even traditional faiths, piety and kinship ties survive in slums, wearing disguises paradoxically supplied by their own massified versions. The slum may even have its version of classicism. It is not what classicism should be according to classicists, but what classicism often is, when bowdlerized and converted into its popular versions for easy digestion and saleability in a market.
>
> Second, the slum creates its own culture out of the experiences of the slum itself; out of the close encounters between the different time periods and diverse cultures telescoped into the slum; out of the impact of 'strange' communities, ethnicities and world-views on the individual; and out of interactions with the alien world of impersonal institutions that have begun to penetrate even the more sleepy South Asian Communities. (Nandy 1998, pp. 6–7)

2   This feature of cities in India eluded the attention of Kaviraj while listing three spheres of the admixture of the ideas of public and private in the city of Calcutta. See 2011, p. 243.

3   I have elucidated the disguised aspect of the pre-modern in India while combating modernity (2013).

References

Descartes, R. (1985), 'Discourse on Method', in John Cottingham, Robert Stoothoff and Dugald Murdoch (trans), *The Philosophical Writings of Descartes, Vol. 1*, 111–51, Cambridge: Cambridge University Press.

Kaviraj, S. (2011), 'Filth and the Public Sphere: Concepts and Practices about Space in Calcutta', in his *The Enchantment of Democracy and India: Politics and Ideas*, 238–73, Raniket: Permanent Black.

Nandy, A., ed. (1998), 'Introduction', in *The Secret Politics of our Desires: Innocence, Culpability and Indian Popular Cinema*, 1–18, Delhi: Oxford University Press.

Raghuramaraju, A. (2011), *Modernity in Indian Social Theory*. New Delhi: Oxford University Press.

Raghuramaraju, A. (2013), *India and Philosophy: Ancestors, Outsiders and Predecessors*. New Delhi: Oxford University Press.

Sarkar, S. (1997), ' "Kaliyuga", "Chakri" and "Bhakti": Ramakrishna and his times', *Writing Social History*, 282–357, New Delhi: Oxford University Press.

Shah, A. M. (29 December 2012), 'The Village in the City, the City in the Village', *Economic and Political Weekly*, XLVII (52): 17–19.

Tagore, R. (1924), 'City and Village', *The Visva-Bharati Quarterly*, II (3): 215–27.

Part Three

Seeing/Doing: Mediatization, Passive Publics and Dissents in Images

The visual challenges the conception of the public sphere as the linguistic domain of critical articulation. It is often understood as purely affective and pre-cognitive, something that bedazzles the intellect and silences critical thought. Perhaps the suspicion of the visual leads Paul Virilio to comment that the public image is replacing the public space (2012). The articles in this part, while remaining vigilant about the possible misadventures awaiting in the complex domain of the image, explore the critical and affirmative powers of the visual. They attempt to overcome the many difficulties in theorizing the visual by exploring the political stakes in the formal elements of the photograph, chromolithographs, cartoons and cinema.

The theoretical approach towards the visual in its relation to the public sphere as critical space is fraught with several difficulties. The investment of the aesthetic theory of the image with power and ideology is well acknowledged, for instance, in the history of propaganda films, especially the case of *Triumph of the Will*, and Hegel's lectures on art (see Mitter). In this regard, Patricia Hayes remarks that the study of photographs is often constrained by the critical thought concerning the relation of the photographic image to surveillance and power on the one hand and the aesthetics of the visible on the other. On the one hand, emphasis on surveillance tends to avoid the problems of form and affect to focus on the significant, even though aesthetic aspects too have a relation to power. On the other hand, the purely aesthetic attention brought to the visual is unable to register those images that are important for sociopolitical struggles. Hayes studies the photographs that have participated in the vocal/

print culture towards the formation of a new post-apartheid public sphere. Documentary photographs in black and white may claim an authentic status as the representation of the harsh socio-economic conditions of life. Gaudy colours are often associated with a non-intellectual sensibility. The black people in the post-apartheid society may not accept such representation, not because they challenge the conditions depicted in the photographs, but because they challenge the signifying binary of racism – blackness/whiteness – operating in the monochrome. Not merely a formal problem in the domain of aesthetics, colour poses questions about, the history of colour and the colour of history. Colour seems to be the membrane of the photographs which opens up the conscious to the unconscious. Ledochowski, the South African photographer, began to colour his black-and-white photographs because black-and-white photojournalist photographs are *of* the people but the colour photographs turned out to be *for* the people. Photography opens up new contact zones between the viewers and those who stand behind the camera in creating new possibilities of participation and action.

Arunima explores the relationship between art and the public sphere through the works of the painter Raja Ravi Varma, India's first public artist, while engaging critically with the theoretical background that dominated the conception of public art through most of the twentieth century, especially Adorno and Benjamin. Exposure and accessibility to the world given by the spaces of modern gallery and museum are not enough to constitute the public reception of works of art. The public here is not exhausted by the spaces of modern gallery and museum. Ravi Varma's colourful, human-like portraits of the gods and goddesses were criticized by the traditionalists and the modernists alike, but gained popularity among the aesthetically unschooled in the Indian public. Arunima cautions us against seeing this unique event in art history through the available distinction between high and low art. What were the conditioning aspects of the specific recipient public? Illuminating the cultural debates regarding the availability of techniques of painting and the contestations for eminence in Indian art history, Arunima argues that it is the auto-didact painter Ravi Varma's engagement with non-Indian naturalist form, and the specific techniques to render this form, that made his works into popular art. In addition to maintaining a certain equation between the figure of woman and the nation, which is not unique to him as a modern Indian painter, Ravi Varma feminized the canvas by drawing the women of Indian mythologies such that it cultivated a new mode of desire for the visual. The lower caste of India were not allowed entry into Hindu temples (a practice that has not ended entirely) and hence did not have the visual or tactile access to the idols that the upper castes possessed. Ravi Varma's lithographs, a precursor to photographic prints, not only made the gods and goddesses visible to the lower castes, but also allowed the latter to take possession of the former, bringing them into lower caste homes and workshops. It is the materiality of the chromolithograph as a desirable, cheap and reproducible object that enabled it to contract the divine power and cut across the curated space of the gallery towards the public space of mass circulation and the private space of worship and ownership.

Devadawson's chapter explores the dimension in which cartoons combine graphic protest and public dissent. She studies the cartoons which came out during the recent anti-corruption protests in India led by the Gandhian activist Anna Hazare. They articulate the dissent arising from the public movements which were opposed to the state understood as the monopolist of corruption. The objective of the cartoons was to expose the manner in which the anti-corruption movements shaped by the public were systematically distorted and steered by the traditional media. Anna Hazare's movement was initially organized through social media and then mobilized through television. The cartoons which expose the spectacular nature of contemporary resistance movements in their desiring relation to the corporate media are also a part of this very spectacle. By their very nature cartoons and caricatures draw out this extra dimension that is produced by their reflexivity into the space of the very public spectacle that is questioned by the creation of that dimension. Devadawson shows how cartoons perform this difficult act of self-criticism by and for the media by working simultaneously on the registers of the figure and the text and by blurring the boundary between cartoons and caricatures. Their criticism of *publicness* is channelled through a certain figure of public authority in India – the saint. Anna Hazare attempted to canonize himself by simulating the figure of Gandhi, the saint exemplar for modern India. In this sense, then, the leading public figure of the spectacle is already a caricature. However the Indian saint figure is expected to both be public, being accessible at all times to those in need, *and* to practice detachment, especially from action, whether individual or collective, wherein his spiritual value entirely lies. The value of the saint lies entirely in this practice of detachment. Unlike Socrates, the typical Indian saint figure is not committed to the public use of reason and speech. He might undertake a vow of silence even at the heights of a public movement. However, the anti-corruption movement also demanded complete public access to information about the conduct of the state. Yet its own leadership derived its efficacy from its ability to be detached from the acts of public speech, debate and conduct. In the mediatized society where the openness of the public sphere is usurped and enclosed by media networks, the cartoon form struggles to find a balance between the difficulties of representing the unfolding spectacles and the need to represent the self-critical dimension of the media. The graphic distortion that produces caricatures, and the disjunctive relationship between the figure and the text, could be seen in the light of such a difficult task.

Susmita Dasgupta rethinks the idea of a discursive public sphere and its transformations in the context of post-independence Indian cinema. The cinematic image, unlike the painting, has no frames marking the boundary between the represented and the unrepresented and, hence, makes it possible for life to flow into it and inhabit the cinematic world. The Indian cinema grew up alongside the Indian freedom movement which emphasized the moral transformation of the individual who, infused with the values of modernity, would demand political power for her full development. According to Dasgupta, it took care of the intimate sphere of this transformation, leaving the political sphere to the Indian National Congress. In popular cinema actors mattered more than the characters played by them and their directors. Those who rose to the status of screen divinities with large fan followings led well-guarded private lives, glimpses of which were accessible to their fans only through gossip. The individual viewer who enters the world in the frameless image is educated in sociality through the publicness offered on the screen, and this cinematic public sphere drew the individual cinemagoer into a dark intimate world. In this sense, cinema redrew the distinction between the private and the public. For Dasgupta the significant transformation of the nature of this Indian cinematic public is the recently growing proximity between cinema, advertisement and television whereby cinema starts to lose its status as a public sphere and become an object of consumption. The proliferation of multiplex theatres and DVDs has privileged the viewer over the film as it increasingly provides the setting for the advertisement of consumable products, lifestyles and for its own special elements like song and dance numbers. The stars have now left their intimately private abodes to attend public events, advertise products and participate in TV reality shows. The focus has shifted from socializing the emotional to transforming the body and from ideology to objects of consumption. As the intimate sphere becomes destitute and is conjoined to the illuminated public world of consumption, the individual viewer becomes free to acknowledge his alignment with cinema. The space vacated by cinema is taken up by what Dasgupta calls the 'civilizational terror industry'. Indeed, the ferociously private or anonymous life of the suicide bomber vanishes in the public spectacle that the vanishing life creates. Through the clippings of this spectacle of vanishing life, the TV news programmes merely satisfy his addiction for the visual instead of guiding the viewer through new modes of individuation.

9

The Colour of History: Photography and the Public Sphere in Southern Africa

Patricia Hayes

Introduction

I start with what is perhaps a throwaway comment in Paul Virilio's essay *The Vision Machine*. At one point in the discussion of technological change, visual penetration and social surveillance, Virilio refers to the public space giving way to the public image (1994, p. 64). I call this 'throwaway' because it materializes in a long line of critical thinking that is suspicious of vision and the ways it is put to use by large forces such as the state (Tagg 1988; Sekula 1989) or global capitalist enterprise (Berger 1972). These questions have exercised scholars in southern Africa to some extent. It is also a growing post-apartheid and postcolonial question in this time of expectation of capitalist expansion on the African continent, when the new African middle class is being hailed as one of the greatest untapped new markets on the globe.

But it is not long ago that activists and artists in southern Africa attempted to use visuality, in this case photography, to create new publics, to join in the occupation of spaces such as the street and make them more public by producing and circulating images of them filled with protest. In this way, I want to suggest, they helped to develop something approaching an inclusive public sphere that was not only critical of the apartheid state but also self-critical. This brings me to interrogate Virilio's 'suspicion'. In any consideration of visuality and the public sphere, there are implicitly two commonly understood features of the public sphere that would be hypothetically at risk. These are firstly its vocality (as opposed to visuality) and secondly its criticality. For most, the idea of the public sphere is premised on speech and text, and words imply cognition, with associations of intellection. Put very simply in neo-Kantian terms, the split between cognition and aesthetics means that the image is often associated with affect, with feeling and with a psychic terrain that older literature has even termed 'pre-cognitive' (Rohde 1998, p. 190; see also Sekula 1978). More recently debates range across those in political philosophy who insist that affect and cognition are deeply interlinked and cannot be separated (Kingston and Ferry 2008); art and literary studies tracking 'explosions of information' that produce 'implosions of meaning and the release of affects' (Van Alphen 2013) which problematizes the cognitive/aesthetic split in new ways; and media theorists who argue that both the visual and the textual are 'mediums of cognition' even if their modes of transmission differ (Belting 2011, p. 10).

Here I wish to critically examine the implications of Virilio's statement by following certain interplays around photography at times of growing political mobilization and state repression in southern Africa in the late twentieth century. My main focus is on the 1980s that represent the climax of anti-apartheid militancy. I am not referring to one homogeneous movement, but heterogeneous organizations, ideologies, campaigns and groups who at some important junctures come together. A central issue is whether a criticality can emerge from human engagements with pictures, or whether these are just surfaces that distract, spectacles that bedazzle and cause a suspension of the intellect or worse. There is a long history of the 'denigration of vision' in critical thought: elements of Baudrillard, Foucault and Debord are frequently cited here (Jay 1994; Reinhardt 2013). Certainly a suspension of the intellect is also explicit when Virilio mentions instrumental uses, such as in advertising, or propaganda. Is the photograph then 'a silence that silences' (Sekula 1989, p. 344)? Or is it as Samuel Beckett has suggested 'a stain on the silence' (cited in Morris 1989, p. 22)?

'The denigration of vision' as Martin Jay puts it in *Downcast Eyes* (1994) is not altogether helpful here. Perhaps a more productive way to think about photography in the 1980s in southern Africa is to see it as similar to, or even part of, print culture. Like the book or the newspaper, this has a very public character. It circulates, it builds communities of those who have seen it or heard about what it portrays. Its relationship with nationalism has been argued in many contexts. I am proposing this route because the material that I work with, call it broadly photographs and history from southern Africa in the late twentieth century, constitutes a field of debate that is usually constrained between two disciplinary paradigms. These are critical theory dealing with surveillance and power, and art, especially those critical and art historical discourses that have gone through a phase of consigning most photographs dealing with political events and social conditions to the veritable dustbin of history (Enwezor 2006, 2010).[1]

In thinking about photography and the public sphere in the 1980s, I examine statements by photographers reflecting on their practice, specifically those who were part of the progressive photographic collective Afrapix that was founded in 1982. Afrapix photographs found their way into many local bodies, trade unions and community-based organizations and were also circulated overseas among solidarity organizations. It was about 'South African stories that were unheard'.[2] An important magazine had emerged called *Staffrider*, which published stories, poems and artworks especially by black authors who could not easily find publication elsewhere and which now included photographs. Afrapix also had its own magazine, *Full Frame*, that appeared at irregular intervals. A number of Afrapix photographers by the mid-1980s made their living from acting as stringers or agency photographers but would still contribute some of their work to the collective. Afrapix grew later in the 1980s to include over twenty photographers around South Africa who contributed to a weekly pool of photographs, from which a package would be selected every Friday that was sent to London to be received and then redistributed through the International Defence and Aid Fund.[3] The irony became that with harsh press restrictions in South Africa under State of Emergency powers, viewers outside South Africa began to see far more photographs of the internal political struggles and repression than did South Africans themselves.

One of the co-founders of Afrapix was Omar Badsha, who was deeply connected with art and politics in Durban. Political circles included Communist Party members, leftist theorists, informal debating groups and Black Consciousness philosophy that was on the rise in the early 1970s with Steve Biko's writings. Badsha later joined the ANC underground and did organizational work in the huge informal settlement of Inanda outside Durban (Hayes 2011a). Badsha was an artist before becoming a photographer. Inspired by worker militancy in Durban, where the 1972 strike was the beginning of significant trade union activism in South Africa, he worked for the Chemical Workers Union and this is where he realized that photography would be crucial in building worker education. He acquired a Leica camera from Cassim Amra, who ran a photo society in his neighbourhood, and started to keep what he called a visual diary. He encouraged others to contribute pictures and started putting up prints on the walls of meeting rooms and halls where workers would see other scenes of labour and organization. In a socio-economic environment where education was very poor and made more so by Bantu Education policies under apartheid, pictures were used for worker education very deliberately.[4] Visual literacy was used to counter illiteracy and build on semi-literacy among workers.

Omar Badsha couches the struggle of activists and politicized artists in terms of shifting the centre and of bringing the margins into the centre. To do this, progressive photographers had to constitute new publics. In fact the spatial metaphor of the public sphere is very apt here (Young 2000, p. 160), given that photographs would reconstitute the spaces of labour and political action that activists wanted to transpose (Edwards 1999) into new spaces of viewership that could become a public. We could say that photography produces new contact zones between the world photographed and viewers who see it and unlocks the potential for participation or action. Azoulay develops this sense of such a zone as a political space through her concept of 'the event of photography' that does not end, linked to the notion of a citizenry of photography outside sovereign power (2012; see also Reinhardt 2013). There are problems with transposing such models generally to the southern African situation, but for our purposes here the discussion will focus on the question of publics generated by viewership, and their emerging cohesion (or not) around certain issues.

Critical images

To return to the question of how critical these spaces were, it is necessary to emphasize that there were times when censorship made the circulation of words so difficult that photographs gained a particular salience in the complexity of what they could aspire to communicate. Certain things could not be said or written but they came to be visualized and communicated across media (see Figure 9.1).

One particular photograph which remains very strongly in public memory even today is that of another Afrapix member, Eric Miller. Miller photographed a night police raid on the COSATU (Congress of South African Trade Unions) headquarters in Johannesburg in 1987 in a tense period during the big railway workers' strike. This made it on to the front page of the progressive *Weekly Mail* (now *Mail and Guardian*) newspaper in a brief twenty-four-hour period between the lapsing of one annual State of Emergency and its renewal in parliament the next day. The South African mainly urban middle-class public who saw the newspaper had the surprise of seeing multiple levels of the trade union building at night, and a series of rooms like a grid, COSATU officials being harassed and held hostage by police. The illuminated rooms shot from another building across the road look like cells or frames on a contact sheet. The photograph offers a window on what the state is capable of, the powerlessness of detained individuals, their atomization. But the state's usual power over visibility is disrupted. In fact the photograph is disrupting the police order with a new visual order. There is even a reference to the photographer's presence in the gaze of the one policeman who sees him. The apartheid state that normally succeeds in hiding its actions is opened up to the viewer, in this case apparently with something of a shock. It is the opposite of Virilio's public image that replaces the public space, for this is an image that certainly created new publics, even if this public appears to have been largely white.[5]

Miller describes this and other scenes to which he was exposed as 'surreal'. They were hard to absorb and process, given that the state produced a huge web of lies and half-truths.[6] But there is more to it. Why does the photographer invoke the notion of the surreal? Is it because of the abyss between what is said and what is done? Is it because things are ripped out of their presumed normal reality? Or is it the opening of consciousness to the possibility of the unconscious, a borderland thinly held by the membrane of the photograph?

Photographs were capable not only of opening a wider public space but also of deepening the criticality of the public sphere by sparking references across new images in conversation with known ones. Many commentators have pointed out the resemblance between some of William Kentridge's frames in *Ubu Tells the Truth* (1996–7) and Miller's photograph of COSATU House (see Figure 9.2). The life of the image went on, materializing in new ways.

In Kentridge's animation the horror of a known narrative is taken up as he adapts accounts from the Truth & Reconciliation Commission of the political detainee who fell to his death from a police headquarters at John Vorster Square during interrogation. Police habitually blamed such deaths on suicide. It is doubtful whether anyone then could have photographed such a fall to death but the associations of Miller's photographed structure with its vignettes of violation are taken further in Kentridge to replay such incidents as a trope of state violence and torture. In this argument COSATU House is transmogrified into the headquarters of the security police. It is an image of repression that goes on and on.[7] Hans Belting emphasizes that it is not the medium that is in the middle between the image and the viewer: it is the image that is in the middle. The viewer's body is also a medium and it is the work of the imagination to fill out (in this case perhaps) the limits of the document – here the documented image. As Belting reminds us, 'images cross media and show accumulations of several different media in one and the same place' (2011, p. 5).

It could be argued that the apartheid state is an easy target for critique because of its injustices, however difficult its repressive apparatus made those criticisms especially in the State of Emergency from 1986. In such a struggle with its dichotomies of collaboration and resistance the temptation is to demonize the state and its supporters and institutions (apartheid/Afrikaners/police/military) in a simplistic way. However there is much photographic work to attest to very subtle portrayals of ordinary Afrikaners, notably by David Goldblatt (1975) (see Figure 9.3).

The other danger in such a polarized situation is to heroicize those who undertook to oppose apartheid. There is a large stock of photographs that build up an image of suffering and resistance of the afflicted that I have written about elsewhere (Hayes 2012). In other words, the danger becomes the propagation of a black-and-white impression of South Africa's past, present and, by implication, future. This is very dangerous because it makes criticism of the liberation movements very difficult and feeds a tendency towards a monumental African nationalism with its heroic icons.

This is where a particular line of photography by Omar Badsha becomes very interesting. Because of the multiplicity of his political influences, he was better than most at pointing to the discrepancies between political mobilization and the development of a broad public sphere, even as he unconditionally risked his life for the ANC underground in KwaZulu-Natal. To some extent he became critical of the kind of publics constituted by the political struggle, especially where the rally or mass meeting is the main mechanism of recruiting support for a campaign or an idea. A multitude is of course good, and crowds and marches were photographed to encourage those involved and convince everyone that the anti-apartheid movement inside South Africa was huge (see Mayekiso 1996). But Badsha started to depict the distance and even verbosity of the leaders and speechifiers. Across different bodies of work he draws parallels between religious and political forms of mobilizing converts, where people are divided into the leaders and the led. He often photographs the faces of the listeners (Figures 9.4 and 9.5).

Vocality itself is visualized and implicitly critiqued. The prosthetics of public vocality and its scale are the subject of many photographs, with loudspeakers and microphones. Often the speaker is distant from the audience. The meaningfulness of what is being said or exhorted in the political speech is in question in photographs of audiences and auditors in halls or at gatherings, with their faces suggesting many shades along a continuum of attentiveness to boredom or possibly scepticism. Most often men are the speakers, and very often women the listeners. Badsha contemplated an exhibition of photographs of men with loudspeakers, but it was regarded as too critical and his closest comrades advised him not to do it.[8] It was not regarded as a good time to critique one's own political movement. Thus these critical references are sprinkled across his archive but have never been edited or curated into a solid statement. Badsha did, however, publish his picture of the ANC leadership after their return from exile or imprisonment who share the stage but are not unified, and the suggestion is there that they are already visibly separating into tense rivalries (see Figure 9.6).

To say this is a very prescient picture is of course easy and teleological, but indeed the state of what we might call a public sphere in post-apartheid South Africa is not strong. Politics is dominated by competing groups of ANC strongmen, many of them increasingly remote from their constituencies and absorbed by their own baronial power struggles. There is a strong sense of fragmentation and post-apartheid abandonment of citizens. Socio-economic change has only affected a very small proportion of the mass of South Africans and explosive localized protest is common in the poorest areas.

One of the most telling and humble things that Badsha says is that he feels many people did not understand what he was trying to do at the time. This is where the larger archive becomes important, as the storage site of photographs for use further down the line. Indeed photographers were not just concerned to constitute new publics and make an impact on the present. Most of them also self-consciously believed that they were photographing history. Such a notion is of course very widespread in photography generally. In her recent book *The Camera as Historian*, concerning late nineteenth-century amateur history societies in England which systematically sought to photographically document their provincial heritage, Elizabeth Edwards writes: 'The promise of photographs was to grasp time and rematerialize it. Photographs extend the reach of the temporal beyond relations between the present and the past, to the future as well, creating an archival grid, through which the past might be accessible in an imagined future' (2012, p. 7). Afrapix member John Liebenberg working in Namibia recalls attending workshops by the collective's co-founder Paul Weinberg who advocated the use of good quality black-and-white film and thorough darkroom processing to produce better-quality negatives that would transcend the needs of immediate press photography and serve through time (Liebenberg and Hayes 2010, p. 22). Of course this tonal depth to black and white would also bring more credit to the photographer. It is at this point, then, that I wish to bring in what is said about the colour of this history by those who were the subjects of these photographs.

The colour of history

It is a very obvious thing to say that to think of these photographs is to think of history, the 'last thing before the last' as Kracauer put it (1969). Edwards argues suggestively that photographs reconstitute the space and time of history (1999). But there is more to it than a straightforward notion of the photograph as the trace of the past, an index of something that has been. Edwards has gone further to ask the crucial question, *what kind of history is a photograph?* We are still trying to answer this. To go even further, perhaps we should be asking, what kind of photograph is history? For as Eduardo Cadava suggests, 'Photographic technology belongs to the physiognomy of historical thought ... there can be no thinking of history that is not the same as thinking of photography' (1997, p. xviii).

It seems that we are still trying endlessly to grasp the relationship between this technology, this medium and the passing by of life. Hans Belting makes a clear distinction between the medium and the image and says that we still do not really know what an image is. Belting argues that an image only inhabits a medium, be it a painting, a photograph, a screen, and is then transmitted into or through the body, which is also a medium, though images can repose there for very long periods of time until reactivated by some trigger or association. Images are presented or externalized through a medium and then internalized or not, and so on. The photograph is only one carrier of the image, though I would argue it is a seminal one since the mid-nineteenth century. This is not the place to pursue all these questions in detail, but Belting's framework is useful in providing a vocabulary to delineate how different human subjects do or do not internalize images that are carried across space and time through the medium of photography. This has implications for thinking about the public sphere in relation to visuality, a relation that is by no means as straightforward as we might think and which can involve an intense back and forth between image producers, situations and consumers.

An issue that is very salient here is the refusal, dismissal, rejection, critique or dislike of certain kinds of photographs by many people in southern Africa.

Sometimes it might be that the photographs appear to be meaningless, that people cannot connect with them. This is of course not a constant (Belting 2011). But how are we to think about the phenomenon that many South Africans who reside in townships, who were themselves (or their parents before them) the subjects of social documentary anti-apartheid photography, actually dislike such photographs and do not wish to engage with them? Such views can be heard from many sides, from older township residents to first-generation university students, besides the more critically aware photographers who are from, or have close ties with, township communities or popular neighbourhoods. To reiterate the problem: many of those who were intended to be the beneficiaries of the awareness that such public photographs were supposed to raise actually reject them. It is not just that people dislike photographs depicting poor socio-economic conditions, violence or armoured vehicles and police occupying township spaces. It is the *black-and-whiteness* of these photographs that is central to the rejection.

This fracturing between photographed and photographer/viewer (crudely put) can be addressed at several levels. The most immediate and indeed growing response has been for scholars to address more 'private' bodies of photography, personal or family photographs and widespread practices around vernacular photographies (Peffer 2013), to suggest what kinds of photographs people did want. The latter is an increasingly rich and promising field of enquiry. Another less obvious response has been to maintain the focus on 'documentary' photography and explore the complexities within bodies of work produced by photographers whose work was more ostensibly public, but whose archives remain largely unexplored. Just as the personal archives of South African families have not come under much scrutiny, so have the archives of many photographers been outside scholarly visibility and more general awareness. Numerous photographers only made public a small proportion of their actual work in response to either 'the market of photography' (Hayes 2011b), or the stringent demands of the 1980s anti-apartheid mobilization, or a culture of co-operation and comradeship that placed less emphasis on individualism. There is an enormous spectrum between what has been visible and what has been out of visibility: photographed but not seen. In a sense these latter cases problematize the more simplistic formulations of the public and the private in photography (Liebenberg and Hayes 2010; Hayes forthcoming 2015).

It is from within this paradigm of a more blurred boundary between public and private photography by individuals who describe themselves as photographers that the exploration around visuality and the public sphere needs to go. A central phenomenon that arises here and leads to a productive set of frictions is colour itself. As stated earlier, there are local discourses of denigration of black-and-white 'documentary' photographs of social conditions in townships. The issues that transpire are colour, as in race, and colour (or lack of it) in the photograph. Many of the sensitivities arise from the class and racial background of numerous photographers. It might not be going too far to say that in the 1980s it is those without colour (benefitting from the structured invisibility of whiteness) who photographed – not in colour – those with colour. There is something crucial here, even if we consider a number of black photographers who were doing the same kind of work. As many township-dwellers see it, whites photograph blacks in black-and-white. It is true that depending on the skill of the photographer and the darkroom printer there are many tones of silver and grey, but the spectrum is enfolded between those two poles.

How is this denigration articulated? Terms like ugliness, misery and poverty are used in relation to what people see of their lives in these black-and-white photos. People would rather have beauty. Santu Mofokeng, a photographer who was born in Soweto, the largest black township in South Africa, says that he does not know any Soweto resident who would buy a print of his black-and-white work on everyday life in the township (Hayes 2009).[9] I think it tells us an enormous amount about how people thought, and still think, about apartheid, from different sides of the racial spectrum.

If people reject this colour of their history, then what is the colour of the photograph/history that they want? There is a need here to look at the question of colour – not in more personal, vernacular or art photography – but in documentary itself: the colour of history, as it were.

Again I shall focus on two photographers (and their audiences), both of whose accounts move strikingly in and out of a vocabulary of the public and the private. The first is a photographer who in a sense crossed the colour lines, Chris Ledochowski. Ledochowski grew up in a Polish émigré family who were part of liberal intellectual circles in Johannesburg in the 1960s and 1970s. He studied art in Cape Town and lived in the mixed race area of Harfield, befriending the respectable and unrespectable alike. He himself took on the intonations and lifestyle of the Cape Flats. As he says, 'I am not some removed kind of First World person going into a Third World situation.'

Ledochowski was called up to do national military service but his reluctance to engage in violent acts against 'fellow South Africans' resulted in psychiatric intervention of the most dubious kind. As political mobilization picked up in the 1980s, he did film and photographic work for political organizations and joined Afroscope and then Afrapix under the influence of Omar Badsha. In time he developed his own critique of the majority of the work that was being done, including his own black-and-white work, some of which was included in Badsha's famous edited volume of 1986, entitled *South Africa: The Cordoned Heart*. He began to change his practice through the influence or indeed pressure of close friends and associates in the Cape Flats, especially in Manenberg where he spent much time. This primarily meant that he 'started to see what colour is about'.

> This colour business, we documentary types have been pushing it out of the way because it's too difficult for us, so stuck in that black-and-white mode. We were trying to show the dismal poverty, all the clichéd stuff, through arty black-and-white photography.[10]

Ledochowski, however, negotiated the turn in a unique and idiosyncratic way. He took large format black-and-white photographs for their quality and sharpness and then hand-coloured them afterwards before giving or selling the print to the person (Figures 9.7 and 9.8).

The portrait style he developed references famous old Cape Town studio practices but also what some commentators call 'coloured' pictorial sensibilities. These include expectations of very high-quality, conventions of framing and a commitment to longevity. All of this, as he says, is an old Cape tradition. 'And you park there for five generations, on the wall' (Figure 9.9).

Ledochowski started with portraits and wedding pictures for private use but then decided to rework his existing documentary prints in the same way for public use. He worked with his own serial accumulations of media traces (Belting's phrase) of an image by reworking black-and-white into colour and metamorphosing the possibility of a photograph, 'almost fictionalizing through colour'. He describes this turn to colour as turning the viewer around, a confrontation with their expectations:

> But you force the viewer, you force them. That's my thing, aim, you see ... with those coloured-in things. I forced you to look at this photo that is so dismal but coloured you have to look at it in a different light, you see. It can actually be quite beautiful.[11] (Figure 9.10)

We come to Ledochowski's best-known photograph, Mandela's first public speech in the Parade in Cape Town after his release from prison in February 1990. Ledochowski makes large prints of the Mandela picture and sells them at a reasonable price, especially so that customers in the Cape Flats can afford to have it. His purpose is so that working-class people can also have history on their walls and in colour (Figure 9.11).

For a while then, before advertising billboards and the new phase of capitalism took hold of visual culture in post-apartheid South Africa, it would seem that apartheid is in black-and-white, and freedom is in colour.

Colour divides?

Ledochowski of course is not unique in his generation in having to think about colour, but he confronted it in a different way to other photographers. His associate Paul Weinberg went to the Netherlands in the late 1980s on behalf of Afrapix, was exposed to the new range of colour film and saw great potential in the shift, which was in fact on the brink of the digital turn. He came back trying to persuade fellow-photographers to change over to colour and survive into the future in a more viable way in the face of international competition. But it was largely resisted and became one minor issue in the broader arguments the progressive photographic community was having. Afrapix itself was torn apart by arguments over funding, direction, careerism and a more collective culture. It shut down in 1992 but its legacy has been very strong, and its training agenda was carried over into the Market Photo Workshop in Johannesburg which still trains photographers from every kind of background, in both analogue and digital photography.

South Africa's most internationally recognized photographer, David Goldblatt, had very strong opinions about colour in the 1980s, even though after 2000 he shifted to colour film that he continues to develop and then digitally scan and print. His earlier objections were technical but had aesthetic ramifications. He says that earlier it was 'extremely difficult because it was such a limited palette. One was stuck with this very pretty image, this very saccharine image. Too sweet and too easy.' He, in fact, now spends an inordinate amount of effort draining the colour from those 'sunny skies and Chevrolet blues. This deep, deep blue sky', to the extent that the tonalities might even start to resemble black-and-white (Figure 9.12).

Goldblatt now remediates photographs taken with colour film through 'de-saturation' to get the attenuated effects he seeks, which he mastered previously with black-and-white.[12] Goldblatt thus drains colour to get the range of shades and tones that he wants from the 'elusive' landscapes that he photographs. What does this do to history?

Michael Taussig refers to the association of colour with warmth or heat, colour and *calor*, as Isidore of Seville put it centuries ago. In his book concerning 'the colour of the sacred' Taussig quotes various authors who see colour as something alive, like an animal (2009, p. 6). He argues that colour pushes us beyond a purely visual approach to vision, that it is part of a bodily unconscious. 'Color vision becomes less a retinal and more a total bodily activity ...' (2009, p. 6). There appears to be a hierarchy around colour, an elitism, a class distinction between refinement and vulgarity that Taussig touches on when he quotes Goethe on the way 'people of refinement' avoid strong colours and gravitate to either black or white (2009, p. 3). In Proust, colour is associated with the formerly colonized other of the French and British empires (2009, p. 5). In South Africa, the colour preferences of township residents are often dismissed as kitsch, or to use Goldblatt's term, 'saccharine'. Thus, as in apartheid, colour divides.

In the hierarchy of values around different kinds of photographs over time (including believability and gravity), colour printing was often associated with advertising and so was less believable. Mieke Bal also draws attention to the gender associations and hierarchies around colour (2013, pp. 234–74). Overtly alongside commerce it was anti-intellectual, even vulgar. But as Taussig argues, 'Colour snatched from commerce' leads to a 'sense of the metamorphosis whereby – thanks to colour – *form undoes itself*' (2009, p. 23). When genres and formats break their boundaries, it suddenly makes apparent those elements that have gone into their construction, maintenance, reproduction and habituation as either a documentary photograph or an advertising picture, for example. Some of this force comes out in the turn to colour after the transition to democracy, notably by Zwelethu Mthethwa initially and later Muholi, Veloko and many others (Godby 1999; Garb 2011; Enwezor 2010), though their focus remains largely portrait subjects. Much of the critical work devoted to these artists foregrounds the portraiture aspect and new explorations of personhood, with the issue of colour becoming secondary again.

Badsha has argued that there were two visual cultures in South Africa during the 1980s. Colour appears to be integral to this. Is the dislike for the spareness and bleakness of black-and-white that dominated print culture and the desire for colour and beauty in the ghettoes a sign that the two worlds could never meet and that the processes of building a public sphere by the late 1980s were obviously very incomplete? Is the main centre of the public sphere and its dominant aesthetic always too far from the township in South Africa? Or can we draw something more from this colour problem? Do people bring meaning to the public sphere/history through their personal worlds, where colour is their preference and the personal relates to important pasts where marginal histories are lodged, as in the ancestral portrait for five generations on the wall? Is colour something that people of colour feel gives them control in their personal worlds? But as Auge reminds us, 'The collective imaginary … we cannot easily separate from the personal imaginary' (cited in Belting 2011, p. 56). This points to a more fluid boundary status between public and private, where the issue of colour ('form undoing itself') allows for a more problematic sense of the notion of 'public' in a place like South Africa.

Notes

1 Enwezor has, however, recently refigured his approach with the serious overview of the apartheid era jointly curated with Rory Bester. See Enwezor and Bester (2012).
2 Interview with Paul Weinberg by Patricia Hayes, Farzanah Badsha and Natasha Becker, Durban, 18 July 2003.
3 Interview with Di Stuart by Patricia Hayes, Farzanah Badsha and Natasha Becker, Johannesburg, 28 July 2003. Interview with Paddy Donnelly (formerly of the International Defence and Aid Fund) by Patricia Hayes, London, 29 May 2003.
4 Interview with Omar Badsha by Patricia Hayes, Farzanah Badsha and Natasha Becker, Cape Town, 6 January 2004.
5 Interview with Eric Miller by Patricia Hayes, Cape Town, 5 August 2002.
6 Ibid.
7 While numerous commentators see a degree of inter-mediality between Miller's photograph and COSATU House and Kentridge's *Ubu* work, Kentridge himself has stated that the influence of certain photographs on his work has only been indirect. Interview with William Kentridge, *Sunday Independent*, 7 October 2007.
8 Interview with Omar Badsha by Patricia Hayes, Pretoria, 23 June 2004.
9 Interview with Santu Mofokeng by Patricia Hayes, Farzanah Badsha and Mdu Xakaza, Johannesburg, 24 July 2005.
10 Interview with Chris Ledochowski by Patricia Hayes and Farzanah Badsha, Cape Town, 27 September 2002.
11 Ibid.
12 Walkabout with David Goldblatt for the exhibition *Intersections Intersected* (digital recording), Michael Stevenson Gallery, Cape Town, 19 January 2008.

References

Azoulay, Ariella (2012), *Civil Imagination: The Political Ontology of Photography*, London: Verso.

Badsha, Omar (1985), *Imijondolo: A Photographic Essay on Forced Removals in South Africa*, Text by Heather Hughes. Durban: Afrapix.

Badsha, Omar (2001), *Imperial Ghetto: Ways of Seeing in a South African City*, Maroelana: South African History Online.

Badsha, Omar and Francis Wilson, eds (1986), *South Africa: The Cordoned Heart*, Prepared for the Second Carnegie Inquiry into Poverty and Development in Southern Africa, Cape Town: The Gallery Press.

Bal, Mieke (2013), *Endless Andness: The Politics of Abstraction according to Ann Veronica Janssens*, London: Bloomsbury Academic.

Belting, Hans (2011), *Anthropology of the Image*, Princeton: Princeton University Press.

Berger, John (1972), *Ways of Seeing*, London: British Broadcasting Corporation & Penguin.

Cadava, Eduardo (1997), *Words of Light: Theses on the Photography of History*, Princeton: Princeton University Press.

Debord, Guy (1977), *Society of the Spectacle*, Detroit: Black and Red.

Edwards, Elizabeth (1995), 'Jorma Puranen – Imaginary Homecoming' in *Social Identities* 08/1995; 1: 317–32.

Edwards, Elizabeth (2012), *The Camera as Historian: Amateur Photographers and Historical Imagination, 1885-1918*, London and Durham: Duke University Press.

Enwezor, Okwui (2006), *Snap Judgements: New positions in Contemporary African Photography*, New York: International Centre of Photography.

Enwezor, Okwui (2010), 'Photography after the end of documentary realism: Zwelethu Mthethwa's colour photographs', in Zwelethu Mthethwa (ed.), *Zwelethu Mthethwa*, 100–15, New York: Aperture.

Enwezor, Okwui and Rory Bester, eds (2012), *The Rise & Fall of Apartheid: The Bureaucracy of Everyday Life in South Africa*, New York: International Centre for Photography.

Garb, Tamar (2011), *Figures and Fictions: Contemporary South African Photography*, Göttingen: Steidl.

Godby, Michael (Spring/Summer 1999), 'The drama of colour: Zwelethu Mthethwa's portraits', *NKA: Journal of Contemporary African Art* 10: 46–9.

Goldblatt, David (1975), *Some Afrikaners Photographed*, Johannesburg: Murray Crawford.

Hayes, Patricia (November 2007), 'Power, secrecy, proximity: a short history of South African photography', *Kronos* 33: 139–62.

Hayes, Patricia (2011a), 'Seeing and being seen: politics, art and the everyday in the Durban photography of Omar Badsha, 1960s-1980s', *Africa*, 81 (4): 1–23.

Hayes, Patricia (June 2011b), 'The form of the norm: shades of gender in South African photography of the 1980s', *Social Dynamics*, 37 (2): 263–77.

Hayes, Patricia (2012), 'Unity & struggle', in Okwui Enwezor and Rory Bester (eds), *The Rise & Fall of Apartheid: The Bureaucracy of Everyday Life in South Africa*, 342–47, New York: International Centre for Photography.

Hayes, Patricia (2015 forthcoming), 'Okomboni: compound portraits and photographic archives in Namibia', in Christopher Morton and Darren Newbury (eds), *African Photographic Archives. Research and Curatorial Strategies*, 177–95, London: Bloomsbury.

Jay, Martin (1994), *Downcast Eyes: The Denigration of Vision in Twentieth-Century French Thought*, Berkeley: University of California Press.

Kentridge, William (1996–7), *Ubu Tells the Truth*, Johannesburg: William Kentridge Studio.

Kingston, Rebecca and Leonard Ferry, eds (2008), *Bringing the Passions Back in: The Emotions in Political Philosophy*, Vancouver: University of British Columbia Press.

Kracauer, Siegfried (1969), *History: The Last Things Before the Last*, Princeton: Markus Wiener Publishers.

Kracauer, Siegfried and Thomas Y. Levin (Spring 1993), 'Photography', *Critical Inquiry*, 19 (3): 421–36.

Liebenberg, John and Patricia Hayes (2010), *Bush of Ghosts: Life and War in Namibia 1986-1990*, Cape Town: Umuzi.

Mayekiso, Mzwanele (1996), *Township Politics: Civic Struggles for a New South Africa*, New York: Monthly Review Press.

Morris, Wright (1989), *Time Pieces: Photographs, Writing, and Memory*, New York: Aperture.

Peffer, John (2013), 'Together in the picture', in *Chronic* (published by *Chimurenga*), 19 April.

Reinhardt, Mark (2013), 'Theorizing the event of photography', *Theory and Event*, http://muse.jhu.edu/journals/theory_and_event/v016/16.3.reinhardt.html, 16 (3).

Rohde, Rick (1998), ' "How we see each other": subjectivity, photography and ethnographic revision', in Wolfram Hartmann, Jeremy Silvester and Patricia Hayes (eds), *The Colonising Camera: Photographs in the Making of Namibia History*, 188–204, Cape Town: University of Cape Town Press.

Sekula, Allan (1978), 'Dismantling modernism, reinventing documentary (notes on the politics of representation)', *The Massachussetts Review*, 19 (4): 859–83.

Sekula, Allan (1989), 'The body and the archive', in Richard Bolton (ed.), *The Contest of Meaning: Critical Histories of Photography*, 343–89, Cambridge, MA: The MIT Press.

Tagg, John (1988), *The Burden of Representation*, Minneapolis: University of Minnesota Press.

Taussig, Michael (2009), *What Color is the Sacred?* Chicago: University of Chicago Press.

Van Alphen, Ernst (2013), 'Explosions of information, implosions of meaning, and the release of affects', in Patricia Spyer and Mary Margaret Steedly (eds), *Images that Move*, 21–30, Santa Fe: School for Advanced Research Press.

Virilio, Paul (1994), *The Vision Machine*, Bloomington and Indianapolis: Indiana University Press.

Young, Iris Marion (2000), *Inclusion and Democracy*, Oxford: Oxford University Press.

Colour versions of these photographs can be found online at http://www.bloomsbury.com/uk/the-public-sphere-from-outside-the-west-9781350028340/

10

Ravi Varma's Many Publics: Circulation and the Status of the 'Artwork'

G. Arunima

Raja Ravi Varma is possibly India's first *public* artist, inasmuch as he was self-consciously concerned about creating a taste for art among his Indian contemporaries. Having said that, it is worth clarifying that speaking of 'public' art is not easy in an era when museums and galleries were first being established in India (as indeed in many parts of the world). For the most part, there's a general common sense that is fast becoming convention that public art, either permanent or temporary, is that which is 'commissioned for sites with open public access. These are located outside conventional [museological or private] locations and settings' (Zebracki et al. 2010, pp. 786–95).[1] This is despite the fact that Hilda Hein, philosopher and museum studies scholar, had, in the mid-nineties, expressed profound scepticism regarding this. In a short piece on the subject, she argues that

> strictly speaking, no art is private ... but neither does art become 'public' simply in virtue of its exposure and accessibility to the world. Publicity has social and political connotations that are untranslatable to public access. Conventionally, the term 'public art' refers to a family of conditions including the object's origin, history, location and social purpose. (Hein 1996, pp. 1–7)

Indeed, as she demonstrates, much of pre-Renaissance art in Europe, often seen as 'religious', was what would in contemporary terms be called 'public', inasmuch as it was often produced by collectivities and signified a common spirit. While modern notions of 'publicness' differ radically from the idea of spiritual unity, conveyed by medieval art, the problem that Hein raises is equally significant.

> [Instead] the concept of *a* public has become so problematized that putative works of public art demand justification in terms of qualitatively unrelated

analyses of public space, public ownership, public representation, public interest, and the public sphere. Rarely does a work satisfy in all these dimensions. (Hein 1996, p. 2)

Moreover, what is also at stake is the manner in which the audience is implicated within a work of art, as a participant, making the artwork 'inherently political' (be it revolutionary, or conservative, ideology) (Hein 1996, p. 3).

These positions point to different kinds of issues, all of which converge on the problem of conceptualizing the relationship between art and the public sphere. This chapter is an attempt to do so by engaging a body of Ravi Varma's artworks and thinking about these in relation to his art practice. Here the two bodies of paintings that I am concerned with are those pertaining to Indian mythology and the genre paintings of women that often utilized a portrait form.[2] Both these were also made available as chromolithographs.[3]

Art, artists and publics

Ravi Varma's self-conscious decision to make his art readily available via the medium of chromolithography requires serious thought. Coming out of the fine art tradition, he chose to publicize his work in a variety of ways. These included avenues that were just becoming available to the Indian artist – mainly, the art gallery (Bombay, Calcutta, Madras) and the art exhibition (the first ever exhibition in Trivandrum was one of Ravi Varma's paintings – see Venniyoor). However, he also took recourse to chromolithography, which enabled the creation of cheap multiple copies of his paintings. The fate of Ravi Varma's art was determined, interestingly enough, by this act of engaging with cross-class 'publics'. Revered in his lifetime by the art-viewing English-educated elite and the print-consuming masses alike, and denounced by the ideological triumvirate (Havell, Coomaraswamy and Nivedita) that set the aesthetic norms for the *swadeshi* artists, Ravi Varma's popularity continued unabated among the largely 'unschooled' Indian public. This was due, to a large extent, to the popularity of his portrait-based artistic style and academic naturalism that captured people's imagination.

Given the current state of art historical knowledge it is impossible to estimate either numbers or the composition of a gallery-viewing audience in late nineteenth-century India. However, lithographs (like other popular art products like the *bat-tala* prints) seemed to have a well-established market, and circulation, by this time. Ravi Varma's setting up of a lithographic press in Girgaum in 1892 (Thakurta, p. 95) then predictably brings to mind the question of art in the age of technological reproducibility (or mechanical reproduction, as in the earlier translations), the implications of which have been famously set out by Walter Benjamin and have since become part of art critical and historical dogma. Closer home, the *swadeshi* ideologues in their attempt to define an Indian aesthetic as one whose formal and conceptual essence would be rooted within an Indian tradition found both Ravi Varma's artwork and practice wanting. Even though it was Ravi Varma's academic naturalism that they considered condemnable, his lithographs too were denounced as a cheap device for ensuring easy popularity among the artistically untutored. The *swadeshi* argument seems curiously to be anticipating Adorno and Horkheimer's fears about the culture industry representing 'enlightenment as mass deception' (2002). Demarcating the boundaries of art, a problem that was intrinsic to the anxieties of high modernism, was obviously of concern to them too; here it was the ambivalent status of a painting as art once it had been rendered as lithograph that was of particular concern to them. I would suggest that this was because the high/low binary in relation to art is deeply implicated within, often unarticulated, notions of what constitutes an ideal audience or public. This in turn is often determined by contexts of circulation. Therefore, in such instances, it is not merely the technological manipulation of art (as in the case of lithographic proliferation) but the nature of the 'public' too that such 'manipulated art' reaches that determines the status of the 'artwork'.

Benjamin's argument about technological reproducibility[4] and its implications for unmooring photography from the 'auratic' constraints of art are too well known to require a detailed elaboration here. Briefly, he makes a case for the liberatory possibilities produced by technology in dislodging artwork from its conditions of production. In the context of painting, he suggests, this provided both the artwork and the artist with an exceptional status by emphasizing uniqueness and originality as essential prerequisites of both. The chromolithograph, a precursor and, for some time, contemporary of the photograph, however, has never received similar or serious artistic or theoretical reflection. My interest here is not to provide an assessment of the de/merits of the intermediate technological form. What I find more intriguing is Ravi Varma's championing of this form which in the context of the nineteenth century, I would suggest, is tantalizingly difficult to assess. This is because, at one level, you have an auto didactic artist in the colony, excited by naturalism and the academic realist form, looking for a way to popularize this. The now-known pedagogic impulse behind his desire notwithstanding (he wished to create a taste for art among the people), what is striking is that he wanted his work to reach a wider and undefined audience than it could have had his paintings been restricted to the gallery or to the private homes of the elite. Some of the new work on nineteenth-century art in India examines lithographic traditions in Maharashtra and demonstrates that the Ravi Varma Lithographic Press wasn't the earliest of its kind in the region (Pinney 2004). However, what is of significance is not so much the vintage of the press but this rather unusual route, indeed initiative, that the artist seems to have taken to circulate his work.

What we have here then is a 'modern' artist supremely unconcerned with, or possibly unaware of, what reproductions might do to the supposed 'auratic' properties of his artworks. What makes Ravi Varma quite unique for his time was his ability to simultaneously work in different capacities – as a commissioned artist, mostly for the elite across the country, and as a chromolithographic entrepreneur, making at least some of the same artwork available to a larger audience. In an important critique of Habermas's idea of the bourgeois public sphere, Oskar Negt and Alexander Kluge point to the neglect of plebeian and proletarian public spheres, a charge which Habermas subsequently acknowledged when he wrote that he realized that 'from the beginning a dominant bourgeois public collides with a plebeian one' and that he 'underestimated' the significance of oppositional and non-bourgeois public spheres (1993; Kellner 2002). In a sophisticated rethinking about publics and counter-publics, Michael Warner argues that a 'public is always in excess of its known social basis' (Warner 2002, pp. 49–90). While he focuses mainly on the literary public sphere, by examining texts across a broad historical spectrum, starting from the early modern period in Europe, he is concerned mostly with the foundational principles for understanding the idea of public(s). I wish here to develop his idea of the public sphere as a 'constitutive and normative environment of strangerhood' to think not merely about publics but, by extension, what implications this might have for artworks. A public in this sense is distinct both from community, as it is from class. In other words – as an 'environment of strangerhood' – it moves beyond the 'bourgeois'/'plebeian' dichotomy. By fore-fronting the centrality of circulation, especially of an artwork that as chromolithograph might reach people cutting across class, I would suggest that Ravi Varma managed to summon into existence different publics for his art. I shall explore further implications of this in the last section of this chapter.

Yet, if there are indeed oppositional 'public spheres', then the question of the circulation of the 'artwork', and its status as 'art' or otherwise, takes on a new dimension. In this light, it would be important to discuss not merely the abstract work of art, but the specific images that would possibly be affected by this circulation across different public spheres, as indeed the effect of the possible commodification of art or the likelihood of manipulative consumption and passivity that Adorno and Horkheimer so feared as the outcome of the culture industry.

Form and appeal

In the context of the curious history of Ravi Varma's artistic career, from reverence to revulsion, the issue of assessing the formal properties of his art becomes particularly relevant. This was because the denunciation of Ravi Varma's work by the *swadeshi* ideologues, in deriding the 'western' influence of naturalism on his art, were not merely drawing attention to his 'un-Indianness'; it was also a critique of the form itself. In addition, despite the formal influence of naturalism, Ravi Varma's subject matter varied quite a lot – from portraits to more genre paintings of women and Hindu mythology. However, despite this, most art historical writing tends to treat his work as homogenous and undifferentiated. An exception here is Tapati Guha Thakurta, and her early essay on women and calendar art has a detailed examination of a large body of Ravi Varma's genre paintings of women (see Thakurta). Nevertheless, despite her nuanced iconographic reading, she suggests that there is something intrinsic to the 'combined core of religious/mythic/feminine imagery in Ravi Varma's paintings' that fed into an art critical and aesthetic opinion in Bengal that was responsible in producing a 'middle class cultural hegemony' (Thakurta 1991, p. 94). Yet, she also says that the formal aspects of his work (naturalist, academic realist) held within it an ability to 'produce mass appeal' (ibid.). What makes Guha Thakurta's argument interesting is that she does not focus excessively on the chromolithograph as a debased form, which would 'naturally' appeal to the masses. Instead, she suggests that it was the form, and naturalism, that held appeal across the board at this particular juncture, especially within the art critical circles in colonial Bengal, which accounted for Ravi Varma's popularity. While art historically she is right in marking this moment, as indeed the later aesthetic shift that would denounce precisely this form as 'un-Indian', I would suggest that the reasons for naturalism's appeal need to be unpacked much further.

Of women and Gods

The story of Ravi Varma's painting and chromolithography is one in which both women and gods loom large on the canvas. That the artist taught himself how to draw by copying European academic realists, especially the French history painters Boulanger and Bouguereau, is now the stuff of art-historical lore.[5] Yet, it's worth bearing in mind that as history painting, and realism, in Europe was varied, across artists, genres, subject matters and impulses, so was it in Ravi Varma's own work. This is particularly apparent when one looks at the formal differences in the artist's paintings of women. I would argue that if one were to treat these paintings as heterogeneous, where the significations and communications of the works shift in relation to space, contexts and publics, then it would be possible to revaluate Ravi Varma's work within a far more nuanced understanding of art rather than within a restrictive reading of what constitutes an ideal Indian aesthetic. In part, this is to move away from current normative practices of art history and criticism, which despite recognizing the *swadeshi* argument as a particular (albeit-definitive) moment within a discussion on defining an Indian aesthetic appears to echo its anti-naturalist premises. If the charge against Ravi Varma was that of being derivative, well then so was the Bengal school. The only difference was that now 'Indian' artistic traditions (and post-Okakura, Asian generally) became the resources with which to refashion the new aesthetic. Therefore, it ought to be possible to have a discussion on Ravi Varma's work without subjecting it to the indigenist *swadeshi* critique (and some of the contemporary revival, and interest, in Ravi Varma clearly stems from such an impulse).

Elsewhere I have argued that Ravi Varma was so closely associated with the genre of portraiture that it was almost akin to his signature (2003). What is equally significant here is that the bulk of the subject matter of his portraits (and portrait-based paintings) was that of women who, through his repetitive manipulation of the image, came to allegorize the nation. Ravi Varma's 'representational dilemma',[6] in many ways, was to find the perfect face and body, and finally we find him settling for a feminine figure that exuded an aura of wealth, leisure and, significantly, sensuousness. Ravi Varma's India(n)/woman was conceived within an erotic, luminescent imaginary; his self-trained hand, often lacking in perfect geometry, or exact dimensions or proportion, still managed to celebrate women's voluptuous corporeality. Even a wistful Damayanti[7] or a despairing Draupadi[8] was visualized as buxom, bountiful and, ultimately, desirable. I would suggest that perhaps it was the circulation, and immediate popularity, of such an image of womanly desirability that invoked the self-righteous wrath of the *swadeshi* artists of Bengal, whose India (and womanhood) was idealized within an aesthetic of austerity.[9]

Equations between women and the nation or depicting land as woman are not unusual. In India, the Bengal school, and by the 1930s Amrita Shergill, would do precisely this, albeit with great stylistic variation and, indeed, aesthetic emphasis. This is a trend that would become popular in many parts of the world – early twentieth-century Irish nationalist art was replete with realist portrayals of the putative nation as woman (see Martin 2003). However, Ravi Varma was one of the earliest Indian artists, especially of the colonial period, who feminized his canvas as much and in the manner in which he did. I would argue that the 'India' of his canvas is far more a geographical notion, self-professedly devoted to depicting ethnic diversity, rather than its more modern, twentieth-century, geopolitical variant.[10] Equally, by invoking a sensuous womanhood on canvas, he not merely gave subjectivity to those who were conventionally excluded from the emergent Indian public sphere, he also created new modes of desire. The circulation of his lithographs widened the possibility for women's appropriation, and refashioning, of this subjectivity. This is the reason why, despite the *swadeshi* critique, Ravi Varma's images have had a long and enduring life. Ironically, it's the afterlife, and circulation, of his women that have provided the space for the contemporary reclaiming of the artist himself, making us rethink, once again, the relationship between art and its public(s).

Ravi Varma's unselfconscious pastiche allowed him to recast his Indian models along the lines of European women idealized by academic realist art. It also permitted him to humanize his gods and goddesses in a manner that was inconceivable to the Bengal school, who felt that it was precisely this stylistic democratization of his naturalism that eroded art of its spiritual essence. However, for the consumers of his devotional themes, Ravi Varma had made heaven appear intelligible and palpable, but, perhaps far more importantly, at hand, and readily available.

Sites of circulation

The circulation of the chromolithographs is therefore both about the image and its afterlife; the artwork's heterogeneity is thus simultaneously determined by its formal properties and by its circulation within diverse spaces and differing publics.

In a recent argument, Kajri Jain states that

> the moment of iconic perception of the gaze, and the icon-as-object dissolves in the immanence of the subject, god. Unlike the cult object of (Walter) Benjamin, an essential aspect of the icon is its visibility, its availability for darshan (seeing or being in the presence of the holy), and the elimination of distance between the viewer/devotee and both the form and the substance of the icon, all of which are ultimately the same thing. (Jain 2007, pp. 57–89)[11]

If one were to extend this reading to Ravi Varma's lithographs, particularly of gods, one encounters a moment of, possibly unintended, radicalism in the colonial Indian context. Venniyoor's biography claims that

> the popularity which these pictures gained among the people led to the establishment by the artist at his own expense of a Lithographic Press in Bombay for the purpose of printing his works in colours and placing them within the reach of the masses. By this means he could create among his fellow subjects a love for the fine arts, and nothing he thought would appeal to their feelings and emotion so much as religious and mythological subjects with which they are so familiar. (Quoted in Venniyoor)

Potentially, then, Hindus across caste could own Ravi Varma's lithographs. In a period where untouchability was the order of the day and temple entry forbidden to most of the lower castes, such access to divinity certainly possessed an immense transformatory potential. Equally, the lithograph enabled people across class to not merely see and develop 'a love for the fine arts' but also touch and possess something that would hitherto have been out of their reach. The immense popularity of Ravi Varma's paintings and the retention of his imagery within popular memory were also to do with the democratizing possibility of this technology.

Christopher Pinney makes a similar argument for Dalit groups in central India (Bhatisuda, Madhya Pradesh) in the contemporary period (see Pinney 2004). On the basis of a detailed examination of deities, patterns of worship and faith practices, he argues for a 'corpothetical' approach where the eye (and by extension vision itself) becomes a way of binding the devotee with the chromolithographized icon. This is an idea he develops through a reading of Michael Taussig's important work *Mimesis and Alterity*. Here Taussig elaborates the importance of the symbolic, and the sensuous, in the context of

Cuna Indian shamanism through a detour through Benjamin (and Adorno and Horkheimer). In doing so, he argues against the primacy given to Enlightenment rationality but makes a case for image-based, 'sensuous' communication that exists as an alternative to language. More recently, however, Mark Paterson, in an attempt to elaborate the 'archaeology of the "technologies of touch" – or the haptic – makes a case for rethinking the importance of tactility' (2007). I would agree that there is something particular about 'touch', especially in a world where both people and deities have been deemed 'untouchable' and, indeed, 'unseeable'. In the nineteenth century, the availability of lithographs would have enabled the then 'untouchable' castes to not merely touch but also to 'possess' gods.

It is here that I wish to refine the idea about 'darshan' that is central to both Jain and Pinney's arguments. They suggest that the centrality of seeing, and being seen, is integral to the idea of 'darshan', and that the notional locking of gazes enabled within the interocular space of a temple precinct is what both endows the encounter with spiritual meaning and also transforms the meaning of 'audience' itself. While I agree that within certain contexts of Hindu worship seeing (and being seen) can certainly have such a spiritual connotation, it is still worth remembering that no temple gives any worshipper, barring a few Brahmin priests, access to the inner sanctum sanctorum, or indeed the idol itself. This is true even for the castes who had hitherto been permitted some entry into the temples, and it continues to be the same even today. Therefore, within the context of temple-based worship, all 'seeing' then is notional. More recently, in a gesture that is both unconscious and therefore ironic, many temples have begun to hang chromolithographic reproductions of their idols outside the inner sanctum, thereby endowing these with divine power. However, what it makes explicit is the inaccessibility, as object of viewing or possession, of God to the ordinary worshipper. Yet devotees throng temples to get a glimpse of gods at appointed times when the shrine doors are 'opened'. This sighting is always conditional on the specificity of this temporality – of the opening of doors – and is meant to provide specific spiritual benefits. Yet, it is perfectly possible to worship without this witnessing, as is attested to by the fact that most temple visits by devotees occur outside the very small windows of 'darshanic' opportunity. The tactile, and in this case the possibility of touching and possessing the chromolithographic images of gods, then begins to acquire meaning because it also implies the possibility of a very different mode of worship within private and domestic contexts.

The importance of tactility needs also to be read alongside another vector – the materiality of the chromolithographs. In an important intervention in the theoretical discussions on photography, Elizabeth Edwards and Janice Hart argue about the need to see photographs not simply as images but also as physical objects.

> Photographs are both images *and* physical objects that exist in time and space and thus in social and cultural experience. They have 'volume, opacity, tactility and a physical presence in the world' (Batchen 1997, p. 2) and are thus enmeshed with subjective, embodied and sensuous interactions. (Edwards and Hart 2004, p. 1)

Lithographs too can be said to have similar properties. And indeed in the case of the Ravi Varma images, both of gods and women, which have had such a long afterlife in India, quite often these lithographs become objects of display in the homes of poor and ordinary people. What is significant here is that these occupy the same space as a body of other 'display' objects – from calendars, with pictures not necessarily of gods (see Uberoi), to personal photographs and other memorabilia. The possibility of such a democratic, and horizontal, sharing of space is undoubtedly a result of their materiality and 'objectness'. Here their value appears to lie, at least equally, in their being available for ownership, possession and display, as in the particularity of their image content.

The lithograph then is not merely a cheaper, reproducible and printable version of the 'artwork'. It possesses within it, precisely because of these qualities, the possibility to destabilize the work of art. In a recent argument on contemporary popular and installation art, Yashodhara Dalmia looks at the way in which artists across the world have parodied the status of the 'work of art' and blurred the boundaries between the gallery and public spaces and between the spectator and the object (Dalmia 2002). The lithograph and its reproducibility then was the first moment in the destruction of the idea of the 'work of art'. Its availability, across publics, meant a constant invitation for a participation in the invention of its meaning and significance.

In the case of Ravi Varma, it is these different publics, sites of circulations, modalities of possession, patterns of display and meaning making that have kept him alive in national memory. Indeed, he is the one artist who is seen as infinitely reproducible – an act that only enhances his value in the popular mind. The cheapness and cross-class availability of the Ravi Varma images pose serious questions to the manner in which discussions on 'art' are still loath to cut themselves free of the exclusivity of gallery curating and market valuation. They also remind us of the urgency with which circulation and publics need to be factored into discussions of art, its value and indeed aesthetics itself.

Notes

1 The piece by Zebracki, Van Der Vaart and Van Aalst is a good example of this.
2 As this discussion is not iconographical, in the conventional art historical sense, I shall simply provide hyperlinks to a few of the better-known examples of both these genres, most of which are now available in the public domain, including on the internet.
3 In his 1992 essay, Pinney retained the older term oleograph for these.
4 Howard Caygill proposes 'technological reproducibility' as a more accurate translation of the original German usage.
5 Both the early biography of the artist in Malayalam and Venniyoor's authoritative text attest to stylistic influences on the artist.
6 This is the phrase used by Geeta Kapur to unpack Ravi Varma's aesthetic choices and painterly strategies.
7 http://www.indiapicks.com/Indianart/Images/R_Varma_Hansa_Damayanti.jpg.
8 http://wiki.phalkefactory.net/index.php?title=Image:Ravi_Varma-Draupadi_carrying_milk_honey.jpg.
9 See for instance Abanindranath's *Bharat Mata*. http://www.artofbengal.com/abanindranath.JPG.
10 G. Arunima, 'Raja Ravi Varma and the Vision of "Modern India"', unpublished paper, presented at the Tenth International Conference of the Forum on Contemporary Theory, Baroda, on 'Thinking Territory: Affect and Attachment towards Land in South Asia', December 2007.
11 This argument has been elaborated in Jain, 2007.

References

Arunima, G. (2003), 'Face Value: Ravi Varma's Portraiture and the Project of Colonial Modernity', *The Indian Economic and Social History Review* 40: 1.
Benjamin, W. (1969), *Illuminations: Essays and Reflections*, New York: Schocken, pp. 217–52.
Caygill, H. (1998), *Walter Benjamin: The Colour of Experience*, London: Routledge.
Dalmia, Y., ed. (2002), *Contemporary Indian Art: Other Realities*, vol. 53, Marg Publications.

Edwards, E. and Hart, J., eds (2004), *Photographs, Objects, Histories: On the Materiality of Images*, New York: Routledge.

Hein, H. (Winter 1996), 'What is Public Art? Time, Place and Meaning', *The Journal of Aesthetics and Art Criticism*, 54 (1): 1–7.

Horkheimer, M. and Adorno, T. W. (2002), *Dialectic of Enlightenment*, trans. Edmund Jephcott, Stanford, CA: Stanford University Press.

Jain, K. (1992), 'Of the every-day and the "National Pencil": Calendars in Post-Colonial India', *Journal of Arts and Ideas*, 27–28: 57–89.

Jain, K. (2007), *Gods in the Bazaar; the Economies of Calendar Art*, Durham: Duke University Press.

Kapur, G. (August 1989), 'Ravi Varma: Representational Dilemmas of a Nineteenth Century Indian Painter', *Occasional Papers on History and Society*, New Delhi: Nehru Memorial Museum and Library.

Kellner, D. (2014), 'Habermas, the Public Sphere, and Democracy: A Critical Intervention', viewed 30 April 2014.

Martin, E. F. (Spring 2003), 'Painting the Irish West: Nationalism and the Representation of Women', *New Hibernia Review*, 7 (1): 31–44.

Paterson, M. (2007), *Senses of Touch: Haptics, Affects and Technologies*, Oxford: Berg.

Pinney, C. (Autumn 1992), 'The Iconology of Hindu Oleographs: Linear and Mythic Narrative in Popular Indian Art', *Anthropology and Aesthetics*, 22: 33–61.

Pinney, C. (2004), *'The Photos of the Gods': The Printed Image and Political Struggle in India*, London: Reaktion Books.

Taussig, M. (1993), *Mimesis and Alterity: A Particular History of the Senses*, New York: Routledge.

Thakurta, T. G. (1991), 'Women as' calendar art' icons: Emergence of pictorial stereotype in colonial India', *Economic and Political Weekly*, 91–9.

Uberoi, P. (28 April 1990), 'Feminine Identity and National Ethos in Indian Calendar Art'. *Economic and Political Weekly*, 25 (17): 41–8.

Venniyoor, E. M. J. (1981), *Raja Ravi Varma*, Trivandrum: Government of Kerala.

Zebracki, M., Vaart, R. V. D. and Aalst, I. V. (2010), 'Deconstructing Public Artopia: Situating Public Art Claims within Practice', *Geoforum*, 41: 786–95. http://pages.gseis.ucla.edu/faculty/kellner/papers/habermas.htm.

11

Personal Convictions, Public Performance: Representing Anna Hazare

Christel Rashmi Devadawson

It is exciting to study pictorial satire on the subject of Anna Hazare's 2011 public protest in Delhi against the Lokpal bill because it reconfigures paradigms of thought concerning public space. This chapter studies graphic protest primarily but not exclusively from the *Hindustan Times* (Delhi edition) through August 2011. This newspaper is a useful starting point for any study of popular culture in contemporary Delhi because it is the English daily with the widest circulation.[1] I will try to contextualize the study of these images with reference to the development of the 'saintly' tradition in Indian politics. This tradition makes it possible to interrogate the way in which individuals who apparently renounce the world actually use their personal charisma to alter processes, institutions and the public sphere that contains both. Such a relationship between personality and process usually develops with great intensity during a period of crisis, spontaneous or simulated. Public crisis in its turn is unfailingly the subject of numerous representations across multiple media. These include print and television journalism, live performance and social media networks. In such a world, graphic satire in the form of political caricature and comic strips occupies a contested space. On the one hand, the commentary offered by pictorial dissent on popular protest helps us develop our understanding of a range of issues. These include collaboration and resistance in mass mobilization, the traffic of images across media that redefine the dialogue between the personal and the political, and the visual conversations that take place among various constituencies. On the other hand, pictorial satire interrogates resistance movements with at least as much scepticism as it reserves for the institutions they protest. I will outline some of the literary and theoretical contexts that frame the visual texts and then analyse specific pictorial representations.

Performativity and the saintly tradition

The pioneering depiction in modern times of the relationship between the ascetic and the public sphere in India appears in an 1895 short story by Rudyard Kipling entitled 'The Miracle of Purun Bhagat'. In this story, Purun Das, a gifted and public-spirited prime minister of a princely state, announces his retirement at the height of his fame. 'He had used his wealth and his power for what he knew both to be worth; he had taken honour when it came his way; he had seen men and cities far and near and men and cities had stood up and honoured him. Now he would let these things go, as a man drops the cloak he no longer needs' (Kipling 1937, p. 326). Purun Das renounces his life as the chief public servant of his state to pursue a personal quest for enlightenment. He remains true to his mission for many years. An onrushing landslide, however, leads him to save the villagers who honour him as a saint. Having now refashioned himself as Purun Bhagat, he realizes that he needs to return to the world of action to organize their rapid evacuation from their village lest they die. He does this successfully, at the cost of no life other than his own. In the process, however, he comes to wonder whether he has obeyed the dictates of the *Bhagavad Gita* in undertaking an appropriate course of action. This issue perplexes Purun Bhagat, particularly when he reverts briefly to his earlier efficient self as a paragon of administrative efficiency and zeal. 'He was no holy man, but Sir Purun Das, KCIE, Prime Minister of no small State, a man accustomed to command, going out to save life' (Kipling 1937, p. 338). Indeed, he wonders whether he has lost the singleness of purpose that led him to set aside the world of affairs and choose the path of renunciation. The use of litotes – the figure of speech intended to carry dramatic emphasis – suggests the intensity of this debate. What constitutes appropriate action for one who has given up the world? If Purun Bhagat continues to believe in his identity as a public servant, he acts according to the expectations of his office. In that case, he can scarcely describe himself as an ascetic. If he believes himself to be a recluse, it would seem that his attachment to the homely devotion and affection of his village community runs dangerously deep. Kipling encodes many allusions to the *Bhagavad Gita* that centre on this issue. His resolution of the short story comes close to the classic formulation of the *Bhagavad Gita*.

   'Performing the duty prescribed by nature, one does not incur sin ... one should not abandon a natural duty though tainted with evil; for all actions are enveloped by evil, as fire by smoke. One who is self-restrained, whose understanding is unattached everywhere, from whom affections have departed, obtains the supreme perfection of freedom from action by renunciation' (Telang 1882, p. 127).[2]

Kipling's Purun Bhagat remains the fictional prototype – in literature about India – of the public figure who renounces the world of action only to intervene in it when duty calls. Unimpeachable integrity, iconic success in the material world and a strong commitment to the world of the spirit thus become features that the popular imagination associates with such a hero. All this is unquestionable. What continues to be debatable, however, is the definition of 'appropriate' action. Should the ascetic return – for however noble a purpose – to the public sphere, with what powers will the popular mind credit him? On what terms will such a stellar figure orchestrate public re-enactments of private conviction? More disturbingly, what will be the impact of such a return on the politics of popular culture?

Received wisdom on the subject usually enters a caveat on the dangerous durability of urban myths that develop around movements alternating between intervention and renunciation. Indeed, a common caution on the subject warns readers that, 'like snails, myths slither through the history of mankind safely protected by their shells' (Balbu 1976, p. 49). The slime of pestilence coheres around such urban myths, their characters and their narration. Nonetheless, if we are to understand the evolution of participatory democracy in present-day India, we need to study the alternating rhythms of asceticism and interventionism in the world of popular politics.

Contemporary political theory about democracy in India is usually wary of the impact of such personal appeal on the world of political and social process. The following analysis is a typical comment on the impact of a charismatic individual on a relatively fragile and developing democracy such as that of India. It makes its point through angry irony.

> The Sarvodaya ideology which inspired the Vinoba (and later Jaya Prakash) mission is somewhat easily stated. The law does not act on conscience, being an insignia of state coercion. The way of state coercion is not the way of social transformation … [Hence] the task of [social] conversion must lie only with charismatic figures, who have shunned political power, who are gifted with the 'grace of god,' and are prepared for martyrdom in pursuit of a noble cause. (Baxi 1990, p. 111)

The politics of personal conviction might seek to bring about social reform, but the price paid for such a movement is high. When people see a division between state rule and the individual conscience, and believe that only the latter can effect social improvement, they prioritize the individual conscience above state rule. At such a point, the individual conscience is likely to be every whit as coercive as any form of state authority. What, however, of the popular practice that seeks to domicile itself within this theory? How do diverse modes of representation depict the movement? These and other related issues make more sense when we turn from context to text – in this case, a cross-section of visual texts that comment on the crusade led by Anna Hazare.

The most obvious characteristic of pictorial satire on the subject is that it draws the reader's attention to the performativity quotient of Hazare's movement. It reminds the reader that Hazare's agitation is a carefully choreographed performance. To begin with, it uses intertextual references to place the movement in the context of other, less exalted, public shows. This comes across vividly in an early representation by Jayanto (Figure 11.1). Jayanto distorts the figure of Hazare, so that it appears with a hugely swollen head, and a puny body to declare 'I accuse you of betraying the nation's trust, dashing our hopes, and bringing shame to all Indians …!'[3] The strident tones of this rant appear as part of the paraphernalia of public protest. Other belongings on display include a token mat, a glass of water to support Hazare through his fast and a manifesto that he clutches in his left hand. Physiognomic distortion indicates reduction

Figure 11.1 Jayanto, *Hindustan Times*, 14 August 2011.

by size, perhaps the most common of ploys in the world of political caricature. Indeed, Jayanto's cartoon contains one of the first principles of the grammar of graphic satire. When graphic dissent literalizes metaphor, it uses a visual image to illustrate a linguistic figure of speech with which the popular imagination is already familiar. A somewhat dated summary sets out this fundamental premise. 'It is the strength and the danger of the cartoonist that he appeals to this tendency and makes it easier for us to treat abstractions as if they were tangible realities. The cartoonist, in other words, merely secures what language has prepared' (Gombrich 1971, p. 128). In Jayanto's illustration, the swollen head is an attempt by the graphic artist to literalize and thus overstate the verbal metaphor that usually indicates conceit. Conversely, the shrunken trunk and limbs indicate that – beneath the inflated public persona – the movement has no real body or substance to it.

The response to Hazare's diatribe comes from a snatch of conversation between two tiny commentators who stand beside him. One of these, in the manner of a television reporter eager for a 'Breaking News' scoop, extends a microphone towards Hazare and asks eagerly, 'He means the government?' His more blasé interlocutor standing behind him replies, 'No, the Indian cricket team!' Unlike Hazare's speech, that hits the reader with the force of a direct address, two speech bubbles contain the observations of the commentators. This representational tool enables the cartoonist to give the protagonist the privilege and authority to address the reader directly, while he places the remarks of characters on the fringe at one remove from the reader and from visual reality. At the same time, Jayanto inflates the central character only to deflate him almost at once. Television journalists might hang on every utterance by Hazare to boost channel ratings, even if an anti-government tirade seems a twice-told tale to most viewers. The cartoonist, however, gives us a Hazare figure whose concern is with the dismal overseas performance of the Indian cricket team. During the months of July, August and September in 2011, England defeated India comprehensively in all forms of the game.[4] Jayanto's illustration belongs to the middle phase of this unfolding debacle. It reminds his readers of what the future might hold for both kinds of public spectacle. The cartoon does not merely downplay Team Anna by suggesting that it may be looking at a loss as total as anything experienced by the cricket squad. It also suggests that both Team Anna and the Indian team are perhaps only enacting scripts with which they are already familiar in rehearsal. If this were not the case, there could scarcely be any grounds for conversation between the two.

Graphic protest and the politics of visuality

Pictorial protest also signals the sense in which – in a political culture that revels in performance – Hazare's agitation is just one among many shows. Jayanto looks back on Independence Day 2011 with a deliberately ironic deployment of colour (Figure 11.2).[5] The backdrop is awash with saffron, but a bright white light beats down on two figures in the centre of the cartoon. Amitabh Bachchan, as anchor of season 3 of *Kaun Banega Crorepati* (the Indian version of *Who Wants to Be a Millionaire?*), is a sorry travesty of his former self. The 'angry young man' of the nineteen-seventies is now an ageing figure with coloured hair, a white goatee and ridiculously flared bell-bottomed trousers. As he hunches himself over his laptop, he asks the clinching question, 'Kaun kaun bana hai crorepati?' (Who are those who have become millionaires?). Bachchan's question parodies the patter of the conventional quizmaster. By asking for the identity of the beneficiaries, the questioner also alludes to the endemic nature of corruption in public life in India, against which Hazare launched his campaign. Across from Bachchan sits his celebrity guest for the evening, Anna Hazare. The splash of green beneath their feet completes the colour-coded reference to the Indian tricolour. Jayanto repeats the earlier distortion of a head significantly larger than its torso, with a notable difference. In the earlier cartoon, dismay is writ large on the puffy

Figure 11.2 Jayanto, *Hindustan Times*, 16 August 2011.

cheeks of the reformer, whose zeal leads him to address the reader directly. In this later panel, the crusader closes his eyes in sanctimonious satisfaction. He replies unctuously, 'Sabko lock kiya jaye!' Hazare's pun alludes to the query that the KBC host routinely makes before he seeks the participant's confirmation. In the standard KBC format, the host asks, 'Lock kiya jaye?' ('Shall I lock your answer?'). He then adjures the computer, 'Lock karo,' (colloquially, 'Freeze that answer!'). After this, participants cannot change their reply. In Jayanto's representation, however, Hazare answers Bachchan's question by insisting that all are corrupt and should face imprisonment.

Two visual details, however, make Hazare's indictment of Indian political culture less telling than his supporters might wish. Neither Bachchan nor Hazare looks the reader in the eye. Bachchan casts his eyes down as he looks down at the keyboard through the lenses of his spectacles. Such a glance ensures that Jayanto's Bachchan engages neither with his guest nor with the reader. Jayanto's Hazare keeps his eyes tightly shut. Even while he clutches the manifesto entitled 'Fast' in his left hand, and waggles an admonitory right forefinger, he does not connect either with his host or with the reader. The facial creases on Jayanto's Bachchan suggest the weariness of an old roué. Simultaneously, Jayanto's Hazare – his eyes shut tight lest they see the wickedness of the world – suggests the moral fatigue of an all-too saintly confessor. Engrossed as they are in their self-fashioning, the characters choose not to see anything beyond their carefully constructed selves. This refusal to look past the self suggests two related issues. Both Bachchan and Hazare seem to insulate themselves from the world of the reader, to play their part with the perfection they think it deserves. Hazare – as much as Bachchan – sees himself as a performer or actor before the masses, rather than a leader who identifies with their cause and rallies them in the name of a crusade larger than themselves.

The other visual detail that gives the show away, literally and otherwise, is Jayanto's use of colour. When we see a panel of pictorial protest that uses the three shades of the tricolour immediately following Independence Day, we might expect it to be sceptical about the national idea. Certainly, the concept of a nation state that celebrates its independence by becoming a televised show for home entertainment carries this charge of criticism. Equally, however, Jayanto ensures that the triple-coloured limelight beats down unsparingly on Bachchan and Hazare. This suggests that they are as much a part of the show as is anyone else. The show and its showmen alike fly the flag in front of the whole nation. Jayanto's Hazare comes across as being a part of the national project that he criticizes. He is also a showman, an actor who is complacent about his own performance. Like Bachchan, he seems to have eyes for nothing beyond the role he plays.

Both panels of graphic dissent review Hazare's crusade ironically. Their use of physiognomic reductionism reminds readers of the way in which the performer bulks more largely in his mind than does his movement. By underscoring the idea of crusade as performance, they remind their readers that what appears spontaneous is actually a carefully rehearsed sequence of events. A rehearsal presupposes a script, written by a team that does not necessarily appear itself. Instead, it sends its star actor to go through the motions before the audience. Spontaneity on the part of the players gives way to the great moment that needs careful orchestration. In both cases – the interview with two media persons and the opening question on KBC – the grand climax takes the form of a sound bite for television. If indeed corruption is endemic, it needs a stronger check on it than performance alone.

Perhaps because Jayanto is one of the few graphic satirists to play the role of an illustrator as well, each panel tells its own story. Pictorial protest does not often carry a narrative charge. For one thing, its panels focus on specific issues in an episodic manner. For another, satire sometimes loses its cutting edge to the need to tell a story. Jayanto however, risks the combination of fiction and dissent. He also manages to use colour as an instrument of critique, not merely as a means to carry the storyline forward. There is a slight lowering of dramatic temperature, however, when Jayanto uses caricature. His attention to physiognomic detail is less close than the care he takes over setting, gesture and conversation. Jayanto's parodic Bachchan works well. However, the Hazare figure (particularly as the campaign fades from public memory) is more likely to come across as the generic Indian politician, whom the popular imagination sees as the epitome of corruption. To purists, weakness of line in caricature – particularly when it leads to blurring or transposition of identities – is unforgivable.[6] In Jayanto's case, though, the title of his panel, 'tooning in', suggests the possibility that real figures mingle with animated cartoon characters on the same plane of reality.[7] Toons and people share space on identical terms. Jayanto's pictorial dissent suggests multiple ways to construct and deconstruct political and cultural identity. Do people become toons when they become creatures of political ideology? How do we, as readers, need to understand their role-playing? Are toons more or less alive than are human beings? The underlying significance of these apparently different questions is the same. Pictorial dissent does not only remind us that performance has its own codes and protocols. It also makes out a case for its own kind of truth claims. The idea for instance that Jayanto's Hazare looks all too like the archetypal dishonest politician, in Gandhi cap, spectacles and dhoti kurta, is a telling comment on the way in which the campaign against corruption bears investigation itself. Otherwise, toon and human being would not need to resemble each other so closely.

Pictorial protest manages to remain consistently sceptical towards the Hazare campaign and towards the opponents of the crusade as well. Shreyas Navare, whose column for the print and website versions of the *Hindustan Times* carries the title 'Dabs and Jabs', also assigns a content-specific caption to each panel. His panel 'big deal' responds to Rahul Gandhi's intervention in the stand-off between Team Anna and the central government[8] (Figure 11.3). Navare reworks the circus – an image that he often uses to analyse contemporary politics – for the purpose. He divides the panel into a conversation between two figures. Navare's India is a young man in a blue T-shirt, black jeans and floaters. When we see him, he is in free fall. This is an interesting visualization of the demographics of the Hazare crusade because the majority of its supporters in Delhi were young, literate and urban. Navare's India looks a little like Jughead Jones from the series of *Archie* comic books, except that he lacks Jughead's crown. High above the clouds, he perspires angrily as he holds out a yellow handbill that screams out 'Wanted' through its caption. The handbill features a paratrooper with the label 'Jan Lokpal' who has his parachute open.

Figure 11.3 Shreyas Navare, *Hindustan Times*, 27 August 2011.

In conversation with the India character is Navare's Rahul Gandhi, who wears his standard white kurta pyjama suit with white sneakers. He also wears a white dunce cap with an orange pompom and has a green trooper's backpack strapped onto him. Clearly, there is more than one way to fly the national colours. He carries a couple of yellow and orange party balloons in his right hand and dangles a teddy bear from his left. The stuffed toy is the only one in free fall who looks petrified. Though the teddy bear wears a Gandhi cap, the resemblance to politicians appears generic rather than specific. Its physical features do not mimic either those of Hazare or his opponents. Navare's India, though young – as his clothes and actions suggest – is not juvenile. Navare's Rahul, however – as the markers of party balloons, clown cap and teddy bear suggest – seems immature. A speech bubble encloses words that underscore adolescence: 'Lucky you that I'm *so* clever!' The speech within the bubble, in its callow colloquialism, may be infantile. A newspaper sheet that lies along the by-line, however, carries the headline that details the offer. This is that the government should assign the Lokpal or national ombudsman a status comparable to that of the Election Commission. Matters have come to such a pass that a negotiator who drops into the crisis in the guise of a circus-artiste gets a hearing. As always, however, Navare leaves the last word to his mascot. This takes the form of a donkey in the lower right corner of the frame who barks out his views. In this case, the donkey yelps, 'I'm *not* Rahul!' This alludes to the saying 'I am Anna' that many people sported as a slogan on their clothes or headgear during the campaign to show their solidarity with Hazare.

By using the image of the circus, Navare distances himself from both sides. He ensures that his readers get a chance to understand the construction of identity on both sides of the ideological divide. At the same time, he ensures that his readers understand clearly that they are spectators and not performers themselves. The circus is a spectacle that depends on meticulous training, rehearsal, timing, colour and skill. Not for a moment need we believe it to be spontaneous or unplanned. It has to do with the painstaking construction of identity to stage a spectacle that is profitable for the organizers and enjoyable for the spectators. Moreover, circus always has a safety net for its performers, whether or not this is visible to its spectators. We need to consider what the equivalent might be in the domain of populist politics.

Finally, Navare makes his critical distance apparent by having the mascot yap his tagline. On the one hand, he is careful to stand aside from Rahul Gandhi's point of view by the remark, 'I'm *not* Rahul!' In a more circumspect way, Navare is also careful to remind the reader that he views the Hazare camp with some criticism. The tagline alludes to the comment in Marathi, 'Me Anna ahé' (in English, 'I am Anna'), that Hazare's supporters wore on their headgear and dress to demonstrate their solidarity with their leader. Whether the caricature inscribes its convictions on its heart is debatable, but it certainly does not wear them on its sleeve. That belongs to the spectacle of populist politics.

The construction of identity

The relationship between the construction of identity and its representation in pictorial satire is a complicated issue. Graphic protest can sometimes read like a palimpsest. A layer of irony might well inscribe itself upon another. At times, it obliterates the one beneath and at others draws attention to it in surprising ways. A good example of this is the panel by Vishwajyoti Ghosh that accompanies the column 'Red Herring' by Indrajit Hazra. Hazra's article carries the subtitle, 'Anna horribilis'[9] (Figure 11.4). Hazra analyses the support that the

Figure 11.4 Vishwajyoti Ghosh, *Hindustan Times*, 21 August 2011.

crusade seems to attract across the political spectrum. He wryly recognizes that 'this mob is ideologically blind'.[10] He cautions that there is a huge gap between the stated, if limited, goals of Hazare's crusade and a revolution as far-reaching as that of 1789. Hazra reminds his readers that many who follow Hazare enlarge their own significance by fashioning themselves as latter-day Robespierres. Hazra concludes, 'Silly, self-righteous but effective Anna isn't storming the Bastille. He just walked out of Tihar.'[11] Ghosh's panel with the series title 'Full Toss' that is alongside Hazra's article has a mob of young men and women wearing a range of costumes: dark trousers, green shorts, khaki knickers. All their shirts carry the slogan 'I am Anna'. At the centre of this mixed group – in which many fly the tricolour – is a ludicrous authority figure in the form of a thin, tall constable. He is the same height as the *lathi* that he uses menacingly to keep off the lone elderly member of the group. The constable demands angrily of the latter, '… and who are you, old man?' He does not recognize him as Anna Hazare. Hazare is the single senior citizen in the motley crew and the only person not to wear the identity-slogan. He goes unrecognized, therefore, not just by the constable but also, probably, by his supporters as well. They are so absorbed in the construction of their identity that they do not recognize their leader.

This panel raises many questions. Ghosh, a member of the Pao Collective that includes graphic novelists such as Amitabh Kumar, Sarnath Banerjee, Vishwajyoti Ghosh, Orijit Sen and Parismita Singh, speculates on the fluid nature of the relationship between fact and fiction. A commonplace concerning certain kinds of graphic fiction is that even when events are historical, the narrative that holds them together is personal. We might well inquire whether this collage of 'new-wave journalism and personal diary' is at work in Ghosh's cartoon panel (2010). On one level, it functions as an illustration to Hazra's column that focuses primarily on two concerns. One is the way in which Hazare's crusade attracts support across the political spectrum. The other is the way in which Hazare's supporters derive their identity from their role in the campaign.

Ghosh's panel depicts both these concerns, but we might wonder whether it develops a perspective of its own. I think it does, because it takes the discussion to the next level by suggesting complications that might arise. It reminds readers that Hazare's supporters – in their zeal to extend their identity through their support of the movement – make it impossible for people to recognize Hazare himself. Interestingly, age and gender do not function as markers of identity. Instead, advertising tools such as slogans, flags and T-shirts operate as indicators. The Hazare persona – when supporters translate it visually – crowds out Hazare the human being. Additionally, the slogan in Delhi is more likely to be the *englished* and urbanized version of the original Marathi, 'Me Anna ahé'. Moreover, if it is possible to construct identity along these lines, people might then rehearse and perform identity on occasions far removed, perhaps, from the original.

This idea takes on a fresh dimension in a subsequent panel by Ghosh that depicts Hazare as Bhishma who lies on a pillow labelled 'Democracy' and waves the tricolour[12] (Figure 11.5). The bed of arrows on which he reclines includes some marked 'Anti-Anna', 'Govt.', 'Media' and Team Anna', among others. He is in full view of a host of tiny symbolic figures who speak the familiar slogan, 'I am Anna', in speech bubbles as they too fly the flag. In Hindu mythology, Bhishma is a complex leader. He takes a vow to renounce his claim to the throne of Hastinapur and to remain celibate so that his father Shantanu can

Figure 11.5 Vishwajyoti Ghosh, *Hindustan Times*, 28 August 2011.

marry the woman he loves. His renunciation pleases the gods who grant him the status of *Sweccha Mrityu*, one who can choose the time of his death. Bhishma stands as grandfather to both the rival dynasties of the Kauravas and Pandavas. When they go to war, Bhishma reluctantly takes the field on the side of the Kauravas, whose army he commands. Knowing that he stands as the only real obstacle between the Pandavas and the victory they deserve, Bhishma tells Arjun how to defeat him. As Bhishma lies dying on a bed of arrows shot by Arjun, he discourses on kingship and statecraft to Yudhishthara, the eldest of the Pandavas.

Judged solely by such an outline, it seems as though Hazare is a latter-day Bhishma. He wears his moral purity with pride, stands above party-politics, pays in physical and spiritual terms for his life of renunciation and is accessible to all who seek his knowledge of the arts of war and peace. Above all, the state needs to allow him the dignity of self-directed choice in terms of the nature and duration of his involvement with public affairs. Nonetheless, to accept such an easy equivalence is surely to beg the question. The moral high ground to which Hazare in particular and Team Anna in general lay claim is open to challenge. As the accompanying 'Red Herring' column by Indrajit Hazra suggests, no single cause can so entirely appropriate public space. However critical we might be of our public institutions, and of the slow rate at which democracy evolves, we cannot allow the tyranny of a pre-set timetable to govern legislative process.

'The pursuit of letting things take their own sweet time is the greatest of our ideals: it won us our freedom. It gave us our democracy. Let us commit ourselves to avoiding the mad rush to do everything that is important. We owe that to the people of India' (Hazra 2011).

As always, irony governs the column. Yet this closing paragraph underscores the need for the gradual evolution of a participatory democracy. A nation cannot hurry through a game-changing moment. Change comes slowly and painfully. It costs the individual and the community a great deal in human life, in time and in pain. Hazare may not be as morally or politically unassailable as Bhishma Pitamah. The situation, however, is sufficiently significant to merit comparison, largely because this time the panel focuses not just on the predicament of an individual but also that of a larger community. However flawed the whole might be it is larger than the sum of its parts. The burden of performance rests not just on the shoulders of the leader but also on those of the people to whom he discourses.

The community and the individual

Conversely, when the community is absent, the Hazare figure loses its political and moral presence. This is particularly true of the graphic satire that responds to the resumption of the Hazare crusade in December 2011. The lead story in the *Navbharat Times* of Thursday 2 December 2011 discusses the issue of the exclusion of the lower bureaucracy from the remit of the Lokpal bill through a curious pair of visual representations. The banner features a photograph of Virender Sehwag diving at nets, in preparation for the Indian cricket team's tour of Australia. Below the photograph is a caricature of a scowling Hazare, seated before a set of uprooted wickets, with the bails flying into the air. The stumps carry the labels – transliterated into Hindi – 'C B I', 'bureaucracy' and 'P M' denoting the three areas excluded from the Lokpal's jurisdiction. Hazare, though stumped, does not walk. He looks as though he is the sole participant in a sit-down strike or *dharna*. The descent into farce seems to have begun.

This sense of the ludicrous intensifies when the crusade recommences. 'Tooning in' returns to the attack, with Jayanto's representation of a visibly older Hazare, looking out over an empty *maidan* in Mumbai, with a one-word query, 'Jan?' (Figure 11.6). It seems to make little sense to speak of the Jan Lokpal bill, or the people's bill – as opposed to that brought by the government – if the *jan*

Figure 11.6 Jayanto, *Hindustan Times*, 28 December 2011.

or people are no longer present. We might legitimately ask whether there can be public space without the public. In a sketch drawn just before this, Jayanto shows his readers the emptying-out of the virtual world. To illustrate an article that carries the title 'Twitter, Facebook not abuzz with Anna support',[13] he gives us three end-of-year revellers who urge each other, 'Yaar ... just support online and party!' The tweeple flee, and the people follow suit.

This brings us to the final question concerning the nature of the relationship between pictorial protest and public dissent. Clearly, there is little easy traffic across this frontier. As a rule, cartoon concerns itself with situation and caricature engages with the individual. A noteworthy feature of representations of the Hazare crusade, however, is that cartoon overshadows caricature. Representation of the group predominates over representation of a leader. Pictorial satire thus leads its readers to involve themselves with the movement, rather than with the leader alone. The performance of politics and the politics of performance become the object of study rather than the charisma of the individual. It thus leads readers to question not just Team Anna, but also, more importantly, their own roles as spectators and participants. Pictorial protest is radical not because of the images of dissent it makes available but because it leads its readers to see dissent itself as being sometimes a show without an audience, a performance without a public.

Notes

1   For the eighth consecutive time, the *Hindustan Times* topped the 2011 Q4 of the Indian Readership Survey, released by the Media Research Users' Council with an Average Issue Readership (IIR) of 22.24 lakh in Delhi and the NCR. See *Hindustan Times*, 6 March 2011, 1.

2   I quote from this edition because it comes from a series with which Kipling was familiar, as well as being the translation that his first readers were most likely to know.

3   *Hindustan Times*, 14 August 2011, 8. All references are to the Delhi edition only. All references in this chapter to the work of Jayanto Bannerjee will use only his first name, following his usage for purposes of the by-line. Jayanto has worked as comic-strip creator, illustrator and cartoonist with *Tinkle*, *India Today* and the *Asian Age*, and is currently with the *Hindustan Times*.

4   England won the Test series 4–0, the One Day International series 3–0 and the T-20 series 1–0, captained by Andrew Strauss, Alistair Cook and Stuart Broad, respectively, in the three forms of the game. M. S. Dhoni led India in all three.

5　*Hindustan Times*, 16 August 2011, 7.

6　For David Low, the political satirist who created Colonel Blimp to resist Hitler and John Bull simultaneously during the Second World War, caricature was the single most important weapon of pictorial dissent, since it deployed 'tabs of identity' to facilitate recognition and thus critique. Subsequent cartoonists, particularly mainstream Indian satirists, have largely followed his theory and practice.

7　The 1988 niche film *Who Framed Roger Rabbit?* (directed by Robert Zemeckis and released by Touchstone pictures) first set up this visual conversation across the divide between people and cartoon characters.

8　*Hindustan Times*, 27 August 2011, 14.

9　*Hindustan Times*, 21 August 2011, 12.

10　Ibid.

11　Ibid. The storming of the Bastille is a romanticized grand moment in the French Revolution of 1789. Believed to be a citadel of political and cultural repression, the symbolic value of its fall in July 1789 was immortalized by Delacroix. Its practical and strategic value was limited by the fact that at the time of its fall it contained only nine prisoners. Hazra's conclusion refers to the release of Anna Hazare once it became clear that his detention in Tihar jail increased popular and political support for the movement.

12　*Hindustan Times*, 28 August 2011, 12.

13　'Lukewarm reception', *Hindustan Times*, 27 December 2011, 8.

References

Anon. (2011), 'Lukewarm reception', *Hindustan Times*, Tuesday, 27 December 2011.

Barbu, Zev (1976), 'Popular culture: A sociological approach', in C. W. E. Bigsby (ed.), *Approaches to Popular Culture*, London: Edward Arnold, pp. 39–68.

Baxi, Upendra (13 January 1990), 'The recovery of fire: Nehru and legitimation of power in India', *Economic and Political Weekly*, 25 (2): 107–12, 111.

Ghose, Anindita, *Hindustan Times*, Mint Lounge, 13 March 2010, posted by The Pao Collective, http://paocollective.wordpress.com/14 March, 2010/06 March 2012.

Gombrich, Ernst (1963), *Meditations on a Hobby Horse*, 2nd edn, London: Phaidon, 1971.

Hazra, Indrajit (2011a), 'Anna horribilis', *Hindustan Times*, 27 August 2011.

Hazra, Indrajit (2011b), 'The game-changer', *Hindustan Times*, 28 December 2011.

Kipling, Rudyard (1895), 'The Miracle of Purun Bhagat', The *Second Jungle Book*, rpt *The Jungle Books I and II*, Sussex edn, vol. xii, London: Macmillan, 1937.

Telang, Kashinath, trans. (1882), *The Bhagavad Gita with the Anugita and the Sanatsugatiya*, Oxford: Clarendon.

12

Looking for Habermas in Cinema as Popular Entertainment – Cinema as Public Sphere with Special Reference to India

Susmita Dasgupta

Introduction

The idea of the public sphere as constituent of the modern society and its politics, as a condition for the emergence of a constitution-based state and eventually for democracy and of the modern welfare state was extensively explored by Jurgen Habermas (1991).[1] The importance of Habermas's treatise on the public sphere emanates from the extensions of concepts of the various spheres of human activity – namely the state, politics, family and economy – which intersect one another in the public sphere, generating ideas and public opinion relating to the mutuality of the above-mentioned spheres. The way these various spheres of social life reinforce or repel one another has important consequences for the modern state and a functioning democracy. The present chapter explores the various ideas that Habermas explores in his conceptualization of the public sphere in the context of the Indian popular cinema.

India is the world's largest film-producing nation[2] and its cinema, especially Bollywood,[3] now underlies the parameters of the global visual culture; it will not be wrong to say that much of the credit for sustaining India as the world's largest democracy[4] goes to its popular cinema which has produced a cultural and a moral density for people to develop a shared culture and universal norms and a sense of a larger society, if not a nation. It is the contention of this chapter that the cinema in India is the public sphere and the interesting manifestations of the cinema have important implications for the shared norms of Indian society.

What is the public sphere?

The public sphere is really not a concrete space but a set of discussions, discourses and reasoned debates around issues in a manner that circulates them into a group of people who then emerge as opinion makers. The aim of such public opinion is to contain the absolute power of the sovereign and direct the same towards the fulfilment of interests of the society that constituted what Habermas describes as the private sphere, namely the economy and the family (Habermas 1991, pp. 25–37).[5] The public sphere, which is actually a set of conversations, discussions, debates, petitions and prayers around and to the state, presupposes and inheres the civil society, a term which he borrows from Hegel. For Hegel, the civil society is a set of relationships which accrues among individuals who look beyond their selfish interests and their position of merely being in the society towards becoming people who speak for the society as a whole. For Hegel, the civil society is rooted in the person's idea of an ideal state and a space where 'ideas' towards the ideal are formed through discussions.[6]

But Habermas adds a few more attributes to this civil society by asking who exactly are its members and how does a civil society come into existence? He finds that such societies come into being through the meeting of educated and literate minds reading literature and engaging themselves in fruitful discussions of artistic products. The people who can access the products of culture are people with money because they are lettered and well-read but also because of their meeting spaces, which are at coffee houses, salons and in reading rooms in England, France and Germany respectively. In fact, among the above three, the coffee houses of England seem to be the most accessible to the 'public', people at large, while salons and reading rooms are often extensions of private homes of the well-to-do. However, the people who participate are not always familiar and, while property and education were uncompromised qualifications for its members, being a recognizable face from the established families was not. Clearly, these spaces of literary circles reflected the emergent bourgeois class, a class in the sense that they defined themselves with respect to property and education, both of which under the circumstances of an emerging capitalist order could be achieved and not inherited instead of being identified with respect to communities, language, sectarian order or positions held in government. Such literary circles were later to emerge, along with the development of the printing press and journals, into political spheres via the route of public opinion (Habermas 1991, pp. 47–52).[7]

A worthy observation may be made between civil society groups and the public sphere. The groups raise and discuss issues, which subsequently inheres the public sphere. Transformations in the composition of the civil society itself change the contents and the structure of the public sphere. It is contention of this chapter to suggest that with the emergence of the cinema public spheres appear to have changed across the board because of deep changes in the nature of civil society and the associative patterns of human beings.

In India, royal courts, village panchayats, Hari Sabhas, Vaishnav Akhras, temple trusts and other similar spaces of interaction were public spheres. After the emergence of the printing press, the rise of the novel and the publishing industry the public space dissolved and inhered in small discussion groups and circles. During the freedom movement, the public sphere actually rose in its true form. There were groups of ideologically motivated friends, there were women's social service groups, religious associations like the Brahmo Samaj and the Ramkrishna Mission, there were political parties contending the monopoly of the Indian National Congress and there were various watchdog groups like the Anushilan Samity and other youth organizations that sometimes took active part in communal clashes but equally helped in relief camps. Whether the Hari Sabhas of medieval India or the Anushilan Samity of modern times, these groups, much like their European counterparts in the coffee houses, discussed and debated ideas of society, its rules, laws of events. The main points of differences between these groups and the European civil society organizations are that while Europe discoursed much regarding the nature of the modern state, discourses in India pertained more towards the ideal society, which sometimes contained the requirements of the king to uphold dharma, or, what is the same thing, the ideal way of being for the society. The role of the cinema must be looked at from these perspectives.

Cinema as public sphere

The cinema is a unique innovation of our times; it is a combination of every form of art which has ever existed for mankind, namely painting, music, art, dance, pottery, crafts, architecture, dress designing, ornament designing, make up and others. All of these are rolled under technology to produce something that presupposes universal appeal cutting across class, culture, creed and community. The universal appeal and the universal circulation of the cinema largely derive from its economics; it is expensive to produce cinema and until and unless it can access a large market, it cannot sustain economically until and unless it collects revenues from large volumes of sale of tickets. Economics and the technology of the large screen and it being an audio-visual medium make cinema itself a public space. Discourses and debates in the cinema appear to have had a circulation among the cine-going public and cinema has been able to create its own public, which becomes active in the public space.

Just as the public sphere has its coffee houses and salons, cinema has its journals, film clubs, fan clubs, film parties, gossip magazines, star interviews and memorabilia, all discussing how some films are good and some could have done better and some are avoidable. What underlie these discussions are sets of normative propositions about what an ideal film should be and how it should appeal to its viewers as universal truth. Film stars who try to experiment with different kinds of roles, which challenge their established image among their fans, are usually constrained because of the normative hold of cinema over its viewers.

The way in which cinema visually overpowers its viewers, towers over them and grasps all their attention by its projection on a large screen accompanied by loud sound and music in a darkened theatre, absorbs the viewer within its frames. Cinema interestingly loses its frames once the viewer encounters it and the latter makes it a continuation of her life and her journey. The public sphere which the cinema creates, interestingly, is not one of debates and discourses over ideology, though ideology is very systematically the objective of its narratives, but rather of styles, attitudes, values and other such attributes which help the individual attain a semblance of respectability as a social being in the public sphere. The crucial factor of cinema being the public sphere rather than something that invokes the public sphere emanates from its characteristic of losing its frames.

When the cinema loses its frames to its people, it becomes a life to be led by the people as characters and participants in that life. Identification happens with cinema as it happens nowhere else. The risk that cinema carries with it is not that it would influence politics and business but that it might itself emerge as politics and business. Narratives and stock characters help people assume their most advantageous positions as players in their real life, take up apt performative stances. The politics of cinema lies just here: it neither challenges the state nor the society but purports to become a self-contained society in itself. The factors through which cinema acquires this attribute is contained in its very technology.

The cinema presents to us a moving image – a moving image in the scale in which it comes to be exhibited to us becomes the defining pace of our world. The cinema provides us the pace of our times; we tend to adjust our step with the pace in films. The visual culture tends to be dictated by cinema; television serials tend to have similar scale of sets in them and commensurate levels of gloss; the advertisements have similar faces, with similar expressions as characters in our films; our drama tends to be set to the pitch of cinematic drama and so on. Cinema, in a way, sets the pace of our societies. This it does by its framelessness, its scale of display and the range of its dimensions.

Scholars have often said that the cinema represents the modern day myths. The crucial difference between cinema and myths is that myths are supposed to be cosmic truths and hence fixed in time. The viewers are fully aware of cinema's fleeting temporality and regard it as the defining truth of the moment. Myths are truths while cinema should be true. Viewers want cinema to be true while they know that they believe myths to be true. Despite the timelessness of myths and the temporality of cinema, the myth-like quality of cinema derives once again from its universality. Cinema assumes that it speaks about everyone though not everyone accepts a film. There are many who have not liked *Mughal-E-Azam* or *Sholay* or even *Sound of Music* but this does not alter cinema's intention. Cinema intends to appeal to everyone just like myth does.

In its universality and temporality, while defining how the world ideally should look at the present moment in the viewers' life, the cinema emerges as the public sphere. Just as the Habermasian public sphere decides what the values should be for the present moment, what kinds of ideals the society should pursue at the defined moment in time, the cinema too defines the stance that an individual must adopt towards her world so as to be best fulfilled in her life's objectives. In the way the cinema assumes morphology, like the Habermasian public sphere, it contends politics; but where the cinema becomes anti-politics is in the way it renounces any ambition of becoming the state and instead focuses on the individual. The individual addressed in the cinema is a universal individual who is supposed to relate to cinema irrespective of her class, caste, creed and community and in this abstractedness of her being constructed; she is also supposed to become apolitical. In the universalization of the viewer lies her depoliticization.

Political sphere and cinema

Despite the fact that cinema raises political questions and questions political morality and the ethics of public life, the cinema is not political precisely because it isolates the viewer from her moorings and absorbs her as a viewer of itself. Yet, interestingly, because the viewer is absorbed by the cinema into its frames, the viewer ceases to be merely private and emerges as a social and a public being. The public being of the viewer is not with respect to her real existence but in a virtual existence in which she lives her life as a character in cinema and relates to the cinematic world where she is thoroughly ensconced not in a cocooned space but in active relationships to other virtual characters. This life is virtual and hence non-participative in the earthly realm; but it acquires every attribute of a perfectly participative person. This is the greatest contribution of cinema in the depoliticization of its viewers.

In the Habermasian text, the eighteenth and the nineteenth centuries were watershed centuries when the public sphere was formed; the main reason for the public sphere to exist was to negotiate with the monarchical powers to gain greater autonomy for the emergent bourgeoisie. The bourgeoisie, a section of individuals capable of earning incomes as entrepreneurs, producing goods and commodities by the use of machines and energy à la Kantian lemma of objectifying imagination, now demanded equal political power/patronage to consolidate their economic powers. While the Hegelian Idea of the civil society helps the bourgeois attain a space from which he negotiates with the state, Habermas's public space is extended to include many values and ideas which the bourgeois regards as the ideal but knows to be contrary in the real world. Thus, Hegelian aesthetics are contained in his civil society and eventually in the reason of the modern state; Habermas's aesthetics are under cloud in the real world but surface in the novels of the times being read in the confines of homes and among like-minded friends. Reading clubs, book clubs, salons and coffee houses, and the changes in the layouts of private homes with the emergence of the drawing room in English houses, point to a public sphere which is separated out from the political sphere, quite unlike the Hegelian idea of the civil society in which the two are collapsed. Habermas says that the family becomes the ground in which the fine sentiments of a cultured humanity are played out, knowing full well the market sphere was underscored by greed and other sentiments far from being fine or humanitarian or both (Habermas 1991, pp. 151–7).[8]

When we look at the Indian scenario, we observe a sudden change in the architecture; it is not so much that homes have changed, but certain kinds of homes are now in the forefront. These are the homes of the rich and upper-class individuals, who have courtyards at the centre with balconies framing rooms all around the courtyard. This is a sea change from homes that were designed like forts, as among the officers and nobility of the Mughal era. Satyajit Ray's films *Charulata* (1964) and *Shatranj ke Khilari* (1977) show the contrasts in architecture very well. While in *Charulata* we see a Habermasian public sphere, which develops inside the home's demarcated public area, where Charu's husband discourses with fellow intellectuals about novels, poetry and religious texts, in the latter film we observe two men, placed in the middle of the public sphere of the nobility as upholders of state power, sink into the privacy of their own world defined by the game of chess. The chessboard becomes the world and an excuse for the players to withdraw.

Nineteenth-century India was a world where the emerging public sphere, as in the Brahmo Samaj or other such associations devoted to social reform and modernity, negotiated with the political powers in order to seek support for the state in reforming society. The exercise of power of such public spheres was over an obscurantist society that seemed to lose its refinement by the day. The Ramkrishna Mission, established in the penultimate years of the nineteenth century, actively distanced itself from any political engagement; instead it drew upon rich patrons like the princely states, especially Rajasthan, to fund its social activities like education, famine relief, education for girls, development of professional skills and so on. Therefore, the public sphere in India seemed to be placed squarely inside the social sphere, addressing issues of the private life. In a way, the public sphere in India raised private affairs into public debate. The public sphere during this time dwelt in the reproductive economy of the society.

The novels which were written during this time, especially by Bankimchandra Chattopadhyay, were in total opposition to the values of the Brahmo Samaj: bravado instead of refinement, aggression, revenge and political rebellion against the Mughal powers constituted the major themes of his work. In the later novels like *Bishbriksha*, *Rajani* and *Indira*, Bankim writes about powerful individuals who are more in the spirit of the Brahmo Samaj. Bankim graduates from political assertion to social reform. What I intend to point out is that the novel was born in India in a different context than in Europe, though Walter Scott and Dickens inspired Bankimchandra greatly.

The birth of the Indian National Congress in the early twentieth century brought about sweeping changes in the Indian scenario.[9] The congress-led freedom movement was one of the largest mass movements of the modern world. The reformed individual, infused with values of modernity, was now supposed to demand political power for her fuller development. Political agency was seen as facilitating a holistic development of personality. The birth of the cinema happened in this space; and after some films on mythology and epics, the Indian cinema shifted towards romantic love. Romantic love was seen as the finest realization for human beings, modernizing societies in the process of accommodating and facilitating romantic love. Romantic love was seen as the fullest realization of the self, a self which the politics of the congress was trying to project as an autonomous political being. It seems that the cinema and the politics of the congress divided up the personal space between them: cinema took on the intimate sphere while the congress took upon the political sphere. In both these cases, the private individual along with her privacy was raised to the public sphere; India's public sphere is about the private lives of individuals whether it is politics or the cinema. The cinema has aided India's project for democracy through the freedom struggle against colonialism by a constant effort of raising the privacy of individual lives into the public realm of shared ideas and values about life and how individuals should ideally behave.[10]

Private and the public of cinema

One of the important ideas of Jurgen Habermas in his work on the public sphere is the manner in which the public and the private have combined into producing the nature of the public sphere. In the context of monarchy, the public was there for all to see and hence forts and palaces and other insignia of royal power were part of being public but were produced by private individuals, whose spaces were guarded away from the public. This peculiar production of the public by the increasingly guarded space of the private spells a monopoly of power (Habermas 1991, pp. 10–12).[11] The cinema in India is similar to the monarchical power of Europe. It is public, for no one is excluded from its viewing, but film stars and directors and producers of cinema are hopelessly private people, guarding themselves from the public eye, refusing to emerge in the public space and very often also avoiding bringing in any opinion in newspapers or television on political subjects. Film stars have however fought political elections as candidates of one political party or the other but they have used politics to consolidate the social power earned through their public recognition. Such crossover from the cinema into politics has not made them public persons or political leaders. The persona of M. G. Ramachandran, at once the hero of Tamil cinema and the leader of his political party, the Dravida Munnetra Kazagham, or DMK, drew public recognition as an individual from both arenas. His politics and cinema remained separate; his presence in politics was only a reinforcement of his popularity in cinema. As a political leader, M. G. Ramachandran was important, but he had a very different persona in politics than on screen; the politics of Ramachandran did not emanate out of his cinema, though cinema helped him to already have a place in his people's hearts when they cast votes for him.

The intensely private space of the cinema makers and the public nature of its exhibition create a kind of monopoly of the cine makers with respect to the production of ideas; there is really no scope to validate how much the viewers really agree with such productions or whether the framelessness of the cinema hands them a set of rules which appear as the givens of their lives. Whatever it is, the neatness of the cinematic form, the discovery of pace, the presentation of movement of bodies on the screen present its own logic of solutions and make the cinema appear to its viewers as if it is life. The presentation of cinema as life creates its own privacy; people feel shy to admit that they are influenced by cinema and that the cinema has failed to fool them while presenting itself as reality. Outwardly people try to deny that they have been influenced by cinema while inwardly they put themselves down in place of the stars they like. Film stars are our secret selves.

When people feel shy to outwardly admit that they have been influenced by the cinema for the fear of public ridicule, they secretly seek others who have similarly taken to cinema. Fan circles are like secret circles, gossip magazines are circulated beneath the classroom desks and views on private lives of stars exchanged through hushed whispers and smothered voices. When cinema is publicly discussed or reviewed, it is done in a manner of scrutinizing, where the discussant tries to be as removed as possible from the object of discussion. This distance is forced upon and between the cinema and its fan because the cinema produces a reason purer than the pragmatic reason of reality. Reason that is put forth by the politics of the modern state and the democratic process of universal franchise often conflicts with the pure ideals pursued by the cinema. The ideals of the cinema are themselves born out of public reason and pursued as pure, too idealistic to be pursued in the pragmatic world. People who take cinema seriously are thus supposed to be naïve.

The desire of sceptics to regard cinema in terms of everyday plausibility tries to put a frame around the medium. Academic studies of the cinema are basically concerned with placing this frame. Fans, on the other hand, are readily dissolved into the frames of the cinema. Cinema is not reflective of the public sphere: it is the public sphere. It generates a certain level of privacy within the private self of the individual in which it then creates its own 'publicness' in which fans, unseen to others, find a role for themselves in the world upon which they impose the reason of cinema. Cinema divides the fan's self into a private and public; there is at first a retreat into the private from socially defined roles and then, within the private self, searches for the public. The entire business of cinema becomes a secret life, which emerges into the open with vengeance when it finds an opening like the persona of M. G. Ramachandran who enters the more pragmatic sphere of politics.

The 'private' of the cinema, which is a private sphere within the private, becomes public when a film is popular. Films such as the ones made with social messages or that are openly critical of the society like Shyam Benegal's *Ankur* (1974) do not seem to be able to create this vast public of secret private selves. Shyam Benegal is a film director of great reputation but not quite considered a popular director regarding box office collections. Another film, *Zanjeer* (1974), released in the same year gave India its megastar Amitabh Bachchan. *Ankur* and *Zanjeer* were both placed against the social classes with entrenched privileges; both films ended unrealistically with the protagonist fulfilled and vindicated. Yet *Zanjeer*'s hero could take charge of his life and actively bring about solutions; solutions happened to the protagonist of *Ankur*. The main point of difference between *Ankur* and *Zanjeer* appears to be the fact of social agency and the forms of these films differed because the latter had to make individual agency seem believable while the former did not have such a task to undertake. *Zanjeer*'s speed of events, its form of developing an entire biography of the hero instead of making him a social type, reducing the supporting cast to stereotypes created by cinema produced before it, its positioning of a problem and the imagination of a solution and then pursuing the imagined solution as the inner dynamics of the film, make *Zanjeer* have a distinct formula. The formula, which is a typical arrangement of the form of the narrative, ensures that the hero always wins, whether actually or, as in *Deewaar* (1975) where the hero dies, morally. The victorious hero becomes the victorious 'I' of the viewer who then takes the stance of the hero in the story of her own life.[12]

Popular cinema is marked out by the stars: fans recall films by their star cast and not by their directors. Directors place frames, stars work inside them and it is only natural to recall cinema by its stars. It is through film stars that cinema unites the privacies of the private selves of people, binds them into a secret community of believers and thus secures their orientation towards a consensual sphere. The consensus that a successful democracy requires comes not from the ideology of the political sphere but from cinema through the identification of people with characters in films, which are viewed universally. The cinema offers people a common game to play and this creates a sense of society where many differences in ideologies and even interests are tolerated. The cinema cuts across differences in politics, straddling differences in society. It sometimes unites people with diverse backgrounds into a communion. The power of cinema is to generate a new sense of life, a kind of 'book' to live by its rules.

Transformations in the private and public in cinema

Just as the public sphere undergoes a transformation in the Habermasian schema as the relationship of the private and the public changes, cinema too undergoes transformation with a change in the public and private aspects in it. Cinema became the monopoly that it is because of the use of technology, an expense that few could afford and which kept the production of cinema the preserve of a privileged few. The increase in the affordability of technology, especially the digital camera, made more people capable of affording the use of the cinematic medium and films of all kinds proliferated. The privacy of the small group of filmmakers collapses as more and more directors and producers come in the fray. The monopoly now shifts from producing and directing cinema towards distribution. Small filmmakers do not get viewing spaces and abnormally high rents for theatres or television spectra make film distribution difficult. As the cinema production becomes public, its viewing is confined to being more and more private. The monopoly over what gets shown is compromised; instead, the monopoly extends now to those who exhibit films. Film theatres increasingly take on the appearance of private salons, tickets are prohibitively priced and the audiences exercise choices in viewing. Accordingly cinema has now become varied, showing various kinds of new compositions, and the formula of the cinema that revolved around the protagonist's problem-solving programmes is now giving way to many new ways of accessing the world of the cinematic characters. The variety in cinema, however, takes away from the medium its consensus-building property. Cinema is, therefore, no longer the other side of the coin for democracy.

In India, the genre of popular cinema has undergone a sea change; while there are box-office formulaic films such as *Dabbang* (2010) or *Rowdy Rathore*

(2012), there are films like *Khosla Ka Ghosla* (2006), *English Vinglish* (2012) and the entire genre of crossover cinema, which are realistic in contrast to being formulaic.[13] The space for a variety of cinema is made possible by the entry of a new class of film producers and directors, made possible due to the wider affordability of film-making technology. The wider bouquet of offers has cut through the universal audiences and the rise of the multiplex that caters to smaller but niche audiences shifts the power from the films to their viewers. Such a shift in power from the film to the viewers has curtailed the cinema's power to be an overarching reality and hence to be the public sphere itself; instead there is now a frame around the films, discussions on cinema and views of critics taken ever more seriously. Film studies rises as a discipline, which objectively dissects cinema as if it were an object, distanced, out there, to be consumed. Cinema as consumption has risen before us almost as a cult and has punctured the power of being a reality for its viewers.

Nowhere is the culture of consumption more evident than in the progressive closeness between cinema and advertising. Music directors, play-back singers and film directors have worked for advertisement films ever since advertisement filmmaking emerged; Lata Mangeshkar's voice would ring out for the analgesic tablet Saridon. But making advertisement films was never a reason for producers to fund directors' projects or working in advertisements a path to making it big in cinema. Models are incubating film stars and directors like Balki and Pradeep Sarkar are essentially advertisement filmmakers.[14] Such closeness would not have been possible if films were also not projected as consumables rather than machinery for expressing the soulful angst of its protagonists. The crash of the song in cinema, its relegation into background music, the rise of 'item numbers', which are stand-alone dance performances, and the use of camera angles and cuts and of colours show that the cinema has moved beyond the spectacle and inheres the space of visual aesthetics pursued together with advertisement films, hoardings, shopping malls, luxury hotels, landscape gardens, high-end apartment blocks, town planning and civil constructions such as bridges, flyovers and airports.

The films of today are far cries from the days when camera-persons pursued aesthetics by tracking the loose tresses of hair across Meena Kumari's face or eyelashes on the drooping eyelids of Madhubala; cinema today focuses on bodies. The actors no longer invest in coiffeurs; instead, they focus on six packs. The face is today passé; the body with its six pack is in focus. The proliferation of gyms across cities, even in small towns, caters to the private world of individuals in which they wish to emerge like film stars. The focus on bodies rather than on emotions, the focus on consumption instead of ideology, has strangely brought cinema into the world of objects where it is far freer for an individual to publicly acknowledge her alignment with the medium. Films have all along dictated fashions for the society as a whole; today designer brands define fashion for films as well as its viewers. The filmic world and the viewers' world are today in tandem with very little reason for cinema to take over the lived-in space. The viewer no longer has to make a secret of her wish to be filmic; she does it openly by organizing theme parties or pursuing, not fashions, but the brands that films endorse.

Apropos to the above, film stars are no longer ensconced in their high privacy; they are now everywhere. They endorse advertisements, appear for private functions, dance on the stage and entertain people in reality television – in short, far beyond what they do in films. The film today exists beyond its frames and instead of absorbing the world into itself, the cinema now walks into the wider world to mingle into its daily conundrum. There is now a reverse effort; there is an effort of the world to look like the cinema – wedding parties, birthday parties, the digital camera, mobile phone video cameras, the uploading of photos on social networking sites.

These changes have affected the public sphere of public opinion on politics and the performance of the political class. The rise of the Hindutva or the Islamic terror where each side competes with the other in putting up equally spectacular riots and bomb blasts, where each side recruits secret soldiers, runs secret governments much like fan clubs and reading clubs, shows that the privately endorsed views of which there exists no public legitimacy are now being increasingly put up for public display. In a manner in which the cinema before the present millennium used to be made by intensely private individuals and then set up for public gaze, these acts of civilizational clash are also put up for public display and hence attempts to hold a monopoly over the 'show business'. The space vacated by frameless cinema is now attempted to be taken over by the civilizational terror industry.

The rise of terror and the decline of cinema in its frameless avatar reveal a new crisis in our civilization. It tells us what our action cinema was trying to convey over the past four decades, that our ideologies and institutions, our judgements and opinions, emanate from and circulate within a narrow band of society in full control of its privileges. The desire of a certain section to gate-keep privileges from wider segments of prospective claimants also lies at the core of our institutionalization, and institutionalization in the Habermasian schema is a certain way to shrink out the public sphere. The rise of institutionalization is the death of the public sphere.

Film scholars in India have often observed the modernization project of the popular cinema in India; it is evident that cinema stood in lieu of institutions which could carry the modernization project in Indian society. The rise of terror as a visual spectacle and the decline of cinema as a routinized object of consumption show that, technologically, cinema seems to have exhausted its visual capabilities. Today audio-visuals are everywhere: the internet, downloadables in the form of YouTube, electronic photo frames, live shows, television and so on. There is perhaps nothing further to be attained, terror being perhaps the newest form of visual and which absorbs every individual into its frames by making them possible victims. This scale of Thanatos[15] is the greatest challenge of our present civilization and a curse cast upon us for pursuing our visual culture far too much.

Reorganization of the private and the public

Despite the flak that television draws from the civil society, it is perhaps only television that can help us redeem ourselves from the failure of the cinema as the public space. Unlike the cinema, which is finite, television is continuous. It has no beginning or middle or end. It runs just as well in the background. It is invisible because it goes on in the background and satisfies fully the addiction of viewers to visual culture. In its being always on, the television is today frameless. The framelessness of television is nowhere better observed than when viewers mistake the footage of terror attacks as clips from action films. The television is a one stop for everything; one watches films in discs in the television screen, one can use the screen to blow up images from iPads and mobile phones, one can use the television to do one's shopping and even take lessons in English and mathematics. The television actually frames us. We tend to be raised into the television; television at once is installed in our privacy and even more so now because each member has her own set and can watch television on laptops and tablets, and yet it braces us as consumers and through this again sets us up in the public sphere. The public sphere, which emerges out of numerous homogenized individuals all aspiring towards a uniform set of consumer products, can have opinions only as consumers and not as political persons. The consumerist public sphere throttles every kind of social and political public sphere into the institutionalization of democratic politics, where politics becomes a consumer product, with ideologies as shopping carts.

Conclusion

As a conclusion, we might say that the public sphere is threatened by the global and universal rise of the audio-visual culture. The audio-visual culture has the ability to relegate people into privacy, sometimes also into secrecy, and manifest their publicness as exhibitions like terror attacks and exhibitionism in social media and social space by private individuals instead of as opinions which relate to politics and the state. Consumerism is promoted while democracy is thwarted with such transformations of the private and the public.

Notes

1 Jurgen Habermas, *The Structural Transformation of the Public Sphere* (USA: MIT Press, 1991).
2 en.wikipedia.org/wiki/Film_industry.
3 Bollywood is a term to denote the Hindi commercial cinema, or the Hindi popular cinema produced in Bombay, now renamed as Mumbai.
4 en.wikipedia.org/wiki/India.
5 Habermas, op cit. 1, pp. 25–37.
6 www.marxists.org/reference/archive/hegel/works/pr/prcivils.htm.
7 Habermas, op cit. 1, pp. 47–52.
8 Habermas, op cit. 1, pp. 151–7.
9 The birth of the Indian National Congress was in 1885.
10 Popular cinema during the time referred to are *Vidyapati, Chandidas, Street Singer* and *Gramophone Singer*, all produced between 1925 and 1937.
11 Habermas, op cit. 1, pp. 10–12.
12 *Ankur,* directed by Shyam Benegal, was released in 1974. *Zanjeer* was directed by Prakash Mehra and released in 1974. *Deewaar* was directed by Yash Chopra and released in 1975.
13 These are popular films. *Dabbang* was released in 2010; *Khosla Ka Ghosla* was released in 2006. *Rowdy Rathore* and *English Vinglish* were released in 2012.
14 Balki directed *Cheeni Kum* (2007) and *Pa* (2009). Pradeep Sarkar directed *Parineeta* in 2005.
15 Thanatos is the Greek god of death.

References

Ankur (1974), motion picture, India. Produced by Blaze Film Enterprises; directed by Shyam Benegal.

Charulata (1964), motion picture, India. Produced by R. D. Bansal; directed by Satyajit Ray.

Dabbang (2010), motion picture, India. Produced by Arbaaz Khan, Malaika Arora Khan and Dhillin Mehta; directed by Abhinav Singh Kashyap.

Deewaar (1975), motion picture, India. Produced by Gulshan Rai; directed by Yash Chopra.

English Vinglish (2012), motion picture, India. Produced by Sunil Lulla, R. Balki and Rakesh Jhunjhunwala; directed by Gauri Shinde.

'Film Industry' (n.d.), wiki article, viewed on 25 April 2014, en.wikipedia.org/wiki/Film_industry.

Habermas, J. (1991), *The Structural Transformation of the Public Sphere*, Cambridge, MA: MIT Press.

Khosla Ka Ghosla (2006), motion picture, India. Produced by Ronnie Screwvala and Savita Raj Hiremath; directed by Dibakar Banerjee.

Marxists Internet Archive (n.d.), *Hegel's Philosophy of Right*, viewed 25 April 2014, www.marxists.org/reference/archive/hegel/works/pr/prcivils.htm.

Rowdy Rathore (2012), motion picture, India. Produced by Sanjay Leela Bhansali and Ronnie Screwvala; directed by Pabhu Deva.

Shatranj Ke Khilari (1977), motion picture, India. Produced by Suresh Jindal; directed by Satyajit Ray.

Zanjeer (1974), motion picture, India. Produced and directed by Prakash Mehra.

Part Four

Inside Out: Individuation, Digitization and New Global Publics

How does the public make possible, and is in turn made possible by, what it is not? That is to say, the specific domains that make up the public, such as the private and the juridical, are instituted within the public sphere through public reasoning. The sectioning of institutional spaces and the laws governing their divisions, functions and inter-operations are constituted within the public sphere, which is not separable from these constituting processes such that the public sphere would be a totally isolated system without any effects on other domains. The role of reason in the theatre of the public sphere has been challenged by many philosophers and theoreticians of politics in the twentieth century (Gramsci, Althusser, Foucault). Instead, a distinct ontology of individuation emerged from the work of Gilbert Simondon (1924–1989) in the 1960s. Simondon's predecessors (Leibniz, Bergson, Canguilhem) and successors (Gilles Deleuze) are difficult to pin down. However, his theory of individuation of the technical, the psychic and the biological object came to dominate the researches of many thinkers. In placing the emphasis on individuation, the chapters in this part, as it were, succeed him, although each of the chapters engages with the question of individuation of the public sphere differently. Bernard Stiegler's is the only text that directly alludes to Simondon; Pramesh Lalu theorizes individuation through the notion of encounter which, for him, takes place between two historic eras towards a possible better future; Mohammed and Mohan place individuation firmly within reason without ever reducing the individual to the general. The chapters study the processes of individuation which constitute and are constituted by the public–private divide.

Today, the place of individuation is contested in societies. Some would argue that it takes place in the schools and others would say it is in religion.

Stiegler's second contribution to this volume poses the question of individuation in the context of social networks, big data and WikiLeaks. He shows the three processes of individuation through which the common space becomes public space: the psychic, the collective and the technical. Drawing upon Simondon, Stiegler shows that the psychic individuation happens only through collective individuation. The psychologically individuated private individuals come to encounter the public thing in other psychic individuals and they individuate themselves into collective individuals. History is the constitution of the new temporality in the encounter with the public sphere. The Greeks encountered this bipolar – the psychic and the collective – individuation in the myths of Hermes and Hestia. In *Technics and Time* Stiegler expounded the myths of Prometheus and Epimetheus, which tell us that technicity is constitutive of man through the default of his being. Mortals, in the experience of this default, came to killing each other. They lacked the political knowledge which would enable them to live together in and through the multiplicity of individual types by emerging from the multiplicity of their technics. Hermes gave them the specific knowledge that involves the technics of justice and shame. This knowledge is also an interpretative therapeutics. However, this medicine is also marked by the deficiency of being and hence can turn out to be poison: it is the *pharmakon*. It is through care that this accidental default is turned into a necessary one. That means the default is individuated not only technologically but also collectively. The public sphere is the space of these three individuations – psychic, collective and technical. Politics is the knowledge of those who share this space. Today collective individuation proceeds as democracy. The relation between the private and the public has been turned into an object of relational technology. Today digital technology is the *pharmakon*. As with any technical individuation the digital can be a cure and a poison. It could link psychic and collective individuation or destroy that link through dis-individuation. The digital culture marks a break with the legacy of the bourgeoisie public sphere which is also the legacy of the French Revolution. It opens a new public space, a new public thing and also a new politics. It offers a therapeutics for psychic individuation. It overcomes the opposition between production and consumption and also between synchrony and diachronic thereby opening new and intense modes of psychic individuation. However, through encoding it may also lead to the destruction of the private sphere.

Premesh Lalu argues that the digitization of the archive of apartheid in South Africa poses new questions about the relationship between knowledge, power and technology. This archive is not a storehouse of raw materials for history writing but an apparatus which served racial subjection. The constitution of the post-apartheid public sphere needs to begin by questioning the prevailing conceptions of the archive and the modes of governmentality that it upheld. Concerns about ownership, intellectual property and political economy, while critical, need to be coupled with an understanding of the consequences of the overlap of knowledge and technology. The nationalist struggle against apartheid seems to have missed these questions, partly due to its preoccupation with the disciplinary techniques which functioned as the conditions for underdevelopment. It failed to see the historical account of liberation struggles as produced under the conditions of Cold War. Nationalism unwittingly reproduced the instrumental view on technology and also on the archive as prosthetics. How can we constitute the archive of the liberation struggles when the Cold War narratives of change that legitimized these struggles have lost their legitimacy in the postcolonial space? The postcolonial is not a state but an event which opens up the future for the task of setting to work on the colonial conditions of knowledge. The postcolonial archive in South Africa has to be seen as a place where a politics of history can be made meaningful and effective. Digitization has to respond to this demand by operating from the standpoint of production. This task for a post-apartheid archive, articulated by Lalu, is waiting to be elaborated in the light of the individuation processes Stiegler has sketched for the digital natives of this century.

Anish Mohammed and Shaj Mohan turn the entry of a new digital technology into an occasion for thinking an old being, *reason*, by means of a bypass between Leibniz and information theory in order to reintroduce the principle of sufficient reason. They suggest that big data and information metaphysics constitute the latest version of the principle of sufficient reason with certain displacements. The principle has been understood as governing the necessary and sufficient conditions of all things. Leibniz, they argue, formulated the principle of sufficient reason to make freedom thinkable in a totally determined world that is surveyed by a benevolent God. Mohammed and Mohan oppose the engineering exigency of information theory, which is now the unchallenged metaphysics that determines the course even of the sciences, with the metaphysical exigency of the principle. Replacing causality with correlations, excising the exigency of existence, information is held ontologically prior to probability, which is chance indexed to a survey-able world. Mohammed and Mohan find in cyberspace a new epoch of politics: not so much a 'utopian arena of equality, friendship and power' (Wertheim 1999) or possibilities of mobilization extending existing public spheres (Wilhelm 2000; Dahlgren 2001, 2005) or proliferating sectional publics (Sassi 2000) and 'smart mobs' (Rheingold 2002). Rather, the system will be able to detect the zone where the unpredictable can arise and will make efforts to ensure that these zones of unpredictability are closed off, reminiscent of the film *Minority Report* based on the short story by Phillip K. Dick. This removal of contingencies will prevent the arrival of Being but it also presents a new opportunity for politics.

All three chapters in this part thus investigate the capabilities and the limits of the public sphere at the crossroads between two epochs – the analogue and the digital, in Stiegler's terms. They deepen the Kantian plea for the public use of reason and extend it beyond Habermas's communicative conception of the public sphere. The focus on individuation allows the chapters to stay clear of the liberalist oscillation between individual and society and, instead, to place the birth of the public at the level of conceptuality and reason. This can be taken up in the light of the problem posed by Caygill in Part I about the availability of conceptuality to explore the *arcanum* of the state and also civil society. The potent afterlife of the narratives guiding digitization and the extraction of information points to the public sphere as a formation that continues to be shaped by geo-power. It entails information metaphysics and the interpretation of 'reason' constituted therein through the collaboration of contemporary data technologies and the ascendancy of statistics as the method to address, or rather to listen to, society.

13

Literate Natives, Analogue Natives and Digital Natives: Between Hermes and Hestia

Bernard Stiegler
Translated by Daniel Ross

Introduction

The meteoric rise of social networks is a phenomenon that demands analysis from many angles. On previous occasions I have attempted to conduct such analyses on an anthropological plane, or in terms of a theory of metadata or a theory of attention, or in terms of the Aristotelian question of *philia*. More generally, digital reticulation in all its forms raises the question of what I call technologies of transindividuation – and this was the subject of a seminar I held at pharmakon.fr that addressed the question of reading Plato in the context of social networking, but also, conversely, considered from a Platonic perspective not only social networking but also that question-machine or even mechanized-oracle that is Google.[1] The angle I would like to pursue here, and in the aftermath of the publication of diplomatic cables by WikiLeaks, is an examination of the question of *social engineering* in terms of what, for more than two millennia, has stabilized itself under the name of the *res publica*, the public thing.

The historical contradiction

What is the public thing – which is also to say, the public cause? It is the thing – that is, the cause – that is not private, which also means that the 'public thing' needs this 'private thing' that it is not. In order for there to be a public cause or a public thing, that is, a public affair, there must be a private thing, cause or affair – the affair being that with which we must do something.

Originally in relation to what it is not, to what it constitutes as such and which constitutes it as such, that with which it forms a dynamic system, a tension and a bipolarity, the public thing is *for* that which it is not but which it makes possible, and which makes *it* possible. The mutual possibility opened up by this bipolarity thus forms a dynamic, constituting what Simondon called a transductive relation: a relation wherein the terms of the relation are constituted by the relation itself, each of these terms being unable to exist without the other, while nevertheless being irreducible to one another.

The *public sphere* and *the public thing encountered there* are thus possible only insofar as a *private* thing, cause or affair is actually encountered. And this encounter – or this relation, which has today been turned into the object of relational technologies – constitutes the sphere of both private affairs and public affairs. Public affairs are possible only between private individuals, that is, individuals who are *psychically individuated* as *incommensurable singularities*, for whom the public sphere within which they encounter one another constitutes the horizon of their *collective individuation*.

These singularities, who meet within this common space called public space, *prophanēs*, not *secret* and thus not *sacred*, where singularities put their singularity into play in an eristic, polemical and agonistic mode, but also in a purely *logical and dialogical* modality of this *public* contradiction – these singularities are *citizens*, through whose acts a new and original temporality is constituted, a temporality that since Herodotus and Thucydides, who are themselves publicly exposed singularities, we refer to as history.

The distinction of the public sphere from the private sphere constitutes the 'historical' epoch of the process of psychic and collective individuation as conceived by Gilbert Simondon and as dynamic bipolarity. Before the appearance of profane society – that is, historico-political society, constituted by its public space – Simondon assumes that societies are constituted by what he calls a 'magic unity': his analysis thereby leaves out those proto-historical societies, such as imperial or Byzantine societies, that belong to the so-called 'archaic' period (Simondon 1989, pp. 162–70). In my view Simondon's analysis is in this way inadequate, but it is not possible to go into this in more detail here.

Be that as it may, Simondon suggests in general terms that the psychic *individual* must be thought on the basis of the *process of individuation* at the heart of which this individual is individuated and not the other way around – magical unity being a stage in which this differentiation remains in some way in limbo. Instead of starting from the process, the philosophies of the subject that appeared simultaneously with the modern age on the contrary take the individual as their point of departure. That is, they grasp this individual as being always already constituted and, as such, as *hypokeimenon proton*, unlike the Presocratics themselves, who applied this term, on the contrary, to what they referred to as *phusis*.

On the basis of this primordial subject, this so-called 'transcendental' subject, these philosophies of the modern age tried to think processes. In relation to the process, the subject would then be the origin, the cause and in this sense the thing, *res*, and would be so as *res cogitans*, or thinking thing, as conceived by Descartes in opposition to the *res extensa*, or extended thing.

To think in terms of individuation, on the contrary, means to begin from the process, from which arises, in the course of this process and as the concretization of this process, the things, causes or affairs of individuals. The history of these individuals, in the sense both of *Geschichte* and *Historie*, begins with writing that makes everything possible by making possible the distinction between public and private. At a later moment of history these individuals come to be referred to as 'subjects', but where these are, first and foremost, *citizens*.

Five theses

Simondon posits that psychic individuation occurs only through its participation in collective individuation, which it is not, but through which it is, and which *is* only through it. I individuate myself psychically only to the extent that my psychic individuation encounters other psychic individuals in a collective individuation, an individuation that is, precisely, not merely psychic but also social.

I would like here to show:

1. that the differential play through which the psychic individual and the collective individual individuate themselves in concert, thus becoming what they are, and transforming themselves through this trans-individuation, is possible only because a technical individuation is also occurring, through which technical objects form a technical system that is itself constantly evolving;
2. that it is through the mediation of technical objects, that is, of things, affairs and causes through which and across which psychic individuals individuate themselves, that psychic individuation can also become collective

individuation, technical individuation concretizing and materializing *in space* the coordinating conjunction in the expression 'psychic *and* collective individuation';

3. that it is through the technical individuation of writing, as mnemotechnical spatialization of the time of speech and, through it, of the intimate and psychic sphere of *phronesis*, which becomes through that *logos*, that psychic individuals can, in the course of the historical becoming of the psychic and collective individual, constitute individuals who think of themselves as being, essentially, citizens;

4. that writing belongs to a wider process of grammatization, one stage of which would be what we today call the digital, referring to an epoch of technical individuation, and that this digital stage of writing could eventually destroy not only the distinction between the public thing and the private thing, but also the distinction between the psychic individual and the collective individual;

5. that it is nevertheless equally true that digitization allows us to imagine the total recomposition of this process, and hence the constitution of a new age of the public thing, and a new age of psychic and collective individuation trans-individuated at a planetary level.

Hermes and Prometheus

The *dynamic bipolarity* that forms the public and the private is already at issue in Jean-Pierre Vernant's analysis of the pairing constituted by the god Hermes and the goddess Hestia. Before citing this analysis, however, it is crucial to point out the fact that, in *Protagoras*, Hermes arrives *after Prometheus and Epimetheus*.

According to the myth of Prometheus and Epimetheus, we mortals are constituted through our technicity, that is, by the fire of Zeus, stolen from the workshop of Hephaestus. Prometheus and Epimetheus endow mortals with their technics, but the latter are only artefacts, that is, *qualities, by default* – through a *deficiency of being*, and as the *signs and scars of the default of origin that brands these mortals with their temporality* and from which derives that *technique which, too, is speech*.

Now, in this test that the deficiency of our qualities constitutes, *the outcome proves to be that mortals kill one another*: empowered by their technics, they nevertheless lack the political knowledge that would enable them to be or to become together in or through that diversity of character that emerges from their technicity – that is, from the diversity of their technics.

It is this political knowledge that, according to Protagoras, will be brought to mortals by Hermes: a knowledge founded on the feelings of justice and shame, *dikē* and *aidos*, which are also techniques, says Hermes, and which constitute the bases of what must be understood as a *hermeneutic therapeutics*.

A therapy, or a therapeutics, is the care we take of that of which we *must* take care. In this case, it is a matter of taking care of the *pharmakon* that technics proves to be, as a power that is also the scar of a *deficiency of being*, that is, of a *default of origin*, a deficiency of the *pharmakon* that can become poisonous but which, through the care we must take, may become *the necessary default* (*le défaut qu'il faut*), the therapy and the *epimēleia* through which *the accidental turns into the necessary*, that is, through which the *pharmakon* is individuated not only techno-logically, but psycho-logically and socio-logically.

This threefold individuation is the challenge of politics as the knowledge of those who share a *public space*, that is, a *space of writing* that intensifies both their psychic individuation and their collective individuation, that is, their unity. Politics is the relation that ties the knot between the psychic individual – that is, the private sphere – and the collective individual constituted by the public sphere.

The psychic individual and the collective individual must be understood as processes of individuation, that is, of transformation, but the myth of Prometheus and Epimetheus teaches us that the processuality of this process stems fundamentally from the technicity of the psychic individuals who together form collective individuals. Technicity is what creates the object of invention, *euriskō*: it is itself, and originally, transformation. That is why we must take into account not two but three processes of individuation: psychic, collective and technical.

What prevents technical individuation from ending in the destruction of psychosocial individuation is political *tekhnē*, as a therapeutics of technical individuation insofar as it is pharmacological, that is, insofar as it binds psychic individuations together so that they together form a collective individuation, but where it is always possible that, on the contrary, this process of individuation may be destroyed, that it may turn into a *process of dis-individuation*.

The *pharmakon* is thus for mortals both a remedy and a poison.

What we are undergoing and enduring today is precisely the imminence of this possibility of dis-individuation, faced as we are with a technological individuation process that seems to be destroying what alone can hold the public and the private spheres together, as what allows them to be distinguished as the two indissociable poles of a transductive dynamic relation.

Today, indeed, the digital *pharmakon*, as technology of 'social engineering', is what tends to *annihilate the private sphere*, which itself tends to become *essentially encoded* and as such to find itself *immediately exposed* within what no longer constitutes itself as a *public* sphere, given that such 'publicity' presupposes a private sphere – which is also to say, *deferred time* (see Stiegler 2009, p. 57) – that we can also call intimacy, the diversity of intimate thoughts constituting, through the space of public contradiction within which this diversity is encountered, a *critical space* that would also be a *critical time, a critical age*.

Hermes and Hestia

The political therapeutics that Hermes brings to mortals is a *hermēneia*: it is an *interpretative* discipline, a *hermeneutic knowledge* that presupposes an interpreter capable of acceding to feelings of *dikē*, that is, of justice, and therefore of injustice, and to the feeling of shame or indignity, and thus also honour or dignity – that shame (see Stiegler 2005a, b) that is also the feeling of stupidity, and it was Gilles Deleuze who told us why.

Political knowledge must know how to take care of pharmacological knowledge, that is, of the *pharmakon* that is itself the result of that efficient knowledge that may always turn into counter-efficiency, which we today call not only counter-productivity but *toxicity* – and this is what is recounted in the story of the sorcerer's apprentice, a tale that illustrates the Greek question, the *tragic* question, of *hubris*.

Hermes, that wandering god and interpreter through whom the immortal gods and mortal *anthropoi* engage in commerce; Hermes, who is also the god of commerce – taking this word in its widest sense – between *oi thanatoi* themselves; this Hermes is the counterpart of Hestia, the god of *common space that becomes public space, that is, also, prophanēs* – Hestia being herself the goddess of that intimate and private sphere that is the *hearth*.

Around this hearth the private sphere is formed and concentrated, wherein the intimacy of a *fire* is maintained. This fire is, at the same time, a symbol of the power of Zeus, of technics that passes into the hands of mortals and of that desire of which Pandora, wife of Epimetheus, is the primordial figure. Fire possesses all these attributes and is that of which Hestia takes care, because fire may be that which warms us, and that in which blossoms, by basking in its warmth, the intimacy of those who desire, but it is also what can inflame and incinerate the hearth, and with it other hearths, and thus the entire city.

The fire of the hearth is as such also the *pharmakon* of which Hestia takes care, which she maintains while preventing it from spreading beyond the hearth; she thus contains it in its very intimacy, which is the meaning of *aidos*, that modesty and shame that is *la vergogne* – the maintenance of the fire, that is, care, through which this intimacy is accomplished (i.e. individuated) as 'desire remaining desire' (Char 1956, p. 59). And we must here relate Hestia, of whom Pandora is the hidden face, to Winnicott's 'good enough mother' (Winnicott 1971).

Hermes and Hestia form a *transductive* pair, and this is what we have learnt from Jean-Pierre Vernant:

> To Hestia belongs the world of the interior, the enclosed, the stable, the retreat of the human group within itself; to Hermes, the outside world, opportunity, movement, interchange with others. It could be said that, by virtue of their polarity, the Hermes-Hestia couple represents the marked tension in the archaic conception of space. (Vernant 2006, p. 161)

> Neither Hermes nor Hestia can, in fact, be viewed in isolation. They fulfill their functions as a couple: the existence of the one implies that of the other. Each is a necessary counterpart to the other. Furthermore, *their very complementarity implies a contradiction or internal tension in each of them that gives their characters as gods a fundamental ambiguity.* (Ibid., p. 174, emphasis added)

This entire pharmacological ambiguity, that Vernant showed elsewhere lies at the heart of the tragic pious practices of Ancient Greece, all of whose rituals are governed by the conflict between Prometheus and Zeus (Detienne and Vernant 1989), is the mark of that which traverses these two figures in linking them together and which is the pharmacological horizon as such. This situation must be related to what Lacan described as an *ex-timacy* (Lacan 1992, p. 139) – which is also the fruit of a *promētheia* founding an *epimētheia* as the two faces (of Janus) from which the pharmacological situation results.

The existence of a *public space*, and of everything that is formed as '*publicity*', that is, as common knowledge, and first of all as understanding of the law, which is also knowledge of *dikē* and *aidos* cultivated and maintained in and by this very sharing, and maintained as one must maintain a fire, the existence of this public knowledge that is the *res publica*, but which must be interpreted privatively, in the intimacy of one's soul, the intimacy of what, in modern times, comes to be called our 'consciousness', all this is based on a *system of publication* – a system the *repression* of which was set in motion by Plato through his tendency to oppose *anamnesis to hypomnesis*.

This public space constituting the *res publica* as space of publication, wherein the *res cogitans* and its *res extensa* encounter one another, is what opens a fund of objectivized and profane knowledge of all kinds, where profane means, precisely, not secret (*pro-phanēs*) and as such public, that is, *exposed to and before critique*. This is the condition of *political law*: of law as what everyone must *submit to on the basis of their right and duty to critique it*, to *transform* it, to individuate it and to trans-individuate it at the core of a new collective process of individuation – all this presupposing the existence of a private sphere that itself constitutes a new process of psychic individuation, the link between the two being what we refer to as citizenship.

It is in this way that the public is distinguished from the private without opposing them, since on the contrary they continually compose and mutually constitute themselves in a transductive relationship. What is public is distinguished from what is private, even while it *constitutes* the private that constitutes it in return, to the strict extent that, between the public sphere and the private sphere, and like Hermes between the hearths, there is circulation: circuits form and transform, and transform what they link together, within which they circulate *as circuits of transindividuation*. To this extent (*mesure*), which is also an excess (*démesure*), *hubris* is always possible, since all of this is thoroughly pharmacological.

The political individuation writing machine

These circuits are those that weave psychosocial individuation as a network both in space and in time – and both in public space and time and in private (i.e. intimate) space and time.

Between the *psychic* individual and the *collective* individual-become-public, that is, *constituted through the 'publicity' of the conditions of its constitution*, was established, in conditions specific to the psychic and collective individuation process that arose in Greece in the seventh century BCE – and which was also in part, but in a very different way, invented in Judea – what we call the *res publica*. Through such a process of *publication* a *doxa* forms, which, after the Reformation and the Republic of Letters, then the constitution of the press as a new age of publication, will eventually, in the modern age, be referred to as *public opinion*. *Doxa*, however, first appears with writing engraved by chisel in marble, and painted in bright colours, for a collective individuation gathered in and by the *politeia* of *citizens, citizens who are such only insofar as they know how to read and write.*

This constitution rests on the knowledge of writing and the system of publication that is the result of this knowledge, a fact that became clear thanks to the historical research conducted by Marcel Detienne and other Hellenists:

> Around 650 BCE, when the first legislative and juridical texts appeared, royalty disappeared, and even the memory of its distant palaces. For a century at least, alphabetical writing had been in circulation: merchants, poets, artisans, private individuals, they all used it, as they pleased and insofar as they understood it. Simple and readable, it is not, it will never be, reserved for professionals. But from 650, with legislators who chose to put the laws of the city into writing, writing changes status. It becomes an operator of publicity, constituting the field of politics. This occurred as a result of the audacity of a few, conscious of the stakes. Solon, more than anyone, affirmed the founding gesture, writing laws 'for bad and for good alike', rather than imposing tyranny or stirring up dissension. Writing made the fundamental rules of life in the city monumental, visible and perfectly readable, so that everyone would submit to them voluntarily. A complex machine served them with support in the Prytanie, in the place of political decision: writing tables erected in the centre of the public space, graphic displays dedicated to the independence of writing. (Detienne 1988, p. 14)

> Displayed in the most prominent places, on the most visible sites and the most frequented areas, steles covered with writing invited 'those who want it to gain knowledge' of its decrees and its laws. Engraved and painted in vivid colours, the letters were meant to be readable by the greatest number. (Ibid., p. 17)

Within the public sphere that was the *politeia*, citizens had equal, isonomic, techno-logical and structural access to public space, that is, to publication, and in particular to the publication of the law, not only insofar as they can read it, and read it to the letter, but equally insofar as they can write it, and, again, can do so '*à la lettre*'.

Literal and analogue natives confront the possibility of a new process of individuation

In the city various *regimes of political individuation* are constituted, that is, regimes of collective individuation founded on '*publicity*', ranging from *aristocracy* to *tyranny* and passing through *democracy, oligarchy* and so on. Plato will order them and register them into a list, ignoring, however, monarchy strictly speaking, which in

France and elsewhere will be overturned by the Republic – and among the items on this list democracy will constitute, especially for the modern West, the political ideal.

Democratic society was truly implemented in France only with the advent of public education. Modern democratic societies, however, were at the same time developing into industrial societies, in which the citizen will be diluted in and by consumerism and in which psychic individuals – as consumers, which the crisis of 2008 showed to be a toxic and addictive state, that is, fundamentally drive-based, poisoning physical and mental environments and combining with a drive-based capitalism that disinvests because it has totally transformed into a machine for speculation – will find themselves dis-individuated and, along with them, so too processes of collective individuation.

This crisis occurred during the same period in which it became clear that the younger generations currently constitute what are nowadays called *digital natives*. With more time I would have shown that in *The Greeks and the Irrational* E. R. Dodds explains the difficulties in Ancient Greece brought by the advent of *literate natives* (1951). It is they who overturn the power of the gerontocracy, among the consequences of which was that social unrest that eventually led to the demand that Socrates drink hemlock – and which in turn led him to ask Criton, just before his death (and these were his final words), to sacrifice a cock to Asclepius. Asclepius: that is, the god of the *pharmakon* who becomes the god of medicine, of therapeutics, but who does so only after having tasted the Gorgon's poison and turned it into a cure, Zeus ultimately striking him down for bringing to mortals the fantasy of immortality, if not its effective possibility.

Be that as it may, what collapsed in 2008 was not the world of digital natives but rather that of analogue natives, that is, of *my* generation, a generation formed by the cinema, by radio and by television, that generation of consumers who are also called 'baby boomers' and who have to a great extent been responsible for destroying the world. It was through a perversion of *lettered, literate reason*, having become *rationalization* – understanding this word in the sense it had for Max Weber, Theodor Adorno, Herbert Marcuse and Jürgen Habermas – that consumerism was established, by combining a *lettered, literate culture*, which must be thought in relation to Martin Luther, with a *mass culture* totally at the service of the capture and destruction of attention (see Stiegler 2010).

In the face of this catastrophe, the digital *hypomnēmaton*, that is, this new stage of writing, seems:

- on the one hand, to close off the public space that emerged from the French Revolution, and from which the industrial revolution immediately followed, and did so as its historical truth, combining a century later with American democracy, which itself emerged from the revolt against the English metropolis, leading to the invention of the *American way of life* that has today been globalized;

- and, on the other hand, to hold promise for the reopening, in a completely different way, of this public space and its thing, and the intimate thing, that is, psychic individuation, provided that this happens as a therapeutics, that is, a politics, that would ultimately be implemented in a way that confronts this *pharmakon* and is *of* this *pharmakon*, not in order to kill off its unprecedented aspect but in order to reinvent citizenship itself.

If I had time, I would try to explain how this unprecedented aspect rests both on overcoming the opposition between production and consumption and on overcoming what seems to oppose the *top-down* and the *bottom-up*, that is, synchrony and diachrony, through the proliferation of metadata in a way that rekindles all those debates opened by Socrates in the fifth century BCE, all those debates that Plato closed off in *The Republic*. I would also endeavour to show that the question of *ethos*, which is the sole basis on which the question of ethics can be thought, is also the question of *aidos*.

Conclusion

The *ethos* is that of mortals, *oi thanatoi*, and the *aidos* that constitutes them as the knowledge of their difference from the immortals – the word *aidos* deriving from Hades, the god who reigns over the dead. This *ethos* is what constitutes a general organology, tying together the psychosomatic organs, artificial organs and social organs (i.e. organizations) through which psychic, technical and social individuations are concretized. In this play of individuations, counter-individuations and disindividuations, there is an ethical question to the extent (*mesure*) that, and in the excessiveness (*démesure*) of the fact that, the *pharmakon* is the law of organology – a law that is itself written, formalized and as such transformed and shared as such (as this sharing, *moira*) in conditions of grammatization.

Does digital grammatization still enable such a law to in fact become a therapeutics and not a generalized toxicity? I believe that it does – and far more than analogical grammatization ever did. But this is a question above all of political economy and not just of ethics: it is precisely the stakes of the economy of contribution, which I also define as an economy of de-proletarianization, that is, of the sharing of knowledge and 'responsibilization' – in the sense that Kant had already begun to think with the concept of maturity in his response to the question, *What is Enlightenment?* (Kant 1991).

Note

1   Available at http://pharmakon.fr/wordpress/le-seminaire/.

References

Char, R. (1956), *Hypnos Waking*, New York: Random House.

Detienne, M. (1988), *Les savoirs de l'écriture. En Grèce ancienne*, Lille: PUL.

Detienne, M. and Vernant, J.-P. (1989), *The Cuisine of Sacrifice among the Greeks*, Chicago and London: University of Chicago Press.

Dodds, E. R. (1951), *The Greeks and the Irrational*, Berkeley and London: University of California Press.

Kant, I. (1991), 'An answer to the question: "What is enlightenment?"', in Hans Reiss (ed.), *Political Writings*, 2nd, enlarged edn, Cambridge and New York: Cambridge University Press.

Lacan, J. (1992), *The Ethics of Psychoanalysis, 1959–1960. The Seminar of Jacques Lacan, Book VII*, New York: Norton.

Simondon, G. (1989), *Du mode d'existence des objets techniques*, Paris: Aubier.

Stiegler, B. (2005a), *Constituer l'Europe: 1. Dans un monde sans vergogne*, Paris: Galilée.

Stiegler, B. (2005b), *Constituer l'Europe: 2. Le motif européen*, Paris: Galilée.

Stiegler, B. (2009), *Technics and Time, 2: Disorientation*, Stanford: Stanford University Press.

Stiegler, B. (2010), *Taking Care of Youth and the Generations*, Stanford: Stanford University Press.

Vernant, J.-P. (2006), *Myth and Thought among the Greeks*, New York: Zone Books.

Winnicott, D. W. (1971), *Playing and Reality*, London: Routledge.

14

The Virtual Stampede for Africa: Digitization, Postcoloniality and Archives of the Liberation Struggles in Southern Africa

Premesh Lalu

The transformation of 'archivistic' activity is the point of departure and the condition for a new history. (de Certeau 1988, p. 75)

A striking feature of post-apartheid South Africa is the ever-expanding debate about the recomposition and refiguring of the archive (see Hamilton et al. 2002). In efforts to stage such a shift, the status of the archive has emerged as a source of uncertainty. In some instances it is perceived as a site of retrieval and representation, in others as a site of power. In yet others, it is viewed as a site where the production of history is already underway. The debate has been conducted in public and academic settings, in scholarly publications and postgraduate seminars, and in institutions of public culture and in relation to the Truth and Reconciliation Commission. Each instance of founding a post-apartheid public sphere, it seems, is dependent on the ability to step out of the shadows of preceding conceptions of the archive and the modes of governmentality it upheld. Apartheid affirmed the idea that the archive was not merely a storehouse of documents but also an apparatus in the service of racial subjection. Emerging from apartheid's grip, the question of refiguring the archive is equally a question of exceeding its normative definition and operation. In order to achieve this, we may have to forego the notion of the archive as merely a prosthesis of power and constellate its activity around the radical singularity of an event. By this, I mean the ability to break with the referential frame of power that dominates our conception of, and approaches to, the archive. Stated differently, as a question: how might the multiplying effects of the archive encompass the singularity of the demand for an elaborated concept of the post-apartheid.

Digital initiatives overlooked the opportunity to engage the problematic of the archive that reflects the mounting debates in South Africa about the politics of collecting. The well-worn categories for selecting materials on the liberation struggle, and their reference to narratives that once provided for the politically constraining choices of the Cold War, threaten to flatten the debate on the archive while manufacturing the paralysis that might ensue from the much-discussed crisis of history (Saunders et al., p. 17). The discussion about digitization requires a different orientation in thought, one that may offer the potential to intensify the debate about the archive, its place in society and its relation to constituting publics and elaborating concepts equal to the challenges of our times. If the demand for a concept of the post-apartheid pressures this assemblage of archive, publics and power, it is to the extent that it calls for a different view about the archive and the crisis of history.

It may be necessary to raise the stakes in the discussion on digital archives by re-articulating the intellectual challenges that confront us in the wake of apartheid. Specifically, I am interested in digital technologies as they affect mainly historical and political archives in, and of, Southern Africa, as these overlap with public debates on the becoming post-apartheid of South Africa. We should not assume a politics of digitization, either on the grounds of the political economy of intellectual resources or on the legal grounds of intellectual property and national heritage. The question of digital archives should not be surrendered to the terms of nationalism or to the presumed inevitability of cultural plunder that underlie narratives of globalization and neoliberalism as presupposed categories – or earlier frameworks of imperialism, for that matter. Rather, the question of digitization of archives of liberation struggles should be located at the limit where the post-apartheid brushes up against the idea of difference that underwrites postcolonial critique. In short, I ask for a re-examination of the intersections of knowledge and technology. Ultimately, both are indispensable for rethinking the relationship between *techne* and *bios* by which the post-apartheid will come to be known.

The creation of digital archives should therefore simultaneously be broached as a question of technology and epistemology. In the process, some care must be taken not to make a fetish of technology for fear, as Theodor Adorno hauntingly put it, of 'a world where technology occupies such a key position as it does nowadays [that it] produces technological people, who are attuned to technology' (Adorno 1998, p. 200; see Masco 2004). In clarifying this statement, Adorno suggests that

> it is by no means clear precisely how the fetishisation of technology establishes itself within the individual psychology of particular people, or where the threshold lies between a rational relationship to technology and the overvaluation that finally leads to the point where one who cleverly devises a train system that brings the victims to Auschwitz as quickly and smoothly as possible forgets about what happens to them there. (Ibid., p. 200)

He concludes that 'with this type, who tends to fetishize technology, we are concerned, baldly put, with people who cannot love' (Ibid., p. 200). There is a tacit reminder in this of Adorno's deep-seated concern for how the effects of technology limit practices of representation in an essay titled 'After Auschwitz'. 'If thought is not measured by the extremity that eludes the concept,' Adorno suggests, 'it is from the outset in the nature of the musical accompaniment with which the SS liked to drown out the screams of its victims' (Adorno 1973, p. 365). The event must therefore be immemorial.

One can only hope that someday the same standards of memory would apply to the violence that, in the name of apartheid, engulfed Southern Africa during the Cold War. For now, suffice to say that in the work of the Frankfurt School we find not merely the concern with representation but also the tendency to view technology as mere mediation and therefore as a separable agency. Technology, Adorno reminds us, has a much more proximate relation to violence. What he does not tell us is that its proximity is equally prevalent in the knowledge/power nexus that Michel Foucault later opened to critical scrutiny (Foucault 1978, p. 23). Digital technology may have substantially reorganized the terms of the cultural industry that once preoccupied scholars of the Frankfurt School.

Generally speaking, the rise of computer technology has generated a fair amount of scepticism about its relation to radically altering the human condition. Many would say that, if globalization was anything to go by, it has facilitated the intensification of capitalist exploitation of the periphery far more than alleviating its burden. Neil Postman, for example, cites David Riesman's caution against over-emphasizing the changes wrought by computer technology. For Riesman 'computer technology has not yet come close to the printing press in its power to generate radical and substantive social, political and religious thought' (in Postman 1992, p. 117).[1] Riesman argues that if the printing press was the gunpowder of the mind, the computer, in its capacity to smooth over unsatisfactory institutions and ideas, is the talcum powder of the mind (Ibid., p. 117). Read alongside the Frankfurt School, we might be called on to rethink the realignments underway with the introduction of computer technology, especially as it places otherwise fraught and fragile institutions and racial formations beyond the pale of criticism. This might mean taking up a critical position in relation to the intrusion of technology into the arenas of knowledge production and, among other institutions, the university in Africa more generally. In the case of the latter, the rise of disciplines such as bioinformatics and nanotechnology has placed the category of the human in direct relation to technology.

A critical model that addresses the relation between technology and knowledge should proceed with further troubling the uncertainty, suspicion and concern that currently surround many digitization projects in Africa. Among humanities scholars, this suspicion is often deferred to the realms of intellectual property rights agreements, copyright issues, ownership, the sustainability of local institutions and related practical considerations of archival capacities and priorities. These are, of course, crucial matters, although their pre-eminence in discussions about digitization suggests a lack of prior political foresight and thought in participating in digitization initiatives. The humanities are for all intents and purposes speechless in the face of the technologization of academic discourse. The disjuncture between archival consideration and epistemological conditions has arguably resulted in rather spontaneous approaches to digitization, which hamper what might otherwise be an intellectually productive and necessary discussion about the archive, technology and political subjectivity in general. One consequence of the drift towards a legalistic framework to deal with the challenges of digitization is the neglect of the larger questions about knowledge necessitated and enabled by digitization. We should not be entirely surprised by the concerns expressed about digitization projects though. Neil Postman makes the insightful comment that 'it is not always clear, at least in technology's intrusion into a culture, who will gain most by it and who will lose most' (Postman 1992, p. 117). Others like Paul Virilio encourage us to understand the change wrought by computerization without, in the process, being bound to an ideological approach (Virilio 2005, p. 8). Virilio also provocatively argues that an emergent techno-science is wrecking the scholarly resources of all knowledge (Ibid., p. 2).

How should scholars in the humanities forge a politics of digitization, one that is scrupulous about the histories, intellectual currents, conceptual developments and institutional dynamics that help to define the conjuncture of globalization, *techne* and *bios*? And how might a conjuncture, threaded through this assemblage, reveal the possibilities of thinking the postcolonial and the post-apartheid simultaneously? How might the discourse of history deal with the inheritance of the archive that is formed almost entirely around the contested nationalist scripts in the struggle against apartheid? To refuse this line of questioning, the archive is to dispose of the possibility that the contestations internal to the emergence of the discourse of history might have something to contribute to the formation of a concept of the post-apartheid. We might agree that the limit of the discourse of history lies in the very modes of evidence of colonialism, apartheid and the Cold War that the archive authorizes. But there has been scant attention paid to the manner in which history as a discourse has become entangled in theories of change that have fallen short of producing an effective concept of the post-apartheid. This problem is compounded by responses to digitization initiatives, which have viewed public access as an end in itself in the debate on the shape of democracy in much of the third world. Technology is treated as a means to an end, without a careful rendering of the mediative role that technology performs in the relationship between archive and history. The concern surrounding digitization initiatives – expressed through legal notions of intellectual property, copyright and national heritage – may have less to do with a sense of cultural sovereignty than with the question of technology and its histories in Southern Africa.

Unfortunately, the critique of digitization, insofar as it targets the global, implicitly produces thinking that is identical to that reflected in the sovereign claims of the nation state. From the vantage of the pedagogy that it authorizes, this thinking remains within the paradigms of imperial war and violence. It says little about the hardening of political sensibilities formed around race and ethnicity in Southern Africa that may otherwise be revealed in a history that took up the question of technology. In other words, what the problematization of digitization offers, currently, remains locked in the framework of development of underdevelopment. Digitization, inasmuch as it touches the question of the archive and history of liberation struggles, seems to require a different critical model.

To lock the critique of digitization in the narrative of underdevelopment is to trap it in the mechanism through which nationalism interpellates the subject of its emancipatory scripts and works to displace colonial governmentality in the contest to name a biopolitics of the future. The archive and its relation to the question of technology, then, may be the place where earlier modalities of biopolitics that were specifically colonial and racial were worked out and now lends itself to the task of understanding how apartheid may in fact be revealed as a biopolitics of the future. Perhaps the only way to interrupt this flow is through requiring that a concept of the post-apartheid be properly attentive to the demand of a postcoloniality that adequately marks a difference with apartheid and the apparatus that sustains its logic.

The archive of globalization

There is much that is misrecognized in the critique of digitization projects in Southern Africa, even when arguments for the digitization have been motivated on the grounds of a nascent public sphere that is the very fault line of the promise of anti-colonial nationalism. Most Southern African digitization projects have targeted documents related to the history of liberation struggles, or, to make it more palatable to the audiences of the West, the archives of the freedom struggle. Given this slippage and emphasis, it is not surprising that digitization initiatives have been so fraught that they have failed to come to terms with the historiographical dimensions of the archives of liberation struggles. Embedded in these historiographies are the bitter contestations about theories of change and conceptions of modes of power. Debates about intellectual property, national heritage and the political economy of digitization obscure the underlying ways in which the archive of liberation struggles are not merely ideological but also intensely historiographical. Much of the historiography of Southern Africa has insufficiently reckoned with the ways in which theoretical and conceptual presuppositions of Cold War narratives register in the documentary traces of the liberation struggles. Rather than thinking of digitization in terms of loss of cultural property, we might think of it in terms of the more severe consequences of the overlap of disciplinary knowledge and technology. While concerns about ownership, intellectual property and political economy are critical, with the rise of digital technologies, we need to understand more fully the consequences of the overlap of knowledge and technology.

Threaded through the anti-imperialism critique, digitization offers one of four possible conclusions. One possible consequence of the digitization of liberation documents in Southern Africa, filtered through critical understandings of globalization discourses, is that it will probably perpetuate the unequal relations between the global North and South. Good intentions notwithstanding, we will perhaps see the rise of vast *technopolies* with powerful resource concentrations that, in our case, will continue to make Africans consumers of knowledge rather than producers of knowledge.[2] This is probably what is implied by the phrase, 'the commodification of information'. Already, we are faced with a situation where the bulk of publishing on Africa is based in Europe and North America, placing the published material outside the reach of a general reading public. As a consequence, we continue to experience expanding levels of illiteracy and high university dropout rates, not to mention the insidious mediocrity that is having an adverse impact on the formation of a viable and dynamic public sphere in Southern Africa. This has been the forfeited promise of modern Southern African nationalisms as they increasingly set out to meet the demands of the apparatus of global governance.

A second holds that digitization may have very negative consequences for the formation of public spheres in post-independence societies. Pierre Bourdieu warns us that one of the effects of globalization and, by extension, the technologization of knowledge is the increasing depoliticization of society (Bourdieu 2001, p. 38). The depoliticizing effects of globalization tend to limit our conception of digitization projects to technical matters of preservation and access. However, since several digitization projects have mainly targeted politically charged collections, this very move is already indelibly politicized. I argue for a mobilization of these political effects in the interests of expanding what can be said about the histories of liberation struggles. It is not enough to dwell on how the liberation struggles were won – it is also imperative to examine their outcomes, their relations to global processes of the Cold War and newer formations of global hegemony, their complex conceptual points of departure from the racial premises of the modern state and their general failure to finish the critique of colonialism. Not only will this hopefully resonate in the domain of intellectual production, but it may also open the mediations of technology in knowledge production to scrutiny and criticism.

A further elision that results from avoiding historiographical considerations is that digitization may in fact be harnessing nascent nationalist tendencies by making available to embattled states the instruments of legitimation. This is an expression of an elite discourse against which many scholars continue to struggle. The resultant optimism surrounding the archive in normalizing power, in one instance, produces a corresponding anxiety about its function as a technology of state, in another. Combined with the technological advantages of cyberspace, many worry about the further instrumentalization of the state. The focus on the history of liberation struggles recasts some well-worn binaries of domination and resistance, but never to exceed ideological scripts. The existence of monopolies over histories of liberation struggles and access to liberation archives highlights the increasing fragility of states, as they become more bureaucratized under the pressures of globalization. It is necessary to inquire into the relationship of technology, elite formations and the instrumentalization of politics in Southern Africa as these are put in the service of state projects.

Finally, digitization also accompanies a growing fear that academic production is being skewed in favour of the wealthy institutions of the global North, where scholarship on Southern Africa does little to enhance the critical debates, as also public debates, about postcolonial social formations. This neglect is supported by the rabid anti-intellectualism taking root in Southern Africa and the transformation of universities into conduits of state developmental goals. This must not be misconstrued as an argument about the banal concepts of insider/outsider knowledges. Rather, it is a reminder that the location of intellectual production is a crucial factor in how many African states respond to academic criticism. Given the ways in which digitization projects are negotiated at an institutional level rather than as part of academic debate, many projects reinforce an already problematic division of intellectual labour.

Historical considerations, as also debates about history in Southern Africa, have been surprisingly absent from the many concerns expressed about digitization initiatives, even when these digital archives are predominantly concerned with history. Cursorily, it is interesting that the matter of digitization should be undertaken without considering how the end of the Cold War entrenched views about capitalism that, in its more recent manifestations, signalled an idea of *exchange* as a universal language. Alongside this, there has been the emergence of a troubling normative discourse, premised on a hegemonic world order, organized around consumption (in archival terms, access), not production. In the various scenarios of digitization, these are the tropes shared by purveyors and opponents of the use of digital technology and resources in education. What is elided in the ascending orders of hegemonic discourse is the element of production by which capitalist relations were once known, comprehended and challenged.

These scenarios hinge on a more fundamental discrepancy at the heart of the archive. It relates to the way the archive is folded into the complicities of knowledge as a necessary condition for colonialism and, later, during the Cold War, apartheid. In Southern Africa, the constitutive relations of power and the further exercise of that power was founded and enabled by a vast disciplinary apparatus. Since the nineteenth century, and in some instances much earlier, vast archives of discipline and punishment have painted a harrowing picture of the complicity of knowledge in achieving social subjection. The archive was never far from the needs of colonialism. Scholars such as Anne Stoler direct our attention to ways in which knowledge was placed in the service of colonial governmentality (2002). In another phrasing of this complicity, Clifton Crais speaks of ethnographies of the state to demonstrate the proximity of knowledge to power in his book *The Politics of Evil* (2004). In *The Deaths of Hintsa* (2009), I show how modes of evidence of the nineteenth-century colonial archive functioned to constrain efforts, by successive generations of nationalist intellectuals, to transcend the limits of a colonial order and racial formation. Crucial to this interdependency between knowledge and the exercise of power, which permeatesthe work of many scholars, is a worry about the practice of collecting 'native life'.

Given this long-standing and imbricated relation of knowledge, archive and power, digitization should not be seen as merely subtractive or additive, or even developmental for that matter. The introduction of digital technology into the realm of archives generates total change to an entire system – its effects are what Postman calls ecological. The conceptualization of the archive is now increasingly up for grabs, and digitizing initiatives are productively giving rise to new contests over the writing of history after apartheid. To enter such contest in the interest of averting the normative narratives of power, it may help to explore the possible ways of aligning the process of crafting a politics out of digitization within the framework of the reorientation currently taking place in the field of knowledge production.

Colonial precedents and Cold War constraints

A major consideration regarding the question of the archive in Southern Africa is its relation to the modular form of the colonial archive. The colonial archive reflects a particular mode of evidence that is a consequence of the rise of new disciplines in the nineteenth century and the requirements of Empire (Lalu 2009). Drawing on the work of Michel Foucault, Edward Said described the specialized disciplines that arose in the nineteenth century in which 'the human subject was first collapsed into swarming detail, then accumulated

and assimilated by sciences designed to make the detail functional and docile'
(Foucault 1978b, p. 710). Said points out that from these disciplines evolved a
diffuse administrative apparatus for maintaining order and opportunities for
study. The emergence of the archive in Southern Africa did not only occur with
the rise of new disciplines, but also with a discourse of race. In Southern Africa,
the conditions of conquest were propelled by the will to know and the will to
power of a specifically racial formation.

Nationalist historiography was an effort at reversing and displacing the
claims built on the basis of the colonial archive, but not under conditions of
nationalism's own making. The rise of segregation and apartheid in South
Africa, the struggle for independence in Southern Africa and the ideological
parameters of the Cold War all gave new meaning to nationalist agendas of
recuperating pasts trampled over by the needs of colonial domination. This was
not a case of history repeating itself first as tragedy, then as proverbial farce.
Rather, it was a case of nationalism's overt concentration on underdevelopment
at the expense of a critique of the disciplinary techniques that functioned as
the condition for underdevelopment. For now, I will argue that nationalism,
in its effort to dislodge the primacy of the colonial script, proceeded to work
within the scripts of the Cold War. The regional experience of apartheid and
opposition to it were produced under the constraint of Cold War ideologies and
their reliance on technologies of domination.

In targeting the history of liberation struggles in Southern Africa, many
digitization initiatives may be leading us back into the impasse in which
nationalism found itself by unwittingly, perhaps, reproducing instrumentalized
notions of technology. The problem arises as the records of liberation struggles
are increasingly treated as information related to the late twentieth century and
not as responses to a longer history of colonialism and its aftermaths in Africa.
It fails to see in the documents of the liberation struggles the discourses that are
essentially vehicles of Cold War ideologies. The inheritance of this Cold War
script is, indeed, of considerable consequence and a key factor in making the
postcolony liveable – even barely liveable. Achille Mbembe has described what
we are up against in somewhat distressing terms:

> In the framework of the strategic ghetto that Africa has become in the aftermath
> of the Cold War, another more basic spatial arrangement and another geopolitical
> situation are currently taking form. Three processes separated in time but
> complementary in their effects are involved in this development. First, the
> processes currently underway are situated within the major ongoing movements

of destroying and reconstituting the nineteenth century state. ... On another level, dynamics that were introduced by colonisation and essentially continued by the independent regimes are grafted onto these processes. Through the mediation of war and the collapse of projects of democratisation, this interlacing of dynamics and temporalities leads to the 'exit of the state.' It promotes the emergence of technologies of domination based on forms of private indirect government, which have as their function the constitution of new systems of property and new bases of social stratification. (Mbembe 2001, p. 39)

Mbembe's assessment implicitly requires us to think our way out of this impasse. His formidable phrase 'technologies of domination' echoes Adorno's caution. Globalization has not merely meant the corporatization of institutions in Southern Africa, but the point at which a sense of hyper-disciplinarity is produced. This sense of hyper-disciplinarity is itself a vestige of the Cold War and entails a growing convergence of discipline and technology. Under these conditions, it is necessary to guard against adding to a heightened sense of disciplinarity that extends its grip on the subaltern subject or results in an intensification of the subaltern effect.

The archives of the liberation struggle in Southern Africa are enabled by the narratives of the Cold War, not only in terms of their theories of change, but also in terms of their motivations, strategies and tactics. The tonalities of intrigue, fear, torture, surveillance and reporting, coupled with arguments about struggles against colonialism and apartheid in Southern Africa, are central features of these narratives. Nationalism in Southern Africa was indelibly marked by the paradigmatic choices made available by the Cold War, even as the end of the Cold War helped to erode the grounds for maintaining the tyranny of apartheid. We might say that since 1990, Cold War narratives have been in jeopardy, deeply suspected for their incredulity: failed promises of change on the one hand; a trail of death and destruction on the other, left in the aftermath of apartheid, which has placed Southern African nationalisms in a compromised position. How, with this inheritance, might we constitute an archival event that exceeds these limitations, even as it erodes the last vestiges of the prevailing discourses of the Cold War as determinate frameworks for Southern African nationalisms? Put simply, how are we to constitute the archive of the liberation struggles in Southern Africa when the Cold War narratives that function as their condition of possibility increasingly lack legitimacy?

The incommensurability between Cold War narratives and the promise of postcolonial futures resembles the growing 'incredulity towards metanarratives'

(Lyotard 1984, p. 6). Digital archives of the liberation struggle seem to have run up against a similar break-up of metanarratives. The digitization of the archive would be compelled not to repeat the logic, terms and concepts specific to the Cold War. And it will have to do this by breaking down the extreme reliance on positivism and reinstalling the place of narrative (if we accept Lyotard's argument) in the domain of the archive. In other words, the creation of digital archives of liberation struggles under conditions which specify the incredulity of metanarratives would have to surrender attachments to ideas of informatics for a more nuanced understanding of an archive if it is to avoid Cold War prescriptions. The archive in this conception is neither a scene of communication in the Habermasian sense (1987) nor a storehouse. Rather, it holds out the challenge to find ways out of an impasse.

If the constitution of digital archives on the history of liberation struggles in Southern Africa potentially fractures the foundational fictions of the Cold War, how might such digitization projects dealing with the evidentiary base of liberation struggles remain attuned to the processes described by Mbembe? How, in other words, might it opt out of this sorry story of the rise of 'technologies of domination'? The promises of emancipation have, it seems, generally folded into expressions of nationalism, nativism and the slippage into the regulations of the market and the discourses of global governance. The history of liberation struggles has been unmoored from their respective universal bearings and globalization has proven to be a detrimental, if not virulent, substitute.[3] By asking for an expansion of what can be said about the history of liberation struggles, I am asking for a reflection both on the break-up of its Cold War dependencies and for a critique of its more recent normalization in the wake of the Cold War. The conditions of possibility for this, I suggest, lie in the way in which the notion of the event has undergone something of a change in the discourse of history. The archive of the liberation struggle may need to be formed around this renewed concept of *the event*.

The archive as postcolonial event

The Cold War conditions in which struggles against apartheid unfolded in Southern Africa require us to rethink both what we mean by the event of history and how the archive might organize itself around such a renewed concept. Herein lies the epistemological potential of digitization, which might both shed light on the conditions of constraint and allow for the emergence of a concept of postcoloniality. Stated differently, we might say that a reformulated concept of event may provisionally be called postcolonial because as it unravels the structures of domination it anticipates the conditions necessary for thinking ahead. Mostly, the designation 'postcolonial' is an allusion to the tasks of setting to work on colonial conditions of knowledge that continue to haunt the frameworks of knowledge.

Historians of Africa have found that the question of the archive in contemporary Africa activates the tensions that once defined the struggle against different forms of domination. The archive is a network of knowledge and power that is fraught with political difficulty, caught between a public sphere struggling to come into its own and nation states bounded by discourses of development, national identity and political legitimacy. The politicization of the archive and its social meaning is derived not simply from the conditions of political conflict that it aspires to communicate as an institution, but by the demands that historians and the discipline of history more generally make on an archive. The inversion of perspective is of profound consequence, particularly in South Africa, where the creation of a post-apartheid archive converges with the need for rewriting national history. The archive is the site where the politics of history are rendered meaningful and effective.

The frameworks for researching histories of liberation struggles in the aftermath of the Cold War cannot be limited to a choice of either 'national' or 'global'. More appropriately, in my view, we should think of frameworks that allow the local and the global to bring each other to a crisis. It is here, I believe, that we should plant the seeds for a politics of digitization, in the midst of an aporia that may activate new intellectual paths to understanding the contemporary world. This would mean making the promise of some digitization projects – to overcome the colonial and Cold War imprints on the archive – the facilitating point for imagining different relations of knowledge production.

Two scenarios may better help to underscore the historical frameworks in which discussions of digitization are taking place. At one level, the digitization of the archive approximates, however inadequately, what print capitalism was for the rise of the imagined communities of which Benedict Anderson speaks. In his argument, the novel, newspaper, census and map created a sphere of unbounded seriality that promoted the replication of the nation form throughout the world (Anderson 1998, p. 10). The nation was imagined through the fundamental technological developments in print capitalism.

At another level, the potentialities of digitization are confronted with the increasing marginalization of the political re-imaginings in and of a world bifurcated by the processes of globalization. This second option for thinking about digitization is perhaps best summed up in a response to the endless productivity assigned to the rise of print capitalism by Benedict Anderson. In considering the proposition of a modular form of nationalism, Partha Chatterjee posed what I think is the most serious challenge to Anderson's discussion of the serialization of nation (Chatterjee 2004, p. 3). Chatterjee wondered what was left to the imagination of the third world if the nation was said to be founded on the modular form of print capitalism. He was not however asking us to think of this other imagination of the third world as merely different from that of the West. Rather, he was asking why it is that if third-world nationalism is made up of the same resources as the West, the third world, nevertheless, always appeared as a failed example of theories of change. Speaking from within the politics of despair, Chatterjee was perhaps pointing out that nationalism appears to have failed to overturn the epistemic conditions that once gave colonialism its motive and subsequently sustained its effects.

Two critical matters flow from this unfortunately truncated outline of the debate between Anderson and Chatterjee. On the one hand, the discussion on technology and society has not sufficiently taken root in Southern Africa. The drive towards digitization prioritizes technological considerations. Digitization seems to be the new-found developmental project of the African state, thereby precluding public interest. On the other hand, there is reason to heed the warning to anticipate a return of the same for those who are constituted as marginal political subjects. In Chatterjee, we might also read the echoes of a plea not to replicate the modalities of the colonial archive by which some are returned again and again to the position of the margin, to the subordinate proposition of the statement. There is, instead, a need in archival disciplines to the problem of technology in the exercise of power. The digitization of African materials should not be aimed at creating minority discourses in the north, or even multicultural syntheses that are eventually returned to Africa for consumption in the name of diversity. Both are highly flawed discourses. Instead, they should clear the space for an investigation in which the post-apartheid recasts the concept of the postcolonial. This would require a greater blurring of the distinction between archivist and historian, perhaps so that we may allow for the possibility to expand what can be said about the history of liberation struggles.

Notes

1 The interest here is in Postman's sense of the limits of technology.
2 The term 'technopolies' belongs to Neil Postman.
3 Lyotard addresses a similar question in relation to the labour movement (1989, p. 322).

References

Adorno, T. (1998), *Critical Models: Interventions and Catchwords*, trans. H. W. Pickford, New York: Columbia University Press.

Anderson, B. (1998), *The Spectre of Comparison*, London: Verso.

Bourdieu, P. (2001), *Firing Back: Against the Tyranny of the Market*, trans. L. Wacquant, New York, London: New Press.

Chatterjee, P. (1993), *Nationalist Thought and the Colonial World: A Derivative Discourse*, Minneapolis: University of Minnesota Press.

Crais, C. (2004), *The Politics of Evil*, Cambridge: Cambridge University Press.

De Certeau, M. (1988), *The Writing of History*, trans. T. Conley, New York: Columbia University Press.

Foucault, M. (1978), *Discipline and Punish*, trans. A. Sheridan, New York: Pantheon Books.

Hamilton, C., V. Harris, J. Taylor, M. Pickover, G. Reid and R. Saleh, eds (2002), *Refiguring the Archive*, Cape Town: David Philip.

Lalu, P. (2009), *The Deaths of Hintsa*, Cape Town: HSRC Press.

Limb, P. (2005), 'The digitisation of Africa', *Africa Today*, 52 (2): 3–19.

Masco, J. (2004), 'Nuclear technoaesthetics: sensory politics from Trinity to the virtual bomb in Los Alamos', *American Ethnologist*, 31 (3): 349–73.

Mbembe, A. (2001), 'At the edge of the world: boundaries, territoriality and sovereignty in Africa', in A. Appadurai (ed.), *Globalisation*, Durham: Duke University Press, pp. 259–84.

Mudimbe, V. Y. (1988), *The Invention of Africa*, Bloomington: Indiana University Press.

Postman, N. (1992), *Technopoly: The Surrender of Culture to Technology*, New York: Vintage Books.

Said, E. (1978a), *Orientalism*, New York: Vintage Books.

Said, E. (1978b), 'The problem of textuality: two exemplary positions', *Critical Inquiry*, 4 (4): 673–714.

Virilio, P. (2005), *The Information Bomb*, trans. C. Turner, London: Verso.

15

Principle of Sufficient Reason 2.0: On Information Metaphysics

Anish Mohammed and Shaj Mohan

Since 2000 the scale of integration of network-based technologies and production networks started becoming visible, for example, in the area of market tracking, where the internet[1] initially kept the index of the market. Soon international capital found it necessary to analyse and program the uneven and, as of now, un-obtained terrain of the international market, tracking sales in each corner of this new market to match production expectations, resulting in the reciprocal determination of the network of capital and the internet. The newly available technologies – big data and the applications of artificial intelligence – are producing centralization and standardization. This does not imply that all actions, such as posting a tweet, will be submitted to a standard. Rather, the standard will be able to 'capture' most of these actions towards centralized processing and programming to predict future behaviours and control them. These technologies form a total circulatory system of all values insofar as values are standardized for techno-circulation; for example, the *like* buttons, the up and down ratings and re-tweets. There is something before us today, and this 'us' is no longer an oppressive generalization of European Enlightenment which grasps the many forms of peoples. Our concretion as the *us* or *one nation under CCTV* is produced by a technological will that we name by the now old concept of surveillance, and we experience it proximately as the loss of the private sphere. Is the loss of the private sphere the gain of the public? Certainly not in the political sense in which the feminism of an era imagined it, though there is much more to entertain us out of the leaks from the private sphere. All windows, doors, walls and devices are the 'Rear Window' of Hitchcock such that we are each found in varying degrees of windowless states; where everything is visible across the boundaries of inhabited space, there is no sense to windows, which are meant as controlled openings, as it stood for the modern sense of autonomy exemplified in Manet's balcony. We are characterized today by a Leibnizian concept – 'Monads have no windows through which anything could come in or go out' (1998, p. 268). It was the charge of shutting the windows of the world to extract all freedom in order to deliver it over as the best world according to the principle of reason that Leibniz found hard to combat. It is evident in a confused way – especially since Heidegger found the essence of technology in Leibniz – that when we concern ourselves with information security and political freedom we are in the domain of the principle of sufficient reason – the principle which grounds the question 'why there is something?' and dominates all domains as the ontological principle.

Even for Leibniz's contemporaries, such a relation between reason and politics was not evident, though it was clear that the principle (*ratio juris*) had a juridical role to play, not merely due to the origin of the notion of a principle out of the juridical grounds of Roman law, nor due to the exigential form of the principle *reason must be rendered*. On the problem of evil, the principle put even God on trial and recovered Him as a renewed clinamen. However, Kant – who divided Leibniz's reason into the court (reason determined as the necessary condition) and the under-trial (reason in its transcendence, a case of which is eminently the principle of sufficient reason as the excess to be determined by the conditions) – was the first one to pose the problematic of politics as governed by a ratio of institutional conditions for reasoning and at the same time towards the end *Reason*. The churning of the pensive heart of the last century rendered reason into a confused zone. It repeated rather ceremoniously the event of Nietzsche's declaration, the end of reason. Reason became a certain indignity and the principle the code of the reactionary. One aspect of reason had already found its limitations in the seventeenth century: that we could not perceive all things necessitated that reason could not be applied to the real total to derive its essence. In the eighteenth century a consensus was emerging that this scenario required the deployment of something akin to reason or its image, which is probability, as Simon Laplace found with respect to Newtonian mechanics. In the nineteenth century, statistical mechanics would appear to dismiss the principle in exchange for the notion of irreversible process and probability as its measure. This exchange would have the traits of a new Platonism, or precisely Leibnizian Platonism: reason is ideal and probability is image.[2] It is said that we no longer live in the age of reason. Instead it can be said that we are *lived* in the reign or principium of 'big data' as the conjuncture of three realities: information, probabilistic reasoning and the evacuation of the domains of reason, including the private. Is there anything left for philosophy if reason, in any of its manifestations, is disallowed? If the zones of reasoning are evacuated, would it be a transgression were one to still philosophize?

Hence, the question that is asked often is 'What is philosophy to do now?' The 'now' is a marker of a spatial zone wrapped by arrows of many correlations,[3] as opposed to determinations which will appear to be too philosophical. There are the various declarations of the 'end of metaphysics' which are at the same time immanent to metaphysics, as Jean-Luc Nancy has shown time and again. The determinations of ends as well as their distributions and their interrelationship in terms of distinctions are among the duties of metaphysics. In spite of all the end-talk of metaphysics we find that there is a more pervasive metaphysics which has the most political effectivity in its history, already determining the courses of even the sciences, namely, the information-metaphysics, which states that 'We can throw the numbers into the biggest computing clusters the world has ever seen and let statistical algorithms find patterns where science cannot' (Anderson 2008). Information-metaphysics does not claim for the sciences a zone of serendipity, but confers on them the power to find, out of massive amounts (Exabytes) of data of nature in its vicissitude, a statistical *fortuna* – 'science can advance even without coherent models, unified theories, or really any mechanistic explanation at all' (Ibid.). This metaphysics can be characterized as 'massive': it gathers all things, being, into a single mass for processing and at the same time it makes manifest all the zones of politics as 'the masses'. In the nineteenth century the people appeared as 'the masses' enduring revolutionary political phenomena which could be distinguished from the other appearances of the people, such as the benign intellectual public sphere and the deleterious revolutionary fronts. The masses arrived as a formation threatening to the governing order under certain conditions but were soon found to be a tamable one, especially through the invention of entertainment. Today, being as information ensures that there is nothing other than masses, making it difficult to call the information-metaphysics a metaphysics for the masses. Indeed, the 'for' is something we will need to enquire into to determine if what is indicated by the term 'we' is any more than a for-colonization.

On the principle and the qualities
of necessity and contingency

Leibniz was not the first philosopher to state the most common form of the principle, that is, the assertion that there is a cause[4] for each thing insofar as it is – there is some X_1 such that it is the cause of X_2 insofar as X_2 is. In this form the relation between causes and reasons are confused, and we step away from the true understanding of the principle as ground. Hegel noted that

> Leibniz opposed the *sufficiency* of ground mainly to causality in its strict sense as the mechanical mode of action … partial determinations are comprehended by their causes, but their connexion, which constitutes the essential feature of an existent, is not contained in causes belonging to the sphere of mechanism. (1969, p. 446)

The principle is ground insofar as it has exhausted the indeterminate in the possible to render it as essence such that it involves exigentia, or such that the possibles can make 'their claims upon the attention of a benevolent creator' (Rescher 2001, p. 154) for passage into existence; cause is merely an event determined in accordance with this ground. We should not confuse Leibniz with the ordinary language understanding of the difference between cause and reason where cause refers to external reality and reason refers to the internal representations of the external reality. The relation between essences, ground and the existent is given by Leibniz, in his mature years, in terms of the distinction between two different qualities of truths – necessary and contingent. Necessary truths, when expressed in propositions, are those which include their predicate in the subject. For example, the definition of prime numbers. The predicate-in-subject is a self-evident notion where the contrary of the proposition evidences itself as impossible and this impossibility marks, for Leibniz, even the limits of the divine vision. In cases where the law of identity is directly the content of the proposition, as in A = A, or *those things are equal with regard to one another which are equal to the same thing*, the quality of necessity of the proposition is obvious. On the other hand, in cases of complex propositions where there are many terms involved, the distinct intuition of necessity must be preceded by understanding and the finite analysis of the terms involved; the definition of prime number – *a prime number is that natural number higher than 1 which is divisible without remainder only by 1 and itself* – involves notions such as natural number and modulo (explicitly) and composite number and number theory itself (implicitly).[5] Further, as one moves beyond primary truths the analysis is not only not self-evident, it also calls for leaps within and over domains. For example, to analyse the definition of a *complex number* would require one to move away from the intuitively evident notion of a natural number to that of *imaginary numbers*. Leibniz used examples with increasing degrees of complexity to impart a sense of exigency of reason: the limit cases involving irrational numbers, the numbers for which we cannot render reason yet, which exist through the divine vision of God due to, and hence demand reason from, us, or ask for analyses.

Analysis is called for by the juridical formulation of the principle – *reason must be rendered* – and it reveals the relation between reason and what there is; the rendering of reason brings into view the exigency of the existent, or makes the essential in the existent manifest towards the liminal point where it separates from the possible or what could have been. Without reason being rendered, the existent and us are shared in a disposition of uncertainty and reason is rendered in the manner of providing a relief, or rendering free; or making the setting for the free composition of the existence is rendered by their reason. That is, to render reason is the only *rendering free*. This relief is not limited to domains such as mathematics alone: 'The world, globally, and phenomena, proximate, local, or remote are given to us; it would be an injustice, a disequilibrium for us to receive this given for free. ... Equity therefore demands that we render at least as much as we receive, in other words, that we do so sufficiently' (Serres 1995, p. 90).[6] Then, when we do encounter those things for which rendering reason appears to be beyond our abilities we must not assume that they are without reason. In such moments the principle assumes another form, which is emphasized by Kant in his Analytic – *nothing is without reason*. What matters here is the relation between contingency and reason. Is it proper to conjoin the contingent with exigency through the genitive?

Within the domain of mathematics and beyond there are objects for which a finite analysis does not provide us primary truths, where its predicate-in-subject form is evident, but contingent truths or concepts of freedom. These are truths nevertheless, even though, unlike necessary truths where the inclusion of the predicate in the subject – the very criteria for being true – is available through a finite analysis, these truths are infinitely analysable. We are not to presume, however, that an infinite analysis can be carried through either by us in our essential finitude or even by God, who is originary intuition, since the completion would imply contradiction. Rather, in his divine vision, God can *see* the inclusion of all the predicates pertaining to all the tenses of time such that future contingents are not of problematic judgement and, instead, everything exists objectively as opposed to the subjective succession of alterations or state transitions – God is the benevolent surveyor. Hence, of the world one can speak without regard to subjective succession – 'At a given moment the pyramid prehends Napoleon's soldiers (forty centuries are contemplating us), and inversely' (Deleuze 2006, p. 88). It is in the existence of the contingent, understood as those truths for which analysis is infinite, that Leibniz finds room for freedom:

> Here lies hidden the wonderful secret which contains the nature of contingency or the essential distinction between necessary and contingent truths which removes the difficulty involved in a fatal necessity determining even free things. (1956, p. 412)[7]

Ultimately the experience of freedom is given in the gradation of analysis such that a terminable analysis determines even at the level of denominations necessity and at infinite degree even God will not be able to terminate the analysis which implies the transition of the world from one state to the next is not reversible even though it is perfectly determinable: freedom is established in the gradation of perfection demanded of the analysis and it is found to have an inverse ratio with respect to those analyses which are reducible to the primary truths. This does not imply that there are two distinct kinds of existences: the necessary, which is determinate and reckoned finitely according to its reason, and the contingent or the indeterminate. Rather, all truths and their qualities – necessity and contingency – are determined according to the principle of sufficient reason and the exigency of their being is found in their conceptual whole since the 'perfect concept of an individual substance involves all its predicates, past, present, and future' and God is able to survey all that was, is and will be (Ibid., p. 414). The necessary and the contingent in this sense are qualities – these qualities correspond to the analysis required for each thing: infinite analysis corresponds to the contingent and finite analysis corresponds to the necessary. Then, if all that exists is perfectly determined and takes place under the survey of God, where is the sense of freedom?

Here, one might misunderstand determination as mechanism and Leibniz himself was aware that such a misunderstanding would result from forgetting the difference between cause and the principle, as we found earlier. In a mechanism, when perfectly crafted, all that takes place in it can be called fated. However, the ground for the mechanism eludes the one who makes it just as a perpetual machine to which infinite analysis ought to correspond does.[8] There are ways in which one misplaces cause for reason. One may mistake the conceptual power of denominations – 'whenever the denomination of a thing is changed, some variation has to occur in the thing itself' (1956, p. 414) – for verbal magic, such as when one names a child 'Victoria' and assumes a victorious life for her.[9] An object is of consideration for thought (*à penser*) depending on its exigency, and we experience it as a weighing (*à peser*) in the mind. In such movements of reasoning one is often led by similarity. The word 'grunt' remains the same between the sense of it marking a feeling of effort and the one marking a low-level soldier, though even etymologically they are distant, which can lead one to reason that the low-level soldier is always grunting and hence called a grunt. On the other hand, the two words galaxy and lactose, which belong to distinct domains, the former to astronomy and the latter to biochemistry, are receding from their common origin in the Greek word for milk, Gala. If such freedoms given by language, which ought to open us towards the principle as other than mechanism, are not mistaken for the reason in existence we are led to a non-mechanical and yet well determined region of freedom.

Were the idea of freedom to be derived in opposition to mechanism, it would demand two scenarios of the world – on the one hand a world of whims and on the other a world of pure chance. In the latter there will be no event such that it may dispose towards the act of freedom that modifies it since one cannot expect a relation between the modifying act and the modified event; without the principle of reason, as the sense of action, there is no action.[10] In the former case one presupposes a mechanism that is discontinuous such that it removes the difficulties of thinking the perpetual machine and in its discontinuities what takes place can be named an act, while bearing in mind that this act is without reason to determine it as that which connects it to a subject. These puzzles of freedom condition certain aspects of *information-metaphysics*. The Leibnizian concept of freedom is even more puzzling from the point of view of the mechanism; all events are perfectly determined according to the principle such that there is freedom. On the problem of sins which imply freedom, Leibniz remarked: 'God does not so much decree sins as he does the admission to existence of possible substances whose complete concept already involves the possibility of their freely sinning' (1956, p. 408). That is, we have freedom insofar as existence is perfectly determined according to the principle which is not reducible to mechanism. This is a freedom visible a priori to God. Is it possible to think the concept of freedom as surveyed in advance? What if this survey corresponds to the imperfections of a mechanism rather than the perfections of a principle?

Information-metaphysics

The political question given to us by information-metaphysics is 'Can the world be made predictive?' such that one may anticipate the revolt to come and alter a few variables in the present to prevent its very conditions from taking form – *interventions that leave everything as if nothing happened.* The modification of the world for controlled manipulation, transmission and processing is the essence of information-metaphysics. The word information designates nearly everything today – from sexual relations and war to biology and governance. There are etymological studies, histories and conceptual genealogies both ensuring the classical origins of information and establishing information theory as the opening to a new era of the world: the former is more or less teleological in such a way that the history of philosophy appears to be a chrysalis for information theory and the latter is on the other hand presented as an evolutionary breakthrough, the human insertion of a specific difference to itself.[11] As designated by Hartley as well as Claude Shannon, information is something without tolerance to torsion or that which is equivalent across its transformations such that it can be encoded adequately for the channel and transmitted without loss or gain for its receiver (Hartely 1928; Shannon 1948). This notion introduced various confusions which are still unresolved, including the relation between semantics and signal, which leads to the confusion regarding the objective and subjective aspect of information and its probabilistic estimations. Shannon considered the relation between semantics and information a practically insignificant problem: 'These semantic aspects of communication are irrelevant to the engineering problem' (1948, p. 379). Before him, Hartley considered it the subtraction of the psychological aspects of communication for securing the quantitative notion of information.[12] Accordingly, the principle of information-metaphysics is engineering, where one subtracts the engineer-able material from the given; it is the excision of the exigency demanded of us by the principle of sufficient reason. The engineering problem is well known from the simple Shannon block diagram: sending in a message subtracted from the semantic space with respect to the coding limit imposed by the nature and capacity of the channel (given the noise that creeps into the channel) to achieve a probabilistically measurable reception of the message which is decoded by the receiver. That is, a system set up under an optimization problem. In this Shannon's theory owes to Von Neumann. This material that could be sent and received found a name – the bit – from the paper Shannon published in 1948 standing for the binary symbol system.

While subtracting semantics and metaphysics to gain 'the bit', Shannon also made a correlation with 'the it' or physics by creating a logarithmic function expressing the uncertainty of the next state of the system as expected by the receiver of the messages – thermodynamics. We need not be concerned here with a more popular notion of entropy that is assumed to associate thermodynamics with information theory and is understood as a measure of disorder. The thermodynamic concept of entropy has nothing to do with disorder, whereas information entropy is a probabilistic concept which can be related, analogically, to statistical dynamics. The systematic study of state transition is at least as old as Galileo. For him the problem was describing the state transition of a body, where both motion and rest are considered states. The state of a system appears manifestly as a problem with Leibniz as we have already seen – contingency implies state transitions that are not finitely analysable but perfectly determined. *Equilibrium* defines a process if all the variables (the macro variables of heat, pressure and volume for thermodynamics) in the system are defined perfectly and take constant values. *Quasi-static* defines a process that has state transitions taking place through equilibria at all points of the system. The *reversible* defines the system if it can be returned to its initial state with nearly no exogenous variable intervening in it. On reversal, the system and its environs would appear as if nothing happened. *Irreversible* would be a process in a perfectly determined system where the return to initial state will not be possible without introducing changes into the system and its environment, and where, in spite of having knowledge of its initial conditions, it will be impossible – probabilistically irrelevant – to predict the state transitions. The best-known example is the weather: knowing the temperature at noon of a city today will not enable one to predict the temperature for the next day at noon.

For Isabelle Stengers, the discovery of irreversible processes interestingly enables us in 'breaking the circle of sufficient reason' (1997, p. 28), whereas for Leibniz, the principle is their very ground. Information theory understands that the transmission of information is not a perfect reversible process, given the noise and redundancies. Instead, the theory presupposes a world that can be conditioned such that it is code-able and transmissible. Such a world was available since Galileo which was quantifiable – 'Motion is number' – and qualitatively irrelevant since 'there is no quality in the realm of numbers' (Koyré 1992, p. 14). Today we find that life is determined by code and it is code-able through the four bases that make the genetic material, and DNA is understood as a stable system for coding and storing information. The physical universe is understood as a coded system which computes information – *It from bit* – where the base is somewhat different in being *quantum bit* or *qubits*. However, there is a difference between our times and Galileo who thought that 'Experiment … is a question we put to Nature. In order to receive an answer we must formulate it in some definite language' (quoted in Koyré 1943, p. 347). We have arrived at a conjuncture where nature, which designates whatever is the concern, must be modified such that we can pose predictive problems to it, or it is made non-contingent such that it is accountable. Information implies subtraction of being as information, control (not merely due to the proximity that cybernetics and Weiner had with Shannon) and prediction – the mutual implication of the three terms is the essence of information-metaphysics. It is characterized by three differences from the Leibnizian metaphysics: there is no principle such that it determines the world and gives it in its exigency to us as we give reason to it; there is no mechanistic or causal system determined according to the principle ('Correlation supersedes causation, and science can advance even without coherent models, unified theories, or really any mechanistic explanation at all' (Anderson 2008)); contingency, understood here as the essence of the world, can be controlled and any exigency of the world that is irrelevant to the information-metaphysics must be discarded. In this sense it is not merely correlationism but an action metaphysics that controls our political engagements already and it is asking us to become a new species without, not only the principle of reason, but also mechanism – 'society will need to shed some of its obsession for causality in exchange for simple correlations: not knowing *why* but only *what*' (Mayer-Schönberger, p. 7). We are to assume that the question *why something* refers to causality and the question *what is it?* gets the same answer each time it is asked of each thing – *it is bit*. Information-metaphysics thus implicitly proposes three axioms. The principle of sufficient reason as the ground and its question 'Why' are equal at best to mechanism. Being has a single quality that is contingency which makes any mechanistic enquiry futile. Reason in all its forms is inadequate with respect to what can be thought; what can be thought is data and it is not thinkable for humans at the scale at which it becomes relevant, which is 'big'. The task of information-metaphysics is to discover correlations in being-as-data and to introduce interventions in such a way that the quality of necessity is made to appear. In the next part we will look at this metaphysics and its infrastructure with regard to politics.

Technological grace

We designate as big data the infrastructure of information-metaphysics which has displaced the architecture of reason and the exigency of the principle of sufficient reason. This infrastructure ensures that the conditions given by information-metaphysics are met: the subtraction of exigency out of existence to get information, the gathering of all realms of existence as massive data and the correlational and probabilistic modelling on this data to give predictions. The relations between and within data sets imply rules for state transition for their domains, including those of physics and politics. The amount of data is such that it is beyond the analysing capability of humans, or even of typical computational architectures. There are many leading thinkers of the big data infrastructure who believe that the theorem of conditional probability given by Rev Bayes is the ground of this infrastructure.[13] However, we have seen that information-metaphysics has a more fundamental claim on the infrastructure since it determines what can be admissible to the infrastructure as material for processing. In the last century, the claims of equivalence between the concept of entropy in statistical dynamics and of the logarithmic function in information theory were expressed rather shyly, including by Shannon himself. Now, information theory certainly claims to ground probability as well, following Kolmogorov: 'Information theory must precede probability theory, and not be based on it' (Cover et al. 1989, p. 840).

The industrial architecture of big data has its own exigency. First, the expansion of the computational hardware market is necessary for the existence of the industry; second, the available data cannot be computed by traditional computing systems; investment in large-scale computing architecture is of the kind that demands control of other fields in order to maintain its profitability. The definition of big data will remain as *that which can be computed only by the industrial data architecture*: today it will be petabytes and tomorrow exabytes; it

> refers to datasets whose size is beyond the ability of typical database software tools to capture, store, manage, and analyze. This definition is intentionally subjective and incorporates a moving definition of how big a dataset needs to be in order to be considered Big Data. That is, we do not define Big Data in terms of being larger than a certain number. (McKinsey Global Institute 2011, p. 1)

What is to be understood is that as computational architecture grows, data availability too will increase. There will always be the industrial computational architecture at the cutting edge. This creates a new division in political ordering, between those who can compute big data and those who cannot. The role of those-who-cannot compute big is to generate data – or the designation in the information-metaphysics for the 'masses' is to turn their lives and practices into massive data that can be computed such that their state changes are predictable. Thus, sociologists, scientific laboratories, political institutions and the medical industry are channelled into the big data architecture since there is data generated with respect to these domains on such a large scale – data determines the future of these domains rather than their regional ontologies or their principle of reason.

Astronomy already reveals how the data sets are outside the purview of the astronomers – 'the Sloan Digital Sky Survey began in 2000. ... By 2010 the survey's archive teemed with a whopping 140 terabytes of information' (Mayer-Schönberger, p. 7). In particle physics, the Large Hadron Collider generates 140 petabytes of data and it is stored and processed in an architecture linking 100,000 CPUs (Hey et al. 2009, p. 42). At the social level nearly all activities are provided in the public domain which ought to make us rethink the political status of the category *public sphere*. Google Street View alone maintains 5,000,000 miles of images and it amounts to 20 million gigabytes of data, part of which was collected by illegally snatching data from Wi-Fi connections.[14] Recently, Google initiated a project to send a survey team to your house to record the initial conditions and install a free wireless router to collect all your data, for which you will initially be paid $5.[15] Nearly 50 per cent of American citizens are tracked by their mobile applications, 50 per cent of Apple phone applications track their users and this data is used for predictive processing: for example, a marketing firm, a specialist such as Acxiom,[16] will be able to predict the likelihood of you buying a certain product, given the kind of marketing intervention and the past behaviour; the likelihood of us choosing from Amazon recommendations, which are based on big data, reveal a lot more. These statistics of tracking movements to predict future movements exclude the actions of the surveillance industry, which is far less in comparison, though significant.[17] The election campaign of Barack Obama was driven by a data-intensive behaviour prediction architecture.[18] We no longer vote in elections: the conditions under which our voting behaviour functions are modified such that we cast it predictably or that we validate the elections with our presence. It is not merely prediction or the equivalent of a divine surveyor that the big data architecture implies at the political level, but control. Assume that the system predicts that you are likely to start a revolution the coming weekend at midnight, provided you have the transportation to reach the square where the fellow revolutionaries are. With total integration of all domains (food, clothing, shelter, transportation, communication) as information and the capability to process this information to expect future state transition of variables in all domains, the only step remaining is a subtle intervention which leaves the system as it was or as if nothing happened – an event of technological grace. Such technological grace in the case of you, the potential revolutionary, might be your self-driven Google car's computer shutting down or the car keeping you under arrest in it for the required duration. This infrastructure has taken the form of a new colonialism, with its distinction between those who have the colonizing architecture and those who generate the information material that drives the colonizing architecture. Perhaps this new distinction is at least as important as and coincidental with the known economic distinction between the 1 per cent and the 99 per cent that started the Occupy movements. Notably, its geographical lines continue the old colonial form as most of the large servers are located in America and Europe, and the major corporations possessing the big data architecture and controlling the field are American – IBM, Microsoft and Google.

Conclusion

The principle of sufficient reason has been relieved of its role in knowledge production only recently. Even when it was displaced as the principle that gave two exigencies – on the one hand the exigency of contingent existence as perfectly determined and yet un-analysable, and on the other as the demand of us from existence to give back reason – it continued to exist as that which institutes mechanistic philosophy under the rule *for each thing there is a cause*. Causality itself has now been displaced by correlationism in information-metaphysics. Another aspect of the principle was found to be the meaning of freedom grounded in a perfectly determined world revealing itself according to the qualitative variations of contingency and necessity which was survey-able but not analysable by God. Information-metaphysics reveals that it modifies and excises the exigency of existence to derive information, a discrete quanta, which given in sufficient amount to the big data architecture is able to generate predictions for each state transition in most domains of life and also able to prescribe new rules of transition to effect the quality of necessity. The necessity that 'everything must remain the same' is evident in spite of recent leaks from the level of the state, which shows the un-challengeable reality of information infrastructure, whereas the celebrity leaks from the private domain train us to live that reality. The architecture is sufficiently integrated with all domains such that it can also intervene and ensure controlled paths for events in the form of technological grace. Within the big data infrastructure the public sphere exists as an apparatus that legally generates and captures information. It is a sphere continuous with what we used to call private.[19]

The scenario raises new questions for politics. Since the algorithms used by Google and Twitter have political implications, should they not be published as well? In pressing for a particular set of algorithms (those requiring expensive and centrally managed infrastructure) and moving towards standardization are we not excluding most peoples from it, if not all the people? People end up being the colonized since they can give nothing but data. Since all data are recorded and cured and only later are the decisions concerning the political categories (public, private, anonymous) applied to them, should these categories continue to determine our political discourse with the values accorded to them on the basis of an older problematic or circulatory system? In fact, when one can and often does determine the private – such as the probabilistic course of an individual during a day – from what is available in the public, it shows the public/private distinction being the material of a production function rather than of being a category in political theory.

This chapter is dedicated to Vijay Tankha.

Notes

1   The term internet refers to computational systems that are networked and are potentially connected to all such networks and services using protocols, not exclusively TCP/IP suite. Internet refers today to most things, including the internet-of-things.

2   The new Platonism will take its limit stand with the quantum mechanics debate where the system of experimentation, or the perceived reality and the theory of perception (the gap between the state of the system and its measurement) found themselves inescapably in the domain of probability. This finding, especially in the debates between Bohr and Heisenberg, resulted in a new reality for thought. Probability, not reason, was the step leader of essences. Nature had to be accepted

as the probable reality; in Hegelian terms the real is probable and the probable is the real.

3   Bayesean nets (See Williamson 2005).

4   There are many kinds of causes and the etiology of the term cause can lead to histories of its mutations. Though we are to understand here efficient causality.

5   The theory of numbers is a place where the principle of sufficient reason insists and at the same time questions of the empiricity of mathematics are raised. For example, Goldbach's conjecture and the questions regarding Mersenne primes are asking after the ground of numbers themselves. The fact that quests of numbers are run by large-scale computation and that there are probability distributions for numbers do not in any way remove the problem of the ground, rather the quest is effected by the ground itself.

6   Serres would see in the principle an a priori juridical ground established between us and the world; we are to be in the world and be received by it only under the condition or due to the reason that we render it something back – 'What can we render to the nature that gives us the given. … The balanced answer would be: the totality of our essence, reason itself' (1995, p. 90).

7   It is evident that we have stepped over the distinction between those propositions whose negation implies contradiction and those whose negation indicates possibility. Since the principle determines all connections it can be seen that even equality of the terms is so determined by the principle.

8   However, if we correct ourselves of the errors involved in translating the Greek αἴτιον into cause we will not find ourselves in the treasury of freedom. See Rescher (1967).

9   This too relates back to the principle which denies any extrinsic denominations to things at all and instead refers to the predicate-in-subject form which is governed by the principle.

10 Donald Davidson's studies of action focused on the meaning of acting and he established a specific region for the principle as that which makes sense of the very word 'action'. See Davidson (2001).

11 For a recent biblical introduction to mythology of information and a sketch of the information-metaphysics see Gleick (2011). For a critical and historical account of the arrival of information as a political concept see May (2002).

12 The mathematics itself, the relation between the number of symbols available for coding (in English 26 alphabets and in binary arithmetic 0 and 1) and their uncertainty (rather than entropy), in an additive form as logarithmic functions were set in place by Hartley. Indeed, in Hartley, the engineering necessity involved in the subtraction of the quanta, information, is evident (Hartley 1928).

13 See Silver (2012).

14 http://www.bbc.com/news/technology-22252506.

15 http://www.nakedcapitalism.com/2013/11/wolf-richter-how-much-is-my-private-data-worth-google-just-offered-me.html.

16 http://www.nybooks.com/articles/archives/2014/jan/09/how-your-data-are-being-deeply-mined/.

17 http://www.bbc.com/news/technology-25231757.

18 http://www.nytimes.com/2013/06/23/magazine/the-obama-campaigns-digital-masterminds-cash-in.html?_r=0.

19 Mark Zuckerberg, the CEO of Facebook, asserted recently that privacy is irrelevant and an impediment for the new business models. See http://www.theguardian.com/technology/2010/jan/11/facebook-privacy.

References

Anderson, C. (2008), 'The End of Theory: The Data Deluge Makes the Scientific Method Obsolete', *Wired Magazine*, 23 June.

Cartwright, N. (2007), *Hunting Causes and Using Them: Approaches in Philosophy and Economics*, Cambridge: Cambridge University Press.

Cover, T. M., Gacs, P. and Gray, R. M. (1989), 'Kolmogorov's Contributions to Information Theory and Algorithmic Complexity', *The Annals of Probability*, 17 (3): 840–65.

Davidson, D. (2001), *Essays on Actions and Events*, 2nd edn, Oxford: Clarendon Press.

Deleuze, G. (2006), *The Fold: Leibniz and the Baroque*, London: Continuum.

Gleick, J. (2011), *The Information: A History, a Theory, a Flood*, 1st edn, London: Fourth Estate.

Hartley, R. V. L. (1928), 'Transmission of Information' July, 7(3): pp. 553–63.

Hegel, G. W. F. (1969), *Hegel's Science of Logic*, New York: Humanity Books.

Heidegger, M. (1977), *The Question Concerning Technology and Other Essays*, New York: Harper Torchbooks.

Heidegger, M. (1991), *The Principle of Reason*, Bloomington and Indianapolis: Indiana University Press.

Hey, T., Tansley, S. and Tolle, K. (2009), *The Fourth Paradigm: Data-Intensive Scientific Discovery*, 2nd edn, Redmond, Washington: Microsoft Research.

Kelly, K. (2002), 'God Is The Machine', *Wired Magazine*, December, Issue 10.12, p. 4.

Koyré, A. (1943), 'Galileo and the scientific revolution of the seventeenth century'. *The Philosophical Review*, 52 (4): 333–48.

Koyré, A. (1968), *From the Closed World to the Infinite Universe*, Baltimore: John Hopkins Press.

Koyré, A. (1992), *Metaphysics and Measurement*, London: Gordon and Breach Science Publishers.

Leibniz, G. W. v. (1956), *Philosophical Papers and Letters, Volume 1 and 2*, Chicago: The University of Chicago Press.

May, C. (2002), *The Information Society*, 1st edn, Cambridge, MA: Polity Press.

Mayer-Schönberger, V. and Cukier, K. (2013), *Big Data: A Revolution That Will Transform How We Live, Work and Think*, London: John Murray (Publishers).

McKinsey Global Institute (2011), *Big Data: The Next Frontier for Innovation, Competition and Productivity*, San Francisco: McKinsey Global Institute.

Rescher, N. (1967), *The Philosophy of Leibniz*, New Jersey: Prentice-Hall, Inc.

Rescher, N. (2001), 'Contingentia Mundi: Leibniz on the World's Contingency', *Studia Leibnitiana*, Bd. 33, H. 2, pp. 145–62.

Serres, M. (1995), *The Natural Contract*, Ann Arbor: The University of Michigan Press.

Shannon, C. E. (1948), 'A Mathematical Theory of Communication', *The Bell System Technical Journal*, XXVII (3): 45.

Silver, N. (2012), *The Signal and the Noise: Why So Many Predictions Fail—and Some Don't*, New York: Penguin Press.

Stengers, I. (1997), *Power and Invention: Situating Science*, 1st edn, Minneapolis University of Minnesota Press.

Williamson, J. (2005), *Bayesian Nets and Causality: Philosophical and Computational Foundations*, Oxford: Oxford University Press.

Part Five

(Whose) Inclusion (Where)?

Some key criticisms of the Habermasian identification of a public, albeit historically bourgeois, sphere – wherein all interlocutors, irrespective of their sociocultural identity and status, engage in rational-critical discourse on matters of common interest leading to will-formation resulting in democratic, political decisions at the state level – have been that this formation excluded many less-than-equal sections referred to as 'subaltern' or 'counter-publics' (Fraser 1992; Negt and Kluge 1993) and continues to either exclude or asymetrically relate to other kinds of discourse, such as religion (Carter 1993; Murphy 1998; Yates 2007). Craig Calhoun points out that 'the issue of inclusion in the more general public sphere' is not adequately addressed in the idea of counter-publics which remain parallel, almost self-sufficient, formations based on experiences and interests and overlooks active contestations (2010, p. 305). Is the 'public' the site of these interlocked discourses, or is it the ascendant discourse that managed to successfully overcome and exclude other contestants? The chapters in this section explore the public–private divide and inclusion by thematizing the entry of the new in relation to the public sphere in four very different ways.

With the number of globally displaced crossing 50 million, both routine and conflicted demographic movements and the range of interactions, and the legal, political and 'humanitarian' challenges generated, fly in the face of the liberal chronotopes of individuals engaged in communicative action as well as the anti-liberal chronotopes of parallel solidarities. Hoff's chapter displaces this altogether-heterotopic approach to the question of 'public' by introducing a kind of new stranger called the *intimate* which is also a familiar being that we avoid thinking about and that spells trouble. A certain binding of modes of action and passion – of affect in the Deleuzian/Spinozist sense – intimacy is proposed as a stratum where affects form and develop histories and are expressed in the public with consequences. For example, both public displays of affection in a conservative country and public covering of the intimacy of the body and skin in a liberal society are dangerous. The latter hints at a life beyond the grasps of its own public norms, and Hoff's suggestion is that the politics of the veil is not really about security as a military/police issue, or the exclusion of religious world views from contributing to the political public sphere, but about a society's insecurity over the explicit announcement by somebody through the veil that there is a certain intimacy that stubbornly insists beneath its publicity. Intimacy is not discontinuous with the public. Hoff argues that our public behaviour is the continuation of our private intimacies, our habitudes which permit our public self-presentation. The mutual introduction of the strata is the telos of the space called public. The training of intimacy is a preparation for public life and is hence also political as it determines how this space will be forged. How do we ensure that all peoples can appear without breaking down their own intimate histories?

Proposing a certain phenomenology that would attune us to various histories of the intimate, Hoff's meditation points beyond the analytical concept of 'intersectionality', borrowed from the US context for the Eurosphere, to understand the positioning of demands of gender equality and ethnic diversity relative to each other (Crenshaw 1989; Ferree 2008; Siim and Mokre 2013). Discussion on intersectionality needs to reckon with non-uniform global situations where the developed world attracts asylum-seeking migration flows while the largest number of forced refugees now exist in developing countries, and a highly significant number are internally displaced. Sloterdijk has exposed the insufficiency of 'contestation' by arguing that the *foam* architecture of our lives today entails reciprocal obstruction, inhibition and interference whose density prevents any unilateral praxis (2005). In her chapter Dwivedi dwells on the issue of refugeehood and migration by using the vampiric figure to make a difference in the interpretations in a series of thinkers of *Mitsein*, starting with Heidegger. The vampire suggests a strata of the old. Their existence is hidden and their survival relies on physical proximity, the intimacy of bites, while their exotic origins lure and threaten the West. The vampiric (as well as zombie) ways of being-with can be said to have undergone a Sloterdijkian densification, proceeding from folklore through high realist literature and expressionist cinema to twenty-first century Scandinavian crime fiction, sci-fi 'survival horror' films and video games, American soaps and chick lit. Dwivedi distinguishes Agamben and Foucault as two inheritors of the philosophical thought of politics that Arendt drew from Heidegger and proposes the concept of a rift-design of politics that preserves the openness for the new even as *it gives* the regimentation of being-with. She revisits Foucault's tripartite sketch for relating to our own time and space politically: the combination of archaeology-genealogy-strategics identifies the possibility of shaking free from a reigning system of governmentality. She translates ontological openness into political openness, suggesting that considerations of refugeehood, too, cannot remain locked in aporias of sovereign power. The aesthetic existence of vampires and zombies across decennia is used as a genealogical index that also invites strategics, as shown in films like *Warm Bodies*.

For Chanter, certain actions demanding equal rights and access to the public in fact already overtake themselves in having staged their political insertion into the public even as they seem to await permission. She extends Rancière's reading of the eighteenth-century French activist Olympe de Gouges to Antigone's political self-insertion into the public whereby two hitherto taboo entities break in: woman and the child of incest. This makes visible, though still blocking the entry of, yet another excluded figure of 'bare existence', namely the slave: Antigone opposes her uncle Creon's move to conduct the last rites of her brother in ways unfit for a royal, but these are the very ways of the slaves, a notion that, Chanter points out, is entangled with the Persians. At this moment in the tragedy, the unconscious of politics becomes available in the way Antigone herself overlooks the division that debars the slave from equal rights. Chanter points out that the political unconscious is not so much about lifting taboos as about a level of dynamism of thoughts and events that are unconscious with respect to the public sphere. The idea regarding the (informal or weak) public sphere is that it contains all the ideas that make up both the public and the private. The business we do in the public is after all sanctioned in the public. But beyond Foucauldian heterotopia Chanter proposes unconscious topias, drawing on the two moments in which Freud found the unconscious of politics: Antigone and also the Moses statue. Rancière finds Freud to have contained it for clinical reasons and yet allowed for the same in his conception of the death drive, but for Chanter there is a third possibility, exercised in art, of the disruptive potential of emotions in 'affective economies' where the state, private economic interest and kinship structures mutually reinforce an exclusionary public sphere. She explores this aesthetic disruption of geographies of security in *Rabbit-Proof Fence*, the cinematic rendition of the narrative of Doris Pilkington Garimara, one of the 'stolen generation' of aboriginal children in Australia.

Wakankar traces the history of a specific opening of reason to publicness which occurs in the historical experience of the Indian Dalit's slavery. A primordial inscription of negativity which is prior to cultural difference and the distinction between the West and the non-West countersigns this opening. This also marks the incipience of conceptuality which is prior to the publicness which constitutes all philosophical concepts including the concepts of the public and the private. In this specific opening we could perhaps locate the secret of caste and race. To arrive at an idea of the public sphere which would include contemporary dalit writers and devotional poets like Kabir, Wakankar finds, is to explore the link between freedom and conceptuality. Only a freedom marked by caste, and re-marked in and as secret, can provide the wherewithal for the modulation of the will opposed to caste. Wakankar argues that the origin of caste is in the origin of sociality itself and cannot be located in the history of the institutionalization of caste. Both dalit and brahmanical thinking share in the incipience of conceptuality, but dalit thinkers differentiate themselves by their access to an originary negativity. Caste is a crypt within the crypt of the negative that opens up both state and the public sphere. This double encryption makes the public-ness of dalit writing possible. Wakankar suggests that the Will can oppose caste only insofar as it was countersigned by a differentiation which is logically and chronologically prior to the origin of caste.

16

Politics in Public: The History of Identity and the Aspiration to Universality

Shannon Hoff

The question of what kind of deliberation and decision-making is appropriate to a democratic political domain is a challenging one, addressed as it is both to the idea of free, democratic participants as well as to the need for determinate and binding decisions. Deliberative democratic theorists such as Jürgen Habermas have derived norms for this process out of a consideration of the very structure of communication itself,[1] and liberal political philosophers such as John Rawls have shown, similarly, that norms for discursive interaction about 'questions of fundamental political justice' emerge from the idea that participants are free and equal yet diverse.[2] The outcome of deliberation in (Habermas's) public sphere or in (Rawls's) public political forum is thought to be legitimate if these norms, shareable by reasonable interlocutors, are met, and existing forms of communication and deliberative outcomes are thought to be capable of being evaluated by these norms. There is much of import in these various attempts, insofar as the restrictions they present to human interaction are conceptually tied to the very character of interaction itself and the very idea of self-determining participants, and thus do not involve alien standards. However, like many basically liberal theories, these accounts of public deliberation insufficiently attend to the actual conditions of human existence and to the practical and structural work it would take to accomplish this kind of interaction, risking thereby, to borrow the words of Merleau-Ponty, a kind of 'mystification' whereby liberal principles become useful means by which 'cunning, violence, propaganda, and *realpolitik*' are concealed (Merleau-Ponty 2000, p. xiii). In this chapter I aim to discuss these 'actual conditions' so as to identify the work that would be required in order that just deliberation about issues of basic political justice be accomplished. I will begin by identifying the significant ways in which our intimate and social *history* with others influences our public interaction, relying on the work of Frantz Fanon. I will then explore the issue of *universality*, showing that, contrary to traditional accounts of public reason and the public sphere, the ideal of universality operates as an *aspiration* produced through interaction in the terms presented by these intimate and social histories. Finally, using the work of Étienne Balibar, I will explore the problems involved with privileging either of these factors – history or universality – over the other, illuminating how interaction in public can be the site of their integration in the mode of what Balibar calls 'civility'. Let us begin, however, by developing a working definition of the distinction between the private and public domains, so as to be able to discuss effectively the nature of the public and public interaction.

The private and the public

However ambiguous, dynamic and open to challenge, there seems to be some kind of line between private and public, discernible not simply in terms of location or size or a similarly quantitative measure but in the qualitative significance that the specific elements of their constitutions – ourselves, others, space and objects – acquire for us.[3] Under typical circumstances, the private is characterized by the dynamic of *familiarity* and by a non-neutral orientation to specific human beings. In private, we generally do not have to introduce and explain ourselves, to reflect on how we might appear so as to give an account of ourselves or to justify our pursuits; the question of who we, our activities, others and our environment are is typically less thematized in private than it is in public. We are more likely to be able to 'relax' and 'be ourselves' than in public, more likely to not experience the feeling of a distinction between 'inner' and 'outer self', between who we feel we are and who we seem to be to others. Even if at times who we are can become an issue or question in private interaction, a kind of unreflective familiarity is the norm. Others are similarly familiar to us; we operate on the basis of a familiarity with them and with what kind of possibilities are available to us in interaction with them. We typically do not ask them to justify their presence in that domain; in its ordinary functioning, it is simply constituted around their presence. Further, private space and the objects within it are typically constituted and ordered in relation to our preferences and pursuits. We move around in space without confronting alien purposes, desires and interests in it and interact with objects without wondering about them. These specific understandings of ourselves, others, space and objects are typical of the private domain, even though the unreflective familiarity of the private can be disrupted by the experience of certain kinds of trouble or uncanniness.

Being in public, however, is typically qualitatively different. In public we interact with those who are less familiar, and we typically are conscious of the fact that we are on display to others for whom our identity is a question. We are 'looked at' in public, in a way that implies a question about who we are and what we are like, and we speak and act in ways that are 'on display', insofar as they are unfamiliar to those with whom we are interacting. Space and the objects in it do not necessarily answer, in principle at least, to our desires, interests and purposes, and in relation to them we have to answer to the desires, interests and purposes of others, since they are also sites for the agency of others.

I draw this preliminary distinction so as to begin to identify the domain in relation to which the concepts of public sphere and the public use of reason have become relevant and to identify the reasons for their relevance – namely, there is no reason to think that the mechanisms of interaction developed in familiar contexts should operate unproblematically with unfamiliar others in a space defined partly by their unfamiliar orientations to it. If the methods of our interaction are not simply up to us – if, that is, we are dealing with other human beings whose acknowledgement of and acquiescence to us cannot be forced – then the question of how to interact with others is pressing. Is there a kind of interaction appropriate to this kind of domain, and, more specifically, what kind of interaction would be appropriate to our attempts to address the specific question of how to structure and organize our living together?

For theorists of the public sphere and the public use of reason, it is precisely this second question that is at stake – broadly speaking, the question about what kind of interaction is appropriate to addressing specifically political questions, to deliberating about the form that living together should take. This question has been answered by reference to the principles at work in communication, and by reference to the formal equality of the participants in communication, but I believe that an adequate answer requires greater consideration of the dynamics involved in actual public interaction with unfamiliar others. Let us identify one such dynamic, investigating how it influences our interaction and how its significance could be appropriately reckoned with: that of the intimate and social histories by which we and our relationships with others are constituted and cultivated.

The history of identity

As developmental psychologists, psychoanalysts and philosophers have observed, we repeat, in ordinary, non-familiar interactions, the patterns of interaction that we have developed with intimate others in private.[4] The way we act in public is powerfully defined by our experience with those with whom we are familiar, who come effectively 'with' us into public, given the way in which they define our sense of ourselves and our orientation to interaction. We are profoundly shaped by others, to the extent that our sense of ourselves as discrete and self-determining can be relatively misguided. Indeed, on my own I may feel out of place in the world, if I have developed a partnership with another person that makes it strange to be out of her company, if I am apart from a family upon which I heavily rely for a sense of self or if I have not yet digested my views with intimate friends. My action ensues from a kind of invisible interaction and unspoken dialogue with other, familiar human beings.[5]

This interaction and dialogue extends beyond the limits of our intimate relations. We are also constituted historically by specific sociocultural ways of life, which can also have a profound influence on our interaction with unfamiliar others. The forms of identification in which we participate often matter quite substantially to our interaction; it makes a difference whether we are brown, white, Jewish, Malay, disabled, aboriginal, female, Dalit, F2M, working class, Tamil, American, mestiza and so on, and it makes a difference whether we and others acknowledge this difference or not.[6] Because of specific historical developments outside of our individual control, we and our interaction are fundamentally defined by our status as belonging to particular groups, by the reasons for the constitution of such groups, by the history of relations and conflicts between groups and by the attachments we develop with those groups by virtue of the significance or trauma we experience as members. This history provides our interaction in public with certain kinds of significance that we ourselves do not invent or control. Because of the phenomenon of history, both intimate and social, we are dealing with much more than people as individuals in our interaction with them: we are implicitly interacting with their parents, their ethnic groups, their churches, their classes, their nationalities and so on, with the specific preferences and orientations of all of these implicated parties and with the ways in which these parties have interacted in the past. Neither of us is ever a generic instance of the idea of a human being essentially defined by discrete individuality.

Frantz Fanon offers a powerful account of this issue – specifically, of how the history of colonialism affects the ways in which people relate to each other and to public space. The first basic thing to notice here is his emphasis on *relation* as that through which individual terms are allotted significance: 'the two congenitally antagonistic forces' of the colonial situation '*owe their singularity* to the kind of reification secreted and nurtured by [this] situation' (Fanon 2004, 2), in which context the black man 'must be black in relation to the white man' (Fanon 2008, 90). To presume that we are dealing solely with individuals is to effectively erase the histories by which their significance is constituted and to misconceive their identity as the result of their decisions and a matter of their responsibility. Fanon's analysis of 'the lived experience of the black man' shows that the colonized subject's self-experience is interrupted and mediated by the 'white man' to the extent that the black man lives in the white man's world, his significance determined by others before he can determine it himself: 'The Other, the white man … had woven me out of a thousand details, anecdotes, and stories' (Fanon 2008, p. 91). The black man need not *cooperate* in the construction of significance: 'The upheaval reached the black man from the outside. The black man was acted upon. Values that were not engendered by his actions, values not resulting from the systolic gush of his blood, whirled about him in a colorful dance' (Fanon 2008, p. 194).

This constitution by the white world has profound consequences for how the black man interacts with others in public, according to Fanon, and these consequences should have an effect on our understanding of the public domain. Whereas public space is often understood to be the open domain of free movement; whereas participants in it are understood to be individuals; whereas peaceful and cooperative discursive relations are construed as the norm; and whereas universal ideals are construed as political liberation, the colonized person experiences the opposite. Space is the domain in which he is held captive by the gaze of another person and in which he is uncomfortable in his body: 'In the white world, the man of color encounters difficulties in elaborating his body schema. The image of one's body is solely negating. It's an image in the third person' (Fanon 2008, p. 90). The norms of peaceful, cooperative discursive relations hypocritically conceal the violent conditions of their emergence, 'the violence which governed the ordering of the colonial world' (Fanon 2004, p. 5), and they legitimate the violence needed to establish them: 'The colonial regime owes its legitimacy to force' (Fanon 2004, p. 42). Further, those who can live as individuals – each 'locked in his subjectivity' (Fanon 2004, p. 11) – can do so because they are not forced to cope with the demands of social reality, unlike the colonial subject: 'I cast an objective gaze over my self, discovered my blackness, my ethnic features; deafened by cannibalism, backwardness, fetishism, racial stigmas, slave traders, and above all ... the grinning *Y a bon Banania*' (Fanon 2004, p. 92). Finally, universal ideals have been imposed upon the colonized subject. When the colonized 'hear a speech on Western culture ... they draw their machetes or at least check to see they are close to hand. The supremacy of white values is stated with such violence. ... In the period of decolonization the colonized masses thumb their noses at these very values, shower them with insults and vomit them up' (Fanon 2004, p. 8). The colonist can be certain that universal ideals will favour him; they reflect to him his power, which was achieved through the oppression of the colonized subject and the institution in that subject of self-doubt. Fanon's response to this one-sided situation is to defend a violent stance of resistance that *refuses* interaction, opposing in its entirety the 'Manichean' world of colonialism for the sake of the renewal of self-worth in the colonized subject. It is to encourage *departure* from the domain of public interaction, which is constituted on the basis of the destruction of the colonized subject.

With these insights, Fanon gives a powerful portrayal of the qualitatively charged character of public space, the possibility of fundamentally distinct and opposed orientations to it and the possibility that refusal to participate could be a politically liberatory gesture. This portrayal explains why interaction in public may be characterized by aggression, opposition and hostility – indeed, why it is at times *appropriate* that this be the case, given the history of interaction between forms of life. It explains why such interaction could involve contributions that are incomprehensible and mystifying. It explains that the proper approach to public interaction might be to anticipate, not rule out of turn, interventions that are oppositional.[7] To impose the rubric of reasoned, respectful discourse on such interaction would be to disallow justifiable opposition and the refusal of discourse, to conceal oppressive and violent relations instead of establishing peaceful relations.[8] To meaningfully grapple with others in interaction requires answering to the historical specificities of their specific contexts, since being associated with them influences how we are able to participate in public, and, indeed, is often the very phenomenon under negotiation in public.

Whereas it might be imagined that the contexts of development and the histories beyond our formation inhibit agency and meaningful interaction, we can in fact see that it is *only* as belonging to and participating in already meaningful worlds that we develop as human individuals – indeed, as human individuals capable of identifying with the projects and pursuits of others. Thus, while some of these developmental contexts are detrimental with regard to our agency and our interaction, the idea is not to be free of such attachments but to be able to develop productive ones, and to organize political life around the necessity of grappling with our ongoing, already-existent, historical determinacy. Because agency emerges only via historical specificity, because contextualization is the very condition of agency, we must deal with the intimate and social worlds of our constitution in order to deal with the real human beings we are. Indeed, it is likely that our political engagement and discourse work better when specificity and the divisions that accomplish it are made into explicit themes for our public interaction.

Grappling with specificity does not require, however, abandoning the project of universality and of developing common aspirations and ideals. Let us explore the phenomenon of political interaction and deliberation further, considering the way in which the experience of a certain kind of identification can be *produced* through attempts to understand the significance of historical specificities.

The production of universality

Thus far we have explored the idea that agency is not fundamentally individual, that the contexts in which we are cultivated are its enabling conditions and that our personal and social histories shape our public interaction. These considerations should inspire opposition to a model of public discourse that would emphasize the formal identity of participants and develop specific procedures for interaction on the basis of this identity. But they can also lead us to a viable approach to identification with unfamiliar others in public, one that works *through* the phenomenon of historical specificity. Let us examine how we are open to an aspiration to universality, even in our specificity.

We are constituted as human individuals through living and developing with others, and in this context we develop an orientation to the world that is substantially shared, through which we are enabled to make sense of the world. On the basis of a primordial openness to and dependence on others, we develop habitual ways of acting, interacting and interpreting, through which the significance of the world and other people comes across to us. Ways of life are ways of orientation to and interpretation of significance.

As such, the relations from which we emerge are both closed and open. On the one hand, they are specific, determinate ways of life involving habitual assertions that 'this is the way the world and we are', and so they operate as a determinate, sedimented and fixed orientation to the world. On the other hand, however, they are open, insofar as specific, interpretative orientations are a mark of our sense that the world demands an interpretation, that there are things in it to be valued and that we are capable of being impacted by it and others. Hence our belonging to specific traditions of interpretation manifests our primordial openness and answerability to others and to the world of meaning.

If this is true of us, then it is also true of others: their originary systems of recognition also give shape to their openness to the world and to others. To foster interaction with such others would require trying to understand the specific character of their orientation and openness to the world – as well as trying to understand the specific character of our own orientation with the help of their perspective. Such understanding would occur not through our asserting our formal identity with each other, but through seeking to illuminate, through communication, the specific frameworks of significance through which the world has become meaningful to each of us.[9] Such understanding has to be *worked toward* and occurs not through an abandoning of the significance of historical specificity but through an attempt to communicate the sense *behind* our different orientations, to see their specificity as a more or less internally coherent way of making sense of the world in co-operation with others.[10]

Operative in this attempt to work towards identification by working through specificity is what we might call an 'aspiration' to universality or to a shared orientation – a gesture towards the ideal presumed by traditional accounts of the public sphere and of public reason. The question concerning how to interact in public would begin here: with identifying how one could develop, through the necessarily determinate form that one's openness to the world takes, an openness to the similarly necessary specificity of another. On the one hand it would entail grappling with one's own specificity, effectively *discovering* one's habitual patterns of perceiving and valuing. Here interaction with unfamiliar others can be extremely helpful, since the one-sidedness and partiality of our patterns of perception and valuing can appear more vividly to these others, and to ourselves when we interact with them. On the other hand it would entail learning about the ways in which the seemingly strange and one-sided patterns of behaviour of others are a meaningful part of their framework of openness to the world and to others.

This kind of learning has to be part of interaction in public if it is to be oriented at all to the possibility of establishing *shared* forms of life, shared principles for the organizational frameworks and institutions by which life together is sustained. Identification with others is something we *earn*, by working through specificity; it is not automatic and capable of being imposed by procedural principles. If we are honest about the inevitability of specificity, however, this identification can be a meaningful aspiration. Here Fanon is again helpful, for his assertion of the significance of specificity is also accompanied by a hope, by an aspiration, for 'humanity' as such. He writes: 'But if we want humanity to take one step forward, if we want to take it to another level than the one where Europe has placed it, then we must innovate, we must be pioneers. ... For Europe, for ourselves and for humanity, comrades, we must make a new start, develop a new way of thinking, and endeavor to create a new man' (Fanon 2004, p. 239). This 'man' is an aspiration, not an assertion of the present existence of a unified group, 'humanity'. In Fanon's work, it operates so as to bolster a certain kind of resolve for the present, to propel the development of a vision concerning what conditions would have to be brought about in order for human beings to be able to say about others that they share in a 'humanity' with them.[11]

Thus far we have discussed the phenomena of history and the aspiration to universality in their positive significance, but there are also specific kinds of violence that attach to each when they operate outside of a relation with the other, in extreme forms. In his 'Three Concepts of Politics', Étienne Balibar identifies forms of violence that correspond to each of these elements and offers the notion of 'civility' as a way of dealing with this violence. Because of the affinity between his work and the themes of universality and history, and because the notion of civility is clearly relevant in relation to the issue of public interaction,[12] I will briefly explain specific aspects of his account and illuminate how they could be useful for developing a conception of the public sphere that does justice to history and the aspiration to universality.

Balibar and the notion of civility

According to Balibar, there is a particular kind of violence attached to the ideal of autonomous individuality that is formally equal to others and the universality of the discourse in which such individuals are said to participate: it is a violence involving the eradication of specificity in the name of an identity that '*float[s] freely* between all roles, between casual, pleasurable (or advantageous) identifications', the flexibility of which is particularly suited to specifically capitalist market relations and thus also attached to the violence attached to them (Balibar 2002, p. 29). This violence of the 'free-floating' stance is implicit in traditional conceptions of the public sphere and public reason, since they imply the possibility that specific forms of identification can be abandoned, which is neither equally possible for people, nor truthful about the extent to which these forms of identification exercise different levels of pressure on human agency, nor sufficiently cognizant about the ways in which they are a manifestation of our fundamental openness. With the idea of the specificity of history, on the other hand, another kind of violence is possible: that involved in taking on a '*single, unambiguous identity*', identifying totally 'with one's role' and in turn desiring the 'elimination of otherness' and of 'mixing' (Balibar 2002, p. 29). This violence implicit as a possibility in the very notion of identity can entail also a violence against other specific identities – a refusal to acknowledge the irreducibility of difference, the multiplicity of forms of identification and the fluctuating character of the meaning of identities.

Balibar advocates a politics of civility as a way of mediating these two extremes, a politics that would regulate 'the conflict of identifications between the impossible (and yet, in a sense, very real) limits of a total and a floating identification' (Balibar 2002, p. 29). Such a politics would take 'as its "object" the very violence of identities' (Balibar 2002, p. 23), understanding that politics is about negotiating interaction and not simply about protecting individuals in their identity, but also understanding that politics involves the interaction of people whose different identities are significant for their political situations. Balibar's argument seems to be that the proper terrain of the political is the phenomenon of relation and interaction, in relation to which identity will always be significant but which it should never dominate. That is, relation has a certain kind of priority in relation to identity, insofar as it is definitive for identity, and a politics of civility would enact a kind of deference to relation over identity, outlawing the extreme forms of violence that would destroy the possibility of interaction. The idea of civility speaks in the name of the political as such, and sustaining the political domain requires answering to the idea that individuals are specific kinds of people in relation to each other but also in principle open to others: their very openness to participation is a marker both of the enabling powers of their forms of identification and of their ongoing capacity to identify themselves differently. Neither the idea of autonomous, free-floating individuality nor the idea of fixed forms of identity answers to the reality of human interaction as such, as both the founding origin and unpredictable future of all human reality.

Let us look at a particular example so as to articulate expressly the way in which both historical specificity and openness to transformation could operate together in ordinary interaction with unfamiliar others in public – namely, the issue of wearing the veil or *hijab*.[13] This issue speaks specifically both to the issue of the historical constitution of identity and to the possibility of communication beyond the traditional boundaries of its relevance. Scholars have aimed to reveal the fact that it does not have a simple, singular significance and thus that it is an example of how the sign of a specific form of identification can also be a singular political expression and a contribution to political communication.[14] Women give various reasons for wearing *hijab*: it is worn as a means of expressing political criticism of the prejudice of the West (Lazreg 2009) and resisting what seems to some to be its desire to annihilate Islam[15]; of asserting political opposition (Killian 2003); of expressing and celebrating one's membership in a larger community (Atasoy 2006); of demanding political respect for religion (Ahmed 2011). To be noticed here is the fact that what could seem to operate as a sign that resonates only within a specific domain of religious significance can take on wider expressive power and relate to terms in other discourses not traditionally associated with that group, bespeaking the way in which meaning flows over the borders of identification. An onlooker, similarly – rather than exercising a distant tolerance, a liberal gesture of false generosity to a foreign other – would exercise *civility* in attempting to develop the capacity to understand these gestures as they are intended, as a piece of an interpretative whole, presuming that, since they are ways of acknowledging specific meanings at work in the world, they have the capacity to communicate beyond the borders of the specific group in which they originate. Further, she could herself be led, through this interaction, to a greater ability to see the specificity of her own cultural practices. She could come to hear, in the gestures of others, a critique of her own culture's lack of concern for the collective support of individual and its reliance on the domination of other cultures. Adopting the virtue of civility here could be the occasion for productive transformation in the mode of greater self-understanding, for civility would assume, as John Gray writes, that 'nonliberal regimes and cultural forms' could 'possess genuine virtues and harbor authentic excellences that are weak, or lacking, in liberal regimes' (Gray 1995, p. 135). Finally, because the commitments expressed through the specificity of wearing *hijab* could be similar to those of the onlooker, understanding this specificity could produce a certain kind of identification. Civility does not require leaving behind one's modes of identification, but involves the recognition that while the particular forms of *expression* that specific beliefs and commitments take may not be shared, the ways in which they are *meaningful* might be. To be a specific being with an intimate and social history is to capture and attest to meaningfulness that is in principle shareable, even if the specific forms of its expression are foreign.

To be in public is to be in a common, illuminated space that is peopled with others whose company we have not explicitly chosen, whose character, interests and goals we do not know and whose influence on us we cannot predict. It is to be in space that we cannot traverse comfortably or confidently – or, if we do traverse it in this way, we have dishonestly suppressed the perspectives of others. It is to encounter objects whose significance is not clear to us, because we will meet others who relate to these objects differently and in so doing shape their significance; through interaction with these others our orientation to these objects could change. It is possible that interaction with others in this domain has the capacity to change us, and thereby to change the significance to us of our intimate and social histories as well as our approach to the very phenomenon of interaction. Interaction, that is, has a certain predominance over identity conceived as autonomous and free-floating. Our interactive pasts have constituted the present, but our interaction in the present contains the possibility of a different future – one to which identity conceived as fixed in a specific way is in a certain way subordinate. The meaning of our specificity and that of others can only begin to be discovered in interaction itself, which has the capacity, therefore, to change that meaning and our orientation to specificity.

Interaction in public is not simply the exchange of already established information through predetermined communicative avenues on the part of fixed selves, but it carries with it the possibility of transformation of fixed selves, of established information and of communicative avenues. It is only in our interaction itself that the process of understanding can take place, and that interaction unfolds on the unpredictable terms and contributions that its participants present to it. As fundamentally unpredictable in this sense, insofar as its participants, its content and its forms are transformable, the public domain operates *without* a law concerning what properly belongs and does not belong. There are risks to this absence of law and structure in public; it can, for instance, become open in principle to people who are opposed to the participation of specific others. But there are also problems with trying to close it and to dictate what kind of interaction is appropriate to it – namely, we render our existing forms of understanding, interpretation and identity absolute, preventing the possibility of a different future for them, and we foreclose the possibility that views that do not meet our standards could be acknowledged, negotiated and understood. To fashion public life so as to preclude this negotiation could be more of a problem than a solution – a symptom of the suppressing, by liberal values, of antagonism, suspicion and mutual dislike.

Conclusion

We are historically and intimately situated, potentially unaware of the prejudices that accrue to us on the basis of that situatedness. We are also exposed and potentially unaware of and incapable of predicting the way in which interaction could lead to our transformation. In our interaction, both old and new meanings assert themselves – the old meanings at work in our development and history and the new meanings available in our interaction. By presuming that individuals interact as individuals and that their interaction can be managed, we effectively attempt to eradicate the significance of both old and new, allowing only the present a say in the determination of meaningfulness. The significance of personal development and social histories to our action and interaction in public, and the possibility that such interaction could change us, should not be underestimated and concealed by a desire to establish norms and strategies for interaction that are shared. We should be open to the possibility that the desire to produce clear-cut procedures for interaction prior to it is a symptom of the fact that, as Fanon might say, we are invested in the perpetuation of patterns of domination and motivated by a desire to close off the possibility of risk.

Notes

1 See Habermas 1984, 1991 and 1998. For a helpful account of various important publications on the public sphere, see Goodnight and Hingstman 1997.
2 See Rawls 1993, 1997.
3 For feminist criticism of the distinction between public and private, see, for instance, Benhabib 1992; Fraser 1985; Young 1990. For a Marxist critique, see Negt and Kluge 1993.
4 See, for instance, Laing 1990; Winnicott 1986; Freud 1962; Russon 2003.

5 For a compelling description of the relationship between intersubjective intimacy and emergence into public, see Jacobson 2010.

6 As John Gray writes, 'the propensity for cultural difference is a primordial attribute of the human species … a species which … exercises its distinctive powers of self-invention in the creation of identities that are not only diverse but also typically exclusive in their natures' (Gray 1995, pp. 112–13).

7 See Eley 1992.

8 There are resonances here between this position and agonistic models of political interaction and democracy. See, for instance, Mouffe 2005; Connolly 2002; Tully 2008.

9 For the idea of establishing a shared reality through 'becoming initiated' into another person's ways, see Russon 1995.

10 See Tully's discussion of reimagining belonging in Tully 1995.

11 For the idea that multiculturalism is a sharing accomplished in living interaction, see Fillion 2008.

12 While conceived of differently than in Balibar's work, the duty of civility is central to Rawls's idea of public reason. See Rawls 1993.

13 For the purpose of this chapter, I use 'wearing the veil' or '*hijab*' to refer broadly to the various forms of self-covering used by women who identify religiously and/or culturally as Muslim.

14 For an account of the diverse reasons at work in wearing *hijab*, see Bakht 2012, esp. pp. 2–4.

15 Karen Armstrong writes that 'the unfolding tragedy of the Middle East has convinced some that the west is bent on the destruction of Islam. The demand that they abandon the veil will exacerbate these fears, and make some women cling more fiercely to the garment that now symbolizes their resistance to oppression' (Armstrong 2006).

References

Ahmed, Leila (2011), 'Veil of Ignorance', *Foreign Policy*, May/June 2011.

Armstrong, Karen (2006), 'My years in a habit taught me the paradox of veiling', *The Guardian*, 26 October.

Atasoy, Yildiz (May 2006), 'Governing Women's Morality: A Study of Islamic Veiling in Canada', *European Journal of Cultural Studies*, 9 (2): 203–21.

Bakht, Natasha (2012), 'Veiled Objections: Facing Public Opposition to the Niqab', in Lori Beaman (ed.), *Reasonable Accommodation: Managing Religious Diversity*, 70–108, Vancouver: University of British Columbia Press.

Balibar, Étienne (2002), *Politics and the Other Scene*, trans. Christine Jones, James Swenson and Chris Turner, New York: Verso.

Benhabib, Seyla (1992), *Situating the Self: Gender, Community, and Postmodernism in Contemporary Ethics*, New York: Routledge.

Connolly, William E. (2002), *Identity/Difference: Democratic Negotiations of Political Paradox*, Minneapolis: University of Minnesota Press.

Fanon, Frantz (2004), *Wretched of the Earth*, trans. Richard Philcox, New York: Grove Press.

Fanon, Frantz (2008), *Black Skin, White Masks*, trans. Richard Philcox, New York: Grove Press.

Fillion, Réal (2008), *Multicultural Dynamics and the Ends of History: Exploring Kant, Hegel, and Marx*, Ottawa: University of Ottawa Press.

Fraser, Nancy (Spring/Summer 1985), 'What's Critical About Critical Theory? The Case of Habermas and Gender', *New German Critique* 35: 97–131.

Freud, Sigmund (1962), *Three Essays on the Theory of Sexuality*, trans. James Strachey, New York: Basic Books.

Goodnight, G. Thomas and David B. Hingstman (1997), 'Studies in the Public Sphere', *Quarterly Journal of Speech* 83: 351–99.

Gray, John (1995), 'Agonistic Liberalism', *Social Philosophy and Policy*, 12 (1): 111–35.

Habermas, Jürgen (1984), *The Theory of Communicative Action*, trans. Thomas McCarthy, Boston: Beacon Press.

Habermas, Jürgen (1991), *The Structural Transformation of the Public Sphere*, trans. Thomas Burger, Boston: MIT Press.

Habermas, Jürgen (1998), *Between Facts and Norms*, trans. William Rehg, Boston: MIT Press.

Jacobson, Kirsten (September 2010), 'Experience of Home and the Space of Citizenship', *Southern Journal of Philosophy*, 48 (3): 219–45.

Killian, Caitlin (August 2003), 'The Other Side of the Veil: North African Women in France Respond to the Headscarf Affair', *Gender and Society*, 17 (4): 567–90.

Laing, R. D. (1990), *The Divided Self*, New York: Penguin.

Lazreg, Marnia (2009), *Questioning the Veil: Open Letters to Muslim Women*, Princeton: Princeton University Press.

Merleau-Ponty, Maurice (2000), *Humanism and Terror: The Communist Problem*, trans. John O'Neill, London: Transaction Publishers.

Mouffe, Chantal (2005), *The Return of the Political*, New York: Verso.

Negt, Oskar and Alexander Kluge (1993), *The Public Sphere and Experience*, trans. Peter Labanyi, Minneapolis: University of Minnesota Press.

Rawls, John (1993), *Political Liberalism*, New York: Columbia University Press.

Rawls, John (Summer 1997), 'The Idea of Public Reason Revisited', *The University of Chicago Law Review*, 64 (3): 765–807.

Russon, John (1995), 'Heidegger, Hegel and Ethnicity: The Ritual Basis of Self-Identity', *Southern Journal of Philosophy*, 33: 509–32.

Russon, John (2003), *Human Experience: Philosophy, Neurosis, and the Elements of Everyday Life*, Albany: SUNY Press.

Tully, James (1995), *Strange Multiplicity: Constitutionalism in an Age of Diversity*, Cambridge: Cambridge University Press.

Tully, James (2008), *Public Philosophy in a New Key*, Cambridge: Cambridge University Press.

Winnicott, D. W. (1986), *Home is Where We Start From*, New York: W. W. Norton & Company.

Young, Iris Marion (1990), *Justice and the Politics of Difference*, Princeton: Princeton University Press.

17

The Rift Design of Politics: 'Let the Right One In'?

Divya Dwivedi

Let the Right One In is the English title of John Ajvide Lindqvist's Swedish vampire novel *Låt den Rätte Komma In*, published in 2004. Lore has it that the vampire needs an invitation to enter habitations and s/he cannot break in, although s/he is free to take up abandoned spaces. In the novel, when the child vampire Eli agrees at her human friend Oskar's insistence to enter his house without his expressly uttering the invitation/permission, she suffers a total haemorrhage moments after stepping in, the blood – of other men – bursting out from her every pore (p. 381). The phrase *let the right one in* is the commandment of the bare schema of politics: inclusion and exclusion. The vampire is imagined according to this schematics of in/out. The vampire does not have an inside of his/her own – blood, a beating heart, soul. S/he is unable to step into daylight and is confined indoors till the night falls when s/he emerges to wait in lonely haunts. To preserve his/her life s/he must find a way to either lure you out or enter your space: desire is the game that s/he sets up in the schematics, not unlike the enclosure of a park converted into a football field by children. S/he seduces in many ways – through her body that resembles humans', through the offer of eternal life and the promise to end to your loneliness. The vampire, due to powers (which include transmogrification, night vision, super strength) of the sub-schematics of the outside that s/he is, acutely perceives the sub-schematics of the inside that defines you. S/he is drawn to the shadows (one thinks of Jung), the gaps in the circuit of social schematics (the loneliness of a weak boy, the needs of a paedophile in Lindqvist's novel) and the taste for adventure where s/he alone can promise fulfilment. S/he offers you a choice – either let her in or keep her out. Either way, you are devastated since the former implies the vampire feeding from your inside and the latter implies your sub-schematics eating into you.

Hannah Arendt saw communities as power relations defined in schematics *among the many*, and politics can take place only in such community of schematics; the vampire would threaten this notion of politics once its import was formulated by Arendt as the right to rights or the right to community. The vampire threatening the community of men is him/herself a peculiar figure reminiscent of man but one who now neither lives nor dies like man, but rather is living-dead. There are many figures proximate to but threateningly different from *man* – the Muselmann (see Levi 1959), refugees (see Agamben 1994), zombies – the last neither think nor seduce nor labour but are popularly seen as defined by the simple drive to feed – and today it is understood that the distinction between *zoe* and *bios* captures them all in its *zone of indistinction*. However, we need to step back to the prior Arendtian conception of politics as the *being-with* of men (rather than man), ontologically prior, that is, to the schematics of specific communities. What if the vampire threatens not community as such but the given schematics, by making it work differently and revealing it by doing so? Lindqvist complicates the zone-of-indistinction schema by introducing Eli, the twelve-year-old vampire, into the Blackeberg community. In an interview he explains that

> where a lot of horror fails ... for me is that I don't care about the people that nasty things are happening to. I mean, you got like this little family, and then the genetically mutated grizzly comes along and he's found a barrel of goo out in the forest so he's become like really dangerous and he kills the boy and the mom, the dad lives. ... I don't believe at all from how they talk to each other that they would really care about one another, these people, and that they're just walking around trying to look good in a movie. (2008)

He had to

> reject all ... sort of 'romanticized' notions about vampires ... and just concentrate on the question: If a child was stuck forever like, in a 12-year-old existence and had to walk around killing other people and drink their blood to live – what would that child's existence really be like? ... an absolutely horrible existence. Miserable, gross and lonely. (Ibid.)

The question this poses is *how does a vampire live among men?* Eli is creative: between the sub-schematics which constitute the in/out she constructs a new inter-schematics that opens new freedoms. She enters Blackeberg accompanied by Haakan, and everyone in the Stockholm suburb assumes them to be father and daughter. Haakan, a school teacher who was dismissed for his pederasty, accompanies Eli, killing residents of the localities that they periodically drift through to provide her with their blood in exchange for the satisfaction of sleeping next to her, watching her naked, and for wads of money with which to return to the city and buy the services of boy prostitutes with a distinct oral schematics – young boys with both sets of teeth removed for better fellatio. Haakan, as the adult, keeps this child at a remove from the vampiric feeding function. That is, she feeds on blood without killing while he kills without feeding: vampiric devastation is mediated by a human. *How does a vampire live among men* is an Arendtian question that nevertheless unsettles the Arendtian position that an existence defined solely in terms of biological necessity is not political. Does this expose a flaw in Arendt's thinking of politics or rather a fork within it? The latter invites us into the latencies in the lines of thought that developed, from Heidegger via Arendt, in the writings of Foucault and Agamben, but especially in their difference.

Arendt and Agamben: The inclusion–exclusion schema of politics

With the *oikos–polis* distinction persisting as the dominant reference point for thinking politics, we continue to approach politics in terms of the schematics of in/out even though we can no longer afford to and must not do so, as evident in the impossibility of practising quarantine against the Ebola epidemic. Politics itself is seen as a region which includes members, qualified by either their attributes of rationality or by their actions. Letting in is already regulated by the insistence on legitimate recourses which seem to be synonymous with political process – that is, permitted by the constitution, constitutional forms of protest, peaceful and non-violent means that do not disrupt civil life. The history of politics would at best be of agitating to end one's exclusion and enter the region of politics, such that the action that precedes and prepares for admittance into the region of politics is itself already political insofar as it addresses this realm from its excluded position and thus becomes included by its own virtue. For example, irregular migrants mobilizing for their rights and speaking out in the public sphere against deportation and other anti-immigration policies delaying or denying them citizenship have been deemed – with an appreciative nod at Arendt – to be 'enacting themselves as citizens even when the law does not recognize them as such' (McNevin 2009; Nyers 2003, p. 1179). It would follow that politics is the act of including or inserting oneself into the political region which is *polis* and citizenship or that which has instituted itself as such by excluding something from itself (politics of politics). Then does politics ask to be permitted into politics, to be let into itself, or does it break in? Prior to Habermasian communicative action delimited by formal or informal public spheres, it asks to be invited but in doing so it is in fact a self-invited guest: is the dominant of this address the emotive, the conative or the metalinguistic? The politics of politics leaves what can be called *the regionalization of politics* intact, only deconstructed.

The vampire, imagined in the inclusion–exclusion schematics of politics, connotes the women and slaves excluded from the Athenian *polis* in antiquity, as well as the modern refugee who is already in the *neighbourhood*, in the camps, slums or ghettoes.[1] The insistence on entering as you are makes the vampire a parasite who feeds on another community, of man, and moves on, or further among men, disguised as man but without being one, without assimilating. However, haematophagous parasitism only reproduces vampires and the dead who do not 'turn' but are drained of blood. Its bio-logic – the becoming one of the two functions of feeding and reproduction – would be autophagy: the ruin of politics in both regions, requiring in response an exclusion beyond all exclusions. The economics and the eco-logic of the schematic limit the demands of politics to setting up parameters of control for this autophagy. The autophagous being at the same time must not be allowed to appear as the schematic of man himself, which is the goal of ideology – there is man, and then there is less and more than man. This schematics of autophagy defines the figure of the Muselmann. Agamben calls this special case, due to its exposure of the limits of the schematic, 'Levi's Paradox' (2002, p. 82). That is, there possibly comes into existence something, a figure, which resembles man but is 'non-man', which arrests the flows in the stratified circuit of politics wherein the play of inclusion–exclusion occurs. This brings us to the limit not of politics but of the inclusion–exclusion schematics of politics which has dominated political thought.

This limit finds a rare illumination in Arendt's *The Human Condition*, where labour, work and action are held to be three kinds of human activities which comprise the human condition. 'Labour is the activity which corresponds to the biological processes of human body … the human condition of labour is life itself'. It entails producing in order to feed and reproduce the species, to which the *oikos* and housekeeping are devoted, to which slaves, women and children are confined in Athens, which also means ties of family (Arendt 1958, p. 7). 'Work is the category that corresponds to the unnaturalness of human existence ... to the "artificial" world of things' which are durable works for use and works of art (Ibid.). Lastly,

> Action, the only activity that goes on directly between men without the intermediary of things or matter corresponds to the human condition of plurality, the fact that men, not man, live on the earth and inhabit the world. While all the aspects of the human condition are somehow related to politics, this plurality is specifically the condition of all political life. (Ibid.)

These activities are separated conceptually and spatially, with labour remaining private and deprived of the public; work pacing between the solitude of the workshop and the exchange market as well as the reificational space of artworks; and action showing itself in the public which is the very place for appearance. Yet, Arendt affirms that they together comprise the *vita activa* that came to be opposed to *vita comtemplativa* in medieval thought: a man can emerge and participate in the public only from out of the more than 'privative' privacy that houses and hides the processes sustaining his bare life, and that it is in order to gain a distance from the cycle of immediacy of nature, of impersonal life and death, which strictly speaking are not recognized by nature, that work is done to create an artificial space of durability that is then 'overlaid' and 'overgrown' by action in word and deed directly between men (1958, pp. 61, 183). Are labour, work and action three categories to which a given human undertaking can be assigned; and is Arendt's a political vision that distinguishes and values content-less action for its own sake among some humans in one zone at the cost of labour and work by the rest in other zones (Kateb 1984; Villa 2007)? For instance, in Wendy Brown's view Arendt was contemptuous of and hostile 'toward the realm of necessity where life is created, reproduced and maintained' by women and slaves (1988, pp. 24, 26–7). Or are these three activities abstractions from or elements of every human activity with one historically obscuring, or even suppressing, the other (see Benhabib 2000; Tsao 2002)? Treating them as abstractions, Roy Tsao draws attention to Arendt's assessment of women's and slaves' exclusion from the Greek *polis* as a 'violent injustice' to them as well as a loss of real life for the beneficiaries of the former's exclusion which only gave the latter a 'vicarious life' (Arendt, pp. 119–20; Tsao, p. 117).

Neither approach clarifies how each of the three activities sustains – historically – the other without devouring it, without collapsing into it (should we say *without including it*?). The collapse occurs, according to Agamben, in the coinciding of bare life (unprotected by, and yet standing before, the law) 'with the political realm [such that] exclusion and inclusion, outside and inside, *bios* and *zoe*, right and fact, enter into a zone of irreducible indistinction' (1998, p. 9, my emphasis). The refugee and the Muselmann of the Nazi concentration camps are two figures of this indistinction, each in itself a zone into which that which would be distinguished from it (the non-refugee or citizen and the non-Muselmann camp inmate respectively) also dissolves. Agamben follows Arendt in identifying the refugee's condition as 'the paradigm of a new historical consciousness' and as 'the only imaginable figure of the people in our day' since it exposes the operation of sovereign power whereby a state of exception, whether provisional or permanent, can strip even citizens of their statehood (Agamben 1995, p. 114 and 1998). The appearance of the refugee is the *future anterior existence* of citizens who will have been subjects of biopolitics. The deconstruction in Agamben of the distinction of *zoe* and *bios*, of subject and citizen, and of the drowned and the saved, is the farthest that the inclusion–exclusion schematic of politics can go. Agamben's recommendation in 'We Refugees' that man's political survival is possible only if we create a space where 'the citizen will have learned to acknowledge the refugee that he himself is' is echoed in the ethic of the witness that, according to *Remnants of Auschwitz*, alone survives 'the ruin of all ethics based on dignity and conformity to a norm' to bear witness to the impossibility of bearing witness when faced with the Muselmann 'who is the human that cannot be told apart from the inhuman' (1994 para. 7; 1999, pp. 69, 82). A politics based on deconstruction is one of witnessing aporias rendered thereby; coming to the moment where the schematic shows no more circulation, although the witnessing itself is the opacity underneath which the inter-schematic is born – such as, the simulation of family between Haakan and Eli, such as the simulation of the Muselmann within man. Not only is 'the camp ... the fundamental biopolitical paradigm of the West' (Agamben, 1998, p. 181, it is also the zone where '[Primo] Levi succeeds in isolating something like a new ethical element' (Agamben, 1999, p. 21).

Agamben gives the name 'Levi's paradox' and 'the aporia of Auschwitz' to this identification of a zone of indistinction between the human and the inhuman in whose structure language breaks off from experience to make witnessing impossible. Acknowledging that Levi premises this aporia on the irrevocability of Muselmannhood, he gives the last word of *Remnants* to those who in fact survived the camp to testify that 'ich war ein Muselmann', and he thereby 'call[s] into question not simply Levi's paradox, but even one of his fundamental presuppositions' namely, that they have no story to tell and their journey is but to the bottom (1999, p. 165). Henrik Nielsen and I have commented elsewhere on these appended testimonies of the Muselmänner and argued that the relation of subjectivity, language and experience illuminated in their narrative leads to a different understanding of community than the aporetic one suggested by Agamben (2013, pp. 6–7). Not the future anterior but the praeterite – both epic and historical – relates (in both relation and *récit*) men and 'non-men' as Levi called the Muselmänner (1959, p. 103).[2] And what they relate is also what Eli tells Oskar: *I must survive.* Within the aporia, as Agamben traces it, the survivor calls the Muselmann 'the figure', but in their narratives the Muselmänner not only call themselves 'I' but refer to others like themselves collectively as 'we' (1999, p. 169).

Agamben draws into the aporetic paradigm the concept of biopower which derives from Foucault's historical ontology of politics. The departure is significant and can be traced back to the fork in Arendt. One path leads from Arendt's influential suggestion of the labour-work-action distinctions to an inclusion–exclusion schematic in which action alone defines the transhistorical region of politics, be it flourishing or diminished: the regionalization of politics. The other path maintains them as a priori elements of a circuit that dispenses historical junctures of politics and leads to Foucault.

Heidegger and Arendt: *Mitsein* and the rift-design

The Heideggerian thought that persists in Arendt is, as is well known, the ontological schematic of *Mitsein* or being-with.[3] An early formulation of this by Heidegger is

> being-with-one-another, being with Others: having the same world there with Others, encountering one another, being with one another in the manner of being-for-one-another. Yet this Dasein is simultaneously being present at hand for Others, namely, just as a stone is there which neither has nor is concerned with a world there. (1992, p. 7E)

To be there is to be-with, amid and between the many in many ways. Arendt insists that politics is grounded in the actions of men with each other and not in the rights flowing from the essence of being human. There-being is being-with, in a manner that is best understood as *transitive* in reference to Heidegger's insistence that the *be-ing* of beings *is not* (not itself a being, an onticoformalization), and that be-ing *is* beings (their be-ing there). That *it gives* is its transitivity. Be-ing must transitively let beings be different in terms of differences understood, including as 'present at hand'. No pure Being of beings can be retrieved on stripping away the understanding, since the latter is the way beings are given as *be-ing*. Be-ing is transitive, since to be is to be something: not be as such but be this or that thing. In this transitivity, the 'not' of be-ing is preserved. Being-with, then, cannot be identified with politics equated with actions between men to the exclusion of work and labour, as these too are modes of the being-with, of the plurality of beings.

The transitivity of being makes for the stratification implied in being-with and given historically – the multiplicity, and errancy, within a giving and of givings, thus altering the static and passive sense of *given*. 'Without errancy there would be no connection from destining to destining' (Heidegger 1975, p. 26). How does such giving come about? – Heidegger uses the term rift design for the simultaneous *a priority* and historicality of being. In 'The Origin of the Work of Art' and 'The Thing', he defines 'work' transitively by emphasizing that 'what is thus at work is so *in* the work' (Heidegger 1971, p. 183). A complex stratification is conceived by Heidegger: the 'world' brought forth, erected or 'set up' by the work, the earth or place cleared or appointed for this erection in this very work, and the conjoined existence of these two strata in the form of a 'rift-design' as an active, transitive and ongoing 'strife' between world and earth which the work itself consists in (Ibid.). World, earth and strife, organized in the design of a rift, can be seen as the stratifying work that comes about as a thing. Both essays speak of the worlding of world – 'world worlds'. 'The thing things world' (Ibid., 170, 181). Heidegger's unusual term 'be-thinged' (*be-ding-t*) indicates this transitivity between thing and world (Ibid., p. 181). In doing so, the thing clears a space for the world to be be-thinged, that is, to be actualized. The world is, more than mere attitude or world view, the very time-space which actualization entails, the becoming a thing of the work. We can understand Heidegger's concept of 'earth' here as this occurring or being, which withdraws into the very occurrence; and the 'world' as the sense which is expanded in the way the thing works, the paths it takes alongside other things – things present, absent, past and futural – and the way it unfolds in its capacity to relate to other things, thus acquiring history, a past and a future. To do so, the thing must stay 'a while', a term understood not only spatially as clearing but also temporally as 'a while'. 'The Anaximander Fragment' elaborates *a while* as simple, but also the complex web of relations that are four-dimensional. Heidegger says that 'The Work belongs, as work, uniquely within the realm that is opened up by itself', so that work is also this opening (1975, p. 167). The work contains the 'essential traits of strife' or of opening, clearing (Ibid., p. 187). 'Rift' or the intimacy of earth and world is 'a basic design, an outline sketch, that draws the basic features of the upsurgence of the clearing of beings' (Ibid., p. 188).

The work(ing) of work for Heidegger is clearly different from that for Arendt, even though the relation between labour, work and action is akin to that between earth and world, or within the fourfold (mortals, gods, earth and sky). This is a self-misrecognition in Arendt of the strife that she sees among the three but ultimately locates in terms of political action in the world of appearance alone.[4] To think the fourfold temporality of 'a while' in which work opens the rift-design, one could well consider the intersecting migratory flows in *Let the Right One in* and its sequel, *Let the Old Dreams Die*, without, of course, treating them as representations of four-dimensional time: post-Second World War camps, the Stockholmers settled in 1950's brand-new suburbs sans history or folk memory, visited unsuspectedly and unpreparedly by the being from the past; the asymmetrical teenage couple, Eli and Oskar, fleeing into an immortal future of clandestine courage and companionship, into which the ailing and ageing couple in the sequel, Karin and Stefan, seeking the vampiric kiss of immortality in the world, follow them with the help of a photograph of the kids waiting pale, gaunt and ready behind a pair of tourists in southern Europe. As though the horror belongs with the courage. Arendt's conceptions of political community and the right to community do not comprehend the transitivity of being-with which is historical. However, her articulation of the historicality of the human condition does. Labour, work and action, comprising the Greek idea of *vita activa*, are constellated differently into historical formulations of the essence of man, and accordingly being-with is regionalized at one point as 'political' in the limited sense and at the another point as 'social'. No doubt, the subsequent epochs that Arendt describes with the help of this analysis of the human condition into labour, work and action carry the suggestion of being in decline from the Greek ideal. Nevertheless, it is simultaneously impossible for her to show the historical shifts such as the rise of the social and the labouring society without appearing to posit labour, work and action *together* as theoretical elements rather than empirical concepts (see also Tsao 2002). These elements are historically put into circulation in circuits within which power, which is to say relations, have been channelized such that the entire circuit sustains (and not simply any instance of human activity as a combination of each element). For example, the distinction of private and public across which labour, work and action are distributed in Ancient Greece is unsettled when the private becomes public after Reformation, obliterates the public and takes its place as the social. That is, the personal, which is not opposed to the public in Greece, appears most clearly only in public where specific men in plural engage with each other without reducing their difference, which shows only in action and not in any attribute. With the rise of the social, the personal vanishes into the behavioural, where everyone shares in the identity of society like a big family. In it the distinction of labour and work too vanishes, as work now produces for consumption in a cycle that begins to repeat nature at another level, and politics becomes management. Labour, work and action are concretely constellated in this circuit even though, for Arendt, politics has collapsed into work, which itself has collapsed into labour, which now comes to define the essence of man as *animal laborans*.

The Greek *polis* is only one epochal world of appearance, given altogether in its being-with the *oikos*, where the being-with is as inclusion–exclusion. Arendt's conception of the essence of politics as political community modelled on the Greek *polis* is a restriction of being-with as such to one of its determinations. To put this in terms of the transitivity proposed here as the essence of *Mitsein*, Arendt finds *vita activa* to be the structure of being-with, but exhausts its transitivity, even as she demonstrates it in its historicality, in a single epoch in her attempt to define politics. Patchen Markell rightly attempts to save Arendt's architecture by showing the tensions and overlaps in its attempt to separate but also relate labour and action through the gated wall constituted by work. (2011, pp. 34–7). However, rather than the architecture of theoretical work 'disclos[ing] its paradoxical problem', as Markell suggests, Arendt's concepts for politics gesture towards a rift-design. While adhering to Heideggerian *Mitsein*, and while sketching its epochal stratifications, she occludes the rift design in which transitivity and stratification are two strokes of a single unfolding that provides the opening for politics. It is in Foucault that the rift design of politics, present but not recognized in Arendt, finds its explicit articulation.

Foucault: Archaeology-genealogy-strategics and the outside

Quite Arendtian is Foucault's exhortation 'to distinguish that which is exerted over things' and that which is 'an ensemble of actions that induce others [other actions] and follow from one another' and, further, relations of communication

(1994, p. 337).[5] These are not separate domains but are always coordinated in 'diverse forms, diverse places, diverse circumstances ... in which these relationships establish themselves according to a specific model' rather than 'a general type of equilibrium' (Ibid., p. 338). The coming about of a given interrelation is historical, comprised of procedures – that produce knowledge which has regular effects of power, that is, of inducing actions of thus constellated people – specific to it, in other words a régime. Each society has its régime of truth, its ' "general politics" of truth' or, as Foucault put it in 'What is Critique?', a 'system of acceptability' to which corresponds the *archaeological* level of his analysis (1980, p. 131; 1997, p. 53). Rather than one knowledge or one power, or power and knowledge each in itself, these concepts 'are only an analytical grid' (1997, p. 52).

This grid can be understood in terms of *rift design*. The archaeological level itself is only one component of the grid, a regime of truth, one stratum. The second is the identification of heterogeneous processes which constitute 'the conditions for the appearance of [this] singularity born of multiple determining elements', that is, a *'genealogy'* (Ibid., p. 57). Genealogy describes the transitivity whereby *it gives/there is* a singular regime, but also 'the breaking points which indicate its emergence', such that the interrelationships comprising a regime 'are in a perpetual slippage' rather than 'one plane only' (Ibid., pp. 54, 58). This means, genealogy identifies conditions, in the mobility and fragility of whose elements dwells a *strategics* that resists, reverses and makes possible the disappearance of that regime. Strategics then is the third component or level of the rift design, where the interrelationships are not 'primary or absolutely totalizing' but 'a field of possibles, of openings, of indecisions, reversals and possible dislocations which make them fragile, temporary ... events, nothing more, nothing less' (Ibid., pp. 58, 60).

Strategics completes the grid and indicates the essential errancy of transitivity, the errancy that connects one model of governmentality to another. Nothing automatic, strategics names the shepherding of errancy by way of discontinuities, local struggles, resistances, in short the question *how not to be governed like that*. Nor is it an *other* kind of agency, least of all the work of a subject, but a room for interactions that errs both ways: this 'perpetual question' does not resist government altogether for it is born in the very (genealogical) conditions of governmentalization:

> As both partner and adversary to the arts of governing, as an act of defiance,
> as a challenge, as a way of limiting these arts of governing and sizing them up,

transforming them, of finding a way to escape from them, or ... to displace them ... *but also and by the same token, as a line of development of the arts of governing.* (Ibid., pp. 28–9, my emphasis)

It conducts both the slippages of elements of a regime and new forms of governmentality in future regimes which are by no means predetermined thereof. For Foucault, 'the power relationship and freedom's refusal to submit cannot therefore be separated' since 'power is exercised only over free subjects' and can be faced with the 'intransigence' of this very freedom – an 'agonism' or a 'perpetual provocation' (1994, p. 342). Although he also calls it the 'intransitivity of freedom', transitivity, which better articulates the entire Foucauldian grid or the rift design that dispenses the errancy of politics of truth, is not *opposed* to the intransigence of freedom, the latter being a component of its historical conduct.

If strife or *agon* is 'the political task inherent in all social existence', and if regimes of truth, or the politics of truth, effectuate 'power relations [that] are rooted in the whole network of the social', then politics itself persists at two different levels in Foucault's analytical grid (Ibid., pp. 343, 345). Thus Foucault articulates the rift design of politics, in which biopolitics would obtain at one level but provoke reversals at the other. The rift of the design, the source of errant transitivity, Foucault calls 'the void' or 'the outside' in another set of writings altogether, those on paintings and literature. Together, archaeology, genealogy and strategics articulate the conduct of the strife, but the fourth fold – where the strife opens and being-with persists and remains 'not' this or that governmentality – this outside in the rift design, or the rift design as the outside of regimes of discourse, Foucault shows, for instance, in *This Is Not a Pipe* and it is not a function of exclusion. Where Heidgger proposed the rift design in a discussion of the thing and the work of art, Foucault does so in his discussion of the relation between things and language, the visible and the sayable in Magritte's work of art. Power relations arise where the visible and the sayable, being and representation, enter into specific regimes of discourse, but they emerge not from necessity but a void that can only be glimpsed through a tearing away of the composed elements, which is what Foucault calls an 'unravelled calligram' (1998, p. 191).

A calligram which arranges words in the shape of the very thing they signify is both tautological in doing the same work twice and destructive since the two workings interrupt each other (1998, p. 191). It is unlike a duck-rabbit picture where instead of two icons dwelling in one signifying line, as here there are two signifiers trying to doubly capture one absent signified. They belong to two orders of lines, the verbal and the visual, that traditionally exist separated from each other in two forms of subordination (Ibid., p. 195). The space of the calligram where they are superimposed gets doubled, being both the blank canvas supporting plastic representation and the paratextual locus launching linguistic reference. Magritte 'unravels' the calligram, and thus the principles of the two orders of lines and space, when he inserts between the image of and the word for 'pipe' the 'not' in that part of the painting which is both painted image and written legend (Ibid., pp. 191–2). Neither the painted words nor the verisimilar image nor the indexical 'this' nor the painting as their common ground – none is a 'pipe'. The 'not' negates painting's principle of resemblance, language's principle of representation and the space which is the ground of these as well as of paratextuality and ostension itself. The 'ensemble' continues 'to employ a calligram where are found, simultaneously present and visible, image, text, resemblance, affirmation and their common ground; then suddenly to open it up so that the calligram immediately decomposes and disappears' (Ibid., p. 202). Between its employment and its shattering, and that of its ground, *nothing* is left: the void. 'And yet in this split and drifting space, strange bonds are knit, there occur intrusions ... destructive invasions, avalanches of images into the milieu of words, and verbal lightning flashes that streak and shatter the drawings' – the rift design (197).

The unravelled calligram 'let the right one in'

Lindqvist's novel illuminates this rift design of being-with by plotting the coming of the vampire into the social life of Blackeberg, where several groups of families and friends struggle to prevent their relationships from completely breaking down. Eli befriends the obese pre-teen misfit Oskar, bullied and sexually harassed by older schoolboys. Another group of friends in the neighbourhood, who have no functional families, return every day to their local Chinese restaurant for company which they can hardly sustain. Two of them, Virginia and Lacke, occasionally get together but do not declare love or try to live together because neither can accept the demands for change and accommodation that this would put on their habits of living, which thus become also habits of relating to others. Eli's entry initiates *both* the impaling of these communities, not only killing some of its members but also leaching relations which tip over their fragile balance when one member dies, *and* returning other relations to a greater intensity or acknowledgement. The phrase 'Let the right one in' is not then restricted to inviting or excluding the vampire, but pertains to every relation among men. It begins to ring out a silent question: care?

The work of the novel *Let the Right One In* is precisely the articulation of this unravelled calligram, not *represented* by Eli, for the diagram is anti-representational, but set up in the ensemble of relations into which Eli is 'let be'. The calligram unravels in the very proliferation of titles for translations and adaptations of the novel. The 2008 Swedish film carried the same title, and in 2010 a Hollywood adaptation closely following the Swedish one but departing in some significant details was made with the title *Let Me In*. In the interview Lindqvist mentions that the shorter title suggested to him was 'Let her in', saying:

> I wonder if they had read the book before they suggested that. But then I suggested LET ME [whatever I may be] IN instead and then they thought that was fine They thought my name was too long as well, they asked if I could change that too. But I wouldn't agree to that [laughs]. (Lindqvist 2008)

He was aghast at the introduction of the reference to gender in the Hollywood title, and although it did not go through, the crucial corresponding change was made in the story presenting Eli unambiguously as a girl whereas in the novel she up to a point appears to be a twelve-year-old girl and then reveals mid-novel to Oskar that she is actually Elias, a genitally mutilated boy who was turned into a vampire 200 years ago.

The three titles together with Lindqvist's fastidiousness compose a calligram of political principles and elements: (1) 'let her in' is a command or an instruction, which as direct speech using the third person speaks to the reader or viewer whereby he/she becomes vicariously the one to whom the story must happen as an experience of horror and of the visitation of a vampire. (2) 'Let me in' is a plea in first person directly from the vampire, the child much like the waif of twenty years in Emily Brontë's novel, bringing the reader/viewer inside the fourth wall. Though there are other instances where characters bang on a door asking for or demanding or forcing admittance, or where they are invited unwittingly, unsuspectingly, the voice insistently projects the second person, screens the third and calls out to both, to us and to the other characters, pronouncing the fact that perhaps it is not heard at all. (3) 'Let the right one in' is unmistakably a maxim, an injunction, an imperative, in the light of which each engaged party, in this literary space or taking place of the work of literature or cinema, which is simultaneously fictional and actual, must make sense of his/her relation to and response to what transpires in that space. Oskar would then be under the spotlight of this imperative, seen or judged in its light. Here the emphasis is on 'the right one', having a knowledge of who it is.

However, recalling that the novel is calibrated with points of coming in, going out and being found before or behind a door, this title-phrase ceases to be an imperative whose community we all, readers and characters together, would form, the ones to whom it is addressed. Instead the titular paratext becomes an invisible calligram, spoken by no one (not the author, not the narrator, not the characters, not the reader/judge/critic), a voice from nowhere contiguous with the story, this anonymous third person who speaks 'let the right one in' and who is not omniscient or universal. In this variation of the three titles what is unravelled is the sub-phrase 'to let', in other words 'let be' or 'let be-with'. The comparison makes this residue more pronounced in its double function: (a) both in its idiomaticity and its grammaticity the phrase is incomplete and itself completes what comes after it, for example, *to let x* or *let y be*, to allow x and y to take place or to be there. Without this x or y it would be impotent. (b) But insofar as it not only completes but lets the very phrase be there, it is the very potentiality of the speech and activity entailed. In this the phrase 'to let' hides in each of the three titles, hiding from their distinction, letting each be distinct, letting there be more than one sense of 'coming in' and of the 'leaving out' or 'coming out' which is implicit in 'coming in'.

The phrase 'let the right one in' alongside the various tellings then indicates less the bare schema of inclusion and exclusion than the rift-design of politics, an unravelled calligram. Oskar and Eli asymmetrically befriend each other in a strangely shared loneliness only once Oskar lets her in after learning that Eli or Elias is a castrated boy – but one who has 'nothing. No slit, no penis. Just a smooth surface' (384). This void in which gender and humanity appear to disappear enables her/his being-with through two centuries, within various communities, and is the void of community itself, from which diverse forms of being-with become possible: her friendship with Oskar, her encouraging him to resist the physical and sexual bullying in school and her saving him from being murdered by seniors in the school swimming pool; but also Oskar murdering Lacke when he finds Eli immersed in her bath-tub filled with blood and tries to kill her to avenge Virginia; and also Haakan's offering his own blood to Eli out of his allegiance to her, then burning himself to avoid their both getting recognized when he is caught, and finally turning into a kind of zombie who hunts Eli down, driven by his reduction to a single function: to penetrate her. Eli asks Oskar to say the words 'you can come in' when she visits his place, not to feed but to share their respective loneliness and exclusion from society. The 'letting' here occurs in both directions, for here it is not the vampire entering to devour, like the refugee feared to devastate the host country, like the Muselmann feared to devastate the self-relation of man by occasioning the consideration 'If this is man'. Rather it is Oskar or the host insisting that the vampire or the immigrant enter by his rules rather than hers. It is Eli who lets Oskar in this time, by agreeing to conduct herself in accordance with his insistence that she enter without the invitation. The inclusion–exclusion schematic fails to note that the rules of conducting oneself transform at the very moment that Eli breaks the vampiric rule at Oskar's behest, instigated by the power of their transgressive friendship: the transgression ripples through the social fabric, tearing it at points (Eli's monstrous massacre of the school bullies to save Oskar, Oskar's flight from familiar life into a dark future with Eli, Haakan's self-incurred yet unforeseen transformation into a singular, zombie-esque impulse).

At the same time, the supernatural concretion of the symbols of the schematic in the vampire's being opens us to think the anxieties, fears, economy and biology of the politics determined by this schematic. The differentiated flows of immigration point to emerging political schematics that the zone-of-indistinction schema occludes. Eli (enacted in the Swedish film by the half-Iranian and half-Swedish actor Lina Leandersson) would represent *irregular* immigrant *geographic* flow, specifically south–north, Oskar's flight the rarer case of north–south irregular migration.[6] Both suggest *demographic* flows in terms of birth and death among undocumented and illegal immigrants which are as difficult to track as the geographic outflows that do not even enter the dominant discourse on either the securitization or the governance of immigration. Haakan's, too, is a kind of outflow but of *status* as he changes from a citizen to a civically, criminally and biologically irregular being.[7] Only one stratum of the schematic of these differentiated and related flows is the inclusion–exclusion regime identified with the state policy and implementation which creates a migrant's 'path into irregularity' of status rather than simply record it (Düvell 2011). This stratum corresponds to the now urgent discourse on refuge and human rights, state resources and national security and controls. Another critical stratum is the manoeuvres of contemporary capitalism which actively generate and sustain irregular migration and status mobility for cheap and pliant labour, and whose participants also include state provisions and actors, traffickers and enclave employers (see Castles 2011). A third is the morbid yet affirmative play of visibility and invisibility that migrants undertake in different ways depending on whether they are compliant, semi-compliant or non-compliant. To be seen is to be detected and deported, to forego wages – much like Oskar hopes to slink away from the school bullies and, of course, like Eli and Haakan – while to remain unseen is to be deprived of acceptable housing, employment, health, banking and the amenities it buys and recourse to law. Locating the political agency of migrants in braving the former dangers to 'come out' and protest publically or to non-cooperate with asylum processing through silence or sewn lips (McNevin 2006, 2013) misses the whole, unfolding schematics as much as celebrating a politics of escape and imperceptibility in the latter strategies (Papadopoulos et al. 2008). Eli is not a parallel to refugeehood since s/he represents the creations of inter-schematics, and their authors should not be identified as those migrants precisely for the reasons Foucault sketched in 'What is an Author?'

Haakan can be read as the anxiety regarding bare life which the popular genre of zombie apocalypse perpetuates, but the pathos-filled, voluntary and dubious stages by which he 'descends' into the comatose state create a different trope than those of flood, horde, invasion, plague invoked in the genre of 'survival horror' (see Stratton 2011). They might be better approached by considering the reverse journey made by the camp's Muselmann survivors who narrate, explain and interpret their experience contrary to the very definition of Muselmann and 'bare life' (see Dwivedi and Nielsen 2013). Like Lindqvist's vampiric one, Isaac Marion's *Warm Bodies* and its film adaptation open an inter-schematic in zombie apocalypse by introducing a difference in the zombie: some are less zombie than others, have minimal speech, an occasional heartbeat and memory flashes, and they develop more of their previous faculties on *eating* the brain of a human prey. Here autophagy enters a new schematics when a zombie falls in love with a human pointing her gun at him. New inter-schematics open in such journeys, 'let' by the rift-design of politics, introducing a difference in man and releasing man equally from essentialist and aporetic schemas. In the words of Karin and Stefan: *Let the old dreams die. We are dreaming new ones* (266).

Notes

1　On the cultural significance of vampire and zombie films and TV serials in the wake of the discourse on terror, security and irregular migration in the past two decades, see Stratton 2011.

2　On the distinction and relation between the two praeterites, see Käte Hamburger 1977.

3 Peg Birmingham traces it to the belonging together or 'jointure' of beings in
the world of appearances presenced in lingering between absences according to
Heidegger in 'Anaximander Fragment' (2013, p. 158).

4 Birmingham points to Arendt's limited awareness of the extent of her debt to both
'Being and Time' and 'Anaximander Fragment' in conceiving action and political
praxis in a common world (2002, p. 192; 2013, pp. 157–62).

5 On the similarity and difference between Foucault with Arendt on their
conceptions of power and biopolitics, see Dolan 2005 and Braun 2007. On other
assessments of the distance between Agamben's thinking of biopolitics on the one
hand and Arendt and Foucault on the other, see Blencowe 2010.

6 Eli is short for Elias in the novel, which refers the reader to Jewish migration,
biblical and historical, in addition to Muslim migrants and 'Islamic terror'.
On the terminology and politics of different immigrant statuses such as illegal,
undocumented, unauthorized, irregular, see Zetter 2007 and McNevin 2013
(p. 183).

7 On geographic, demographic and status flows, see Clandestino Project 2009
(pp. 12–14).

References

Agamben, G. (1995), 'We Refugees', *Symposium*, 49 (2): 114–19.

Agamben, G. (1998), *Homo Sacer: Sovereign Power and Bare Life*, Stanford, CA:
Stanford University Press.

Agamben, G. (2002), *Remnants of Auschwitz: The Witness and the Archive*, trans.
D. Heller Roazen, New York: Zone Books.

Allen, A. (2002), 'Power, Subjectivity, and Agency: Between Arendt and Foucault'.
International Journal of Philosophical Studies, 10 (2): 131–49.

Arendt, H. (1958), *The Human Condition*, Chicago: University of Chicago Press.

Benhabib, S. (1996), *The Reluctant Modernism of Hannah Arendt*, Thousand Oaks, CA:
Sage Publications.

Birmingham, P. (2002), 'Heidegger and Arendt: The Lawful Space of Worldly
Appearance', in F. Raffoul and D. Pettigrew (ed.), *Heidegger and Practical Philosophy*,
191–202, Albany: State University of New York.

Birmingham, P. (2013), 'Heidegger and Arendt: The Birth of Political Action and
Speech', in F. Raffoul and E. S. Nelson (eds), *Bloomsbury companion to Heidegger*,
157–64, London: Bloomsbury.

Blencowe, C. (2010), 'Foucault and Arendt's "Insider View" of Biopolitics: A Critique of
Agamben'. *History of the Human Sciences* 23, no. 5: 113–30.

Brown, W. (1988), *Manhood and Politics: A Feminist Reading in Political Theory*, Totowa:
Rowman & Littlefield.

Castles, S. (2011), 'Migration, Crisis and the Global Market'. *Globalization*, 8 (3): 311–24.

Clandestino Project (2009), *Undocumented Migration: Counting the Uncountable. Data and Trends Across Europe*, Brussels: European Commission, Final Report.

Dolan, F. M. (2005), 'The Paradoxical Liberty of Bio-Power: Hannah Arendt and Michel Foucault on Modern Politics'. *Philosophy & Social Criticism*, 31 (3): 369–80.

Düvell, F. (2011), 'Paths into Irregularity: The Legal and Political Construction of Irregular Migration', *European Journal of Migration and Law*, 13 (3): 275–95.

Dwivedi, D. and Nielsen, S. K. (2014), 'The Paradox of Testimony and First Person Plural Narration in Jensen's *We the Drowned*', *CLCWeb: Comparative Literature and Culture*, 15 (7), http://docs.lib.purdue.edu/clcweb/vol15/iss7/.

Foucault, M. (1980), 'Truth and Power', in C. Gordon (ed.), *Power/Knowledge*, 109–33, New York: Pantheon Books.

Foucault, M. (1997), 'What is Critique?', in S. Lotringer and L. Hochroth (eds), *The Politics of truth*, 41–83, New York: Semiotext(e).

Foucault, M. (1998a), 'This is not a Pipe', in J. Fabion (ed.), *Aesthetics, Method and Epistemology: The Essential Works of Foucault, 1954-84 vol. 2*, 187–204, New York: The New York Press.

Foucault, M. (1998b), 'What is an Author?', in J. Fabion (ed.), *Aesthetics, Method and Epistemology: The Essential Works of Foucault, 1954-84 vol. 2*, 205–22, New York: The New York Press.

Foucault, M. (2000), 'Subject and Power', in J. Fabion (ed.), *Power: The Essential Works of Foucault, 1954-84 Vol. 3*, 326–48, New York: The New York Press.

Hamburger, K. (1973), *The Logic of Literature*, trans. Marilynn J. Rose, Bloomington and London: Indiana University Press.

Heidegger, M. (1971), *Poetry, Language, Thought*, trans. Albert Hofstadter, New York: Harper & Row.

Heidegger, M. (1975), 'The Anaximander Fragment', in D. F. Krell and F. A. Capuzzi (trans.), *Early Greek Thinking*, 13–58, San Fransisco: Harper.

Heidegger, M. (1992), *Concept of Time*, trans. William McNeill, Oxford: Blackwell.

Kateb, G. (1984), *Hannah Arendt: Politics, Conscience, Evil*, Totowa, NJ: Rowman and Allanheld.

Låt den Rätte Komma In (2008), motion picture, distributed in Sweden by Sandrew Metronome and in USA by Magnet Releasing.

Levi, P. (1959), *If This Is a Man*, trans. Stuart Woolf, New York: Orion.

Lindqvist, A. J. (2007), *Let the Right One In*, trans. Ebba Segerberg, London: Quercus.

Lindqvist, A. J. (Interview) (2008), 'The Northlander Sits Down with the Writer of Let the Write One In!', http://www.aintitcool.com/node/38839 (accessed 20 April 2014).

Lindqvist, A. J. (2012), 'Let the Old Dreams Die', in M. Delargy (trans.), *Let the Old Dreams Die*, 237–66, London: Quercus.

Marion, I. (2012), *Warm Bodies*, New York: Atria.

Markell, P. (2011), 'Arendt's Work: Architecture of the Human Condition', *College Literature*, 38 (1): 15–44.

McNevin, A. (2009), 'Contesting Citizenship: Irregular Migrants and Strategic Possibilities for Political Belonging', *New Political Science*, 31 (2): 163–81.

McNevin, A. (2013), 'Ambivalence and Citizenship: Theorising the Political Claims of Irregular Migrants', *Journal of International Studies*, 41 (2): 182–200.

Nyers, P. (2003), 'Abject Cosmopolitanism: The Politics of Protection in the Anti-deportation Movement', *Third World Quarterly*, 24 (6): 1069–93.

Papadopoulos, D., Stephenson, N. and Tsianos, V. (2008), *Escape Routes: Control and Subversion in the 21st Century*, trans. M. Rocke, London and Ann Arbor, MI: Pluto Press.

Stratton, J. (2011), 'Zombie Trouble: Zombie Texts, Bare Life and Displaced People'. *European Journal of Cultural Studies*, 14 (3): 265–81.

Tsao, R. (2002), 'Arendt Against Athens', *Political Theory*, 30 (1): 97–123.

Villa, D. (2007), 'The Autonomy of the Political Reconsidered', *Graduate Faculty Philosophy Journal*, 28 (1): 29–45.

Warm Bodies (2013), motion picture, Mandeville Films.

Zetter, R. (2007), 'More Labels, Fewer Refugees: Remaking the Refugee Label in an Era of Globalization', *Journal of Refugee Studies*, 20 (2): 172–92.

18

The Public, the Private and the Aesthetic Unconscious: Reworking Rancière

Tina Chanter

This chapter stages a conversation around art and politics, drawing on the one hand on Jacques Rancière's conception of politics and on his reflections concerning the role art plays for Sigmund Freud, and on the other hand on work informed by feminist, queer and race theory about the figurative ways in which the shaping of national collectivities occurs. In what follows I engage two different senses of the public in relation to Rancière's work. The first is the formal account of the public sphere he gives in the context of his discussion of democracy. The second is a less formal, more implicit account of that which constitutes a public realm that I think can be found in his discussion of aesthetics. I suggest that it is productive to read together these two ideas of that which is publicly available, especially since politics and aesthetics are intrinsically linked throughout Rancière's corpus.

Governments – and there is no such thing as a properly democratic government for Rancière – occupy themselves in efforts to diminish the public sphere, in order to prevent political actors whose interests are not consonant with the state from taking part in the public sphere. It is in the interests of government to relegate such actors to the private realm, a realm that is thereby constituted as the polar opposite of the public realm. Yet, the very realm that passes itself off as the public realm, over which government tries to maintain control, is itself in reality privatized, in the sense that government is an oligarchy. For their part, those relegated to the private realm attempt to have themselves, and their concerns, recognized as public. In this respect, politics can be understood as the effort to expand the public sphere.

Politics is thus understood as the constant renegotiation of the boundary separating the private from the public sphere. The lexicon Rancière uses to express this negotiation is that the public sphere is the arena in which conflicts between politics and what Rancière calls the police order, which coalesces in this context with the conversion of this or that contingent distribution of places and capabilities into natural right, are played out. The impetus of republican or conservative politics is to effectively eliminate or minimize conflicts between the police order and politics, as if those who govern have a natural right to do so. In other words, the effort is to eliminate politics as such by stabilizing and enshrining as permanent the boundary separating the public from the private (and to disguise the fact that the security and stability of the public realm is in fact premised upon the accumulation and protection of the private interest of wealth).

In the first part of this chapter I expand upon Rancière's understanding of politics and the sense in which it redistributes conventional conceptions of public and private spaces and refigures who counts as political subjects. In the second and third parts of the chapter, still taking my cue from Rancière, but focusing on his discussion of the aesthetic unconscious in relation to Freud, I discuss two works of art. The first, Sophocles' *Antigone*, can be read as a play that concerns itself with the founding or inaugural moment of politics as such. I turn to the ancient Greek tragedy of *Antigone*, a drama that has lent itself to appropriation by a series of political reinterpretations, and to a contemporary film which shares a common theme. They both address themselves to the relationship between kinship and the boundary separating public from private. In considering *Antigone* and *Rabbit-Proof Fence* (2002), I anchor my reading in an account that Rancière offers of the role that art plays for Freud's psychoanalytic conception of the unconscious, an account which, however, I rework. I pay particular attention to the way in which visibility itself is underwritten by certain legitimating narratives that prevent us from seeing, blinding us and eclipsing from view that which might later come to be seen as quite obviously unjust, exclusionary, unequal or racist. Such narratives have often been unselfconsciously woven into the fabric of national collectivities. The distribution and figuration of affects play into the ways in which such collectivities understand themselves.[1] To question the ways of seeing that such narratives legitimate is to interrogate that which passes as sanctioned, publicly accepted mythologies that have established themselves as truths, or as just the way things are.

An instance of political activism that reworks the public/private boundary

Subjects, whose political force is rendered invisible, inconsequential or meaningless by efforts to represent the boundary between public and private as if it were set in stone, struggle to establish public spaces in which their voices can be heard to constitute meaningful political interventions. Thus, for Rancière, the 'democratic process implies: the action of subjects who, by working the interval between identities, reconfigure the distribution of the public and the private' (Rancière 2006, p. 61). A brief analysis of an example Rancière provides of a female political activist who staged a public action in order to effect such a redistribution will illustrate how the reconfiguration of the public and private can occur through political action. In this instance a woman acts in such a way as to inscribe herself in a public realm from which she was previously excluded, in order to contest the basis of that exclusion and lay claim to equality, which, as Rancière insists, 'is not a fiction' (Rancière 2009, p. 48) but which the prevailing political system denied her.

Eighteenth-century French activist Olympe de Gouges took action in order to demonstrate that 'women belong to the sphere of political expression' (Rancière 2006, p. 60). The form of action she took was to insert herself into the public arena, an arena from which women were excluded on the basis of the belief that their sphere of life should occupy the private domain of family.[2] In order to assert the right of women to political representation, and to the vote, Gouges formulated the following argument: if women were considered enough of a threat to warrant the death penalty (and as such were treated as equal to men before the law of the gallows), then they must also be eligible to vote and to play a part in political representation. The logic of this argument appeals to a fundamental human equality that was denied to women in denying them the vote, yet was implied by the fact that women could be sentenced to death. If women 'have the right to mount the scaffold', she maintained in her 1791 'Declaration of the Rights of Woman and of the Citizen', then they must 'equally have the right to mount the rostrum' (Rancière 2006, p. 60). Rancière understands the logic of this argument to be an instance of politicizing the 'opposition of "bare life" to political existence' (Rancière 2006, p. 60). Consigned to the private domestic realm of bare life, women are construed as having no part in political life, as being wholly submerged within and constrained by the realm of necessity, taken up with their supposed duty to reproduce life itself and to maintain biological life with the material, repetitive, manual labour of household work. Construed in such a way, women have no political rights. Yet, if the political threat that women present is acknowledged in the form of holding them accountable for their actions through punishment by death – a fate which eventually met Gouges herself – they must in fact have the very rights that are formally denied to them in excluding them from suffrage. If women have the potential to be so politically disruptive as to be put to death, then must not the very fact that their potential disruption of the state warrants their death also attest to the fact that – notwithstanding the public sphere's denial of their political status – women are already political actors? What Gouges' action achieved was the staging of a political right that women were being denied, thereby making visible women's equality, an equality that the contingent state of affairs of a political order which denied them the franchise was obfuscating.

The argument to extend suffrage, to enlarge the public sphere, in order to include those formerly excluded is both an argument to reconfigure public space and a redefinition of women as not merely occupying the private space of domesticity, but as also capable of crossing over to the public space of politics. Indeed the argument rests upon acknowledging that women have in fact already transgressed the boundary separating private from public, in recognition of which the law has already tacitly acknowledged their equality in judging women eligible for the death penalty. The argument to render suffrage in deed (and not merely in word) universal thus shows the boundaries of the public realm to be permeable and fungible, and at the same time shows the meaning of universality to be in contention. The assertion of women's equality was already underway in that their ability to constitute a politically disruptive force had earned them the 'right' to be punished through death; in order to be consistent women must, so the argument goes, be granted the political rights denied to them by excluding them from the franchise. The extension of equality to women in respect of granting women the right to vote functions then as supplementary to a right that had already granted them equality, the right granting that women are subjects capable of action that merits being put to death.

Antigone's symbolic reworking of her being: The identity of contraries

We have seen that politics operates by constantly pushing the contingent boundaries that are erected to distinguish the private from the public realm.

The latter realm in Rancière's view belongs to everyone but is co-opted by government in the interests of the consolidation of power. These interests coincide with assuring governmental control of the public sphere and establishing measures for the security of its accumulation of wealth, which in turn assures the continuation of government as oligarchy.[3] 'Politics,' says Rancière, 'effectively begins whenever the power of birth is undermined' (Rancière 2009, p. 44), that is, 'when the principle of government is separated from the law of kinship' (Rancière 2009, p. 40). The effective beginning of politics is its distinction from the claim to rule through appeal to aristocratic right, which in the final analysis consists in nothing but the 'power of property-owners' (Rancière 2006, p. 44). Yet, through the submergence of democracy by capitalism (or at least a selective interpretation of capitalism that ensures that the rich continue to get richer, because the government bails out companies deemed too big to fail whenever they face the risk of failure), we seem to have come full circle. Once again we find ourselves in an oligarchy, ironically the very predicament from which the ancient Greeks, so often credited with the birth of democracy, tried to break free.

This transition from aristocratic to democratic rule is one of the issues at stake in Sophocles' *Antigone*, a play in which Antigone's desire to honour her brother in death is articulated against an historical background of aristocratic trappings of the lavish celebration of funeral rites, at funeral processions in which women and slaves were the primary mourners to indulge in what came to be construed as an unseemly display of emotions. Creon is at pains to curb both the ostentatious aristocratic display of wealth and power and what was coded as the effeminizing, slavish and inappropriate display of affect.[4] To the extent that Antigone becomes a spokesperson for the sanctity and importance of kinship bonds, she might be taken to stand for the claims of a fading aristocratic past against Creon's claims for democracy, but the play is more complex than this. Creon's character is more than a little tinged with tyrannical overtones, while if Antigone becomes a placeholder for the affective familial ties Creon's narrow view of the polity cannot contain, as the daughter of the incestuous union of Oedipus and Jocasta, she has much more immediately pressing reasons to uphold kinship than loyalty to aristocratic rule (from which formal structures she would effectively have been excluded as a woman in any case) – namely to uphold the sanctity and individuation of familial bonds that her very existence violates.[5] Neither can Antigone be said to simply stand for a pre-political moment; to be sure, women would have been excluded from politics in the context in which Sophocles writes, yet it is precisely her incorporation into the public realm to which Antigone asserts her right of access when she publicly declaims her deed of burial in defiance of Creon and refuses to keep silent about it.[6] Her stance is further complicated by the fact that in establishing her right to speak, and to be heard, which she does through her persistent performance of self-justification, Antigone implicitly underwrites the absence of any such right on the part of certain others, namely slaves.

Before I develop this point, I want to briefly draw on Rancière's discussion of Freud and art as a prelude to turning back to *Antigone* and finally to *Rabbit-Proof Fence*, in part because I think that Rancière's appeal to the aesthetic unconscious can help us think through why this last point concerning slavery has been largely neglected by the extant commentary on *Antigone* in philosophy and psychoanalytic circles. Publicly sanctioned narratives inform and limit how art, including literary texts, plays and films, is read, received and interpreted. The aesthetic unconscious also provides us with a way of processing how it was that individuals representing the Australian government thought themselves justified in forcibly removing what it called 'half-caste' children from their aboriginal homeland, which is the political, conceptual (and literal) territory explored by *Rabbit-Proof Fence*. If art can offer to aesthetic vision a sensible experience shaped by alternative narratives, there is a chance that it can also open up the possibility of making an intervention in the availability of narratives. It can thereby open up the possibility of decisive shifts of vision that can transform the legitimacy of existing narratives and enhance the legibility of those narratives that the prevailing interests controlling the public realm do not sanction.

The realm of art, as it is configured in the aesthetic regime, constitutes a domain, for Rancière, in which a certain relation between thought and non-thought, knowledge and ignorance or consciousness and the unconscious is at play.[7] To understand what this means, I will focus for a moment on the figure of Oedipus, a figure that comes to play such a fundamental role for Freud, according to Rancière, because he embodies at one and the same time a knowing that is also a radical failure to know. His relation to logos is shot through with the affliction of pathos. For this tragic hero, as G. W. F. Hegel suggests (and it is Hegel, along with other Romantic philosophers, who makes available to Freud, on Rancière's reading, the new model of Oedipus that Freud deploys), to act is also to suffer. Rancière glosses this balancing of logos and pathos under the heading of the 'identity of contraries'. Oedipus is the one whose very insistence on discovering the truth leads him to the failure or limits of his own knowledge, the one whose insistence upon knowing the world confronts him with the impossibility of understanding himself.[8] Confronted with the horror of the true meaning of what he has done, afflicted by circumstances beyond his control, undone by precisely what he took himself to have mastered, he discovers himself to have committed parricide and incest. It is a lack of mastery, an involuntary aspect at the heart of what we take ourselves to know – in short, the unconscious as embedded in what we take ourselves to have authored – that is emblematic of Oedipus.

At a more general level, the claim that Rancière makes is that art and aesthetics constitute a realm in which the unconscious is at work as the thought that does not think, and it is this domain that allows Freud both to make Oedipus such an over-determining reference point and to develop the idea of the unconscious in psychoanalytic theory. Art offers a pre-existing site, then, in which the idea of the unconscious is already at work, and as such, it is what makes possible Freud's theorization of the unconscious. As for Oedipus, what makes him such a crucial figure for Freud on Rancière's reading is the fact that for all his determination to conquer the enigmas and riddles that confront him, he is unable to discern the truth of his own identity; he fails to recognize that it is none other than he himself at the centre of the mystery he attempts to solve. In the end, it is his failure to assert the authority of logos over pathos that constitutes his downfall, and it is precisely the fact that he succumbs to pathos that, according to Rancière, draws Freud to him. It is Oedipus's 'fury' that undoes him, yet although his affect, his pathos, attracts Freud to him, he is ultimately unable to sustain the affective pathos that afflicts his Oedipal heroes, of which Michelangelo's Moses is one (see Rancière 2009). Freud eventually succumbs to the very representative regime from which the new Oedipus with which romantic philosophy provided him broke away. This is in keeping with the therapeutic telos that governs Freud's overall project, a healing narrative that ends up turning into the moralizing impulse to keep under wraps emotions that threaten to signify chaos. For Rancière, if in his interpretation of works of art such as 'The Moses of Michelangelo' (1914) Freud ends up circumscribing the affect that threatens to overtake his heroes, mastering it with the most classical of impulses, the Freud of *Beyond the Pleasure Principle* (1922) nonetheless allows back into his theory the nihilistic entropy of which Rancière thinks Freud is so wary. This occurs in the shape of the death drive. Freud thus in effect reads into art the effective mastery of pathos, only to admit pathos into his own psychoanalytic theory at a later stage.

Rancière does not explore the possibility of a third alternative, which would fall between the closing down of affect in the name of Freud's moralizing mastery and acquiescing to the nihilist free reign of the meaningless of affect. If Rancière is right to suggest that it is affect/pathos that undoes Oedipus, and Sara Ahmed is right to construe affects as circulating between subjects and helping to constitute the borders by which subjects distinguish themselves from other subjects and from objects, I suggest it is productive to construe the relationship between Sophoclean characters in terms of the circulation of affects. Ahmed suggests that 'emotions are crucial to the very constitution of the psychic and the social as objects' and that they 'produce the very surfaces and boundaries that allow the individual and the social to be delineated as if they are objects', such that the work that emotions do and how they signify politically needs to be carefully mapped (Ahmed 2004, pp. 10, 19). In particular, how they circulate according to 'affective economies' and thereby help to constitute the aesthetic unconscious demands our attention. Accordingly, we might say that Antigone becomes the repository of the affects that Oedipus, finding himself unable to endure them, transmits to her and that Creon denies altogether – until they come back to haunt him in his denouement, when the burden of that which he has denied – the return of the repressed? – is enough to break his spirit.[9]

I will return to the disruptive potential of emotions and the way in which they signal a departure from the ostensibly rational procedures by which both states and sanctioned narratives justify themselves. For now I want to note that if Freud could not ultimately remain true to his initial affirmation of affect, except by subordinating it to his own, admittedly philosophically unorthodox, Oedipal version of rationality, it seems to me that therapeutic practice that is informed by feminist, queer or anti-racist theory and practice, for example, can interpret affects in a manner that neither capitulates to their meaninglessness, nor advocates overcoming them in the name of the status quo.

How might the idea of the identity of contraries be developed in relation to Antigone? If the true meaning of Oedipus's actions escape his control, if knowing is coupled with not knowing in the figure of Oedipus, in Antigone's case her very existence constitutes an aberration. In her case it is not knowing but *being* that is coupled with its opposite, in the sense that her very identity, who she is in her very existence, presents itself as compromised.[10] As a child of incest, her symbolic position in the kinship matrix violates the rules. Yet she refuses to be defined by her birth, merely as aberrant, simply as a violation, just a fault in the system. She defies what she is, and the impossibility and illegibility of the position she inhabits, by becoming other than herself, by going beyond the unreadable place she inhabits in terms of kinship structure.

She inscribes her own legibility by reaffirming the kinship bond between herself and Polynices, whom she recognizes as a brother, and, as Mader puts it, as *only* a brother (see AL).

If Oedipus knows and at the same time does not know, Antigone is what she is not. If Oedipus has been taken up as a hero of modernity, as one whose epistemic framing of the world is undercut by his ignorance, in Antigone's case it is not how we know and at the same time fail to know the world that is at stake – with all the Kantian overtones that such a formulation carries with it – but rather it is who we are in our very being that is in question. That Antigone's very existence or being is at stake is perhaps among the reasons that existential philosophy (one thinks of Martin Heidegger and Søren Kierkegaard) has been drawn to Antigone. We can add that her symbolic reworking of her status is among the reasons that feminist, queer and postcolonial thinkers have been attracted to the character of Antigone. For here is a character who symbolically rewrites her very being, transforms her very existence, and in doing so rewrites the rules about what it is to be. Antigone defies her being in more than one way. She specifies the meaning of her birth in a way that refuses to acquiesce to a narrative that focuses narrowly on the horror of incest, of which, as her father's child, she is the product. She insinuates herself into a public realm from which the culture bars her, refusing to adhere to the cultural silence and obedience demanded of her, and in doing so she rewrites the meaning of the political. She asserts her birth connection to her brother on the basis of having shared a common womb (rather than construing their connection on the basis of common blood) and thereby emphasizes her matrilineal rather than her patrilineal lineage with its incestuous legacy. She thereby inserts herself into the public realm as someone who takes on the impossibility of the aberrant existence she has inherited from her father and reworks it. She exceeds any designation she might have as either properly or improperly conforming to kinship roles, by speaking up for the way kinship authority subtends the very political system that silences her. She occupies a political space that her very speaking up etches out, as she refuses to be contained by the private, pre-political space to which the cultural expectations of the ancient Greek world out of which her character emanates would have constrained women.

Yet, even as she carves out a space in which her voice can be heard, Antigone plays a part that is complicit in the silencing of other voices, a part that is consonant with her aristocratic identity.[11] She might be a female character – and so not entitled to speak out publicly as far as Creon is concerned – but she is also an aristocratic character in a family of royalty, and thus at least succeeds in getting an audience in the figure of Creon, who is, after all, her uncle as well as the newly recognized king of Thebes. One can draw out Antigone's complicity by focusing upon just one moment of the play, a moment however that I think is symptomatic of a network of instances, which, taken together, attest to a motif that runs throughout the Theban cycle, yet one that has not been paid thematic attention. It is the moment when Antigone says she would not have buried her brother had he been a slave, a moment that for the most part has been read over by philosophical and psychoanalytic commentary, but one that, I suggest, has been taken up by literary and dramatic reworkings of *Antigone*. I will not belabour the point, as I have developed it elsewhere (see Chanter 2011). My emphasis here is that if, as Rancière argues, Romantic philosophy made available a new model of Oedipus that Freud took up and inscribed as having universal applicability, one might also argue that the contingency Rancière thereby works into psychoanalytic theory opens up the possibility of a more radical reworking and a more radical contingency. If there can be a new Oedipus, there can be another type of tragic hero, differently gendered, differently sexed, differently raced. Rather than Oedipus providing the universal reference point, feminist and queer responses to psychoanalysis have taken up Antigone as the tragic anti-hero. Beyond this, we might look not just to the philosophers for a new model of Oedipus, but also to the theatrical appropriations of *Antigone* in all their multiplicity, across continents and in the wake of postcoloniality, which have produced a series of Antigones, each of which speaks to the specificity of the political crises out of which every new iteration of Antigone is born. Such Antigones bear witness to the moment that philosophy and psychoanalytic theory has typically read over, the moment in which the possibility of Antigone speaking and being heard is achieved through her complicity with a system that continues to see slaves as unworthy of being granted the humanity that Antigone has been understood to grant her brother in affording him a 'proper' burial – that is a burial that conforms to the religious practices of ancient Greeks.[12]

Redistributing the sensible: *Rabbit-Proof Fence*

If there can be more than one tragic hero, if there can be a female tragic hero, then there can also be non-European, non-Greek heroes. Taking our impetus from a rich international tradition of sister-figures to Antigone, a theatrical and performative legacy that interrogates the European inheritance of tragedy, we could go one step further. I am suggesting that the systematic neglect of the motif of slavery characteristic of the reception of *Antigone* by the Western theoretical tradition might be seen as an instance of the aesthetic unconscious at work. This not knowing inhabits the most detailed of commentaries, the most thorough knowledge of Sophocles. At the same time, the dramatic rebirth of Antigones in diverse political contexts attests to the limits of representation established within and by political and intellectual regimes and to a reworking of those limits, a rebirth that affectively reworks both Oedipus's failure to know and philosophy's failure to notice the motif of slavery.

Rather than turn to this rich legacy of Antigone figures (again, this is work I have done elsewhere) I turn here, in the final move of my argument, to consider a film that interrogates the mandate of the Australian government to intervene in kinship practices in the name of white racial hegemony, a film that explores the underside of that which begins to make itself felt in certain appropriations and interpretations of *Antigone* – namely the recognition that kinship structures are enmeshed in systems of slavery, and in racialized systems, since when Antigone speaks up for her brother as kin, she also speaks up for the free world, as distinct from that of the enslaved. My motivations in taking up this film are multiple. First, the film demonstrates how deeply kinship regulations are infused with racial connotations. In this sense, it brings to the forefront that which tends to get buried alive (along with Antigone) in Sophocles scholarship, namely that the question of who counts as kin is heavily implicated in what Orlando Patterson has called 'social death'.[13] If consideration of the implication of kinship in ethnic injunctions is at best oblique in most discussions of Sophocles, in *Rabbit-Proof Fence* it is central. There is an official injunction to marry outside a group defined by its racial parameters and distinguished by its allegedly primitive mode of life. Kinship practices are engineered by cordoning off a whole group of people on the basis of the colour of their skin and way of life as inappropriate marriage partners. Taken from their families and from the land they know, the 'stolen generation' of aboriginal children were deposited in schools to learn, in the words of Doris Pilkington Garimara, 'how to live like the white man'.[14]

A second motivation for taking up *Rabbit-Proof Fence*, which is the story of a fourteen-year-old Mardu girl, Molly Kelly, and her two younger 'sister-cousins', as Pilkington Garimara calls them, is that it provides a way of shifting from the model of the universal applicability of Oedipus that Freudian and Lacanian psychoanalytic models tend to take for granted.[15] At the same time, it facilitates a reworking of the Eurocentric inflection feminist rejoinders to Western psychoanalytic theory and philosophy tend to preserve, still orienting themselves towards Greek heroes. Even non-Western appropriations of *Antigone* preserve this orientation insofar as their reference point remains Greek tragedy, which has been passed down, more often than not, via colonial systems of education.

Thirdly, *Rabbit-Proof Fence* illustrates how a white colonizing nation conceptualizes itself according to racialized assumptions that are woven into the fabric of society, in a way that might be thought of in terms of an aesthetic unconscious. Fourthly, in looking to *Rabbit-Proof Fence*, I am looking to art itself, rather than to the philosophers, not for a new Oedipus, nor even for a new Antigone, but for a new type of tragic hero altogether, one that brings into question the borders defining subjects as distinct from objects, individuals as distinct from communities. In reading this film alongside Ahmed's understanding of affects as not belonging to discrete subjects, but circulating between subjects in such a way that this transmission helps to constitute who counts as a subject and who does not, and at the same time helps to delineate subjects as belonging, or not belonging, to specific communities, I suggest that *Rabbit-Proof Fence* can be understood to rework any connotation tragic heroism might have acquired that equates it with individualism.[16] A community previously relegated to anonymity finds a voice in *Rabbit-Proof Fence*. At issue is a cultural mode of seeing that is specific to a communal way of life valued by indigenous communities, but not valued – and to all intents and purposes not even visible to – those who set themselves up as their 'protectors'. Making visible that which is rendered invisible through cultural hegemony, where the latter is understood as a systematic inability to see, or what also might be elaborated as a failure of affective investment, is what is at issue here.

Finally, and most importantly for this chapter, I propose that the film illustrates what Rancière calls the redistribution of the sensible. In doing so I suggest that it provides an example of how visibility itself is orchestrated in advance by the sanctioned narratives that circulate and come to be recognized as synonymous with the realm of appearances itself and how seeing things through the eyes of others differently affectively positioned from ourselves can open up the possibility of challenging those narratives.[17] Legitimating different narratives is a way of transfiguring the public domain of that which passes for common sense as self-evidently true.

Taking these points into account, the film offers us a way of thinking through how something like an aesthetic unconscious can inhabit the best of intentions and how such intentions can be structured through radical blindspots, structured, in this case, through the assumption of white privilege, which takes on genocidal overtones. The aesthetic unconscious allows us to approach fundamental failures of vision that structure what passes for knowledge, failures of vision that allow those affected to dismiss a way of life as invalid because it does not conform to oligarchic, Western lifestyles and styles of government. A. O. Neville, the 'chief protector of aborigines', played in the film by Kenneth Branagh, believes that the genocidal acts in which he engages in relation to aboriginal peoples is 'for their own good'.

In 1931 Molly (Everlyn Sampi), along with her younger cousins, escaped from Moore River Settlement, to which they had been forcibly removed, and set out on foot to find their way back home by following the fence from which the film derives its title, *Rabbit-Proof Fence*. The fence had been erected in a vain attempt to keep the rabbits that had been introduced to Australia by the English from ruining agricultural crops. When the three girls, Molly, Gracie (ten) and Daisy (eight) escape from Moore River Settlement, they find their way home by following the fence, which provides them with a road map. Seeing the fence through their eyes is a way of redistributing the sensible. Against all the odds, the girls walk the 1,200 miles home, defying police attempts to find them. The film puts in question the effort of government to impose racial homogeneity by intervening in kinship practices. I read the film as one in which the legitimating narratives that serve to frame that which is publicly sanctioned as visible are aesthetically displaced. Sanctioned narratives, precisely because they confirm and corroborate ruling powers, circulate more or less invisibly in their work of legitimation, as they encourage, verify and reward behaviours that conform to the version of events that governments espouse. When displacements and disruptions occur, the mythical frameworks that organize and orient national collectivities, but which are not always made readily available for interrogation, can present themselves for reworking.[18] Sanctioned ways of seeing are those that are most readily publicly available, which are facilitated by unarticulated myths that limit and constrain in advance the possibilities of vision, predisposing us to see that which we habitually see, that which we are allowed to see, that which available narratives suggest, corroborate, encourage and confirm. We are presented with something that appears as permanent, as though this is the only appearance possible. This is what Rancière refers to as the police distribution of the sensible.[19]

Concluding reflections

I have suggested, with reference to the motif of the identity of contraries, which Rancière develops in relation to Oedipus, who knows at the same time as he fails to know, that Antigone is at the same time as she is not. When Antigone defies the narrative that circumscribes her as aberrant and becomes other than that narrative, she makes an intervention not just at the level of knowing but also at the level of being. We could say that the point at which an epistemic framing of what is possible and what is not comes together with, or collapses into, an ontological or existential reframing of possibilities *in such a way as to present itself for interrogation* is also the point at which the public realm becomes susceptible to reconfiguration. At the point of rendering visible this collapse, or merging, that is, at the point that the difference between knowing and being, epistemology and ontology presents itself as indiscernible, that is, *their very indiscernibility becomes discernible,* so too the emergence of different legitimating narratives becomes possible. The passage that marks such a transition is one that can be specified both as a movement of knowing and as a movement of being, or, more precisely, as a movement in which a certain type of knowing and being are understood to underwrite one another. Legitimating narratives circumscribe in advance the possibilities of not just recognizing individuals as equal, but also transforming the standards according to which equality is judged. They also limit available interpretations of the very narrative works of art that can shape affect in such a way as to be transformative and the frames of visibility that dictate interpretative schema.

Throughout *Rabbit-Proof Fence* there are many shots of the fence, seen from various angles and framed in various ways, visually, narratively and politically. Such a moment occurs in the opening shot of the film, for instance, a long, unbroken aerial shot, which begins with a bird's eye view of an expanse of water, before panning over what turns out to be a landscape, but which presents itself at first as indeterminable. We are not sure what we are seeing immediately. And this very indeterminacy is at the heart of the film. For what we see when we see the rabbit-proof fence, what we see when we see the land it cuts across, whether we see a barren inhospitable land or whether we see a homeland, is precisely what is affectively, politically and philosophically at stake.

Notes

1 The work of Falguni Sheth and Sara Ahmed contributes to an understanding of the metaphorical work that emotions do in shoring up certain configurations of the public as if they were immovable and unchangeable, and in understanding how certain associative meanings operate to de-legitimate particular subjects as unruly or threatening. See Sheth 2009 and Ahmed 2004 (hereafter CE).

2 Olympe de Gouges also argued for civil partnerships and for the abolition of slavery.

3 That the law of accumulation has in fact taken on a life of its own, which has been divorced even from the classical principles of capitalism (which require the failure of companies that fail to remain competitive) and reserved for a preservation of the existing balances of power/wealth, was very clearly demonstrated in 2008. Governmental bail-outs of companies and banks to the tune of hundreds of billions occurred when certain companies were considered 'too big to fail'.

4 On the relation of Antigone and Creon to democracy see Honig 2013. On the relation of women to mourning practices see Taxidou 2004.

5 Creon's alignment with democracy is hardly unequivocal, given his tyrannical tendencies, as Haemon bluntly points out: his father will not listen to the murmurings of city, to the voices of the people, which are in sympathy with Antigone. The point here is to resist a reading of the play that assimilates Antigone and Creon to a representative framework, in which they simply stand for competing claims, which is how Hegel has tended to approach *Antigone*.

6 Judith Butler has emphasized Antigone's emphatic insistence on publicly laying claim to her act of burial (2002). Clifton Spargo elaborates the theme of the pre-political in 'Antigone: Toward a Theory of Apolitics' (2014).

7 By the aesthetic regime, Rancière designates the regime of art that succeeds the representative, classical regime. The representative regime is, at bottom, based on the view of art that Aristotle puts forward in the *Poetics*, and involves a certain ordering of what can be seen and what can be said according to a social hierarchy. The aesthetic regime disrupts the representative regime.

8 Although Rancière develops this idea in a post-Kantian register, one can also see how such a construction would lead very easily to recognizing in a modern Oedipus Kantian overtones.

9 The fact that Antigone is the Sophoclean figure made, in the end, to bear the brunt of affective familial ties, that she is the one to shoulder the burden of the affects that prove to be too much for Oedipus, is not something Rancière explores. Yet the affective pull of tragic poetry is intricately tied to Plato's condemnation of it, a condemnation that is implicated in the ancient Greeks' effort to distinguish themselves from what they considered to be effeminizing Persians. While Hegel makes of Antigone a pure tragic hero, he also limits her understanding of the ethical to the intuitive.

10 In developing this thought, I am drawing in part on Mader 2010 (hereafter AL).

11 It remains open how far this is inadvertent or unconscious on Sophocles' part, or whether it is in fact a deliberate strategy and it is merely the Western tradition of interpretation that has been slow to recognize its significance.

12 Antigone's specification that she would not have defied the law had her brother been a slave can be interpreted as a recognition that funeral rites for non-Greeks differ from those of Greeks. Persians were represented by Greeks as exposing their dead on funeral pyres, rather than burying them beneath the ground (a practice that was in fact current among Persians, but which some have suggested was exaggerated in Greek characterizations of their enemies). Antigone's anxiety about the exposure of Polynices' corpse can therefore be read as an anxiety to distinguish him from a slave (given the ease with which the categories of Persian and slave slid into one another for ancient Greeks).

13 Orlando Patterson, *Slavery and Social Death: A Comparative Study* (Cambridge, MA: Harvard University Press, 1982).

14 The record of a true narrative handed down to, and originally told by, Doris Pilkington Garimara, the daughter of Molly Craig, is retold by Jennifer Bassett 2008 (p. 5). The story formed the basis of Philip Noyce's film *Rabbit-Proof Fence*. I have been unable so far to procure the original version.

15 Rancière addresses the theme of universality, but does not follow it up as rigorously has he might.

16 In fact, if we accept the structuralist conception of tragedy whereby ancient Greek tragedy was a vehicle for the city putting itself on trial, a means of political critique in which the relation between characters reflect back to the city the tensions that beset it, it is not clear that individualism applies to the reception of tragic heroes in Ancient Greece. See Jean-Pierre Vernant and Pierre Vidal-Naquet 1965/90 (p. 247).

17 There are ties that bind Molly to the land from which she comes and to which she belongs and which she knows and loves, ties that are insignificant to those who seek to wrest her from that land. These ties of belonging are at the same time communal ties, ties to a shared way of life, which includes a vision of the land that is inaccessible to the police, whose search fails to find her.

18 While it is impossible to tell exactly how much, if at all, the impact of *Rabbit-Proof Fence* (2002) fed into the change of heart witnessed on the part of Australian government, which under John Howard had refused to grant the official apology that Kevin Rudd did in fact grant in 2008, I think it is likely that the impact of the film (which was widely seen) on public opinion played a role in this shift. See http://www.theguardian.com/film/2002/oct/27/features.review1 (accessed 12 January 2014).

19 There are one or two subtle signs in the film that a shift of authority, a shift in vision, might be possible at some future point, as when the tracker sent to bring the girls back to the Moore River Settlement, after repeatedly being frustrated in his efforts to do so, acknowledges that Molly is 'clever', conceding an attribute that Neville manifestly denies her, and then after a moment's pause simply adds these words, which need no further commentary: 'She wants to go home'.

References

Ahmed, S. (2004), *The Cultural Politics of Emotion*, New York: Routledge.

Bassett, J. (2008), *Rabbit-Proof Fence*, Oxford: Oxford University Press.

Bulter, J. (2002), *Antigone's Claim: Kinship Between Life and Death*, New York: Columbia University Press.

Chanter, T. (2011), *Whose Antigone? The Tragic Marginalization of Slavery*, Albany, New York: SUNY.

Honig, B. (2013), *Antigone, Interrupted*, Cambridge: Cambridge University Press.

Mader, M. B. (2010), 'Antigone's Line', in F. Söderbäck (ed.), *Feminist Readings of Antigone*, 155–72, Albany: New York: State University of New York Press.

Rabbit Proof Fence (2002), motion picture, HanWay Films, Australia. Produced by Philip Noyce, Christine Olsen and John Winter; directed by Philip Noyce.

Rancière, J. (2006), *The Hatred of Democracy*, trans. Steve Corcoran, London: Verso.

Rancière, J. (2009), *The Aesthetic Unconscious*, trans. D. Keates and J. Swenson, Cambridge, MA: Polity.

Sheth, F. A. (2009), *Toward a Political Philosophy of Race*, Albany: State University of New York.

Spargo, C. (2014), 'Antigone: Toward a Theory of Apolitics', in T. Chanter and S. D. Kirkland (eds), *The Returns of Antigone: Interdisciplinary Essays*, Albany: State University of New York Press.

Taxidou, O. (2004), *Tragedy, Modernity and Mourning*, Edinburgh: Edinburgh University Press.

Vernant, J. P. and Vidal-Naquet, P. (1965/90), *Myth and Tragedy in Ancient Greece*, trans. J. Lloyd, New York: Zone Books.

19

Law and Bhava: Notes Towards a Treatise on Freedom

Milind Wakankar

The movement this chapter charts is twofold: there is at first the itinerary of freedom, in its transition from the self-concept (or Concept) in its primary locus in negativity. The secondary movement is that of the dalit (untouchable) idea of primitive slavery, which appears to make a crucial, if secondary, inscription in the concept at the point of original negativity. I want to show how this inscription takes place at a point prior to cultural difference, prior to the distinction between Occidental or non-Occidental reason. I speak of freedom: one could well speak of the open. This would imply the light of an effulgent 'public-ness', a publicity that inaugurates the public use of reason. My point is: what does it mean for us to think freedom, not out of the generality of the self-concept in its primary inscription, but out of the *particularity* of the negative in its secondary inscription? In plain terms: I wish to argue for a universal account of freedom from out of the specific history of slavery; this would reverse the tendency in accounts of freedom, wherein the latter is understood as a universal horizon from which all particular claims are to be assessed. In short, what does it mean to think freedom or the open *at* this singular moment of a secondary inscription? What implications does this have for the relation between the open and the secret, between the lighted clearing that is the open and the return to the dark past that is also part of the movement of openness? Thinking (dalit) slavery in this way allows us to 'hold open the open', so to speak, but always in cognizance of that which remains hidden. This is, I would argue, the secret of caste and 'race': a throwing out there and a holding back in, but one that always makes possible a *transition*. I like to think of this as a transition to a new idea of the open, a new script for freedom.

Let me first lay out the stakes in the Indic or Brahmanical scene of the emergence of the self-concept. *Bhava*, the Indic term for the self-concept, was not always tied to emotion or psychological states. Here, I want to argue for its role in the movement of conceptuality. I understand the latter as an instance of ontology: thinking provides the framework by which human beings define their relation to history. To inhabit the concept is to lay claim to humanity (being human) as thinking being. Note that thinking as such is determined by its proximity to the negative; it turns back on itself (the negative negates itself) and thereby produces one side of immediacy, which we might characterize as difference. However, difference itself cannot but have a relation to identity. The oscillation between the two was for Hegel in his *Science of Logic* characteristic of 'identity-in-difference'. We learn much about Hegel when we follow Heidegger's life-long engagement with his *Phenomenology* but pre-eminently his *Logic*, where the subject of thought (not to be mistaken for the self or the 'I') is for Heidegger 'developed fully' in its 'dignity' (Heidegger 1973, p. 31).

This is not to say that *bhava* in its modern meaning, as 'emotion', can have no purchase on conceptuality. My point is that we must relocate *bhava* on the cusp of the transition from political psychology to political thought, which is to say the movement from *bhava* as understood in the philosophy of spirit (the shapes of human thought through history, between anthropology and psychology) to *bhava* as that which is lodged in the moment of the self-concept within holy reach of the idea of freedom. In this, I am encouraged by recent work in dalit conceptuality such as Gopal Guru and Sundar Sarukkai's book, *The Cracked Mirror*, which instructs us in how to read *bhava* beneath the level of emotion.[1] (The complete re-engagement with psychoanalysis this would necessarily involve is outside the scope of this chapter but is eminently within the ambit of my current work on freedom.)

My task here is informed by the need to preserve the specificity of the dalit account of ontology. Nonetheless, I am impelled to find a counter-echo of dalit conceptuality in a non-dalit discursive setting. The imperative is to enter into the immanence of conceptuality, to follow its internal logic. The historical experience of dalits is the incontrovertible tie to exteriority here: I am aware of its urgency as it is expressed in dalit politics and activism. My object is to follow the arc of dalit conceptuality as it opens out to embrace not just non-dalits but also the possible moorings of a new notion of sociality. It is here in the work of freedom that one can find in dalit thought the surest sign of how the question of race, caste and slavery is not only a matter of historical redressal: it is a question of philosophical self-reconstruction within the resources available in conceptual change. This is why one can imagine here a treatise on freedom.

The element of absolute, Purna, in Patil

I want to begin with a passage from the work of the influential non-Brahmin thinker in the anti-caste movement, Sharad Patil. At the outset, we should note that he is drawn here to a dialectical (*anityatavadi*) reconciliation of what for him are the two aspects of the concept of freedom. Noteworthy is the fact that he does not couch these juxtapositions in the idiom of cultural difference – which is to say that he does not make claims for the superiority of the one over the other.

> The [notion of the] Spirit, *visvacaitanya*, bequeathed to us by the upper classes of the Occident and the [notion of the] *parbrahman* [Essence] which is the legacy of the upper castes of India together comprise the original fund of cognition [*dnyanace nidhana*]. To accede to it is to attain freedom, release and salvation. It is not merely that this form of release or freedom is available to man within the limits of his natural and social stage of evolution and to the varying extent to which he is enabled to comprehend it; it is a matter of his being able to retrieve this fund of freedom [*svatantryanidhi*] in the [very element] of the 'absolute [*poorna*]' – such is the fundamental metaphysical concept of human freedom, regardless of whether the latter is spiritual or temporal [in nature]. (Patil 1988, p. 106)[2]

Again, what is unprecedented here is the following implication: *that the self-concept of freedom is not accountable to cultural difference.* (Note: I will henceforth render Hegel's term '*Begriff* [literally, *Be-griff* or self-grasping] as 'self-concept' in order to distinguish it from the everyday usage of the word 'concept'. I want to avoid the word 'Notion', now eschewed in Hegel scholarship; on the other hand, placing 'Concept' in upper case would rob it of its logical movement, freezing it as though it were a substantive. The reader is to be alerted to the dangers of taking 'self-concept' to imply 'the concept of the self'.) To be sure, there is an elective affinity, one might say, between Spirit as *Geist* and Essence as *Parbrahman*. But weighing on that co-occultation is not just the entire gamut of associations encapsulated, for instance, in the title of Rosenzweig's landmark work, *Hegel and the State* (1915)[3]; nor is it only a question of the specific place of the Advaita-Vedantic notion of 'brahman' in the trajectory of Brahmanism as it is charted for instance in Jotiba Phule's incendiary anti-Brahmin text, *Gulamagiri* (1873). Those vicissitudes involving their by now well-documented historical emergence represent a secondary moment; the primary moment is attained when and if the two – *Geist* and *Parbrahman* – relate to each other as aspects of conceptuality in its immanence to itself. So a mere nexus in Occidental and non-Occidental Brahmanism would have yielded a facile polemical possibility here (abstract ideas imposed interestedly on two sets of material conditions or some such passing ideological salvo), which Patil resolutely circumvents. Instead, in a manoeuvre that seems to me of profound significance, he moves the polemical driving-wedge of his anti-Brahmanism to the primary moment where the bond between the two ideas across the cultural rift is now more than a bond; it is nothing short of a bind. This binding together is derived from within the structural transformations involved in identity-in-its-relation-to-difference but always ever in the element of the absolute, *poorna*. Again, Patil's emphasis is less on the limits of a specific form of historical inquiry, even less on its ideological provenance (the elite or *abhijat* origins of the two ideas are self-apparent and can therefore be stated loosely here by Patil: 'upper classes ... upper castes'); his stress is on 'being able to retrieve' (*jevhada kadun gheta yayil*) freedom in its plenitude (*nidhi, nidhana*), a plenitude available only in the ether of the absolute.

But, what *is* this element of the absolute in its Hegelian specifications? By token of the ontological ambition of the *Science of Logic* (1811–16), we might say that it is the self-belonging of negativity to itself, the point at which it is united with itself neither in the simple immediacy of Being with its interminable oscillation between being and becoming, nor in the posited immediacy of essence by virtue of the reflexive shine (*Schein*) of opposites. Negativity is absolute only if it is *im*mediate to itself, which is to say that the mediation of itself with itself is not posited outside itself (on the side of difference) nor posited within itself (on the side of identity). Neither *Geist* nor *Parbrahman* refer to anything but the self-reference of the negative; in them the turning back of the negative on itself is no longer premised on the specular inwardness of the 'I'. Here at this point, subjectivity will have made way for the negative.

It is here then that the self-concept will have attained in its self-conscious grasp of itself its proximity to right. This proximity is delimited by Hegel in such terms as the 'sacrosanct'. The lines from the great treatise on *Recht* (1822) are well known: 'Right is any existence at all which is the existence of the free will. Right therefore is by definition freedom as Idea.' 'It is precisely because right is the existence of the absolute self-concept or of self-conscious freedom that it is something sacrosanct' (Hegel 2008, pp. 29–30, Hegel's italics removed). Whether it is freedom as the self-concept or the self-concept as freedom, what is clear is that both are tied to the self-reference of the negative. It is in negativity itself, in its movement from and to itself, to be sure in its 'return' to itself, that freedom attains the ontological rigour of the self-concept.

Put differently, in the self-reference of the negative both freedom and the self-concept find each other; the self-concept will have freed itself for itself in absolute alienation. Freedom is the ether in which the self-concept relates to its own negativity, a negativity that it has made its own. By the same token, in 'the beginning is the end', implying that the end and the beginning of this freedom are one in the self-concept, which is itself one with the absolute. So the self-concept is nothing if not incipient, wherein the beginning

> contains both, being and nothing. … But further, that which begins already *is*, but *is* also just as much *not* yet. The opposites, being and non-being, are therefore in immediate union in it; or the beginning is their *undifferentiated unity*. (Hegel 2008, p. 51)

Thus, to merely state the coming together of *Geist* and *Parbrahman* is to imply an indifferent unity, one where the two components stand side by side and where their relation is external to themselves. An 'undifferentiated unity' on the other hand would imply that their unity is not-yet-differentiated; it is the moment prior to difference where the 'is' and the 'not yet' coexist. Beginning preserves the negative as though in secret. So, we might say that the self-concept is already one with the negative at the beginning; moreover, this incorporation of the negative prior to difference *per se* is already a prefiguring of the end. The self-concept in the end is thus the self-concept that has restored itself to itself by virtue of the very negative that was contained in it in secret.

Bedekar's Marathi Hegel-Book

To this idea of the negative that lies at the core of the itinerary of the self-concept, grandiose in its rigour and lofty in its reach, what we see in Patil is the counterposing of an originary negation, one that is prior to the affinity between the self-concept and the negative. To uncover this originary negation, Patil is compelled to broach the history of conceptuality, which is also the history of freedom, from another point of entry: the origins of the state. Note that this is *not* an archaeology of the state as it was conducted by such historians of late Indian antiquity as Romila Thapar and R. S. Sharma. This is a genealogical endeavour propelled by the problem of the originary institution of social life. For at the core of that moment when the social was put into place is *also* the secret of caste; the 'also' directs us to the function of caste as a millennial supplementation (filling in and exceeding its gaps) of Indian sociality. Two implications are worth noting here. First, Patil seems to say, all manner of ontological questioning (and especially the kind of questioning that deserves the name 'ontology' precisely because its movement is at the level of the itinerary of being in the self-concept) maintains itself in a close proximity to the problem of the negative or (which is the same thing) to the problem of the self-concealment of the negative. Second, ontological questioning of this kind is marked in the very rigour of its delineation of the trajectory of the self-concept as secret by a *further* mark, which is the mark of caste and race in primitive slavery. It is not in happenstance that the archaeology of the institution of the state is the point of departure for a genealogy of caste/race. Another way of putting this is to say that freedom in its adequation of the self-concept traverses the mark of originary negation left behind by caste. Only a freedom marked in this way by caste, and re-marked *in* and as secret, can provide the wherewithal for the modulation of the will opposed to caste. At the heart of Patil's researches, therefore, is the forging of a will that seeks, very much in the manner of Ambedkar, nothing less than the extirpation of caste distinctions. But Patil is uniquely attentive to the need to uncover the secret of caste at the heart of the origins of the state, for again it is only ever in the domain of the conceptual that a genuine relation can be forged between freedom and the will.

Patil's 1982 classic, *Dasashudranci Gulamagiri* (henceforth 'DG'), could well be called the 'Anti-Kane', since so much of its polemical force as well as its substantial evidence are derived from the mammoth five-volume history of Hindu law written between 1930 and 1962 by the legal scholar Pandurang Vaman Kane (1997). The central criticism of Kane in Patil's book is directed at the former's reluctance in the *History of the Dharmashastra* to take into account the problem of primitive slavery. The difference between the two projects is salient: Kane sought nothing less than the sources for Hindu law understood as the legitimizing basis for caste; Patil hoped to uncover the secret of caste. But, this secret was not always on offer in the history of the institutionalization of caste; instead, one had to look for caste at the origins of sociality itself. It is for this reason that the work of the sociologist Iravati Karve became crucial; now the investment in the theory of kinship is definitive in the entirety of Karve's oeuvre and is characteristic of her late work on the Mahabharata, *Yuganta*. What brings Patil and Karve together, placing them in an instructive sequestration from Kane, is their shared interest on the bases of social life; one might say that the question of sociality is *the* source of the political, whereas Kane reads law as though he were collating the Pentateuch of the Hindu tribal nation – yet, his work is usefully 'amateur' in a way that more recent works on Hindu law cannot afford to be, determined as their motives are by the entire history of work on law in the German nineteenth century after the epoch of biblical hermeneutics.[4] In his book, on the other hand, Patil would seem to have sought to traverse the entire domain of 'ethical life' under the sign of right (in the sense of Hegel's '*Sittlichkeit*'); we only have to look at the titles of the book's chapters to detect this convergence of questions around something like the basis of law in right – Ancient Vedic Society, The *Kulta* and the *Ganika*, Mother Goddess/Bhumata, The Feminine State/*Strirajya*, Marriage, *Yadnya*/Sacrifice, *Dasa*/Slavery. This is Hindu law turned inside out, a 'philosophy of right' drawn from the sources for human being-with-in the world. Except that the demarcations of alterity are imposed not as a horizon looming ahead but at the outset. The book is also marked by its Engelsian emphases; this explains the recurrent recourse to the notion of the mother goddess and to matriarchal and matrilineal societies, not to mention the institution of marriage. Like the historian Rajwade (and Dange who made much of this aspect of Rajwade), Patil too is drawn to the idea of a primordial expropriation of the feminine bases of sociality. It is almost as though, at the point at which the taboo on incest and sexual licence (*svair sambhoga*) was imposed by dint of proto-heteronormative sanction so to speak, at that very instance one is given to see the vanishing traces of feminine forms of sociality and state. Even as the ur-forms of feminine sociality slowly recede, the miraculous persistence of such forms (as though in a lab) is ensured in matrilineal Kerala. This thread in Patil's argument runs not just through the 1982 text but in everything he has written since.

For our purposes, what is of great interest is the trace of the feminine at the originary institution of sociality. From Patil's perspective, Karve's cardinal error is to have read *dnyati* as a synonym for *kula*, clan. One could speculate that almost all the work that has been done on the origins of the state from Thapar through R. S. Sharma to Burton Stein (notwithstanding that his notion of the 'segmentary state' is drawn from Aidan Southall's study of the East African Alur),[5] not to mention the notion of kinship that marks Ranajit Guha's narrative of the death of Chandra, the entirety of this august body of work rests on the assimilation of dnyati to *kula*. So for instance for Karve, 'the *kula* can also be called the *dnyati*, as in *Gebruderschaft*, and to the extent that it remains tied to landed property can be taken to be *vikulvivahi*, exogamous' (Patil 2008, p. 47).[6] But for Patil the point is precisely to dissociate *kula* from *dnyati*. It is to go back to origins of human society, which is to say the evolution from horde to gathered mass (*saman, samaj, samaaj, samajya*). If the *kula* was in this sense the primitive unit of sociality, a unit of the *saman*, it is the ensuing differentiation that is of great importance. For this is the time of the break-up of the primal mass into phratry or moiety. Patil's emphasis is on the nature of this primitive differentiation: he wants to argue that at every step the differentiation took place along the lines of a divide that was at once patriarchal and brahmanical. *Dnyati* and *gotra* as instances of the paternal line precisely for this reason carry within themselves the original secret of caste. The patriarcho-Brahmanical institution of the social presupposes the original divergence of the *kula* along Brahmanized lines.

The surest sign that Patil's argument stems from the tradition of the critique of caste is his radical divergence from the master-narrative that has been woven around Hindu sociality since the beginnings of Indian social science, but also earlier in the twentieth century in the work of such thinkers as Hazariprasad Dwivedi. From Dwivedi to Dumont (I make this sweeping gesture to draw attention to a running thread in all modern characterizations of Hindu social life) caste is understood to be the pre-eminently cohesive factor in Indian sociality. It is that which, as the minimal instance of the social bond, makes Hindu society both pliant and rigid with regard to its internal distinctions (See Wakankar 2010). As opposed to this metaphysics of caste, Patil proposes a radical ontology where Hindu society originates from a primal differentiation, a fundamental divergence within the mass as *kula*: here it is crucial for him to note that the *dnyati* is 'as a phratry' (Patil 2008, p. 25) that which breaks away from the *kula*. What guarantees this original divergence? Patil does not answer this question but one might say that therein in that ancient rift lies the secret of caste.

The secondary inscription of the negative

A primal differentiation prior to the divergence in person, property and civil society – such a difference-before-difference was of moment for Patil because he remained committed to maintaining the relation between freedom and the self-concept. This is why one can speak here of the incipience of conceptuality in the dalit critique. We saw earlier how this relation between freedom and the self-concept is the forge in which a will is to attain *Bildung*, achieve gestalt. Now if the will (in democratic politics, or more strictly political society) is to be able to perform this gesture of opposition to caste, it must have counter-signed something earlier, something both logically and chronologically anterior. This is of course the primal differentiation we have seen, but as I have tried to argue this differentiation in a sense explores a terrain that is prior to the link between freedom and the self-concept as marked by Hegel, and is docketed in the tradition of ancient philosophy that yielded the notion of the *Parbrahman* to Sankara's Vedanta in late antiquity. This is a remarking of the mark: but what does it yield in terms of the principle of individuation? Both *Visvacaitanya* and *Parbrahman* are followed in the very movement of their metaphysical impetus by the notion of personality on the one hand and *purush* on the other. In order to develop the idea of an individuated will that speaks to the primal differentiation in the origins of freedom, Patil must reach beyond Hegel.

Reaching beyond Hegel: let us pause to gauge the nature of the polemical gesture involved here. Above all, this means that the critique of Brahmanism can no longer rest on the supposed obduracy of Brahminical thinking in its adherence to abstraction, as opposed to the inherent materialism of dalit thinking. The fact is that both Brahmanical and dalit thinking meet in the moment of the incipience of conceptuality; what is crucial for the dalit critique, to my mind, is the point at which the incipience of dalit conceptuality departs from this shared origin in the incipience of conceptuality as such. Shared beginnings to be sure (let us bring to mind Patil reading Kane, and Kane in his disavowals of dalit experience as though he has already read Patil!), but secreted in that starting point lies a moment unavailable to Brahmanical thought, which is a certain originary negation.

The philosophical tools needed to undertake such an inquiry are simply waiting for us to be gleaned in the work of such rigorous historians of philosophy as Dinkar Bedekar. Bedekar's life-long reading of Marx and Hegel yielded his triumphant opus, *Hegel: Jivana ani Tatvadnyana* (1966) – a text that is virtually a teaching text for the dalit-Marxist tradition in Marathi-speaking Western India. Now Bedekar's project is at some remove-from-the-dalit critique; certainly, one cannot find in his sizeable oeuvre any sustained engagement with caste; this is curious, given his vastly important work on the social and philosophical bases of religion in antiquity: his work explores Brahmanical philosophy but from a 'non-dalit' perspective.[7] Sadly, his untimely death in 1973 left untried what would have been a logical extension of his late researches into the point of convergence between ancient religion and the origins of caste.

Yet, where Patil and Bedekar meet is at that point, where the self-concept as freedom and freedom as self-concept converge. What is crucial for our purposes is the fact that Bedekar dedicates almost a third of his Hegel book to the analysis of Hegel's *Logic*, in a manner that is I daresay unique in the literature on Hegel in the Indian languages. In turning now to Bedekar we will have completed something like a diptych of identity and difference. Patil's proposition on freedom led us to the idea of the absolute, broached at some point in the trajectory of the negative. We entered into this issue on the side of the subterranean workings of *Geist*, especially in its relation to the self-concept (*Be-griff*). Here, with Bedekar, we are enabled to explore the question of freedom on the side of the *Parbrahman*. It is at this point that we are called upon to turn towards Bedekar's renditions of the key moments in the *Logic*. I cite an explicatory passage in the first of the two long chapters on the *Logic* in his Hegel book.

> We can then proceed to describe the three *bhava's* that constitute the structure of the concept [*paribhava-vyuha*] in Hegel. ... These are entitled *bhava-matra* (*being*), *bhava-mithuna* (*essence*) and *bhava-samavarta* (*self-concept*). (Bedekar 1966, p. 113)

What is at play here is a critique of Advaita Vedanta that runs through the course of Bedekar's book. For him, missing in that school of thinking is a genuine account of the *poorna* as absolute.

> Now if we turn in [the ontological lexicon implied in] our Science of Logic [*tarkashastra*] to such pragma [*padartha*] as 'dravya', 'guna' and 'karma' on the one hand and such notions [*kalpana*] as 'paksha' and 'hetu' we do not find anything bordering on the concept, *bhava-samavarta*. And if we were to move 'beyond' Logic, so to speak, and attend to the metaphysical, we come across mere oppositions of the following kind: 'ekatva-anekatva', 'param-artha and vivarta-rupi artha', and 'neyartha and nitartha.' Here the idea of a *brahman* that is characterized by *ekatva* [unifying unity] and by the quality of being 'ekameva advitiya' [the wholly singular] is certainly on offer, but then the consummation of *ekatva* itself is to be achieved only after the cessation of *vivartarupa anekatva* [the manifold of the multiple]. [On the other hand,] Hegel's *samavarta bhava* [the that returns to itself as concept] is geared not towards a *nirakarana* [negation] or a cessation [*nirasana*] but towards a *samavartana* (or *sangrahana*

[a gathering together]), and for this reason the kind of final *ekatva* [unifying unity] foreseen in the Indian philosophical lexicon is greatly different from the notion of *ekatva* one finds in Hegel. (Bedekar 1966, p. 115)

Bedekar is critical of the kind of negation of time and change (the manifold of the multiple) that is merely tied to a cessation. There is a Heraclitean conundrum here: how to account for change (transformation, metamorphosis) by imposing on it the idea of a unifying unity but without simply negating change itself. For a simple negation would imply that what is not change, which is to say substance, would perdure in the face of change but not without bearing within itself the trace of the non-changing. Which would mean that the next moment in the trajectory of the self-concept is inevitable: one would find that the very impetus of temporality would return substance to changeability. By this token, change would have to turn itself towards substance, which in turn would induce the reverse movement in the direction of change and so on. For Bedekar this mode of conceptual oscillation does not adequately grasp the self-concept itself as a 'gathering together' (*sangrahana*) of these moments, a gathering together that transpires in the work of the self-concept on itself – which is to say: change and time internalized, into-reflected and introjected into the life of the self-concept itself; and hence the self-concept understood under the sign of Hegel as *samavartana*: identity (*sama*)-in-difference (*vartana*).

Bedekar is for this reason critical of the very idea of the negative as it is elaborated in the leading schools of Indian philosophy from Sankhya to Nyaya through to Vedanta. And yet, when it is incumbent upon him to render Hegel in Marathi, he has recourse to a vocabulary of negativity yielded by Vedanta in its long history. Relying on the remarkable book-length essay by Paul Hacker on '*Vivarta*', one might say that what Bedekar falls back on is an idea of the negative that is in this instance prior to the notion of a simple negativity that he believes is ubiquitous in the scene of Indian Logic (1953). Hacker himself had tried to argue that Vedanta in its many schools had been epistemologically ambivalent with regard to the phenomenal appearance of the world in general: Vedanta before and after Sankara had tried to argue that such a world was infra-cognitive or nescient – secondary and possibly false – when compared with the idea of the world gained through an insight into *Brahman*. Yet, in text after text, the schools of Vedanta went on to provide some of the richest accounts of how we understand the world, even if under the shadow of delusion. *Vivarta* (literally, the turning [*vi-*] of the turn [*vartate*]) then refers us to the negativity inherent in all the ways in which we make sense of sensory stimuli.

Here we must enter with Bedekar into the internal life of the self-concept. The task cut out for ontology is prescribed for it in a double session; advisedly one must use the word 'ontology' itself with the greatest caution. On the one hand, there is the rigour that is incumbent upon us as we track the *bhava*-as-self-concept, where Bedekar reads the Indian tradition with his eye on the Hegelian concept understood in its Logic. Second, we are called upon to comprehend the self-concept-as-*bhava*. Here, beyond the self-defined projects of a Bedekar and a Hegel, there will have been, *below* the level of translation, a re-marking of the negativity at the heart of the self-concept by a second negation – one that announces itself as prior. This anteriority of the negation that befalls the negativity secreted at the heart of the self-concept, this primary negation, is the work of the 'turning of the turn' or the '*vivarta*'. By dint of this turn, the entire range of Hegelian conceptuality (the self-concept in all its moments) is re-inscribed. Let us look again at Bedekar's renderings, placing them beside his own references to Hegel's terms (albeit in their English, not German, renderings): *bhava-matra* (*being*), *bhava-mithuna* (*essence*) and *bhava-samavarta* (*self-concept*). The very movement from being to becoming is marked by a tendency closely related to *vivarta*, which is *vikar* or *vikriti* (Bedekar takes the latter from Sankhya). Being-in-itself is the first moment in the determination (*vyakrita*) of being, which Bedekar renders as determinate being, *niyata sat*. Now determinate being is itself subject to determination/*vyakriti*, because of which:

> This second *vyavritti* arises in the opposite direction as though it were a *pratiprasava*, toward the origin. *Niyata sat* [determinate being] when exposed to the *vyavritti* moves toward *aniyat sat* [indeterminate being] or *sat* [being as such]. This is what Hegel has described as *svaniyat purtabhava* (*being-for-self*). Merely the purest instance of *sat* (*being*) cannot at all attain the *bhava* that is *svaniyat purtabhava*. The latter assimilates two instances, the instance of *sat* and the instance of the *vyakrita bhava* (*being-for-other*). The second instance is attained by the *vyavritti* of the first; whereas to adequate *svaniyat purtabhava* one would need a second *vyavritti*. Hegel calls this secondary *vyavritti* [the locus of a] *purta-vyavritti* (*absolute negation*). (Bedekar 1966, pp. 128–9)

What is crucial here is the curious double signature of negation (call it *vivarta* or *vyavritti*) at the very instance of the absolute negation. Now as a reader of Hegel, Bedekar is careful to insert in parentheses the English approximates of the original German; on the other hand, as a reader of Sankhya and Vedanta, there is a tendency in Bedekar himself to weigh in on the work of the *vya* – or more strictly the negating *vi* – in *vyakrita/vyavritta*. How can we account for the invisible work of the negative, issuing forth from the other side of the cultural rift? Reading *bhava-as-self-concept* is one thing (this is the project of translation); vastly different is the task of detailing the *self-concept-as-bhava*, which inaugurates a scene of something like an internal counter-signature. Could one argue that the notion of a 'secondary *vyavritti*' is an unprecedented rendering of the self-concept, exotic and exorbitant in every way, entirely outside the ambit of cultural difference, translation, orientalism and its critique, and so on? I want to insist that in this 'secondary *vyavritti*' the self-concept itself will have been re-inscribed, re-marked – but, most crucially, that this re-marking happens *at the level* of the self-concept. And, it is because it happens at the level at the self-concept that we are afforded here the gift of a breakthrough in ontology itself.

We should recall that Hegel's ambition is to dislodge the subject or the 'I' from the scene of self-reference. The self-reference of the self in Fichte is the self-reference of the negative in Hegel. The attainment of the absolute is accomplished by means of a relentless introjection or intro-reflection of difference and its moments. In the end, if the self-concept itself becomes the very instance of 'identity-in-difference', we can say that it will have synoptically addressed the gamut of ontological predication. Yet, when we read Patil and Bedekar, we find that a second internal negation has transpired, and only ever at the level of the self-concept. For Patil, it is the secret of caste at the origins of the state that provides the basis for the self-concept as the freedom to think, the freedom to forge a will. In Bedekar, it is the double negation, *vyavritti*, wherein the paleonymy, so to speak, of words and meanings comes to re-inscribe the self-concept from within. In both instances, a crypt has been generated inside the very crypt of the negative. A crypt within a crypt – the ethics of this encryption will be the perennial legacy of these thinkers to the continuing engagement of the dalit critique with the lexicon of philosophy and the social sciences. Insinuated in the encryption is a profound divergence between Patil and Bedekar (the secret of caste is 'unconcealed', so to speak, only to Patil) but also a coming together, this time not across the rift of cultural difference, not even the rift between dalit and non-dalit, but across the internal rift that is the negative itself. A non-meeting then, and one that can only ever hold true under the sign of the subjunctive. *In nuce*, by dint of their rigorous investment in the work of the negative, they make it possible for us to return freedom to its domicile in the absolute, *poorna*; but not without having also laid the grounds for a transition to the open staked at the level of the self-concept in its proximity at once to the negative and to the secret. Slavery, publicity, openness – these moments in the trajectory of the negative (haunted at every moment by the secret of caste and 'race') redefine in an infinitesimal way the very openness of the open.

Notes

1 I have discussed this book at length in 'Topics in the New Dalit Critique', forthcoming in *Comparative Studies in South Asia, Africa and the Middle East*.

2 This text was first published in *Satyashodhaka Marxavadi*, August 1982. While in the process of revising this chapter for publication in this volume, I learnt (12 April 2014) that Sharad Patil had died. This chapter is I hope a worthy tribute to the spirit of this last great iconoclast of the Marathi anti-Brahmin tradition.

3 Franz Rosenzweig, *Hegel und der Staat* (Berlin, 1920).

4 See, for instance, Donald 2010, which exemplifies the problems inherent in this tradition of legal-historical scholarship inaugurated both by legal scholars such as J. Duncan Derrett as well as outstanding philologists such as Patrick Olivelle.

5 The key essays have been usefully brought together in Kulke 2004.

6 Cited in Patil 2008, p. 47; from Karve, *Kinship Organization of India*.

7 See his son Sudheer Bedekar's editions of Bedekar 1977a, b.

References

Bedekar, D. K. (1966), *Hegel: Jivana ani Tatvadnyana*, Pune: Vishwavidyalaya Prakashan.

Bedekar, D. K. (1977a), *Dharmacintana*, ed. S. Bedekar, Pune: Samaj Prabodhana Sanstha.

Bedekar, D. K. (1977b), *Dharmashraddha: Eka Punarvicara*, ed. S. Bedekar, Pune: Padmagandha Prakashan.

Donald, R. D., Jr. (2010), *The Spirit of Hindu Law*, Cambridge: Cambridge University Press.

Hacker, P. (1953), *Vivarta: Studien zur Geschichte der Illusionistischen Kosmologie und Erkenntnistheorie der Inder*, Wiesbaden: Franz Steiner.

Hegel, G. W. F. (2008), *Outlines of the Philosophy of Right* (1822), trans. T. M. Knox, revised, ed. and intro. Stephen Houlgate, Oxford: Oxford University Press, 2008.

Hegel, G. W. F. (2010), *The Science of Logic* (1812–13, rev. 1831), trans. George di Giovanni, Cambridge: Cambridge University Press.

Heidegger, M. (1973), *The End of Philosophy*, trans. Joan Stambaugh, Chicago: Chicago University Press.

Kane, P. V. (1997), *History of the Dharmashastra*, Pune: Bhandarkar Oriental Research Institute.

Kulke, Hermann, ed. (2004), *The State in India 1000-1700*, Oxford: Oxford University Press.

Patil, S. (1988), 'Samagra Svatantrya va Samta: Adhyatmika va Bhautika', in ed. Sharad Patil, *Abrahmani Sahityance Saundaryashastra*, Pune: Sugava Prakashan, pp. 103–21.

Patil, S. (2008), *Dasashudranci Gulamagiri*, Shirur, District Pune: Mavalai Prakashan, [1982].

Wakankar, M. (2010), *Subalternity and Religion*, London and New York: Routledge.

References to Introductions

Balagangadhara, S. N. (2013), *The Heathen in his Blindness: Asia, the West, and the Dynamic of Religion*, Delhi: Manohar Books.

Bhargava, R. and Reifield, H., eds (2005), *Civil Society, Public Sphere and Citizenship: Dialogues and Perceptions*, New Delhi: Sage Publications.

Bloch, A., Sigona, N. and Zetter, R. (2014), *Sans Papiers: The Social and Economic Lives of Young Migrants*, New York: Pluto Press.

Calhoun, C. (1993), 'New Social Movements' of the Early Nineteenth Century', *Social Science History*, 17 (3): 385–427.

Calhoun, C. (2010), 'The Public Sphere in the Field of Power', *Social Science History*, 34 (3): 301–35.

Carter, S. (1993), *The Culture of Disbelief*, New York: Basic Books.

Castles, S., Haas H. de and Miller, M. J. (2013), *The Age of Migration: International Population Movements in the Modern World*, 5th edn, Basingstoke: Palgrave MacMillan.

Cohen, J. L. and Arato, A. (1992), *Civil Society and Political Theory*, Cambridge, MA: MIT Press.

Crenshaw, K. (1989), 'Demarginalizing the Intersection of Race and Sex: A Black Feminist Critique of Antidiscrimination Doctrine, Feminist Theory and Antiracist Politics', *University of Chicago Legal Forum*, 140: 139–67.

Dahlgren, P. (1991), 'Introduction', in P. Dahlgren and C. Sparks (eds), *Communication and Citizenship*, 1–26, London: Routledge.

Dahlgren, P. (1995), *Television and the Public Sphere: Citizens, Democracy and Media*, London: Sage Publications.

Dahlgren, P. (2001), 'The Transformation of Democracy?', in B. Axford and R. Huggins (eds), *New Media and Politics*, 64–8, London: Sage Publications.

Debord, G. (1995), *Society of Spectacle*, trans. Donald Nicholson-Smith, New York, NY: Zone Books.

Dirlik, A. (1994), 'The Postcolonial Aura: Third World Criticism in the Age of Global Capitalism', *Critical Inquiry*, 20 (2): 328–56.

Eley, G. (1992), 'Nations, Publics, and Political Cultures: Placing Habermas in the Nineteenth Century', in C. Calhoun (ed.), *Habermas and the Public Sphere*, 289–339, Cambridge, MA: MIT Press.

Esser, F. (2013), 'Mediatization as a Challenge: Media Logic Versus Political Logic', in H. Kriesi, S. Lavenex, F. Esser, J. Matthes, M. Bühlmann and D. Bochsler (eds), *Democracy in the Age of Globalization and Mediatization*, 155–76, Basingstoke: Palgrave Macmillan.

Esser, F. and Strömbäck, J. (2014), *Mediatization of Politics: Understanding the Transformation of Western Democracies*, Basingbroke: Palgrave Macmillan.

Ferree, M. M. (2008), 'Framing Equality. The Politics of Class, Gender and Race in the US, Germany and the Expanding European Union' in S. Roth (ed.), *Gender Politics in the Expanding European Union. Mobilization, Exclusion, Inclusion*, 237–56, New York: Berghahn Books.

Fraser, N. (1985), 'What's Critical about Critical Theory? The Case of Habermas and Gender', *New German Critique*, 35: 97–131.

Fraser, N. (1992), 'Rethinking the Public Sphere: A Contribution to the Critique of Actually Existing Democracy', in C. Calhoun (ed.), *Habermas and the Public Sphere*, 109–42, Cambridge, MA: MIT Press.

Fraser, N. (2007), 'Transnationalizing the Public Sphere: On the Legitimacy and Efficacy of Public Opinion in a Post-Westphalian World', *Theory, Culture & Society*, 24 (4): 7–30.

Goldberg, G. (2010), 'Rethinking the Public/Virtual Sphere: The Problem with Participation', *New Media & Society*, 13 (5): 739–54.

Habermas, J. (1962/89), *The Structural Transformation of the Public Sphere: An Inquiry into a Category of a Bourgeois Society*, trans. T. Burger and F. Lawrence, Cambridge, MA: MIT Press.

Habermas, J. (1984), *The Theory of Communicative Action. Vol. I: Reason and the Rationalization of Society*, trans. T. McCarthy, Boston: Beacon.

Habermas, J. (1996), *Between Facts and Norms: Contributions to a Discourse Theory of Law and Democracy*, trans. W. Rehg, Cambridge, MA: MIT Press.

Habermas, J. (2006), 'Religion in the Public Sphere', *European Journal of Philosophy*, 14 (1): 1–25.

Hallin, D. and Mancini, P. (2004), *Comparing Media Systems*. Cambridge, MA: Cambridge University Press.

Herman, E. S. and Chomsky, N. (1988), *Manufacturing Consent: The Political Economy of the Mass Media*, New York: Pantheon Books.

Herman, E. S. and McChesney, R. W. (1997), *The Global Media: The New Missionaries of Global Capitalism*. London: Cassell.

Hjarvard, S. (2013), *The Mediatization of Culture and Society*, London: Routledge.

Joshi, S. (2001), *Fractured Modernity: Making of a Middle Class in Colonial North India*, New Delhi: Oxford University Press.

Kalpagam, U. (2002), 'Colonial Governmentality and the Public Sphere in India', *Journal of Historical Sociology*, 15: 35–58.

Keen, P. (2007), 'When is a Public Sphere not a Public Sphere? Thoughts from 1795–96', in A. Benchimol and W. Maley (eds), *Spheres of Influence: Intellectual and Cultural Publics from Shakespeare to Habermas*, 151–74, Bern: Lang.

Klancher, J. (1987), *The Making of English Reading Audiences, 1790–1832*, Madison: University of Wisconsin Press.

Koser, K. (2005), *Irregular Migration, State Security and Human Security*, Geneva: Global Commission on International Migration.

Laclau, E. and Mouffe, C. (1985), *Hegemony and Socialist Strategy: Towards a Radical Democratic Politics*, Verso: London.

Lippmann, W. (1997), *Public Opinion*, New York, NY: Free Press.

Lundby, K., ed. (2009), *Mediatization. Concept, Changes, Consequences*, New York: Peter Lang.

McLuhan, M. (1964), *Understanding the Media: The Extensions of Man*, New York, NY: Mentor.

Mitchell, W. J. T. (2012), *Seeing Through the Race*, Cambridge, MA: Harvard University Press.

Mitter, P. (1992), *Much Maligned Monsters: A History of European Reactions to Indian Art*, London: University of Chicago Press.

Murphy, A. (1998), 'Rawls and the Shrinking Liberty of Conscience', *The Review of Politics*, 60 (2): 269–76.

Muthukumaraswamy, M. D. and Kaushal, M., eds (2004), *Folklore, Public Sphere and Civil Society*, New Delhi: IGNCA and Chennai: NFSC.

Negt, O. and Kluge, A. (1993), *Public Sphere and Experience: Toward an Analysis of the Bourgeois and Proletarian Public Sphere*, trans. P. Labanyi, J. O. Daniel and A. Oksiloff, Minneapolis: University of Minnesota Press.

Orsini, F. (2002), *The Hindi Public Sphere 1920–1940: Language and Literature in the Age of Nationalism*, New Delhi: Oxford University Press.

Pojmann, W. (2008), *Migration and Activism in Europe since 1945*, Basingstoke: Palgrave Macmillan.

Rawls, J. (1987), 'The Idea of an Overlapping Consensus', in Samuel Freeman (ed.), *John Rawls: Collected Papers*, 421–48, Cambridge, MA: Harvard University Press.

Rawls, J. (1997), 'The Idea of Public Reason Revisited', in Samuel Freeman (ed.), *John Rawls: Collected Papers*, 573–615, Cambridge, MA: Harvard University Press.

Rheingold, H. (2002), *Smart Mobs: The Next Social Revolution*, Cambridge, MA: Perseus Books.

Roberge, J. (2010), 'The Aesthetic Public Sphere and the Transformation of Criticism', *Social Semiotics*, 21 (3): 435–53.

Roberts, J. M. and Crossley, N. (2004), 'Introduction', in N. Crossley and J. M. Roberts (eds), *After Habermas: New Perspectives on the Publics Sphere*, 1–28, Oxford: Blackwell.

Sassi, S. (2000), 'The Controversies of the Internet and the Revitalization of Local Political Life', in K. Hacker and J. van Dijk (eds), *Digital Democracy: Issues of theory and practice*, 90–105, London: SAGE Publications.

Siim, B. and Mokre, M., eds (2013), *Negotiating Gender and Diversity in an Emergent European Public Sphere*, London: Palgrave.

Sloterdijk, P. (2005), 'Atmospheric Politics', in B. Latour and P. Weibel (eds), *Making Things Public: Atmospheres of Democracy*, 944–51, Cambridge, MA: MIT Press.

Stiegler, B. (1998), *Technics and Time: The Fault of Epimetheus*, Stanford: Stanford University Press.

Tuathail, G. Ó. (2005), *Critical Geopolitics: The Politics of Writing Global Space*, London: Routledge.

Virilio, P. (2012), *Lost Dimension*, Los Angeles: Semiotext(e).

Wertheim, M. (1999), *The Pearly Gates of Cyberspace: A History of Space from Dante to the Internet*, London: W. W. Norton & Company.

Wilhelm, A. G. (2000), *Democracy in the Digital Age: Challenges to Political Life in Cyberspace*, London: Routledge.

Williams, R. (1983), *Culture and Society 1780-1950*, New York, NY: Columbia University Press.

Yates, M. (2007), 'Rawls and Habermas on Religion in the Public Sphere', *Philosophy and Social Criticism*, 33 (7): 880–91.

Index

Figure 9.1 COSATU House, 1987. Courtesy of Eric Miller.

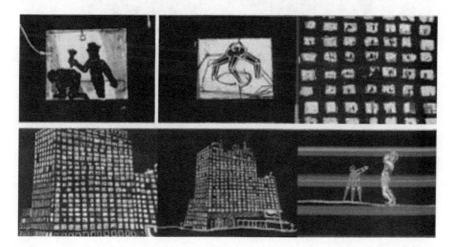

Figure 9.2 Stills from the film *Ubu Tells the Truth*, 1996–7. Courtesy of William Kentridge.

Figure 9.3 The commando of National Party supporters that escorted the late Dr Hendrik Verwoerd to the party's fiftieth anniversary celebrations. De Wildt, Transvaal (North West Province), 31 October 1964. Courtesy of David Goldblatt.

Figure 9.4 Man with loudspeakers, Badsha Pir birthday celebrations, Grey Street, Durban, 1981. Reproduced from Badsha 2001, p. 108.

Figure 9.5 Chief Gatsha Buthelezi, head of the KwaZulu government, at unveiling. Reproduced from Badsha 1985, p. 65.

Figure 9.6 Newly elected ANC leaders, Durban, 1991. Reproduced from Hayes 2011a, p. 562 and Badsha 2001, p. 108.

Figure 9.7 Mr and Mrs Van Zyl, ca 1985. Black-and-white photograph and hand-coloured print. Courtesy of Chris Ledochowski.

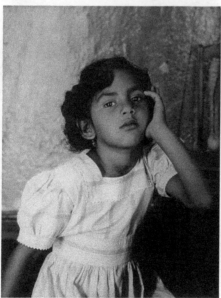

Figure 9.8 Fatgiya, Harfield Village, 1985. Courtesy of Chris Ledochowski.

Figure 9.9 Wedding Bonteheuwel, 1984. Courtesy of Chris Ledochowski.

Figure 9.10 Purple rain, Cape Town, 1989. Courtesy of Chris Ledochowski.

Figure 9.11 Mandela's first speech at the Grand Parade, Cape Town, 1990. Courtesy of Chris Ledochowski.

Figure 9.12 Richtersveld. Courtesy of David Goldblatt.